OUTLAWING THE SPOILS

Ari Hoogenboom

★ ★ ★ ★ ★ ★ ★ ★ ★ ★ ★ ★

OUTLAWING THE SPOILS

★ ★ ★ ★ ★ ★ ★ ★ ★ ★ ★

A History of the Civil Service Reform Movement

1865-1883

★ ★ ★ ★ ★ ★ ★ ★ ★

University of Illinois Press, Urbana, Chicago, and London

1968

FOR DAVID DONALD

PREFACE

Civil service reform was a live political issue in the post–Civil War United States. It made and broke presidents, would-be presidents, and a number of lesser political figures. No other American movement has claimed more intellectual and social leaders. The fervor of these molders of public opinion was almost religious. One cried out as he died, "I have spent my life in fighting the spoils system," while another referred to fellow reformers as "saints." [1] Verses praising reform and damning the spoils system were set to music and sung at reform gatherings.[2] The concentration of prominence, influence, and fervor in the civil service reform movement made it a powerful force in American politics.

Traditionally, historians have viewed the civil service reform movement in simple terms of "good" versus "evil." "Good" reformers were outraged by the "evils" of the spoils system and attacked it. Historians rarely, if ever, have ascribed ulterior motives to these reformers but rather have held them up as worthy examples for future generations.

Matthew Josephson is an exception. Influenced by Karl Marx and Max Weber and writing during the "Great Depression," he claims industrial and later financial capitalism dominated the post–Civil War era. Josephson stresses that the civil service reform movement was a businessman's movement designed to take the reins of gov-

---

[1] George William Curtis *et al.* to _____, New York, May 17, 1889, printed form letter in National Civil Service League Papers, National Civil Service League, New York; Dorman B. Eaton to Silas W. Burt, Washington, March 3, 1884, Burt Collection, New York Historical Society.

[2] Henry Lambert, *Civil Service Reform Campaign Song: Tune, "The Old Granite State,"* copy in National Civil Service Reform League Papers.

ernment away from the rude spoilsman, whose power was based upon political assessments and plunder derived from the civil service. Thus the function of the movement, according to Josephson, was to make the political party dependent upon contributions from businessmen and amenable to the business point of view. After 1880 and 1881, Josephson claims, even the industrial capitalist became disgusted with the spoilsman and clamored for civil service reform.[3]

Josephson is not the only author to find a deeper meaning in the civil service reform movement. A distinguished political scientist, E. E. Schattschneider, sees reform as a presidential weapon used in the Executive's unending struggle with Congress. He argues that American political parties have always been decentralized; that power, including the actual control of patronage, has been lodged in the hands of the local political boss rather than the President; and that congressmen—mere minions of the boss—"have extracted patronage from the national government for the benefit of local party bosses at the cost of the public reputation of the president, who has been forced to prostitute the public services for the advantage of the local bosses in order to get their consent to his legislative program." The complete abolition of the spoils system would crush the boss, would increase the power of the President, and would help create a centralized party system. Schattschneider argues that Presidents have been consistent supporters of reform while congressmen have conspicuously opposed it.[4]

Social psychology as well as political science can contribute to an understanding of the civil service reform movement. Certain historians have recently viewed reformers, such as abolitionists and progressives, as members of a "displaced class" who became frustrated when they were no longer politically, socially, or economically dominant, and who achieved self-fulfillment by attacking a convenient whipping boy.[5] This view has become so controversial that the term "displaced class" arouses bitter hostility among many historians. Nevertheless, this view deserves as careful consideration as

[3] Matthew Josephson, *The Politicos, 1865–1896* (New York, 1938), pp. 276–277, 319, 321–323.

[4] E. E. Schattschneider, *Party Government* (New York, 1942), pp. 137–140. The quotation is found on pp. 139–140.

[5] Richard Hofstadter, *The Age of Reform: From Bryan to F.D.R.* (New York, 1955), pp. 131–173; David Donald, *Lincoln Reconsidered* (New York, 1956), pp. 19–36; George E. Mowry, "The California Progressive and His Rationale," *Mississippi Valley Historical Review*, XXXVI, No. 2 (September, 1949), 239–250.

any other hypothesis that has been advanced to explain reform movements.

Who is right? The answer to this query lies in a history of the civil service reform movement and in an analysis of its personnel. Who were the civil service reformers, why did they become reformers, and what was the impact of reform upon politics and upon the civil service itself? It is my hope that the following study will help answer these questions.

My research leads me to suggest that the civil service reform movement fits into an "out" versus "in" pattern. The post–Civil War political world was not what the "outs" expected it to be. In their disappointment, they turned to reform. "Civil service reform," Benjamin F. Butler jeered, "is always popular with the 'outs' and never with the 'ins,' unless with those who have a strong expectation of soon going out." [6] The master spoilsman has supplied my text.

Early attacks on the spoils system by "outs" were designed to embarrass their political enemies. Later Charles Sumner and Thomas A. Jenckes seemed to time the introduction of their civil service reform bills to confound Presidents Lincoln and Johnson. Although Sumner pursued his plan no further, Jenckes continued his agitation and eventually received widespread support outside of Congress. Many of these supporters had seen their own political aspirations or those of their friends frustrated under Johnson and after a season of hope crushed by Grant. Blaming the professional politician for their political impotence, reformers struck at his source of strength, the spoils system. As a weapon they used civil service reform, which would convert the public service from partisanship to political neutrality. By the close of the Grant regime, these reformers could not be bought off with patronage. Being consistent men, they refused to turn their backs on reform.

The waning political effectiveness of reformers, before they organized themselves into a pressure group, reflected their declining economic and social power. Civil service reform flourished in an age when the businessman, particularly the industrialist, became the most important element in American society. Although businessmen formed about half the rank-and-file membership of civil service reform associations, very few reformers were industrialists. Indeed,

[6] *Congressional Globe,* 42 Cong., 2 sess., Appendix, 268.

the leadership of the movement was made up almost entirely of professional men—editors, lawyers, doctors, clergymen, and professors—whose families long had occupied an honored position in society.

These reformers had other interests as well as outlawing the spoils system. They started their careers as free-soilers and finished them as anti-imperialists. In the interim along with civil service reform they advocated tariff reform, sound money, and antimonopoly. From the founding of the Republican party to their defection in 1884, civil service reformers were one of its most important elements. As political independents from 1884 through 1896, they helped pick the winner in all four presidential contests. Their history is not only that of civil service reform but also that of a significant, almost crucial, political faction in the post–Civil War era. Their story suggests reinterpretations and adds new shades of meaning to many old questions, such as why reformers abandoned Radical Reconstruction and why President Hayes attacked Roscoe Conkling's control of the New York Customhouse. The thoughts and actions of these reformers comprise an integral part of the political, social, and intellectual history of their time. The object of this book is to mirror the role of civil service reformers while showing the history of their movement.

My debts are many. Professor David Donald of Princeton University not only suggested this book but also guided and criticized it in all stages. Professor C. Vann Woodward of Yale University read the entire manuscript with great care and made numerous suggestions. I also received valuable criticism on the whole manuscript from Professors Richard Hofstadter, Joseph Dorfman, Wallace S. Sayre, and R. K. Webb of Columbia University, Professor Kenneth K. Bailey and Professor and Mrs. Robert Burlingame of Texas Western College, and Mrs. Robert A. McDaniel of the University of Illinois Press. I am also indebted to Professor Jeannette P. Nichols of the University of Pennsylvania for criticism of my chapters on Hayes's administration, to Professor Paul P. Van Riper of Cornell University, to Professor Ruth Keesey of East Carolina College, to Professor Walter Ralls of Hobart College, to Professor Wayne Fuller of Texas Western College, to Professor A. W. Werline of Columbia Union College, to Miss Beth Kantor of Pennsylvania State University, and to members of Professor David Donald's seminar at Columbia University—especially to

Professor Grady McWhiney of Northwestern University, to Professor Irwin Unger of Long Beach State College, and to Dr. Norman Dain of Rutgers University. I am deeply indebted to my mother, Mrs. Ari Hoogenboom, Sr., to my sister, Clara Hoogenboom, and especially to my wife, Olive Hoogenboom, who aided my project from beginning to end.

Librarians contributed greatly of their time and knowledge to this study. My debt to C. P. Powell of the Manuscripts Division of the Library of Congress and to W. H. Bond, Curator of Manuscripts at the Library of Harvard University, is especially heavy, since their collections supplied a large number of my citations. Watt P. Marchman, Director of the Rutherford B. Hayes Library, Fremont, Ohio, was most generous in donating his time to my queries and in making valuable material available to me on interlibrary loan. Other librarians who have been most helpful are Kenneth Lohf of Columbia University Libraries and Mrs. Elaine Woodruff, Librarian of the United States Civil Service Commission. I am also indebted to the staff of the Collection of Regional History and University Archives at Cornell University, Miss Mary C. Venn of Oberlin College Library, Miss Helen C. Drummond of the National Civil Service League, W. Neil Franklin, Thad Page, and Harold E. Hufford of the National Archives, Robert Haynes, Curator of the Theodore Roosevelt Collection at Harvard College Library, Wilmer R. Leech of the New York Historical Society, Wayne Andrews, formerly of the New York Historical Society but now of Charles Scribner's Sons, and Baxter Polk of the Texas Western College Library.

I am grateful to Joseph G. Rayback, editor of the *Historian*, and to William C. Binkley, editor of the *Mississippi Valley Historical Review*, for permission to reprint portions of my articles: "An Analysis of Civil Service Reformers," *Historian*, XXIII, No. 1 (November, 1960), 54–78; and "Thomas A. Jenckes and Civil Service Reform," *Mississippi Valley Historical Review*, XLVII, No. 4 (March, 1961), 636–658.

CONTENTS

I

CITADEL OF THE SPOILSMEN

I

"At present there is no organization save that of corruption," complained Julius Bing of the American civil service in 1868, "no system save that of chaos; no test of integrity save that of partisanship; no test of qualification save that of intrigue." Bing exclaimed to his fellow citizens: "we have to deal with a wide-spread evil, which defrauds the country in the collection of taxes on a scale so gigantic that the commissioners of revenue, collectors, assessors, and Treasury officers—at least those of them who are honest—bow their heads in shame and despair. We have to deal with an evil that is manifest here and there and everywhere." [1] The typical reformer—and Bing was typical—took a dim view of the civil service. It was not as "evil" as Bing's hysterical prose suggested. Indeed, the government would not have functioned at all if corruption and incompetence were as universal as reformers alleged. Nevertheless, professionalism was almost nonexistent in the civil service, and politics permeated it to the core.

At the end of the Civil War the bureaucracy, which reformers were striving to improve, was subdivided into seven departments employing 53,000 workers whose annual compensation amounted to about $30,000,000. Uncle Sam was then, as he is now, the largest employer in the United States. The Post Office Department, with an office in nearly every village, employed more than half of all civil servants. Next in size and in political importance was the Treasury Department with a large office in Washington, sizable customhouses in major port cities, and internal revenue agents dis-

---

[1] Julius Bing, "Our Civil Service," *Putnam's Magazine* (New York), New Series, II, No. 8 (August, 1868), 233, 236.

persed throughout the country. The somewhat smaller Interior Department was also politically significant because of the Land, Patent, Indian, and Pension Bureaus. The remaining War, Navy, State, and Justice Departments controlled less patronage.[2]

The civil service lacked system. Uniformity in personnel policy outside of Washington was by accident rather than by design, and only a loose personnel system existed even in Washington where clerks were divided into four grades, were compensated accordingly, and were examined for competence upon appointment. Other evidences of a personnel system were the provision for supervision of clerks, the fixing of hours by Congress, the experimentation with efficiency ratings, and the tendency to reward the proficient with promotion. In practice, however, the personnel system was primitive. Examinations were farcical, nepotism was common, no real promotion policy existed, and there was neither a training program for new recruits nor provision for retirement.[3] In these respects the American bureaucracy was not unique. British personnel practices —despite progress toward reform—were also primitive, and those of private business were even more backward.

It is difficult to separate policy-making positions from purely administrative positions in the civil service. Perhaps the founding fathers attempted this separation, for the Constitution differentiates between important officers appointed by the President with the advice and consent of the Senate and inferior officers appointed by the President alone, the courts, or department heads. In 1842 policy makers were described by a House committee as either confidential advisers of the President or those able to aid or hinder an administration policy. The "ministerial level" had plummeted to the lowest ranks by 1865; the humblest postmaster was considered capable of aiding or hindering administration policy.[4]

Apportionment of Washington offices among the states and territories according to population was theoretically well established by 1865. Actual practice, however, departed from theory. An analysis of the 321 clerks in the second auditor's office in the Treasury De-

---

[2] Joint Select Committee on Retrenchment, "Civil Service of the United States," *House Reports*, 40 Cong., 2 sess., II, No. 47, 2, 7. Civil servants may actually have numbered 70,000 in 1867. See Appendix A for the number of civil servants at various times.

[3] Leonard D. White, *The Jacksonians* (New York, 1954), pp. 394–398. White's generalizations on the personnel system in 1860 are applicable five years later.

[4] *Ibid.*, pp. 347–348, 394–395.

partment reveals that the northeastern states fared better than southern or western states. In the more specialized Patent Office, areas near the capital almost completely monopolized appointments with the District of Columbia claiming nearly one-third of the ninety-six employees.[5] Western congressmen bitterly protested that the Northeast and the District of Columbia received a disproportionate share of Washington appointments. After the Civil War and Reconstruction their cries were echoed by southern congressmen.

Tenure of civil servants was short and uncertain in the 1860's. Although every department could point to civil servants who had been in office for many years, these workers were the exception. They formed the working core of the civil service, provided continuity and consistency in administration, and trained new recruits. An example frequently cited is that of William Hunter, the Second Assistant Secretary of State, who in 1868 had been employed in the State Department for thirty-nine years. Unlike Hunter, most civil servants held their positions only a short time and anticipated early dismissal. Tenure varied, with offices requiring a high degree of technical knowledge retaining their employees the longest. In 1868 twenty-seven of the fifty-five officers in the New York assay office had been employed more than ten years and forty-five of them had worked there more than six years. The office of the United States Treasurer, however, is more representative. A tally taken in December, 1867, found that 219 of the 282 employees had been appointed within the preceding four years. Only five individuals had been employed over ten years.

The training and backgrounds of civil servants differed widely. For positions requiring technical competence—such as jobs in assay offices and in the Patent Office—men of ability were secured and retained. In other offices, background was less exacting. The 282 employees in the Treasurer's office were a motley group. They numbered in previous occupations "7 accountants, 13 bankers, 18 bookkeepers, 27 clerks, 1 detective, 2 druggists, 1 editor, 5 farmers, 1 hackdriver, 1 housekeeper, 1 hotel steward, 16 laborers, 1 lawyer, 1 machinist, 1 manufacturer, 8 mechanics, 14 merchants, 2 messengers, 1 minister, 1 page, 1 porter, 1 postman, 2 salesmen, 1 sculptor, 12 students, 1 surveyor, 24 teachers, 2 telegraphists, 1 county treasurer, 1 waiter, 1 washerwoman, 1 watchman, and of no particular oc-

---

[5] *Register of Officers and Agents* (Washington, 1866), pp. 25–29, 129–131.

cupation, 112." [6] These appointments were not the result of haphazard policy. They were the fruit of the spoils system.

The spoils system, though hoary in some aspects, had grown with
democracy; it was no accident that the two developed side by side.
With frequent elections decided by large numbers, democracy forced
politicians to build elaborate organizations to influence voters. The
best assets in building a "machine" were local, state, and federal
employees whose jobs depended upon politicians. With the application of pressure these civil servants would contribute both
time and money to their patron's political wars. Frequent elections,
however, meant frequent changes, for winning politicians would
force their political enemies out of office. By 1865 the spoils system
(like democracy) was well established and rested on three major
principles: appointment primarily for political considerations, congressional dictation of most appointments, and rotation of officeholders.

Appointment of officers for political reasons had early precedents.
In the British colonial service in America offices were secured
through political connections, just as they were in England. The
Revolution and the launching of the federal Constitution brought
little change in personnel recruitment. Although Washington made
few removals—and none for political reasons—his appointments
became increasingly partisan. He wrote in 1795 that he would not
"bring men into any office of consequence knowingly whose political
tenets are adverse to the measures the general government is pursu-
ing; for this, in my opinion, would be a sort of political suicide." [7]
Washington's successors followed his policy of appointing political
friends to office. As time went on, ability received less and less emphasis. By 1865 capacity was an unnecessary prerequisite for most
offices.

---

[6] "Civil Service of the United States," pp. 23, 40, 203.

[7] On the historic connection between politics and the British civil service, see
Catherine Drinker Bowen, *The Lion and the Throne* (Boston, 1957), *passim*.
Dorman B. Eaton, *Civil Service in Great Britain* (New York, 1880), pp. 91–97, is
particularly harsh on Walpole. See Carl Russell Fish, *The Civil Service and the
Patronage* (Cambridge, 1920), pp. 1, 6–16, on spoils in the British colonial service
and in Washington's administration. The roots of the spoils system did not escape
the notice of Edward Channing, *A History of the United States* (New York,
1905–25), IV, 56. "The 'spoils system,' indeed, instead of being an invention of
Jacksonian Democrats or Jeffersonian Republicans, was an inheritance from the
Federalist Presidents and by them had been built up on colonial and English
precedents."

The Constitution gave Congress no right of appointment, but by 1865 that body dictated most civil service appointments. From the beginning of the government, congressmen steadily increased their influence for it was impossible for the President and department heads to know all candidates for offices. As early as the close of John Adams' administration, congressmen were normally consulted upon federal appointments in their districts, and by Abraham Lincoln's administration post office appointments were completely turned over to them.[8]

Congressional control of patronage was simplified by rotation of officers, which was firmly established by 1865. Rotation had been practiced occasionally before the American Revolution, and during that struggle it was required by many state constitutions to keep officeholders in close contact with the people. The Articles of Confederation had fixed terms for executive officers in the territories, and the federal government continued this policy. By the end of John Adams' administration, justices of the peace in the District of Columbia were appointed for five-year terms.[9] A Tenure of Office Act was passed in 1820 which created the machinery for a "clean sweep." By limiting to four years the terms of certain offices—primarily regional ones in the Treasury Department—congressional control of government service was increased. The act's effects on partisan politics were obvious from the start. Former Presidents Jefferson and Madison were both alarmed. Candidates for offices appeared whenever commissions expired, and John Quincy Adams noted that rotation was "more congenial to republicans out of than to those in office." Both James Monroe and Adams, however, reappointed worthy officers, and Adams even recommissioned men actively opposed to his re-election.[10]

Andrew Jackson's presidency did not mark as sharp a break with the past in practice as it did in theory. The first President to espouse

---

[8] Leonard D. White, *The Federalists* (New York, 1948), p. 83; Harry J. Carman and Reinhard H. Luthin, *Lincoln and the Patronage* (New York, 1943), pp. 70–71.
[9] Fish, *op. cit.*, pp. 80–85.
[10] Leonard D. White, *The Jeffersonians* (New York, 1951), pp. 387–390. "The classes of agents affected [by the Tenure of Office Act of 1820] were district attorneys, collectors of the customs, naval officers and surveyors of the customs, navy agents, receivers of public money for lands, registers of the land offices, paymasters in the army, the apothecary general, the assistant apothecaries general, and the commissary general of purchases. Not affected were pursers, Indian agents, postmasters, or any of the accounting and clerical officers and employees stationed in Washington." *Ibid.*, p. 387.

the theory of rotation, Jackson argued that the duties of all officers were so simple—or could be made so—that any intelligent person could quickly master them. The loss of efficiencies supposedly gained after years of service was offset, according to Jackson, by destroying the idea that the office was the property of the holder. Although Jackson swept virtually all his opponents from the lucrative presidential offices (important posts filled by the President with the Senate's consent), relatively few inferior officers were proscribed. By the end of his second term only about 10 per cent of the civil service had been removed. Nevertheless, the spoils system continued to grow during Jackson's administration. Spoilsmen added a practical defense of rotation to the theoretical view that rotation was democratic, and argued openly that hope of office held the parties together. An administration, they claimed, which distributed patronage impartially courted its own destruction.[11]

Both parties were soon thoroughly committed to spoils policies; in making appointments party considerations, not ability to perform public duties, were of utmost importance. Although Martin Van Buren made few changes at the beginning of his administration, he demanded personal as well as party loyalty when seeking re-election. Despite its previous attacks on rotation in office, the Whig party under William Henry Harrison rotated Democrats out of office in 1841. The Democrats returned under James K. Polk, who replaced 13,500 of the country's 16,000 postmasters and used patronage to implement his program. Both the Whigs under Zachary Taylor and the Democrats under Franklin Pierce continued spoils practices. James Buchanan went one step further and rotated Pierce's appointments out of office even though they were fellow Democrats. William Marcy, who earlier had said "to the victors belong the spoils," now complained that he had never intended to pillage his own camp and observed that "Pierce men are hunted down like wild beasts." Under the Republican administration of Abraham Lincoln, 1,457 incumbents of the 1,639 presidential offices were removed. In addition, the occupants of many offices were changed two and three times between 1861 and 1865. The Civil War and the accompanying fear of disloyalty aided this almost complete pro-

[11] James D. Richardson, *A Compilation of the Messages and Papers of the Presidents 1789–1897* (Washington, 1896–99), II, 448–449; Fish, *op. cit.*, pp. 125–126; White, *The Jacksonians*, pp. 307–308, 317; Arthur M. Schlesinger, Jr., *The Age of Jackson* (Boston, 1946), p. 47.

scription. The spoils system had triumphed; the alternation of party control had been basic in bringing it about.[12] Ironically, a half century later frequent change of the party in power would have the same effect on the merit system.

II

Pre–Civil War protests against the spoils system were neither widespread, deep, nor well directed. The extension of the spoils system accompanying the rise of democracy was popular and was even regarded by many as reform. Early complaints were sporadic, aimed at the President, and made primarily by congressmen who failed to realize it was they and their colleagues who abused the patronage. Furthermore, those who opposed spoils practices were usually out of power, but once these "outs" were "in" the evils of the system seemed to vanish. Opponents of the spoils system tended to belong to the Federalist-Whig-Republican political tradition. Democrats, who were not "out" very often before the Civil War, were committed ideologically to frequent change of officers. Indeed so strong was their commitment to rotation and so well did they realize its political value that despite being "out" for twenty years Democrats virtually ignored civil service reform until 1880. During and after the Civil War attempts to reform civil service came primarily from dissident elements within the Republican party.

Despite differences between prewar and postwar efforts, early attacks on the spoils system were the seeds of the civil service reform movement. In 1811 Josiah Quincy, a Federalist representative from Massachusetts, attacked the evils involved in man's passion for office. Quincy feared that congressional independence would be subverted by executive abuse of the patronage. Although he hoped to influence public opinion as well as influence his colleagues in favor of reform, neither responded. Fifteen years later Thomas Hart Benton's proposal to reduce Executive patronage by transferring it to Congress was essentially a political attack on President John Quincy Adams by an ardent Jacksonian.[13] After Jackson became President the Whigs challenged his power of removal. Henry Clay,

---

[12] White, *The Jacksonians*, pp. 309–315, and Fish, *op. cit.*, pp. 134–172, discuss rotation from Van Buren to Lincoln. Carman and Luthin, *op. cit.*, p. 331, agree that Lincoln made a complete sweep.

[13] White, *The Jeffersonians*, pp. 386–387, 390–393; Charles Eliot Norton, ed., *Orations and Addresses of George William Curtis* (New York, 1894), II, 9.

who only a few years earlier had urged Adams to use the civil
service for partisan ends, now led the attack against executive abuse
of the appointing power while Benton significantly remained silent.
Specifically, the Whigs launched a drive to repeal part of the Tenure
of Office Act of 1820 (the four-year law) and to require the President to submit reasons for making removals. Once again, those
favoring this "reform"—Clay, Daniel Webster, John C. Calhoun,
Thomas Ewing, and Hugh Lawson White—were opponents of the
administration. The Whigs momentarily forgot "reform" when they
gained the presidency in 1841, but their lapse of memory was as
short-lived as their triumph. Before the end of John Tyler's administration they were again the opposition, and in 1844 one of their
senators, James T. Morehead, offered an elaborate report on the
evils of patronage. Despite the shallowness of these early Whig attacks, they did expose the dangers of rotation in office.[14]

These harmful effects were soon apparent. No longer was there
prestige attached to being a civil servant. Political obligations of
officeholders took precedence over their public obligations. Not
only was political orthodoxy demanded of officeholders, but they
also were required to contribute time and money ("assessments")
to political campaigns. Under these circumstances, efficiency suffered
and the career service was whittled to the bone.[15]

To correct this situation, Congress instituted examinations to
determine proficiency. These examinations had precedents—Jefferson had used them in certain branches of the military service, and
the Jacksonians had continued and expanded his program. In addition, certain British agencies had for many years selected agents,
teachers, and engineers through examinations, which frequently
were competitive and open to all.[16] The United States followed
Britain's example, but from a distance. A House committee headed
by Thomas W. Gilmer, a States Rights' Virginian, unsuccessfully
recommended in 1842 that clerks be examined after appointment
but before entering service. Unlike other early congressional "reformers," Gilmer was not motivated by political hostility; he was
genuinely interested in retrenchment. Nine years later, the Senate

---

[14] White, *The Jacksonians*, pp. 40–42, 323–324; Fish, *op. cit.*, pp. 140–142.
[15] White, *The Jacksonians*, pp. 325–346.
[16] White, *The Jeffersonians*, pp. 362–364; White, *The Jacksonians*, pp. 363–365;
Eaton, *op. cit.*, pp. 155–168, covers the introduction of examinations in Great
Britain.

requested executive department heads to provide a plan for examination, classification, graded pay, and systematic promotion. Without the help of Secretary of State Daniel Webster, who was hostile to the idea, a plan was reported in 1852 and was enacted the next year by a Democratic Congress.[17] The service itself demanded these innovations; neither public opinion nor any political party had called for a system of examinations. No one outside of government circles seemed to be interested.

The law of 1853 classified most of the 700 Washington clerks into grades and required that incumbents as well as appointees be examined before receiving commissions. All classified clerks in Washington were examined before July 1, 1853, and only a "few" were found incompetent. These "pass" examinations were not competitive and if honestly administered merely insured a minimum standard. Although the public service derived some benefit from this legislation—which was in force until the passage of the Pendleton Act in 1883—examinations were frequently farcical. Yet the setting up of a minimum standard provided machinery to prevent the retention and future appointment of the worst incompetents.[18]

This advance toward a career service was followed by an abortive step in 1856. Ironically Secretary of State William Marcy, who gave the spoils system its name, suggested a statute, which Congress enacted, requiring that twenty-five well-qualified consular pupils be selected by examination or by other means. Before any pupils could be selected, Congress repealed the law and temporarily crushed the trend toward a career service.[19]

The need for further regulating government service became urgent in the 1860's. During the Civil War, most experienced Democrats were swept from the federal service, while its functions and personnel expanded rapidly. Abnormal conditions caused inefficiencies, which magnified the problems of administration. At the request of Secretary of State William H. Seward, John Bigelow, Paris Consul-General, enthusiastically reported in 1863 on competitive examinations used in France to select customs officers.[20] On April 30, 1864,

---

[17] Select Committee on Retrenchment, "Retrenchment-Reorganization of Executive Departments," *House Reports*, 27 Cong., 2 sess., IV, No. 741, 24; *Congressional Globe*, 32 Cong., 2 sess., 897; White, *The Jacksonians*, pp. 150–152, 365–366.

[18] *Ibid.*, pp. 365–375; Fish, *op. cit.*, pp. 182–183.

[19] White, *The Jacksonians*, p. 374.

[20] Fish, *op. cit.*, p. 210. Bigelow was not enthusiastic about having to write this report. He resigned but reconsidered when Seward asked him to stay on. Margaret

Charles Sumner, Massachusetts Republican senator, introduced a
bill providing for competitive examinations administered by a civil
service commission. This system was similar to that eventually
adopted, but Sumner did not strongly urge the passage of the bill
and asked that it be tabled.[21]

Sumner's objectives are not clear. Ostensibly, he wished to eliminate inefficiencies in the civil service, but his timing suggests that
partisanship may have been a motivating factor. In 1864, Sumner
opposed Lincoln's renomination, and although his bill had been
ready for three months, he did not introduce it until the Lincoln
machine—manned by officeholders—triumphed in early precon-
vention maneuvering over the similar machine of Salmon P. Chase.
The attempt to focus public attention on the civil service did not
prevent Lincoln's nomination.[22]

Having long written of his contempt for offices, officeholders, rotation, and the spoils system,[23] Sumner wrote of his bill: "I matured
it alone, without consultation, and flung it on the table of the
Senate as a way of drawing attention to the subject. . . . I do not
doubt that the scale of business now and the immense interests involved will require some such system. We cannot transact our great

Clapp, *Forgotten First Citizen* (Boston, 1947), p. 188. Perhaps Seward wished to
embarrass his archenemy, Secretary of the Treasury Salmon P. Chase, with this
report.

[21] *Congressional Globe*, 38 Cong., 1 sess., 1985. The bill is reprinted in Charles
Sumner, *The Works of Charles Sumner* (Boston, 1870–83), VIII, 452–454.

[22] Sumner mentions his bill in Sumner to Francis Lieber, no place, January 31,
1864, in Edward L. Pierce, *Memoir and Letters of Charles Sumner* (Boston,
1877–93), IV, 191. For details of Lincoln's troubles with the Radicals of whom
Sumner was a leader, see T. Harry Williams, *Lincoln and the Radicals* (Madison,
1941), *passim,* and for information on Lincoln's political machine and his nomination, see Carman and Luthin, *op. cit.*, pp. 228–260. Yet evidence that political considerations led Sumner to introduce his bill is merely circumstantial. On the other
hand, Sumner's bill received support from the *New York Times,* a strong Lincoln
paper whose editor, Henry J. Raymond, became Lincoln's campaign manager in
1864. Raymond hardly would have supported Sumner's bill if he thought it in-
jurious to Lincoln.

[23] Sumner to George Sumner, Boston, June 24, 1846, Sumner Papers, Harvard
University; Pierce, *op. cit.*, III, 149; Sumner to George Sumner, no place, July 31,
1849, *ibid.*, p. 44. Although in the past he had opposed spoils methods when the
Democrats were in office, Sumner now, as chairman of the Senate Foreign Relations
Committee, exerted influence to secure offices for friends. Carman and Luthin,
op. cit., pp. 99, 105, give two examples. See also three letters from George William
Curtis, a future champion of civil service reform, to Sumner, North Shore, [Staten
Island, New York], June 28, 1861, Staten Island, October 27 and December 29, 1862,
Sumner Papers.

concerns without serious loss unless we have trained men. 'Rotation in office' is proper enough in the political posts where political direction is determined, but absurd in the machinery of administration. . . . This is a moment for changes. Our whole system is like molten wax, ready to receive an impression." [24] Sumner patterned his "impression" on British precedents. He was a close student of English institutions, corresponded with leading Englishmen, and, as his bill demonstrates, was well aware of the increased use of competitive tests in the British civil service. Open-competitive examinations had been used in Britain as early as 1853 for selecting appointees to the Indian civil service. Two years later a British civil service commission had been created to supervise examinations for the home service. At first these examinations were primarily noncompetitive, but after 1860 limited competition was generally adopted.[25]

Sumner's bill aroused distinguished support outside of Congress. "I am astonished at the echo to my little bill on civil service," he confided to a friend. Part of the echo came from the Washington *National Intelligencer,* the *New York Times,* the New York *Evening Post,* and the New York *Independent.* Among those endorsing Sumner's bill were Professor Joseph Henry of the Smithsonian Institution; Professor Francis Lieber of Columbia College, who, even while doubting the bill would pass, desired to be a civil service commissioner; Bradford R. Wood of Albany, a founder of the New York Republican party and Lincoln's minister to Denmark; William E. Dodge, Jr., of Phelps, Dodge and Company, New York importer of metals, who sent word that the Union League Club of New York had organized to support the bill; and E. B. Ward, a Detroit businessman who declared that next to crushing the rebellion Sumner's bill was of greatest importance. Josiah Quincy, who at ninety-two was only a few weeks from death, also commended Sumner's measure to reform the evil he himself had attacked fifty-three years earlier. Yet most of Sumner's correspondents and most of the country's press ignored his civil service bill, which was never revived.[26]

---

[24] Sumner to Lieber, no place, May 15, 1864, in Pierce, *op. cit.,* IV, 192.

[25] Eaton, *op. cit.,* pp. 177–223; Robert Moses, *The Civil Service of Great Britain* (New York, 1914), pp. 48–126. On the British civil service, consult the two works just cited in addition to the more provocative J. Donald Kingsley, *Representative Bureaucracy* (Yellow Springs, Ohio, 1944).

[26] Sumner to Lieber, no place, May 15, 1864, in Pierce, *op. cit.,* IV, 192; Dodge to Sumner, New York, May 13, 1862 [1864], Henry to Sumner, Washington, May 14, 1864, and Ward to Sumner, Detroit, May 25, 1864, Sumner Papers; Lieber to

Sumner was also prominent among those favoring competitive examinations for appointees to the United States military and naval academies. In the years before and during the Civil War ineffectual moves were made to secure a uniform system of admission examinations. The Civil War increased interest in and criticism of these academies. While Grant, Lee, and Sherman were hailed as distinguished graduates of West Point, McClellan, Bragg, and Buell were exhibited as incompetents. The 1863 to 1865 boards of visitors to both academies, the teaching staffs, and Secretary of War Edwin M. Stanton criticized the admission policies and requested competitive examinations.[27] Congress ruled in June, 1866, that five nominees by each congressman be examined and the best selected for cadetship at West Point, but dropped this limited competition a few months later.[28] The exigencies of war had also enabled the West Point faculty to discharge poor students. With the end of the war, however, congressmen resumed their old power and sometimes even refused to have their cadets discharged regardless of inability.[29]

Despite the action of Congress, several of its members used competitive examinations to select nominees for the military and naval academies. In 1859, Daniel E. Sickles, a New York Democrat, selected his appointee to the military academy after a competitive examination of twenty candidates. The successful individual—an average student at the New York Free Academy—graduated at the head of his West Point class. Other congressmen, such as Republicans James A. Garfield of Ohio and Henry B. Anthony of Rhode Island, followed Sickles' example and selected cadets by examination. To this pioneering group belonged Thomas A. Jenckes.[30]

Sumner, New York, May 12, 1864, Lieber Papers, Henry E. Huntington Library, San Marino, California. For support by Wood and Quincy, see Pierce, op. cit., IV, 191. Ward was also an early supporter of Thomas A. Jenckes's attempts to reform the civil service. Infra, p. 39, n. 16.

[27] Pierce, op. cit., IV, 191, n. 4; W. E. Crosby, "Competitive Examinations for Admission to the Military and Naval Schools," Nation (New York), I, No. 8 (August 24, 1865), 231–233; T. R. Lounsbury, "The West Point Military Academy," ibid., No. 26 (December 28, 1865), 807–809.

[28] "Congress: Diary," ibid., II, No. 57 (June 15, 1866), 754; Ed. Schriver to Thomas A. Jenckes, Washington, September 28, 1867, Jenckes Papers, Library of Congress.

[29] D. H. Mahan, "The West Point Military School: Its Abuses and Their Correctives," Nation, II, No. 34 (February 22, 1866), 243–244.

[30] W. E. Crosby, loc. cit.; Charles Briggs to Jenckes, Providence, April 12, 1864, and Charles W. Tippitt to Jenckes, Providence, April 28, 1864, Jenckes Papers.

II

JENCKES ASSAULTS THE
SPOILS SYSTEM

The impact of the Civil War upon the civil service was similar to
its effect on the larger social order. The war accelerated developments already under way. The growing bureaucracy swelled ab-
normally and the rotation of officeholders increased. Although the
spoils system controlled more offices more completely than before,
the stress of war exposed its deficiencies and stimulated interest in
reform. In this way, the Civil War contributed both to the rise and
to the fall of the spoils system. It was the war's legacy of Reconstruction, however, that played a greater though more subtle role
in the movement for civil service reform.

I

By 1864, Thomas Allen Jenckes was a leader of the Rhode Island
bar and one of the ablest attorneys in the House of Representatives.
He had been elected a Republican representative in 1862 and remained in the House until 1871, where he was a member of both
the patent and the judiciary committees. It was during these years
that Jenckes became the recognized leader of the civil service reform
movement. Like many others who were to be interested in civil
service reform, Jenckes came from a prominent old New England
family. He was a man of intellectual breadth, interested in literature
as well as mathematics and the physical sciences, who distinguished
himself in college and quickly rose to prominence in a law career.
Although witty in select company, Jenckes was frequently described
as cold and unsocial, lacking enthusiasm and ignoring public opinion. Despite these traits, he engaged in Rhode Island politics when

quite young. In 1840, two years after his graduation from Brown University, Jenckes was elected reading clerk of the Rhode Island House of Representatives. He sided prominently with the conservatives in the Dorr Rebellion, serving as clerk of the Landholders' Constitutional Conventions of 1841 and 1842 and as secretary to the council of the Whig Governor Samuel Ward King. Jenckes was later adjutant general of Rhode Island, a representative in the state legislature, a member of the committee to revise the state statutes, and chief counsel for Rhode Island in her boundary dispute with Massachusetts, which was before the Supreme Court from 1857 to 1861.

Jenckes's ability and interest in sciences led him to specialize in patent law. He was retained as counsel in many important patent cases and revised and improved federal laws governing patents and copyrights. Patent law also served Jenckes as a springboard to his numerous business enterprises. Connection with the Goodyear patent suits led Jenckes into the infant rubber industry, where his Rubber Sole Shoe Company not only made shoes, which the United States government rejected as inferior during the Civil War, but rubber spittoons as well. Another business interest of Jenckes was the American Wood Paper Company, which through its patents monopolized the manufacturing of paper from wood pulp.[1]

At its Royersford, Pennsylvania, plant, this company employed Hugh Burgess, a scientist friend of Jenckes. Both Jenckes and Burgess had good personal reasons for dissatisfaction with the American civil service. A constant annoyance was their failure to receive material sent to them through the mail. Burgess, who forwarded his foreign periodicals to Jenckes, complained of their frequent pilferage. "I duly receive my scientific periodicals," he wrote Jenckes in September, 1864, "but never the papers of general` interest tho mailed in London by the same agent. . . . When do you bring in your Civil Service Bill. It is much needed in the Post Office."[2]

Jenckes, however, delayed introducing his bill until December,

---

[1] The best biographical account of Jenckes is William B. Munro, "Thomas Allen Jenckes," *Dictionary of American Biography,* eds., Allen Johnson and Dumas Malone (New York, 1928–36), X, 41–42. Other sources of useful biographical material concerning Jenckes are *In Memoriam: Thomas Allen Jenckes, Born November 2, 1818. Died November 4, 1875* (Providence, 1876), *passim;* Thomas A. Jenckes Papers, Library of Congress, *passim.*

[2] Burgess to Jenckes, Royers Ford, September 30, 1864, *ibid.* This letter contains the only reference to civil service reform in Jenckes's Papers prior to the introduction of his bill.

1865. The change in the political situation from September, 1864, to December, 1865, is a possible explanation for Jenckes's delay. As a supporter of Lincoln, he might have withheld his bill rather than undermine party discipline in the civil service. Jenckes, himself a dispenser of patronage, appreciated the political potential of the civil service. In addition, he might have reasoned that there was no pressing need for civil service reform either before or after the election of 1864 since Lincoln used the patronage to achieve ends consonant with Jenckes's desires. Jenckes, although a Radical on Reconstruction matters, did not oppose Lincoln; the immediate problem of winning the war subordinated all other questions. After Lincoln's assassination and the restoration of peace, however, Reconstruction assumed a new importance. When Johnson applied his lenient policy in the summer of 1865 and alienated the Radical wing of the Republican party, Jenckes was among those estranged and was ready with his bill when Congress convened. Designed to curtail executive (as well as legislative) patronage, the Jenckes bill was introduced on December 20, 1865,[3] before Johnson "abused" his appointing power and while his civil service policy was still characterized by restraint. Yet the fear that Johnson would use the patronage to implement his Reconstruction policies was real, and, in Jenckes's mind, could have offset the absence of overt acts.

It is possible that Jenckes had better motives for introducing his bill than circumstantial evidence suggests. In a speech before Congress, he later explained his interest in civil service reform. "When I first entered the public service of this Government during the war, I could not but be struck at once at the great difference between the military and naval administrations and that of the civil departments. It led me to inquire into the cause of this great difference, and to see whether such difference existed in the systems of other nations. I found that in England, during the Crimean war . . . great complaint existed against the civil service from its almost total inefficiency, arising, as admitted and proclaimed, from the vicious mode of appointments to office in that service. I learned that the evil in England had almost been entirely cured, and I looked into her

---

[3] *Congressional Globe,* 39 Cong., 1 sess., 98. For evidence of Jenckes's Radicalism, see his remarks on January 11, 1865. *Ibid.,* 38 Cong., 2 sess., 225. Additional evidences are his close friendship with Henry Winter Davis, the ultra-Radical representative from Maryland, his writing an article of Johnson's impeachment, and his narrowly missing election as a House manager of the impeachment trial.

history to find the reason of the change. I found it . . . in the adoption of a wise and practical system regulating the appointments in the different departments of the civil service." [4]

The bill Jenckes introduced was patterned on British precedent. It would have encompassed all federal civil servants except those "nominated by the President and confirmed by the Senate" and certain postmasters whose salaries fell below an amount to be stipulated by Congress. Only persons found best qualified by open-competitive examinations were to receive civil service appointments. Vacancies above the lowest grade were to be filled either by promoting the senior employee in the next lower grade or by administering a special examination for the position. Competitive examinations also were to determine seniority within civil service grades. The cost of the new system was to be met by fees charged for examinations as well as for certificates of recommendation for appointment, promotion, or seniority.

The Jenckes bill provided for an administering board of three civil service commissioners. These commissioners were to be appointed by the President and confirmed by the Senate for five-year terms, and could be removed by the President only "with the assent of the Senate"—a stipulation which reveals Jenckes's fear of Johnson in particular or Executives in general. Besides administering examinations, the commissioners were to formulate a variety of rules, including the definition of inefficiency or misconduct sufficient for removal and the procedure for the trial of accused civil servants. Two further sections of the bill were not mandatory. Department heads could require examination of officers in service before the bill was to have gone into effect and could remove officers failing to qualify. The President also could require the examination of applicants for positions requiring senatorial confirmation.[5]

The Jenckes bill received from the past and gave to the future. Like Sumner's bill, it derived from Great Britain the concept of open-competitive examinations administered by a commission.[6]

---

[4] *Ibid.*, 39 Cong., 2 sess., 1034.

[5] *A Bill to Regulate the Civil Service of the United States, and Promote the Efficiency Thereof*, 39 Cong., 1 sess., Senate No. 430, forms the basis for the ensuing discussion of the Jenckes bill. This bill was introduced in the Senate by Henry B Anthony of Rhode Island and is identical with the Jenckes bill. The only copy located is in the papers of the Senate Committee on the Judiciary, National Archives.

[6] Although Jenckes reputedly carried on an elaborate correspondence with Eng

British practice, however, was not as advanced as British theory. Although a British Civil Service Commission had existed since 1855 and competitive examinations were generally adopted after 1860, admission to these examinations was restricted to political favorites. It was not until 1870 that open-competitive examinations were adopted in Britain. Nevertheless, the Jenckes bill borrowed freely from the British program and passed its borrowings on to the Pendleton bill. Yet seventeen years of agitation were necessary before enactment of the Pendleton bill, which applied to but a fraction of the offices the Jenckes bill proposed to affect.

Agitation was slow in starting. The Jenckes bill made no headlines, drew no immediate editorial comment, and was mentioned as a news item by only a few newspapers. Two weeks after it was introduced, the *New York Times,* apparently unaware of its existence, concluded an article on the "Want of Efficiency in the American Civil Service" with the question "When shall we begin to initiate remedies?" By January 18, 1866, the *Times* was better informed and editorialized that the Jenckes bill "is too good and too much in advance of our civilization to pass as yet." [7] The reform bill also apparently failed to increase appreciably the volume of Jenckes's correspondence. Only five letters resulted, but one of these included civil service memoranda from David A. Wells, chairman of Johnson's Revenue Commission.[8]

Publication of the Revenue Commission's report in late January, 1866, provided a new impetus for civil service reform. Wells exposed frauds, waste, and incompetency in the New York Customhouse—where, he estimated, $12,000,000 to $25,000,000 were lost annually—and suggested reorganizing the entire revenue system.

---

lish reformers, much searching, both in this country and in England, has uncovered only one letter, which was not addressed to Jenckes but indicated that it was also for his use. Charles E. Trevelyan to Charles Loring Brace, London, February 8, 1869, Library of the United States Civil Service Commission. According to George William Curtis, Jenckes placed his English correspondence at the disposition of the Grant Civil Service Commission. *Civil Service Record* (Boston), II, No. 3 (August, 1882), 21.

[7] *New York Times,* January 7, 1866, p. 4, cc. 6–7; "The Public Service—Competitive Examinations," *ibid.,* January 18, 1866, p. 4, c. 5.

[8] Wells to Jenckes, Washington, January 19, 1866, George W. Searle to Jenckes, Boston, January 12, 1866, William Hichborn to Jenckes, Boston, February 14, 1866, William Allen to Jenckes, New York, March 14, 1866, and Isaac Pitman to Jenckes, Providence, March 24, 1866, Jenckes Papers. Correspondence relating to a bankruptcy bill Jenckes sponsored far outweighed civil service correspondence, although there is the possibility that all civil service letters may not have been preserved.

Specifically, he advocated removing the customhouse from politics by modeling on British example an independent board of custom commissioners to test applicants and to make appointments. The newly founded *Nation* enthusiastically proclaimed that the Revenue Commission had called for open-competitive examinations (when it had merely called for tests) and expressed the desire to see all but the highest public places filled by merit. "The whole system of nomination by members of Congress," it cried, "is a monstrous abuse." [9]

The press, in general, though favoring the Revenue Commission's report, ignored its recommendation for examination of customhouse officials. Even George William Curtis, political editor of *Harper's Weekly* and the future's stanchest champion of the merit system, did not immediately advocate competitive examinations as a cure for civil service abuses. Throughout 1866 he recommended a wider division of presidential patronage among the executive department heads, Congress, and the judiciary—a remedy he would later denounce. Johnson's handling of patronage inspired his fear of one-man control.[10]

The politically independent *Nation*, brilliantly edited by Edwin Lawrence Godkin, on the other hand, early and consistently supported civil service reform. When Godkin emigrated from Britain in 1856 he already had a distinguished record as Crimean War correspondent of the London *Daily News*. In America he flirted briefly with law, studying under David Dudley Field, but journalism remained his first love. Godkin's dream of founding and editing a weekly was realized in 1865 when he joined with James Miller McKim, Frederick Law Olmsted, Charles Eliot Norton, and others to establish the *Nation*. Outstanding contributors and particularly Godkin—hard-working, hardheaded, a trifle hardhearted, and very

---

[9] United States Revenue Commission, "Revenue System of the United States," *House Executive Documents*, 39 Cong., 1 sess., VII, No. 34, 44–51; "The Way the Government Is Served," *Nation* (New York), II, No. 33 (February 15, 1866), 198.

[10] See, for example, "Our Revenue System—The Inequalities of Taxation," *New York Times*, February 4, 1866, p. 4, cc. 3–4; "Our Revenue System," *New York Tribune*, January 30, 1866, p. 4, c. 3; "Report of the Revenue Commission—Important Recommendations for the Regulation of Taxes," *New York Herald*, January 30, 1866, p. 4, cc. 4–5; "Frauds in the New York Custom-House," *Press* (Philadelphia), January 31, 1866, p. 4, c. 3; "Custom House Frauds," *Harper's Weekly* (New York), X, No. 479 (March 3, 1866), 130; "Presidential Patronage," *ibid.*, No. 484 (April 7, 1866), 210; "The Appointing Power," *ibid.*, No. 491 (May 26, 1866), 322; "Satraps and Dependents," *ibid.*, No. 506 (September 8, 1866), 562.

hard-hitting—made the *Nation,* to quote James Bryce, "the best weekly not only in America but in the world." Editor for thirty-five years, Godkin reflected and shaped the attitudes of the so-called "best people" and from the start worked for civil service reform. In January, 1866, the *Nation* complained that the New York Post Office was "managed as if it were simply a large hall for political re-unions," and in March it specifically advocated the Jenckes bill, whose principles "worked eminently well in England," and urged purging the civil service of "political partizans destitute of business capacity" as well as "political eunuchs with not force enough to call their souls their own." [11]

Despite the *Nation's* support, civil service reform did not make good newspaper copy in 1866. Newspapers ignored the creation of the House Select Committee on the Civil Service in March, the reporting and recommitting of the Jenckes bill in June, and the passage, also in June, of a resolution offered by Senator B. Gratz Brown of Missouri directing a Senate committee to inquire into the expediency of reforming the civil service. In July, the introduction of Jenckes's bill in the Senate by his friend Henry B. Anthony was also unheralded by the press.[12] The unprecedented struggle between President Andrew Johnson and Congress was far more important than civil service reform, even to the press that later formed the backbone of the movement.

Office seekers did not trim their sails to meet the slight stirrings created by the civil service bill. As Jenckes's actions illustrated, a congressman, even while reforming the civil service, had to dispense patronage to maintain his political position. "When do you think I will get my appointment in the *New York Custom House?*" queried George T. Hammond, the proprietor of the *Newport Daily News,* a few weeks after Jenckes introduced his reform bill. Jenckes did not disappoint him. Hammond was appointed customhouse storekeeper at $4.00 a day.[13] Less than two months after Jenckes

---

[11] *Nation,* II, No. 29 (January 18, 1866), 65; "Congress," *ibid.,* No. 38 (March 22, 1866), 355. On Godkin, see Rollo Ogden, ed., *Life and Letters of Edwin Lawrence Godkin* (New York, 1907), and the more critical William M. Armstrong, *E. L. Godkin and American Foreign Policy, 1865–1900* (New York, 1957).

[12] *Congressional Globe,* 39 Cong., 1 sess., 1342, 1365, 3141, 3450–51, 3825. Anthony, a senator from Rhode Island, apparently had no reform motive for introducing the bill and probably did so simply to oblige Jenckes.

[13] Hammond to Jenckes, Newport, February 1, 1866, Jenckes Papers; *Register of Officers and Agents* . . . (Washington, 1868), p. 106.

introduced his bill, N. B. Durfee, in a letter endorsed with the sinister words "destroy this," reminded Jenckes "of the promise to our old friend Cyrenus Bliss that he should have the Custom House appointment in Tiverton now holden by George Howland." The promise was kept.[14] As was typical of the spoils system, Jenckes's appointees looked after him just as he looked after them. "You will lose the nomination if you don't come home and see to it," the Providence Postmaster warned Jenckes.[15] Like all politicos of his time, Jenckes had a group of friends working in his interest who were rewarded with the spoils of office.

Jenckes, however, did not relish dispensing spoils and did not build a machine. George Manchester, a political lieutenant, repeatedly petitioned for office without success. Although Manchester performed valuable services—keeping Jenckes informed on local trends in politics and advancing his political fortunes at party conclaves—Jenckes seldom answered his letters. Only when his political future was severely threatened in 1870 did he solicit Manchester's advice with the promise of office for reward.[16] Although tardiness in his correspondence was not unusual for Jenckes, his neglect, for the most part, of Manchester's frequent letters and the small number of patronage letters in the Jenckes Papers indicate an aversion to the "practical" aspects of politics. Additional evidence of this aversion was Jenckes's awareness of intra-party discord resulting from changes in officeholders. When the Rhode Island delegation unanimously resolved to make no personnel changes in state offices until after an impending election, Jenckes approved heartily.[17]

II

The future proponents of reform continued to beg and pressure for office, but with less skill than their future opponents. Reformers,

---

[14] Durfee to Jenckes, Providence, February 13, 1866, Jenckes Papers; Cyrenus Bliss is listed in the *Register of Officers and Agents* . . . , p. 101, as surveyor of Tiverton, Rhode Island. The annual compensation for this plum was $200.

[15] W. C. Simmons to Jenckes, Providence, March 11, 1865, Jenckes Papers.

[16] See, for examples, Manchester to Jenckes, South Portsmouth, March 5 and 7, 1864, April 5, 1865, November 18, 1868, and April 25, 1870, *ibid.* Manchester finally got a job in 1875 after Jenckes had left Congress. Manchester to Jenckes, Newport, March 12, 1875, *ibid.*

[17] Jenckes to B. E. Borden, Washington, February 28, 1865, *ibid.*

who had a tendency to regard themselves as repositories of "virtue," were not basically hypocritical in this matter. The consistency of their course lay not in their methods (which they themselves later condemned in others) but in their goal. This goal was an efficient, honest civil service manned with officers drawn largely from their own ranks. Neither competitive examinations nor the idea of letting the office seek the man received their support while they were receiving federal patronage. The diplomatic corps boasted such men as Charles Francis Adams, Sr., of the Adams family; John Lothrop Motley, noted historian; and John Bigelow, distinguished New Yorker. George William Curtis could have had a post in Egypt, and novelist William Dean Howells was repaid for his Lincoln campaign biography with a post in Italy. The spoils system functioned satisfactorily for them under Lincoln, but not under Johnson. It took reformers time, however, to discover their loss of power and to rally around a specific reform program.

The similarities shared by these post–Civil War "professional reformers" are remarkable. Most of them were lawyers, editors, clergymen, professors, and businessmen whose interests were mercantile and financial rather than industrial. The typical reformer came from an old-established New England family and was a descendant of merchants, clergymen, and public servants. He inherited wealth and consequently deplored the crass materialism of the new rich whose prominence, based on vast fortunes, eclipsed his own. The typical reformer was either an Episcopalian or a Unitarian and was a Harvard graduate. Proud of his Anglo-Saxon heritage, he patterned his thoughts and actions after English models. John Stuart Mill was his philosopher and William E. Gladstone his ideal statesman.

Although not organized in 1866, except perhaps for the American Social Science Association, and without an official organ (though the *Nation* and the *North American Review* unofficially spoke for them), reformers advocated a number of principles with consistency. Their nebulous unity had come about through social contacts and political activity. In pre–Civil War days they generally favored free soil rather than abolition and did not think highly of those advocating the latter. Charles Eliot Norton, a Harvard scholar, marveled how James Miller McKim, a Pennsylvania abolitionist, retained "a modicum of good sense and good feeling in spite of long, corrupting association with the most self righteous set of radicals." [18] Reformers, who had leaned toward the Radical wing of the Republican party during and shortly after the Civil War, had a conservative bent which later asserted itself. Immediately after the war they generally advocated Negro suffrage but with educational qualifications, for their prejudices were more intellectual than racial.

In the last decades of the nineteenth century, the cause of the Negro was forgotten while reformers advocated a variety of beliefs stemming from their laissez-faire philosophy. Reformers favored a downward revision of the tariff and were hard-money men. They were hostile to the rapacious capitalist and to monopoly, yet they opposed government ownership or effective regulation of industry. The post–Civil War industrialization of the United States confused reformers, for it was impossible to prevent the growth of monopoly within the framework of their laissez-faire system, which actually fostered monopoly. Reformers were also hostile to organized labor and to immigrants from southern and eastern Europe. Furthermore, their laissez-faire philosophy led them to believe in the ideal of small and efficient government—an ideal which caused them to oppose imperialism and to favor civil service reform.[19]

Reformers felt the effect of Lincoln's assassination and of Johnson's ensuing policies but not as quickly as other Radical Republicans. Despite general agreement with Radicals that the South should not be restored speedily to the Union, reformers were not in the vanguard of opposition to Johnson. In July, 1865, Henry Adams thought Charles Sumner and Richard Henry Dana, Jr., were in "an amusing provincial hurry to get into opposition," and in November, George William Curtis felt sure of Johnson's "honesty." As late as August, 1866, the Reverend Henry W. Bellows, who later became the first president of the New York Civil Service Reform Association, regarded Johnson as "a man of good intentions, conscientious & warmly, hotly, patriotic, however, wanting in taste discretion & discipline." Bellows was "astonished & shocked" by

---

[18] Norton to Godkin, Ashfield, Massachusetts, July 20, 1866, Godkin Papers, Harvard University.

[19] See Joseph Dorfman, *The Economic Mind in American Civilization: Volume Three 1865–1918* (New York, 1949), pp. 3–110 *passim,* for information on the economic views of reformers such as David A. Wells, Charles Francis Adams, Jr., William Graham Sumner, and Francis A. Walker. For a more detailed analysis of civil service reformers, see *infra,* pp. 190–197.

Bostonian hatred of Johnson. Another reformer, Frederick Law
Olmsted, the prewar traveler through the South, kept a restraining
hand on the *Nation*'s editor, E. L. Godkin, in his dealing with
Johnson because he feared that the Radicals in "protecting the
negro, in their wild thoughtless way," would "injure the whole
structure of the government." [20]

The conservative temperament of reformers kept them from
joining the opposition to Johnson until the first half of 1866, although his moves toward early Reconstruction of the South in 1865
had begun to alienate them. When it was thought that Johnson
would use patronage to implement his southern policy, reformers
not only opposed him but also directed their attention toward the
civil service. Although these fears were unfounded, since Johnson
failed to use patronage in a sustained systematic way until the fall
of 1866,[21] they were current in January, 1866. By spring, the *Nation* was convinced that Johnson was using patronage to further his
policy and that certain Republican party elements, which it regarded as disreputable, were planning a third party based on the
spoils with Johnson at its head. The *Nation* reasoned, however, that
passage of the civil rights bill over Johnson's veto had dissipated
the hopes of these "bummers." [22]

Actually, the Radicals, not Johnson, controlled the civil service,
although Johnson did occasionally replace Radicals with conservatives in a haphazard fashion. In April the Radical Senate refused

---

[20] Henry Adams to Charles Francis Adams, Jr., London, July 14, 1865, in Worthington Chauncey Ford, ed., *Letters of Henry Adams (1858–1891)* (Boston, 1930), p
121. Actually, neither Dana nor Sumner really was in the opposition at this time,
but it is significant that Adams thought they were. Curtis to Norton, Staten Island,
November 5, 1865, Curtis Papers, Harvard University; Godkin to Norton, no place,
February 20, 1866, Godkin Papers; Olmsted to Norton, Franconia, New Hampshire, August 26, 1866, Norton Papers, Harvard University. Olmsted reported a
recent conversation with Bellows.

[21] Howard K. Beale, *The Critical Year* (New York, 1930), pp. 120–121. Gideon
Welles, Johnson's Secretary of the Navy, told him on December 18, 1865, "that the
patronage of the Executive had . . . been used to defeat the policy of the Executive." Howard K. Beale, ed., *Diary of Gideon Welles* (New York, 1960), II, 398. Over
a year later, on March 12, 1867, Welles had not changed his mind. He felt that
Johnson and some of the departments had no system of appointments, consequently
the administration made no headway. *Ibid.*, III, 64. Welles was wrong; patronage
could not save Johnson. For a brilliant discussion of Johnson, patronage, and its
limitations, see Eric L. McKitrick, *Andrew Johnson and Reconstruction* (Chicago,
1960), pp. 377–394.

[22] "Congress," *Nation*, II, No. 28 (January 11, 1866), 35–36; *ibid.*, No. 42 (April
19, 1866), 481.

confirmation of Johnson's appointees; and only by a narrow margin were appropriations made for the salaries of postal employees who might be appointed during the Senate's recess in place of officers removed for political reasons. By June, Henry Charles Lea, eminent Philadelphia publisher, historian of the Inquisition, and early reformer, foresaw a Radical victory over Johnson's influence—which never really was a threat—in the civil service. "The office-holders," he wrote, "have found themselves powerless & those who were disposed to bend to executive dictation are beginning to realize that consistency in the long run will prove to be the best policy." By August even Olmsted had a change of heart and opposed the President. His action was paralleled by that of Curtis, who lost faith in Johnson because he acted "from temper." [23]

The August National Union Convention held in Philadelphia distressed reform as well as Radical Republicans. They were convinced that this "arm in arm" convention of moderates was composed primarily of Republicans without political future who joined with Johnson and with former Confederates in an effort to gain power and spoils. "There are a parcel of disreputable worn-out politicians here," Lea reported from Philadelphia, "who are endeavoring to construct a Johnson party, but it is up-hill work, & the cohesive power of public plunder is hardly sufficient to agglomerate around them enough deserters to make any impression on our compact ranks." The convention, however, again called attention to the power that patronage gave the President.[24]

Immediately following the convention, Johnson "swung around the circle" on an intemperate stump-speaking tour. "Johnson," Godkin gasped, "is shocking. He will come to a bad end. He is really stumping the North for Congress. I wonder why his managers do not make him either hold his tongue, or avoid polemics." But Johnson continued to blunder. Taking advantage of the recess of the Senate, which allowed him to fill vacancies without senatorial consent, he vigorously removed officeholders and replaced them

---

[23] "Congress," *ibid.*, No. 44 (May 1, 1866), 546; *ibid.*, No. 48 (May 15, 1866), 610; Lea to Norton, Philadelphia, June 20, 1866, and Olmsted to Norton, Franconia, August 26, 1866, Norton Papers; Curtis to Norton, New York, June 4, 1866, Curtis Papers.

[24] Lea to Norton, Philadelphia, July 4 and 13, 1866, Norton Papers; J. R. Dennett, "Three Days at Philadelphia," *Nation*, III, No. 60 (August 23, 1866), 152. The delegates from Massachusetts and South Carolina entered the convention hall arm in arm.

with his partisans—many of whom were Democrats. This proscription continued until the November elections in which the administration forces suffered a crushing setback.[25] Although the number of Johnson's removals then tapered off, his manipulation of the patronage in 1866 and the threat of either a third party or a revitalized Democracy had publicized the power latent in the civil service.

Corruption in municipal government also alarmed nascent civil service reformers. "The Union party [in local Philadelphia politics], I fear, is hopeless[ly] corrupt," Lea wrote in August, 1865, "& nothing will purify it but a wholesome course of purgation by loss of place." Lea reasoned that public office gravitated inevitably to the most unscrupulous person, and he was considering the organization of a "third party which shall hold the balance of power & exercise it in favor of the best candidates for municipal position, irrespective of party hues." The *Nation* echoed that high taxes and bad government would drive business from New York City to a better-regulated port further South, and later a series of two articles discussing the seamier side of New York life ended by suggesting that "missions, charities, schools, and associations for reform work against wind and tide until we have a good municipal government." [26]

Primary elections in northern cities disturbed reformers. The state exercised no control over these party elections for local candidates and convention delegates. Traditionally, these elections were held in a ward's worst "dive" with swarms of drunk "repeaters" overexercising their franchise rights. The inspectors, usually members of the same intra-party clique, dispensed with the formality of counting votes. In the 1850's, Bill Poole, the Whig-Nativist butcher who was even better at brawling than his Democratic rival John Morrissey, developed the "counting" technique into an art form.

[25] Godkin to Norton, New York, September 1, 1866, Godkin Papers; "The President's Broom," *Nation*, III, No. 62 (September 6, 1866), 191–192; *ibid.*, No. 73 (November 22, 1866), 401. Beale, *The Critical Year*, pp. 120–121, agrees that Johnson did attempt to use the patronage to oppose the Radicals in the fall of 1866, but by then it was too late.

[26] Lea to Norton, Philadelphia, August 26, 1865, Norton Papers; *Nation*, I, No. 9 (August 31, 1865), 258. The *Press* (Philadelphia), January 31, 1866, p. 4, c. 3, argues conversely that the corruption and laxity in the New York Customhouse made that port so attractive to importers that other ports more honestly administered were ignored. Years later, President Rutherford B. Hayes agreed with the *Press. Infra*, p. 157. Bayard Taylor, "A Descent into the Depths. Diversions of the Fourth Ward," *Nation*, II, No. 37 (March 15, 1866), 333.

His winning candidate in a Whig primary election in 1850 received over 5,000 votes although in the general election one month later only 250 people voted for him. By the sixties, primary votes numbering from 4,000 to 7,000 were frequently reported in wards where the party never received more than 2,500 votes and where only 500 attended the primary. Reformers lamented that both Republicans and Democrats kept alive Bill Poole's contribution to political science.[27]

Uneducated voters were a sore trial to reformers. James Parton, the biographer, writing in the *North American Review*, blamed New York municipal corruption on the ignorant swarm of foreigners, primarily Irish, who were cajoled by demagogues of the Fernando Wood type. The *Nation* enthusiastically seconded Parton's views and favored restricting the suffrage by a "good and thorough educational test." It also advocated additional representation for property owners with "at least a veto on votes of money made by the representatives of mere numbers." [28] The proprietors of the *Nation* and many of its readers did not slavishly admire either universal suffrage or majority rule. "Whoever is right, the majority is wrong," Henry Adams, a *Nation* subscriber, wrote the following year, and Charles Eliot Norton, one of the founders of that magazine, urged that "the decline of manners [a matter of utmost importance to reformers] owing to the spread of democracy, and the influence of democracy on high feeling, are subjects well worth consideration." [29]

Despite concern over power latent in patronage and growing municipal corruption, the civil service reform movement did not exist in 1866. Early acknowledgment of the need for competitive examinations by the *Nation* and Revenue Commissioner David A.

---

[27] "Primary Elections," *Ibid.*, III, No. 73 (November 22, 1866), 411–412. For a fascinating account of Bill Poole, see John Lardner, "That Was New York: Martyrdom of Bill the Butcher," *New Yorker* (New York), XXX, Nos. 4, 5 (March 20 and 27, 1954), 41–56 and 38–59 respectively.

[28] James Parton, "The Government of the City of New York," *North American Review* (Boston), CIII, No. 213 (October, 1866), 413–465; Edwin Lawrence Godkin, "The Government of Our Great Cities," *Nation*, III, No. 68 (October 18, 1866), 313. Parton's position was more lenient than the *Nation's*—those already exercising the franchise were not to be disturbed, but in the future anyone who could not read English of "medium difficulty" was not to be admitted to the franchise. Parton, *op. cit.*, p. 460.

[29] Henry Adams to Charles Francis Adams, Jr., Baden, September 4, 1867, in Ford, *op. cit.*, p. 133; Norton to Godkin, Cambridge, March 13, 1867, Godkin Papers.

Wells, both of whom supported reform through the years, was exceptional. Indeed, even Editor E. L. Godkin's 1865 and 1866 correspondence does not mention civil service reform despite the support his journal gave it. Nascent civil service reformers were interested in the federal civil service only as it related to the President's southern policy. They ignored the Jenckes bill, which contained their future program of competitive examinations. Until the end of 1866, men and measure had not combined to become a movement.

III

On December 13, 1866, Jenckes reported a substitute for his bill. This revised measure narrowed the scope of civil service coverage by exempting all postmasters from its operation. The substitute bill also defined the judicial functions of the commission in greater detail, and, in keeping with anti-Johnson sentiment, allowed the Senate as well as the President to require examination of presidential appointees. The bill, like its predecessor, generally excluded applicants for positions requiring senatorial confirmation from compulsory-competitive examination.[30]

The report in Congress of the Jenckes bill occasioned the beginning of a long association between Jenckes and Joseph George Rosengarten, a Philadelphia lawyer whose family engaged prominently in manufacturing chemicals.[31] While Rosengarten was a student abroad, he had become interested in public administration and had collected many books on this subject. Prodded by Hugh Burgess, Rosengarten offered his services to Jenckes after the bill was reported. A few weeks later, the *Nation* published his first offering: an article supporting Jenckes's bill by stressing the "political evils" and the waste of taxpayers' money resulting from the spoils system. Rosengarten called for "prompt action and agitation by merchants, manufacturers, tradesmen, capitalists, railroad and other corporations—by all, in short, who feel where the shoe pinches." [32]

---

[30] *Congressional Globe,* 39 Cong., 2 sess., 109, 835–836.

[31] Their firm, after a series of mergers, became part of Merck & Company, Incorporated. "George David Rosengarten," *The National Cyclopaedia of American Biography* (New York, 1892–1955), XXXV, 272–273.

[32] *University of Pennsylvania Biographical Catalogue of the Matriculates of the College 1749–1893* (Philadelphia, 1894), p. 181; Rosengarten to Jenckes, Philadelphia, December 16 and 21, 1866, Jenckes Papers; Joseph George Rosengarten, "The Civil Service Bill," *Nation,* IV, No. 80 (January 10, 1867), 32.

Two weeks after Rosengarten's article appeared in the *Nation,* Jenckes addressed Congress in behalf of his bill. This speech of January 29, 1867,[33] illustrated Jenckes's grasp of civil service reform and became the model for civil service addresses, just as Jenckes's bill proved the prototype of the later Pendleton Act. Like Rosengarten, Jenckes stressed both the political and the administrative advantages of basing appointments on competitive examinations. He exposed the vicious nature of the spoils system: political activities determined appointments, public servants were assessed for party campaign funds, tenure of office did not exist, and diligence did not lead to promotion. These conditions, Jenckes maintained, kept the civil service filled with disreputable persons who gave it a low social status.

Jenckes next appealed to businessmen eager to cut taxes. He alleged that private business organizations comparable in size to customhouses and large post offices operated far more efficiently. Knowing that retrenchment was popular,[34] Jenckes argued that the merit system would cut taxes by eliminating one-third of the civil servants and would increase by one-half the efficiency of those remaining. It would also save congressmen and executive officers countless hours wasted listening to office seekers.

Even though Jenckes claimed his bill was nonpartisan since he had drafted it during Lincoln's administration, it was hostile to President Johnson. Jenckes admitted he was attempting to check "the centralization of all appointing as well as executive power" in the President. Congress had directed the Joint Committee on Retrenchment, from which Jenckes reported his bill, to investigate the use of the civil service "as an instrument of political and party patronage." Jenckes, therefore, attacked "the direct interference of the Chief Executive in the appointment of officers which by law is vested in the heads of Departments" and the President's claim "to exercise over these chiefs the power of removal without the assent of the Senate." Although Jenckes obviously had Andrew Johnson in mind, he did not mention him by name.

Having catalogued the evils of the spoils system, Jenckes turned

---

[33] *Congressional Globe,* 39 Cong., 2 sess., 837–841.

[34] Since economy in government was in demand, Jenckes's bill was reported from the Joint Committee on Retrenchment, which had been appointed the preceding July to curtail military, naval, and civil expenditures. *New York Times,* July 17, 1866, p. 4, c. 7, p. 5, c. 1, and July 19, 1866, p. 4, c. 1.

to his remedy. To eliminate surplus offices he hoped to institute a new long-term system of appointment based on competitive examinations rather than a short-term plan. Jenckes's description of the civil service certificate as a combined diploma and recommendation that would be recognized in all circles indicated that he contemplated a test of general knowledge rather than specific tests measuring skills for each position. He apparently hoped to follow the European practice of tying the civil service to the universities. Such a system, Jenckes concluded, was not impractical as its enemies alleged, for it was already functioning successfully in Great Britain, France, and Prussia.[35]

A large section of the press responded favorably to Jenckes's speech before Congress. "The newspapers," wrote Rosengarten to Jenckes, "have given such a thorough report of your Bill and speech that the public have the 'Civil Service' well before them." [36] The *New York Times* attacked the spoils system as "costly, inefficient, wasteful, corrupt" and called for its reform. Reform was necessary to curb the "overgrown power" of the presidency, to bring efficiency into an organization of "colossal proportions," and to achieve retrenchment that would ease the "crushing" burden of taxation. A few days later, the *Times* called upon the Republican majority to enact the Jenckes bill. Some papers, however, were not so favorable. Horace Greeley's *New York Daily Tribune* prefixed its two-sentence coverage of Jenckes's speech and bill with the words "The House did little of importance to-day." [37]

---

[35] Jenckes later published supporting material for his bill in a report from the Joint Committee on Retrenchment. The great bulk of this report consisted of appendixes. In one, New York's surveyor of customs maintained that examinations and stable tenure would "unquestionably" improve the quality of appointees, and the deputy collector of the same port asserted that this method would improve the efficiency of workers. Other appendixes reprinted sections of David A. Wells's Revenue Commission report of January, 1866, an abstract by Rosengarten of Edouard Laboulaye's *Education and the Administrative System of Probation in Germany*, information on the French and British civil services, and numerous specimen British competitive examinations. Jenckes's report offered little that was new (only two pages of testimony by New York customs officials) but was useful since it gathered in one volume scattered materials on civil service reform. Joint Select Committee on Retrenchment, "Civil Service of the United States," *House Reports*, 39 Cong., 2 sess., I, No. 8, *passim*.

[36] Rosengarten to Jenckes, Philadelphia, January 31, 1867, Jenckes Papers. See also *New York Times*, January 30, 1867, p. 1, cc. 3–7, p. 8, cc. 1–2; *World* (New York), January 30, 1867, p. 1, cc. 4–6, p. 8, c. 1; *Press* (Philadelphia), January 30, 1867, p. 1, cc. 5–6, p. 8, c. 2.

[37] "The Civil Service—A Question of Efficiency and Retrenchment," *New York*

Supporters of reform were almost unanimously enthusiastic. Hugh Burgess told Jenckes that if he ever got his bill through he "would be the greatest patriot in the country—greater even than the 'Great Commoner [Thaddeus Stevens].' You might put the last named gent into the political saucepan & season him with a Sumner, some Butler, a little Stanton—adding from time to time a few handfuls of the ordinary saviours of their country, (an article not uncommon in the market) boil the whole & you'd get a smoking hot dish of patriotism, & the whole dish shall not have one half the nourishment that a stray whiff of your proposed bill of fare of simple diet has. If you don't get the bill through you have entered the thin edge of the wedge." [38] The *Providence Journal* and *Evening Bulletin* received assurance from their Washington correspondent that the bill would pass and, on January 31, 1867, Rosengarten predicted an early victory. A few days later he was not so confident. Everyone he spoke with said the "politicians" in Congress would "never give it a chance," but he still thought "better of them than that." Rosengarten's main concern was giving civil service reform "life" after it became law.[39]

In Congress, the Jenckes bill encountered strong opposition from Frederick E. Woodbridge, a Vermont Republican lawyer who had engaged in both politics and railroad building. Theoretically the bill was perfect, he argued, but the "natural weaknesses and wickednesses of man" precluded its success. Woodbridge contended that the public service was no more corrupt than private business, that periodical changes of officers in the civil service were wholesome, and that Jenckes's proposed commission—"This great traveling menagerie, this inquisitorial court"—would drain the Treasury. The bill was also "anti-democratic." The merit system was used in class-conscious, aristocratic Britain where rail splitters did not become prime ministers. Competitive examination, Woodbridge concluded, "might work in Belgium, France, or England, where the masses are mere machines; but in free America it will never work."

Jenckes vigorously challenged Woodbridge and spoils practices. A "more vicious system," he exclaimed, "does not exist in any

Times, January 30, 1867, p. 4, cc. 2–4; "Reorganization of the Civil Service—Mr. Jenckes' Bill," *ibid.,* February 2, 1867, p. 4, cc. 3–4; *New York Daily Tribune,* January 30, 1867, p. 1, c. 1.

[38] Burgess to Jenckes, Royers Ford, February 2, 1867, Jenckes Papers.

[39] George W. Danielson to Jenckes, Providence, January 30, 1867, *ibid.,* and Rosengarten to Jenckes, Philadelphia, January 31 and February 4, 1867, *ibid.*

civilized nation on the face of the earth." He then noted that in the United States the military service—a career service—was far more efficient than the civil service and stressed the recent example of Prussian bureaucratic efficiency in the Austro-Prussian War. Finally, Jenckes argued that the merit system was truly democratic, for under it everyone could compete for office in contrast to the limitations of the aristocratic spoils system built on favoritism.

Jenckes's spirited defense failed to convince a majority of his colleagues. Thaddeus Stevens, the Radical leader of Congress, successfully moved to lay the Jenckes bill on the table. Fifty-six Republicans and 11 Democrats supported Jenckes's measure by opposing Stevens' motion; 49 Republicans and 22 Democrats united to kill the bill. This vote of 71 to 67 was surprisingly close and cut across party lines. Although the bipartisan vote reveals no sharp cleavage between political "outs" and "ins," it does outline an urban versus rural pattern. There is an indication of correlation between distance from centers of commerce and decrease of interest in civil service reform. In New England, the more urbanized states of Massachusetts, Rhode Island, Connecticut, and New Hampshire registered no opposition to the measure, while rural Maine and Vermont did not cast a vote for the bill. The New York delegation, except for nine members representing rural districts, voted for reform. In Pennsylvania, all voting representatives from the Philadelphia and Pittsburgh areas supported the Jenckes bill. Of the remaining Pennsylvania representatives, only one favored the bill while ten registered opposition. Finally, the more rural West was more hostile to reform than the urban East.[40]

The Jenckes bill was not the only legislation proposed during the second session of the Thirty-ninth Congress relating to federal offices. In answer to Johnson's recent threat to "kick out" Radical officeholders,[41] the Senate on January 18, 1867, passed the controversial Tenure of Office bill. It required Senate approval of removals from offices, appointment to which necessitated senatorial

---

[40] *Congressional Globe*, 39 Cong., 2 sess., 1034–36. Officially the vote was 72 to 66, but Jenckes changed his vote from negative to positive to enable later consideration of the measure. The tally herein given and the analysis based upon it ignores this move.

[41] Ellis Paxson Oberholtzer, *A History of the United States Since the Civil War* (New York, 1917–37), I, 437–438, says that although Johnson made this threat in his "swing around the circle" he did not carry it out. Congress, nevertheless, used the threat as an excuse.

confirmation. This bill specifically exempted Cabinet members from its operation on grounds that Congress could not interfere with the President's confidential advisers. The House disagreed with the Senate. Reconstruction legislation then pending made military rule of the South appear certain and increased the importance of the Secretary of War. The House, apparently to insure Radical Edwin M. Stanton's continuation in that office, included Cabinet members under the bill and passed the amended bill by a strict party vote. Later, a Senate-House committee rephrased the controversial amendment and vaguely required that Cabinet members be retained in office during the "term of the President by whom they may have been appointed." When on March 2 the bill passed over Johnson's veto, both the House and the public assumed that Stanton was protected.[42]

This Tenure of Office bill was far more congenial to congressmen than was the Jenckes bill. Jenckes's measure went beyond the immediate requirements of the Radicals by providing an independent commission that would curtail congressional as well as executive control over patronage. Many persons regarded the Tenure of Office Act as a reform measure. The opinion was widely held that executive power was dangerously strong and needed clipping.[43] The *Nation* enthusiastically declared, "This bill is undoubtedly one of the most valuable of those of which Mr. Johnson's folly has furnished the occasion, and, coupled with Mr. Jenckes's, would do all that legislation can do for the purification of our politics." Although the *New York Times* thought the "President should have more freedom of action in the case of his own immediate advisers" and preferred the Jenckes bill, it praised the Tenure of Office Act as a reform measure which would bring stability to the service. The Democratic New York *World*, however, questioned Republican ardor for reform. Political expediency, it felt, rather than sentiment for reform assured the passage of the Tenure of Office Act.[44]

[42] *Congressional Globe*, 39 Cong., 2 sess., 550, 970; James Ford Rhodes, *History . . . from the Compromise of 1850 . . . 1877* (New York, 1906), VI, 121, 129–132.

[43] See, for example, "Congress and the President," *Nation*, III, No. 75 (December 6, 1866), 450.

[44] *Ibid.*, IV, No. 84 (February 7, 1867), 101. Two weeks later, the *Nation* "heartily" rejoiced that the Tenure of Office bill was assured of enactment. *Ibid.*, No. 86 (February 21, 1867), 141; "The Tenure of Office Bill," *New York Times*, March 4, 1867, p. 4, c. 2, and "Office-Holding in the United States—The New Law," *ibid.*, March 7, 1867, p. 4, c. 4; "Tenure of Office—Can the President Remove Incumbents Without Consent of the Senate?" *Wòrld* (New York), January 22, 1867, p. 4, cc. 3–4.

III

REINFORCEMENTS
FOR JENCKES

By 1867, the struggle between Andrew Johnson and Radical members of Congress had aroused interest in the civil service. Conservatives and Radicals knew that patronage and power were synonymous, for control of the civil service decided political wars. The Tenure of Office Act and, to a lesser degree, the Jenckes civil service reform bill were Radical attempts to tie Johnson's hands. As a by-product of Reconstruction, civil service reform merely received the attention normally given such a by-product. It could not steal headlines and enthrall millions. Reconstruction thus simultaneously stimulated and stifled reform. In time, however, some of those whose interest was kindled would become convinced of the intrinsic worth of civil service reform and less certain of the value of Radical Reconstruction. These were the "best people," many of whom had joined the Republican party during the antislavery crusade and were recognized by the Lincoln administration. Their elimination from politics by Radicals as well as Conservatives and the corresponding growth of corruption led to widespread interest in civil service reform. Jenckes's supporters increased both in number and power in 1867.

I

The Jenckes bill received new and powerful support from George William Curtis. Exposed early to transcendentalism at Concord and Brook Farm, Curtis never escaped its influence. After the Grand Tour abroad, he embarked on a literary career, becoming one of the most popular writers of the 1850's and associate editor of *Putnam's*

Monthly. Financial disaster struck, however, when this magazine
collapsed. Curtis assumed a debt for which he was not legally responsible and to pay it labored for years on the lyceum circuit. In
the late 1850's, Curtis became an ardent Republican and later
strongly supported the Lincoln administration from his post as editor of *Harper's Weekly,* America's leading illustrated paper. As his
political activities increased, his literary contributions decreased and
were in time limited to his graceful "Easy Chair" essays in *Harper's
Monthly* and to his occasional orations. A gentle, sweet-tempered
man, Curtis was intuitive and emotional rather than rational. His
dear friend, Charles Eliot Norton, was impressed by Curtis' barometric sense of "the atmospheric currents of popular opinion. . . .
The rise or fall of his mercury indicates coming changes. His principles are as firm & clear as the glass tube, but his feelings & his opinions as to modes of action & courses of policy vary with the popular
weather. This makes him an excellent & useful political writer &
actor in such a country as ours & at such a time as this. He is not a
statesman of the first class,—of whom there are none in America just
now—but one [of] the first of the second class." [1]

Working through E. L. Godkin and the *Nation,* Norton launched
a campaign in the fall of 1866 to make his second-rate–statesman
friend a senator from New York.[2] Curtis, although happy to make
the race, saw little hope for success. He reasoned that the honor was
not to be given to New York City, and that neither Horace Greeley
(himself a candidate) nor Theodore Tilton—both powerful Republican editors—would favor him. "The former," wrote Curtis, "thinks
me dainty and too respectable,—the latter, too conservative & timid."
Although Curtis' sensitive nature was not a political asset, "several
journals, both East and West," supported him.[3]

Success, however, did not follow. "Conkling is undoubtedly to be
the man," Curtis wrote Norton in January, "but his friends and

---

[1] Norton to Godkin, Cambridge, February 1, 1867, Godkin Papers, Harvard
University. See Gordon Milne, *George William Curtis & the Genteel Tradition*
(Bloomington, 1956), for the literary aspects of Curtis' career.

[2] Norton to Godkin, Ashfield, Massachusetts, October 12, 19, and 21, 1866, Godkin Papers. Curtis would have succeeded Ira Harris of Albany. The main candidates were Roscoe Conkling of Utica and Noah Davis of Albion, who was backed
by Governor Reuben E. Fenton.

[3] Curtis to Norton, Staten Island, October 26, 1866, Curtis Papers, Harvard University; *Nation* (New York), III, No. 70 (November 1, 1866), 341; *ibid.,* No. 74
(November 29, 1866), 422.

Davis's and Harris's—the three real contestants—have each declared for me as their second choice. Still even that would not
bring it because I am not enough of a politician for the purposes of
the men who make Senators." As if to prove his point, Curtis "declined absolutely" to unite with the weakest candidate against Roscoe Conkling. When Conkling was elected, a *Harper's Weekly* editorial in good party spirit associated him with the "moral intelligence of the party" and exhausted the usual supply of laudatory
adjectives. Not only was he called "a man equal to the hour" but
was also described as "Young, fearless, devoted, able; of profoundest
convictions; of much experience acquired in critical and stormy
times; with all his brilliant powers disciplined and available." [4]

A few weeks later, in answer either to his barometric sense of
public opinion or to a more personal sense of frustration with
politics, Curtis wrote in *Harper's Weekly* favoring the passage of
the Jenckes bill by the expiring Thirty-ninth Congress.[5] Although
tardy, Curtis' espousal of civil service reform lasted until his death
twenty-five years later. In this period he became its most conspicuous and devoted leader.

Other men were driven by continuing corruption to advocate
the Jenckes bill. Even the darlings of reformers got their coattails
dirty. Henry A. Smythe, whose appointment as New York collector
had been widely applauded,[6] continued his predecessor's corrupt
practices with gusto and even improved upon some of them. Goods
that failed to clear customs within a required period of time
were stored in designated "general order" warehouses—usually
owned by a friend of the collector. Smythe went further. Offered
$50,000 annually for the "general order business," he preferred in-
stead 30 per cent of the gross proceeds. This plan had been in operation a few months when a congressional investigation demanded
Smythe's removal. The *Nation* commented that Smythe's own testi-

----

[4] Curtis to Norton, Staten Island, January 2, 1867, Curtis Papers. The rejected
terms were the election of "whichever was stronger now," Davis or Curtis, "and
the pledge of the successful man to support the other two years hence." *Ibid.* "The
New Senator from New York," *Harper's Weekly* (New York), XI, No. 526 (January
26, 1867), 50.

[5] "Reform of the Civil Service," *ibid.*, No. 531 (March 2, 1867), 130.

[6] For example, the *Evening Post* (New York), April 17, 1866, p. 4, c. 1, stated that
Smythe, the president of the Central National Bank and formerly an eminent merchant, was appointed principally at the behest of businessmen, not politicians. He
was described as "a man of unimpeachable personal integrity and of diligent
habits."

mony showed that "the management of the Custom-House . . .
[was] a disgrace," and his exposure demonstrated that no one could
be trusted in office as long as the "present system" continued. Until
the public service became a career even the "purest men" would
"grab" all they could during their short terms of office. "A man who
won't rob," the *Nation* concluded, "now naturally finds his position
untenable." [7]

While indignation over corruption in the federal civil service was
not new, protests were more sustained and concerted after the
Jenckes bill provided a rallying point. When in February, 1867, a
committee inquiring into whisky frauds reported that the high tax
on whisky and the unmitigated knavery of the revenue officers in
large cities caused the abuses, the *Nation* concluded there was "no
reform so much needed as Mr. Jenckes's, but we suspect it will be
some time before Congress will be virtuous enough to swallow it." [8]
Events proved the estimate of congressional "virtue" accurate.

Although corruption occurred on the federal level of government,
it was on the state and municipal levels that it became most blatant
and common. Almost everyone knew by the spring of 1867 that the
votes of New York legislators were bought and sold like "meat in
the market." It was impossible to pass a bill unless a high percentage
of the legislators had been purchased, and agents who facilitated
these purchases did not operate in secret. In New York, bills harmful to wealthy interests were introduced and then withdrawn upon
payment. The *Nation* pointed out that the "knaves" sent to the
legislature by the New York Irish did not "drive this trade. . . .
The main body of the corrupt drove are lawyers, farmers, and what
not from the interior of the State, Republicans in politics, and sound
enough on all the great issues of the day to please Thaddeus Stevens
himself. . . ." [9] Corruption was not the exclusive stock in trade of
the Irish nor the Democrats and was not limited to New York.
Pennsylvania under Simon Cameron could match New York's record. This widespread corruption corroded the democratic faith of
reformers.

While corruption aroused reformers, Johnson's appointments and

---

[7] William J. Hartman, "Politics and Patronage" (Columbia University, 1952),
pp. 137–141; *Nation*, IV, No. 90 (March 21, 1867), 226; *ibid.*, No. 88 (March 7,
1867), 182.

[8] *Ibid.*, No. 87 (February 28, 1867), 162.

[9] *Ibid.*, No. 93 (April 11, 1867), 286.

removals displeased nearly all Republicans. Reformers were outraged by the treatment of John Lothrop Motley, the Brahmin historian from Boston and the minister to Austria. An American traveling in Europe accused Motley of being especially hostile to the
administration. When Secretary of State William Henry Seward relayed this charge to Motley, he resigned, and Johnson insisted that
the resignation be accepted. Motley's close friend, Senator Charles
Sumner, charged that Motley was released to make way for Edgar
Cowan of Pennsylvania. This allegation disturbed the *Nation* even
more since Cowan not only was a supporter of Johnson and his
"policy" but also had recently praised the virtues of rotation in
office. The character of the public service was declining. "Mr.
Lincoln," with one possible exception, the *Nation* exclaimed, "put
into office the best set of foreign ministers we have had in many a
day, and all our representatives at first-class courts for the last six
years have been men who were in every sense of the word an honor
to the country. . . . They are now being removed one by one to
make room for the broken-down adherents of 'the policy,' and if
anything can be done to stop the process, stopped it should be." [10]
Godkin wrote George Perkins Marsh, minister to the Italian States
and contributor to the *Nation*, "I am afraid you will not long be
spared, or any other man of character and standing in the service of
the government. Johnson and Seward seem to have completely lost
their heads & I doubt if there is now any means of avoiding an
impeachment—which I for one—however, it may end, shall look
on as a great calamity." [11]

Reformers' distrust of Johnson grew. His appointment of John
M. Binckley as "acting attorney-general" brought further criticism
from them. According to contemporary reports, Binckley was a
jack-of-all-trades who had been a portrait painter, a land agent, a
newspaperman, and a civil servant before turning to law only three
years prior to his appointment. He had had but one case in court

---

[10] Marjorie Frye Gutheim, "John Lothrop Motley" (Columbia University, 1955),
pp. 258–277; *Nation*, IV, No. 82 (January 24, 1867), 61–62. Motley's behavior disgusted John Hay, a diplomat who had been Lincoln's secretary. "Letters like that
were written to nearly everyone in the service—nobody grew furious & resigned
but Motley. He becomes a high-priced martyr and has the sure thing on a first-
class mission two years hence." Hay to J. G. Nicolay, Washington, February 14,
1867, in Tyler Dennett, ed., *Lincoln and the Civil War* (New York, 1939), p. 277

[11] Godkin to Marsh, New York, January 20, 1867, Godkin Papers.

from which he prudently withdrew before emerging as the President's chief legal adviser.[12]

Most reformers opposed impeachment until January and February, 1868, when Johnson panicked Curtis and Godkin into supporting it by attempting for the second time to remove Secretary of War Stanton.[13] After the initial shock over Johnson's move wore off, these reformers began a retreat. In March, the *Nation* criticized Thaddeus Stevens' denunciation of Johnson for using patronage to secure votes, with the reminder that neither Stevens nor his party voted for the Jenckes bill. Two months later, the *Nation* recognized that nothing would be gained through Johnson's conviction because he was powerless. The Republican party, not the President, controlled the civil service. After Johnson was declared not guilty, many reformers defended Republican senators, who voted for his acquittal, and his eminent counsel William Maxwell Evarts.[14]

A few reformers consistently called for impeachment. One of the leading impeachers in the House was Thomas A. Jenckes. His aid, Julius Bing, congratulated him on his *"powerful & clinching speech"* favoring impeachment. Jenckes, besides narrowly missing election as a House manager at Johnson's trial, had written the article of impeachment which charged the President with illegally attempting to gain control of the army.[15] Henry C. Lea, reformer from Philadelphia, viewed the impeachment as a political, not a judicial, process. After Johnson's acquittal was imminent, Lea, not realizing that the Republican party controlled presidential appointments, wished to continue the effort to convict Johnson in order to gain his patronage. "After all," Lea continued, "the greatest danger to which our institutions are exposed is the scramble for office & . . . the passage of such a measure as Mr. Jenckes's Civil Service Bill would be the panacea for the greater portion of the evils under which

[12] *Nation*, V, No. 110 (August 8, 1867), 101; *ibid.*, No. 112 (August 22, 1867), 141; *ibid.*, No. 116 (September 19, 1867), 221.

[13] "The Crisis at Washington," *ibid.*, VI, No. 139 (February 27, 1868), 164–165; "The Removability of Public Offices," *Harper's Weekly*, XII, No. 586 (March 21, 1868), 178–179. Some reformers never did favor impeachment. Norton argued that "three months of Ben Wade are worse than two years of A. J." Norton to Godkin, Cambridge, March 1, 1868, Godkin Papers.

[14] *Nation*, VI, No. 140 (March 5, 1868), 181–182; "Mr. Wade's Arrangements," *ibid.*, No. 149 (May 7, 1868), 364; *ibid.*, VII, No. 181 (December 17, 1868), 494; "Mr. Evarts and his Traducers," *ibid.*, VI, No. 151 (May 21, 1868), 408–409

[15] Bing to Jenckes, Washington, March 5, 1868, Jenckes Papers, Library of Congress; *Nation*, VI, No. 141 (March 12, 1868), 201.

we suffer, & which threaten to increase immeasurably in the
future. . . ." How Lea reasoned that making Benjamin F. Wade
President would cut down the scramble for office is not clear, but
he did associate impeachment with civil service reform. Lea was
not alone in making this association.[16]

Reform Radicalism reached its zenith during the impeachment
trial of Andrew Johnson, but a drift toward an anti-Radical position was already perceptible. This shift was not made out of sympathy for the South but rather because of widespread corruption
within the Republican party. In the party, reformers were being
eclipsed by professional politicians whose power was based on patronage and in many cases corruption. Reformers initially thought
the politico's Radical views on Reconstruction were "sound," but to
reformers the elimination of corruption in the North (including
the politico who prevented reform domination of the Republican
party) became more important than the Radical Reconstruction of
the South.

Even before impeachment, reformers' favorite journal illustrates
the corrosive effect of corruption upon their Radical ideas. In April,
1867, the *Nation* said, "If the process of reconstruction should be
completed satisfactorily during the coming summer, the question of
legislative corruption, and, in fact, corruption of all kinds, will
probably engage a good deal of attention during the next two or
three years. Much appears on this subject in print, but not half
what one hears in private." By summer the *Nation*, speaking for
"true radicalism," said, "Let us be content with securing equal justice
at the South, and then combine to attack corruptions nearer home."
Two weeks later the *Nation* assailed the idea that the Negro or anyone else had any special claim to office. Corruption had shouldered
aside the Negro, in whose interest the *Nation* partially had been
founded. "The diminution of political corruption . . . is the great
question of our time," pronounced the *Nation* in October, 1867.
"It is greater than the suffrage, greater than reconstruction. . . ." [17]

---

[16] Lea to Norton, Philadelphia, May 19, 1868, Norton Papers, Harvard Univer
sity. E. B. Ward, a Detroit merchant and secretary of the National Manufacturers'
Association, wrote Jenckes that his bill was "of as much importance to the well
being and security of this government, as the impeachment of the president." Ward
to Jenckes, Detroit, April 6, 1868, Jenckes Papers. See Ward's similar letter to
Sumner, *supra*, p. 11.

[17] *Nation*, IV, No. 95 (April 25, 1867), 325; "True Radicalism," *ibid.*, V, No. 107
(July 18, 1867), 51; Edwin Lawrence Godkin, "The Negro's Claim to Office," *ibid.*,

The result of the impeachment trial encouraged Charles Eliot
Norton, not because he liked Johnson, his policies, or the South, but
because it enhanced reformers' chances for capturing the Republican
party. "I think," he wrote Godkin, "we have a better chance now
than we had any right to expect so soon for reforming the party &
freeing it from the burden of the sins of the extremists who have
tried to usurp the leadership. Butler is sinking himself so low, that
he will hardly be able to hold his head above the mire into which
he plunged with native alacrity. The other original impeachers will
share his fate." Lea, however, drew the opposite conclusion. He
thought that control of the party would now rest "more than ever
in the hands of the 'war-horses.' " Significantly, the primary concern
of both Lea and Norton was not Reconstruction but reformers'
chances of controlling the Republican party.[18] To eliminate the
spoilsmen, many reformers eventually allied themselves with the
once-hated southern white. The amnesty policy of the Liberal Republicans of 1872 had its origin in northern, not southern, corruption.

II

The impeachment of Andrew Johnson obscured all other events including efforts for civil service reform. Yet the movement for reform continued and was not the function of prominent publicists
alone. It also involved the work of obscure men, particularly the
clerk of the Joint Select Committee on Retrenchment. Julius Bing,
an individual in straitened circumstances before receiving his post,
commenced in the late spring of 1867 to lay the groundwork for the
civil service reform movement. Passionately loyal to the ideal of
reform, Bing worked prodigiously in his routine duties and also
wrote numerous magazine articles which called for reform.[19]

No. 109 (August 1, 1867), 90–91; "The Republican Troubles," *ibid.*, No. 120 (October 17, 1867), 314.

[18] Norton to Godkin, Cambridge, May 30, 1868, Godkin Papers; Lea to Norton,
Philadelphia, May 16, 1868, Norton Papers.

[19] Bing to Jenckes, no place, May 6, 1868, Jenckes Papers. Very little is known
about Bing. He was not a native American but was acquainted with Charles Sumner, who probably was responsible for his appointment as United States consul at
Smyrna. In 1868, Bing became Crete's diplomatic agent in the United States. Bing
to Sumner, Newburyport, Massachusetts, October 30, 1856, Smyrna, March 24, 1864,
Washington, September 26, 1868, and no place, January, no day, 1869, Sumner
Papers, Harvard University. Bing also wrote a biography of the eccentric, radical,
abolitionist Civil–War-diarist Count Adam de Gurowski. The manuscript is located in the Gurowski Papers, Library of Congress.

One of Bing's articles, usually credited to Jenckes, appeared in the *North American Review* of October, 1867, and is interesting because of its appeal to the "aristocracy." "In the early days of the Republic," Bing stated, subordinate officers as well as Presidents and Cabinet officers "were generally selected from well-known families." Although this custom was no longer in use, Bing assured his readers that the Jenckes bill would restore the original practice. Bing even claimed—with dubious validity since the Jenckes bill did not apply to elective offices—that the country would have been spared Andrew Johnson had the competitive principle been in force. If the civil service commission had examined him, "it would not have required a profound psychological knowledge to arrive at the conclusion, that a man may rise from the tailor-shop to the alderman's gown, and from thence to the senatorial ermine and the gubernatorial chair, and yet be morally and intellectually incapable of presiding with dignity, justice, and ability over the destinies of a great nation." Bing evidently thought the readers of the *North American Review* felt that manual labor did not cultivate "dignity, justice, and ability." Bing's only objection to the Jenckes bill was that it did not create a career foreign service from top to bottom. If ministers and consuls were included under the bill, Bing maintained, they would "become powerful auxiliaries to the increase of the commerce, industry, science, arts and general civilization of the Republic." [20]

The *Round Table,* a New York weekly magazine which appealed to the same type of reader as did the *Nation,* published about twenty articles by Bing between the fall of 1867 and the spring of 1868. Bing thought that the *North American Review,* the *Chicago Tribune,* and especially the *Round Table* deserved commendation for supporting civil service reform, and flattered himself that his own articles had provoked numerous others written on the subject. By January, 1869, the tremendous support civil service reform received from the press was noted in Congress.[21]

[20] Julius Bing, "Civil Service of the United States," *North American Review* (Boston), CV, No. 217 (October, 1867), 478–495. For authenticity of authorship, see Jenckes to Norton, Washington, August 19, 1867, Norton Papers; Bing to Jenckes, Washington, May 22, 1868, Jenckes Papers.

[21] Bing to Jenckes, Washington, May 22, November 26, and December 31, 1868, and Rosengarten to Jenckes, Philadelphia, December 18, 1868, *ibid.; Congressional Globe,* 40 Cong., 3 sess., 269, 747. The founding of the *Nation* was delayed by the existence of the *Round Table,* and the *Round Table's* demise was caused in part by the *Nation's* usurpation of the place it hoped to fill. Frank Luther Mott, *A History of American Magazines, 1865–1885* (Cambridge, 1938), III, 324, 332. Another

Julius Bing's efforts for reform were not limited to magazine propaganda. He distributed pamphlets to congressmen and newspaper editors and alerted Jenckes on a variety of items, ranging from reminders to frank more envelopes to information concerning the reform implications of David A. Wells's latest report. Bing also did personal evangelism. He buttonholed Senator Charles Sumner as well as William D. "Pig Iron" Kelley, the arch protectionist and inflationist who was one of Philadelphia's representatives, and both affirmed their support of the Jenckes bill. Sumner gave Bing several letters that had helped him mature his civil service bill in 1864, and Kelley emphatically said that competitive examinations *"must be popularized!"* Bing wholeheartedly agreed with Kelley and wrote Jenckes, "The great thing is to keep the agitation alive all round." [22]

Jenckes did not need urging to keep "agitation alive." In January, 1868, he corresponded with Nathaniel Gale, a clerk in the Boston Customhouse who supplied him with names of Bostonians interested in reform (mostly merchants and former officeholders). Gale also distributed copies of a Jenckes speech to a commercial convention at Boston, inspired press support for Jenckes's bill, and proposed a "monster" petition from Boston since *"every* body is ripe for it here." [23] Jenckes received further support from the Democratic New York *World* and the New York *Evening Post.* [24]

Certain business organizations also began to advocate civil service reform. In December, 1867, the National Manufacturers' Association, whose interests were mainly in the old Northwest, unanimously adopted a resolution "heartily" approving the Jenckes bill. [25] Its reasons were to achieve tax and revenue reform and economy in

---

article published by Bing was "Our Civil Service," *Putnam's Magazine* (New York), New Series, II, No. 8 (August, 1868), 233–244.

[22] Bing to Jenckes, Washington, November 27, 1867, Jenckes Papers.

[23] Gale to Jenckes, Boston, January 3, 11, 16, 22, 27, and February 4, 1868, *ibid.* The quotation is found in the letter of January 16.

[24] Dupee to Jenckes, Boston, May 9, 1868, *ibid.* Charleton T. Lewis of the *Evening Post* wrote Jenckes of his desire to keep reform alive in the columns of the *Post* as far as it could be made of popular interest. Lewis to Jenckes, New York, April 30, 1868, Jenckes Papers.

[25] Other resolutions favored a protective tariff coupled with the repeal of excise taxes on useful manufactures, further extension of the facilities of the National Banking System into the West and the South, and the funding of the public debt by the issuing of long-term bonds, whose principle and interest would be payable in gold. This organization's president, treasurer, corresponding secretary, and recording secretary all came from Detroit, and four of the five members of its executive council were from cities west of the Allegheny Mountains.

government. It was natural to support civil service reform in con-
junction with opposition to the burdensome and complicated
internal revenue system that evolved during the Civil War. This support of civil service reform was sustained by the New England Manufacturers' Convention held at Worcester in January, 1868, and was
"carried on by a delegation in Washington D.C." later that winter.
Further aid from businessmen was received from James A. Dupee,
who persuaded the Boston Board of Trade to endorse unanimously
the Jenckes bill. After this success, Dupee pressed the Massachusetts
legislature to support the bill, urged the New York Chamber of
Commerce to consider reform, and later asked "gentlemen of influence" to write the Massachusetts congressional delegation backing the measure.[26]

On May 14, 1868, Jenckes again urged Congress to adopt civil
service reform. The bill he spoke for was a substitute that radically
differed from his earlier measures. The alterations, like their pred-
ecessors, reflected the contemporary political scene. Hostility toward
Johnson obviously motivated the proposal for a new department
of civil service headed by the Vice President in place of the earlier
presidential commission. The commissioners would no longer be
removed by the President, and the Vice President would appoint
temporary commissioners pending senatorial confirmation of regular
presidential appointees. Jenckes's speech reviewed material covered by his previous efforts. He stressed the practicability of reform, commented that for the money it spent the United States
received poorer service than any other government, and assured the
House that the merit system would attract "educated, earnest, patriotic, and ingenuous youths." Yet Jenckes more than echoed his
earlier speeches. Research by Bing for a forthcoming report provided Jenckes with proof that nearly all important civil servants
favored reform.[27]

Poor timing by Jenckes, however, again curtailed press response
to his speech. Civil service reform could not compete successfully
for public interest with Johnson's impeachment trial and the approaching Republican National Convention. Gale was "disappointed & mortified" when none of the Boston papers printed

[26] G. B. Stebbins to the manufacturers and businessmen of Providence, Rhode
Island, and vicinity, Detroit, November 15, 1868, Dupee to Jenckes, Boston, April
7 and 13, May 23, 1868, *ibid.*

[27] *Congressional Globe,* 40 Cong., 2 sess., 2466–70.

Jenckes's speech in full. In New York, Jenckes received only short notices in the *Herald* and the *Times,* but the editors of the *Tribune,* never before friendly to civil service reform, commented favorably and printed both Jenckes's speech and bill. This publicity by the *Tribune* indicated the growing significance of reform. This growth was confirmed by M. D. Marsland of the *Financial Chronicle,* who claimed that Jenckes's speech "produced a decided sensation" when reported in the telegraphic dispatches. The *Nation* published an article by Rosengarten, which boasted that the country would be "richer by a hundred millions every year" if it adopted the Jenckes bill and predicted that this bill would do "more to renew and restore and sustain the virtues of the Republic, than all the legislation of the last decade." [28]

As Jenckes persisted with his bill, interest in civil service reform gradually widened. Coupled with the growth of early interest in Boston, New York, and Philadelphia was occasional western support. From California, Henry George, the *San Francisco Times*'s young editor who had endured but had not written of the poverty that led him to question the reality of progress, wrote Jenckes: "I have already advocated the bill in several articles, and do so again this morning. These articles so far as my knowledge goes are the only ones which have appeared in the press of this coast on the subject. . . . I trust I may be mistaken, but it seems to me that the difficulties in the way of your bill are so enormous that it will not pass until the people of the whole country are aroused to its importance, and to secure this popular support it is the duty of every one who himself sees its necessity to do what he can." [29]

Jenckes's speech was followed by his celebrated report of May 25, 1868, which Julius Bing had been preparing for months. In

---

[28] *New York Herald,* May 15, 1868, p. 7, c. 6; *New York Times,* May 15, 1868, p. 8, c. 2; *New York Daily Tribune,* May 15, 1868, p. 4, c. 2, p. 8, cc. 3–4; Joseph George Rosengarten, "The Civil Service Bill," *Nation,* VI, No. 152 (May 28, 1868), 425; Gale to Jenckes, Boston, June 22, 1868, and Marsland to Jenckes, New York, May 19, 1868, Jenckes Papers. There is some confusion concerning the telegraphic report of Jenckes's speech. Rosengarten claimed that it was not telegraphed, and the action of Boston and Philadelphia papers confirms this statement. Yet New York papers obviously did receive a report of the speech, because the *Tribune* printed it and Marsland spoke of it. Nevertheless, the main point is that Jenckes's speech did not receive the publicity it normally would have because of the impeachment trial and the Republican convention.

[29] Henry B. Brown to Jenckes, Detroit, May 25, 1868, E. B. Ward to Jenckes Detroit, June 1, 1868, and George to Jenckes, San Francisco, May 16, 1868, *ibid.*

December, 1867, Bing had submitted to Jenckes and his committee associates three questionnaires for approval. The first contained ninety-one questions for department heads, the second listed eighteen questions for the second auditor of the Treasury Department and the Paymaster General, and the third questionnaire consisted of twenty-five questions for heads of colleges.[30] The circular for department heads was pared down to thirty-seven questions before mailing. Answers to these questions formed the foundation of the Jenckes report.

Bing spent most of January and February classifying and abstracting replies to these questionnaires. Most replies were similar to that of Auditor S. G. Ogden of the New York Customhouse, who *"emphatically"* favored the proposed reform. The questions, Jenckes reported, had been mailed to 446 officers, whose subordinates within the operation of the proposed act numbered 12,819. Of these officers, 362, whose subordinates numbered 11,561, decidedly favored reform while only 12, supervisors of 143 civil servants, were decidedly opposed. The remaining officers were indifferent or evasive in their answers. These figures indicated that reform would be supported strongly within the government service. People writing Jenckes on reform confirmed Bing's survey; over one-third of them either were or had been civil servants. In June, Bing proudly referred to "our" report and said that "the mass of evidence it contains, will stagger the public mind, & constitute perhaps, one of the most extraordinary & interesting records, ever placed before this or any country."[31]

The report became the source book for civil service reformers. Its main body consisted of Bing's questionnaires and sample replies. These printed replies, although overwhelmingly favoring reform, contained a wide range of suggestions for achieving it. Only one hostile reply was printed. John M. Connell, an internal revenue assessor from Ohio, thought "nothing could be more disastrous" than the Jenckes bill. He favored short terms of office and felt the dominant tendency was *"towards making all offices elective."* In conclusion Connell feared, with some justification, that civil service reform

---

[30] Bing to Jenckes, Washington, December 4, 1867, *ibid.*

[31] *Congressional Globe*, 40 Cong., 2 sess., 2470; Bing to Jenckes, Washington, January 23, 1868, and no place, June 19, 1868, Jenckes Papers. From 1864 to 1872, 361 persons wrote Jenckes on civil service reform. Of these, the occupations of 270 have been ascertained and it is found that 99 of them either were or had been civil servants. *Ibid., passim.*

was an attempt by hypocritical politicians to cripple their opponents by restricting patronage which they would use themselves if they could. The remainder of the report included a brief history of civil service reform; quotations from Washington, Jefferson, Henry Clay, and Josiah Quincy; extracts from the contemporary press; expositions on the civil service of China, Prussia, England, and France; and sections of Jenckes's preceding report.[32]

Julius Bing had reason to be proud of his accomplishments. Within a period of twelve months, he had published influential articles in the *North American Review* and *Putnam's Magazine,* had written numerous articles for the *Round Table,* and had done most of the research and writing of the reformer's bible—the civil service report of 1868. In fairness to this obscure and forgotten clerk, the report should be known as the Bing Report. But Bing's reward was his own knowledge of his contribution. "I may flatter myself," he wrote Jenckes, "that the strong breeze raised in & out of Congress is at least in part, due to my efforts." [33]

Despite growing support for Jenckes's measure, there was as yet no organized pressure for its passage. The convention of the National Board of Trade deferred endorsing the Jenckes bill,[34] although it had earlier received business support. Farmers were not interested. One of the few adverse responses to Bing's questionnaire was from James B. Weaver of Iowa, presidential nominee of the farmer-orientated Greenback Labor party in 1880 and of the Populists in 1892. Labor had little sympathy for reform. Only one of

[32] Joint Select Committee on Retrenchment, "Civil Service of the United States," *House Reports,* 40 Cong., 2 sess., II, No. 47, *passim.*

[33] Bing to Jenckes, no place, June 19, 1868, Jenckes Papers. Bing was also largely responsible for the less elaborate report supporting the bill of Senator James W. Patterson, which proposed a competitive system for the United States foreign service. Joint Select Committee on Retrenchment, "Report [to accompany Bill S. No. 587]," *Senate Reports,* 40 Cong., 2 sess., No. 154, 27. Ironically, Patterson is remembered for his connection with the Credit Mobilier scandal. His expulsion from the Senate was recommended in early 1873, but that drastic step was not acted upon since his term expired in March.

[34] John Welsh to Rosengarten, no place, June 8, 1868, and Rosengarten to Jenckes, Philadelphia, June 9, 1868, Jenckes Papers. Fifteen years later, Hamilton A. Hill of Boston addressed the National Board of Trade and claimed that it supported the Jenckes bill in 1868, 1869, and 1870. Hill also contended that while opinion fluctuated in "other circles," businessmen had been unalterable supporters of civil service reform. *Civil Service Record* (Boston), III, No. 2 (July, 1883), 11 Looking back over the years Hill probably got his dates mixed, and he definitely misstated the constancy of business support given civil service reform. Other business organizations, however, did show interest in the late 1860's.

Jenckes's 1864 to 1872 correspondents on civil service reform could be identified as a laborer, and he was a highly skilled employee of the Boston Navy Yard. Reformers, in turn, had little sympathy for labor. "Pray give Henry Wilson a broadside for dipping his flag to that piratical craft of the eight hour men," James Russell Lowell later wrote of his senator to Godkin. "I don't blame him for sympathizing with his former fellow-craftsmen (though he took to unproductive industry at the first chance) but I have a thorough contempt for a man who pretends to believe that eight is equal to ten & makes philanthropy a stalking horse." [35]

The seeming indifference of businessmen, laborers, and farmers did not encourage quick congressional action. The *Nation* stated, however, that civil service reform was growing in "public estimation. The prominent party journals begin to see the absurdity of roaring about corruption as long as a bill of this kind lies unpassed, and are beginning to urge it faintly on Congress." But Congress remained unimpressed. When in July, 1868, Jenckes moved to suspend the rules to enable consideration of his bill, the requisite two-thirds vote was not attained, although a bipartisan majority supported him.[36]

As the election of 1868 drew near, the prospects for civil service reform brightened. Reformers like all other Republicans had fallen under the spell of Ulysses S. Grant. They had been influenced by a forged letter—allegedly written by a member of Grant's staff—stressing Grant's independence of party, his willingness to follow Congress, and his determination not to reward his supporters with office. The last declaration particularly pleased the *Nation*, which said that if Grant really said this, and if he would assist by "authority and example" the passage of the Jenckes bill, "he would do more for the salvation and perpetuation of this Government than he has yet done in the field." [37]

All were attracted to the potential power centered in Grant. Believing that the men surrounding him would determine his views and seeing "all the disreputable politicians of the Republican

---

[35] Lowell to Godkin, Cambridge, May 2, 1869, Godkin Papers.

[36] *Nation,* VI, No. 155 (June 18, 1868), 482; *Congressional Globe,* 40 Cong., 2 sess., 4003.

[37] *Nation,* V, No. 129 (December 19, 1867), 493. The inconsistency of civil service reformers in supporting a man untrained for the presidency was pointed out to the *Nation* by the "Western General of Volunteers," in "Correspondence: Chase and Grant," *ibid.,* VI, No. 156 (June 25, 1868), 510.

party" flock about him, the *Nation* called on the "best men" in the party to "exert such an influence as shall ensure a victory which will require no distribution of plunder." [38] Grant clubs and committees, designed to take Grant's nomination out of the hands of the politicians and prevent the nomination of another, soon sprang up all over the country. In New York City, A. T. Stewart organized a club composed of leading merchants and lawyers, who hoped to influence their various business connections.

The Chicago Republican Convention, which gave Johnson three groans to the tune of the Rogue's March, cheered itself hoarse when it unanimously nominated Grant on the first ballot. The platform on which Grant stood, besides approving congressional Reconstruction and denouncing repudiation, called for "strictest economy" in the civil service and an end to the corruption which Johnson "so shamefully nursed and fostered." [39]

Julius Bing reasoned, as Chicago platform builders hoped reformers would, that the economy clause was meant to include the Jenckes bill. Godkin was not so gullible. After the Democratic Convention in July attacked corruption in the administration, the *Nation* pronounced the declarations of both parties worthless and intended merely to soothe "obstreperous reformers." Only when the Republican party advocated the Jenckes bill in the same manner as it did Reconstruction legislation would the *Nation* regard the party as sincere. Grant, reasoned the *Nation,* would be powerless to stop abuses since senators, representatives, local politicians, and editors controlled appointments. Nevertheless, it supported the Republican party as the lesser evil but reserved the right to "scratch," denounce corruption, and expose mistakes.[40] Its reservations concerned the party—not Grant. Charles Eliot Norton's sentiment that " 'Honesty & Grant,' 'good-faith & Grant' must succeed," could easily have been echoed by the *Nation*. Grant, it was hoped, would oust politicos and help reformers capture control of the Republican party. Civil service reform would have its best opportunity yet under Grant, who knew a good man when he saw one, and who "undoubtedly" would support reform as only a nonpolitically oriented man could.

---

[38] "The Nomination of Grant," *ibid.*, V, No. 129 (December 19, 1867), 505.

[39] Ellis Paxson Oberholtzer, *A History of the United States Since the Civil War* (New York, 1917–37), II, 156.

[40] Bing to Jenckes, Washington, May 26, 1868, Jenckes Papers; "Recent Warnings to the Corrupt," *Nation*, VII, No. 159 (July 16, 1868), 46–47; "Where Shall Honest Men Go?," *ibid.*, No. 161 (July 30, 1868), 84.

The *Nation* evidently had forgotten its earlier view that politicians, not Grant, would control the civil service. To Julius Bing, Grant's imminent election made the "prospects of our success . . . brighter now than . . . at any previous time." [41] Reformers felt triumphant when Grant was elected.

Yet the results of the election were not altogether pleasing to reformers. Inflationist Benjamin F. Butler had been victorious in Massachusetts, and the *Nation* charged that Democrats had succeeded in colonizing Indiana and Ohio with Kentucky voters and Philadelphia with New York voters. Democratic judges in New York City were accused of naturalizing 25,000 ineligible and imaginary persons in time for the election. "No election in the country," cried the *Nation,* "was ever attended by so much fraud." In New York, "every variety of cheating has been practiced." Republican reformers, however, were more aware of Democratic frauds and scandals than of their own party's political assessments.[42]

Rhode Island was a bright spot for reformers. Thomas A. Jenckes was re-elected to the House. Among the congratulatory letters he received was one from Congressman James G. Blaine of Maine. Blaine had voted against reform in February, 1867, and in the future would have reason to hate both reform and reformers, but he desired to be speaker of the next Congress and possibly with that in mind wrote Jenckes: "I congratulate you very cordially on your triumphant re-election— Your return to Congress is hailed with pleasure all over the country on account especially of yr authorship of the measure to purify improve & elevate the *civil service* of the country— Pray advise me of the present attitude of yr Bill. I mean its parliamentary status— Is it in such a position as will insure its being reached & acted on at the approaching session?" [43] Reformers had elected their man to the presidency, their chief advocate was re-elected, and the man who would be Speaker of the House implicitly favored their measure. Reform apparently had triumphed.

---

[41] Norton to Curtis, Manchester, England, July 24, 1868, Norton Papers; "What May Be Expected from Grant's Administration," *Nation,* VII, No. 174 (October 29, 1868), 344; Bing to Jenckes, Washington, October 27, 1868, Jenckes Papers.

[42] *Nation,* VII, No. 171 (October 8, 1868), 281; *ibid.,* No. 172 (October 15, 1868), 301; *ibid.,* No. 174 (October 29, 1868), 341; *ibid.,* No. 175 (November 5, 1868), 361. See the memorandum of William Schindy, chief coiner of the branch mint at San Francisco, dated November 2, 1868. Twenty out of 21 employees contributed from $20 to $100 to the Union Republican State Central Committee. Carl Schurz Papers, Library of Congress.

[43] Blaine to Jenckes, Augusta, Maine, November 7, 1868, Jenckes Papers.

IV

GRANT FAILS REFORMERS

Fervor for civil service reform grew from 1867 to 1869. Although farmers and laborers were indifferent toward the movement and professional politicians hostile, certain businessmen called for reform and growing press support stimulated even further interest. A shift in goals, however, is perceptible. Instead of being a means of tying Johnson's hands and effecting Radical Reconstruction, civil service reform had become for some of its supporters a means of tying the politico's hands and effecting control of the Republican party. Not only would the Jenckes bill change the character of the civil service, it would also deprive the party war horses of their patronage and power. The resulting vacuum could be filled by reformers and their peers. Reformers counted on Grant to help carry out these plans. He, too, was a nonprofessional politician. Certainly he would back the Jenckes bill, and most certainly he would appoint respectable and cultured men to office.

I

Reformers prided themselves upon Grant's nomination and rejoiced at his election. The new President, they predicted, would introduce efficiency and morality into the federal service. The *Nation* reasoned that since Grant's nomination and election were achieved without bargaining he was obliged to no one. Under Grant, the spoils system would end and electioneering would be carried on by a "good" rather than "a very bad class" of workers. "Wire-pullers and orators of the baser sort" would be replaced by men like Jenckes who belonged to the Republican party "not as an end but as a means" of putting their ideas into practice. On December 31, 1868, the *Nation* stated that Grant favored the Jenckes bill.[1] From New York, Samuel Gray Ward reported, "We are in great spirits here about Grant. Especially since he tells the Rail Road land grant people they have nothing to expect from him. There are various other classes of people that it is to be hoped will find in his reign a more stringent atmosphere than they have been used to." "Grant grows daily in my respect & confidence," echoed Charles Eliot Norton and rapturously described the President as "so simple, so sensible, so strong & so magnanimous." The reform element continued to cheer when Grant with "extraordinary skill and coolness . . . foiled" the efforts of Pennsylvania politicians to dictate a Cabinet appointment. "We are in hopes," crowed the *Nation,* "that we have in Grant a man who will break up the present system, and in breaking it up reveal to the country the possibility of being both great and prosperous without the aid of party charlatans." [2]

Although reformers rejoiced when politicians were snubbed, they did not want to be ignored themselves. "If you see a perfectly fit and easy opportunity," Norton wrote Curtis, "I should be glad to have you use it to suggest my name as that of a suitable person for the mission to Holland or Belgium." Curtis wrote to the newly appointed Secretary of State, Hamilton Fish, in Norton's behalf and also asked Senator Charles Sumner to secure the nomination of friends as consuls at both Paris and Marseilles. In addition, Curtis recommended as surveyor for the Albany Customhouse the "honest and faithful" but convivial poet Alfred Billings Street, who, Curtis testified, was merely "enlivened" by drinking and not a drunkard as alleged.[3] After four lean years under Johnson, reformers were as desirous of re-establishing themselves in higher federal offices as they were of instituting a system of competitive examinations in the subordinate civil service. To them, competitive examinations were but an imperfect means [4] of securing their object—the appointment

---

[1] "Grant and the Civil Service," *Nation* (New York), VII, No. 179 (December 3, 1868), 452–453; *ibid.,* No. 183 (December 31, 1868), 541.

[2] Ward to Norton, New York, December 26, 1868, and Norton to Curtis, London, January 29, 1869, Norton Papers, Harvard University; "The Men Inside Politics," *Nation,* VIII, No. 192 (March 4, 1869), 164–165.

[3] Norton to Curtis, London, January 29, 1869, Norton Papers; Curtis to Norton, Staten Island, March 13, 1869, and Sumner to Curtis, Washington, February 18, 1869, Curtis Papers, Harvard University; Curtis to Sumner, Staten Island, February 10, 17, and 23, 1869, Sumner Papers, Harvard University.

[4] Even the *Nation* pointed out that competitive examinations were not a flawless mode of appointment. *Nation,* VII, No. 177 (November 19, 1868), 410.

of well-qualified individuals to all posts. Almost invariably, they found the best-qualified individuals to be Republicans who like themselves were not professional politicians.

Reformers, as well as other Republicans, were soon somewhat disillusioned by Grant's Cabinet and by the method used to assemble it.[5] Not that Grant had consulted the politicians. He had ignored all the accepted formulae and had treated the task of Cabinet-making as if he were hiring servants for his home. Henry Adams went to the Capitol to hear the names announced, eager to join the Executive in taking away the Senate's two-thirds vote and power of confirmation. "To the end of his life," Adams later wrote in his autobiography, "he wondered at the suddenness of the revolution which actually, within five minutes, changed his intended future into an absurdity so laughable as to make him ashamed of it. He was to hear a long list of Cabinet announcements not much weaker or more futile than that of Grant, and none of them made him blush, while Grant's nominations had the singular effect of making the hearer ashamed, not so much of Grant, as of himself. He had made another total misconception of life—another inconceivable false start. Yet, unlikely as it seemed, he had missed his motive narrowly, and his intention had been more than sound, for the Senators made no secret of saying with senatorial frankness that Grant's nominations betrayed his intent as plainly as they betrayed his incompetence. A great soldier might be a baby politician."[6]

As Secretary of State, Grant appointed his fellow-townsman Elihu Washburne—the appointment was honorific. Washburne resigned to go as minister to France with the prestige of having held high office.[7] To the amazement of Curtis and others, Grant replaced Washburne with Hamilton Fish of New York. Although a member of a socially outstanding family, Fish was an unexciting appointment. "A man of good feeling, honest, solid, sound, always of Republican sympathies," Curtis said, "who has made no great blunders,

---

[5] On Grant as a Cabinet maker, see Allan Nevins, *Hamilton Fish* (New York 1937), pp. 108–115; William Best Hesseltine, *Ulysses S. Grant* (New York, 1935) pp. 145–148; Ellis Paxson Oberholtzer, *A History of the United States Since the Civil War* (New York, 1917–37), II, 214–220; James Ford Rhodes, *History . . . from the Compromise of 1850 to . . . 1877* (New York, 1906), VI, 236–241.

[6] Henry Adams, *The Education of Henry Adams* (New York, 1931), p. 262. Un like most reformers at this time, Adams did not fear but favored executive power

[7] An acid-tongued critic remarked that Washburne went to France because he did not know English. Oberholtzer, *op. cit.*, II, 217, n. 2.

but of the most ordinary ability, and a man of no vital relation to the party of today." [8] Fish may have been colorless, but the contrast between him and Washburne was so great that "discriminating quarters" were grateful for his appointment.

Grant's inclusion of his "subscribing" friends in his Cabinet shocked the country. A. T. Stewart, who a few days earlier had given Grant a check for $65,000,[9] was appointed Secretary of the Treasury and Adolph Borie, a rich Philadelphian who had figured prominently in a scheme to present Grant a house, was made Secretary of the Navy. Reformers struggled to maintain their confidence in Grant. Just as they were persuading themselves that Stewart, a businessman free from the intrigues of politics, "might bring good sense to the public service," it was found that a statute of 1789 made merchants ineligible for the position. Grant again shocked the nation by asking that Stewart be excused from the law's operation. When the Senate, under the leadership of Charles Sumner, balked, Grant withdrew his message. The backbone of the opposition to Stewart was the extreme Radical Republican element, which felt inadequately represented in the Cabinet. To please it, the Treasury was given to Radical George S. Boutwell of Massachusetts, whose main qualification for the post was intense political partisanship.

The remaining Cabinet appointees attracted little adverse comment. John A. Rawlins, like Grant and Washburne a native of Galena, Illinois, became Secretary of War. John A. J. Creswell, a Maryland secessionist who had turned Radical Republican, was appointed Postmaster General. Reformers were gratified by the appointment of Jacob D. Cox of Ohio as Secretary of the Interior and of Ebenezer Rockwood Hoar of Massachusetts as Attorney General.

Although the *Nation* was reasonably satisfied with Grant's independent but erratic attempt at Cabinet-making, many reformers had reservations. Always a stronger party man than Godkin, Curtis was representative of reformers who wanted to work through party structure. If Grant "loosens his hold upon the party he loses his chance of real reform," Curtis commented, "and I shall be grievously disappointed if he does not see it more plainly than anybody. I think

---

[8] Curtis to Norton, Staten Island, March 13, 1869, Curtis Papers.

[9] This sum had been made up "by himself and other opulent men, purporting to be purchase money for Grant's home in Washington," which "had been bought by public subscription for Grant for $30,000. What was originally a gift to him was now 'purchased' from him for more than twice as much as it was worth, to be presented in turn to General Sherman." Oberholtzer, *op. cit.*, II, 215–216.

now that he was not wise in holding his tongue so firmly about the Cabinet,—and the *subscribing* element is a little conspicuous in the high places." Nevertheless, Curtis did not lose faith in the President, although it was apparent to him that Grant did "not sufficiently understand political necessities." Rosengarten, too, looked askance at Grant's independence of party. "I don't believe," he confided in Jenckes, "a personal administration, such as the present Cabinet seems to be,—with no wish other than the President's and no counsel or advice or policy of its own, can or ought to be successful." [10]

During the months that followed Grant's election, agitation for civil service reform quickened. In November, a Bostonian sent Jenckes a petition demanding the merit system in the Post Office Department, and a month later another citizen of Boston, who was getting up a petition to support the reform bill, assured Jenckes, "The general feeling is hearty concurrence & sympathy in your efforts." G. B. Stebbins, corresponding secretary of the National Manufacturers' Association, urged business and manufacturing organizations to aid reform by advocating "speedy passage" of the Jenckes bill.[11]

The prospects of the Jenckes bill did appear good. Grant's election and his reported approval of civil service reform carried the bill's popularity to new heights. Senator James W. Patterson of New Hampshire predicted its passage. Nathaniel Gale reported that Bostonians "who had little hope a few months ago are *quite* sanguine now of an early favorable result" and found Boston papers "quite earnest in pushing on the great proposed reform." By February, 1869, an enthusiastic correspondent wrote Jenckes that "every live journal throughout the Country" had endorsed civil service reform. In addition, the annual report of Secretary of the Treasury Hugh McColloch advocated passage of the Jenckes bill as essential to revenue reform, and the Union League Club of New York unanimously adopted a resolution favoring competitive examinations in the civil service.[12]

---

[10] *Nation*, VIII, No. 194 (March 18, 1869), 201; Curtis to Norton, Staten Island, March 13, 1869, Curtis Papers; Rosengarten to Jenckes, Philadelphia, March 12, 1869, Jenckes Papers, Library of Congress.

[11] E. H. Derby to Jenckes, Boston, November 10, 1868, Waldo Higginson to Jenckes, Boston, December 13 and 17, 1868, and Stebbins to the manufacturers and businessmen of Providence, Rhode Island, and vicinity, Detroit, November 15, 1868, *ibid.*

[12] Gale to Jenckes, Boston, November 25, 1868, John Jay to Jenckes, New York,

Further impetus came in December, 1868, when the American Social Science Association joined supporters of reform. Founded at Boston in October, 1865, by a group among whom the antislavery element was prominent, this organization was modeled upon the British National Association for the Promotion of Social Science. Its objectives included the advancement of education "and the diffusion of sound principles on questions of economy, trade, and finance." Sound principles meant hard money, a revenue tariff, and, by the closing days of 1868, civil service reform. Jenckes was invited by the association's recording secretary, Henry Villard, to meet with "professional and business men" of the society. Villard, a German immigrant, had covered the Lincoln-Douglas debates as a journalist and would in time make his mark in finance by completing the Northern Pacific Railroad. The proposed Boston conference, Villard wrote Jenckes, was to be an "informal and private one and simply intended to afford an opportunity for an exchange of views and for consultation as to the best means of bringing about" reform.[13]

Jenckes's Boston trip was a huge success. His activities there consisted of far more than one private conference. He presented his bill before the favorable Boston Board of Trade and spoke on the practical aspects of his measure before a large, distinguished public gathering which included three former mayors of Boston and Senator Henry Wilson. The audience unanimously signed a petition supporting the Jenckes bill before the meeting adjourned.[14]

Encouraged by the success of their Boston venture, members of the Social Science Association decided to hold a similar meeting in New York. Within a week of Jenckes's Boston address, Villard, armed with letters of introduction from Godkin, was calling on "prominent" New York businessmen to organize another meeting for Jenckes. Villard "succeeded in getting some of the first names in New York" on his list and "found everywhere the strongest sympathy for our movement." He also attended to committee work, planned a program, and compiled a list of 1,200 "select persons" to

January 21, 1869, and John W. White to Jenckes, Philadelphia, February 17, 1869, *ibid.*; *Nation*, VII, No. 180 (December 10, 1868), 469.

[13] *Nation*, I, No. 15 (October 12, 1865), 449; Henry Villard, "Historical Sketch of Social Science," *Journal of Social Science* (New York), No. 1 (June, 1869), 5–10; Villard to Jenckes, Boston, December 17, 1868, Jenckes Papers.

[14] Alexander H. Rice to Jenckes, Boston, December 27, 1868, *ibid.*; "Address of Hon. Thos. A. Jenckes, of Rhode Island, Before the American Social Science Association in Boston," *New York Times*, January 3, 1869, p. 1, cc. 4–6.

whom special invitations for the January 16, 1869, meeting were sent. The New York meeting was, Villard reported, "as great a success as the Boston one. . . . Mr. Jenckes spoke very well . . . was greatly applauded and produced a very favorable impression." [15]

The *New York Times* was more critical than Villard. It reported that an audience similar in "respectability and intelligence" was seldom seen in New York but that Jenckes's "address was not equal to the occasion." It was too "congressional" in style with "long-drawn and deliberate commonplaces, the reading of hackneyed quotations from the writings of the 'Fathers' of the Republic, and the swelling periods on the glory of the Union." The *Times* concluded, "What we needed from Mr. Jenckes was not a history of our civil service or quotations from Jefferson and Lord Bacon, but a compact, strong statement, made with some rapidity, of the defects of our civil service, and the modes in which his particular bill would remedy them." [16]

After Jenckes's speech, Villard turned his full attention to enlisting members and raising money for the Social Science Association. Within four days he had collected $600 and had set up a committee of twenty "gentlemen of the highest standing" to carry on the membership drive. Moving on to Washington, Villard succeeded in signing up Grant, Vice President–elect Schuyler Colfax, Chief Justice Salmon P. Chase "and other high dignitaries and a score of Senators and members" of the House. By early February, Villard wrote Jenckes, "Our Association is now rapidly extending its organization throughout the country and we propose, with the aid of our branches, to carry on a regular campaign for reform in the civil service between now and the next winter in the Eastern as well as the Western States." [17] Civil service reform was no longer an undirected interest; with organization, its advocates had become a pressure group.

---

[15] Villard to Fanny Garrison Villard, New York, January 5, 8, 9, and 15, 1869, and Angelot, Orange, New Jersey, January 17, 1869, Villard Papers, Harvard University. "Movement" here probably refers to the Social Science Association and its general objectives.

[16] "Mr. Jenckes' Address on the Civil Service Bill," *New York Times*, January 23, 1869, p. 4, cc. 5–6.

[17] Villard to Fanny Villard, New York, January 21, 1869, and Washington, January 26, 1869, Villard Papers; Villard to Jenckes, Boston, February 5, 1869, Jenckes Papers.

II

Congress, however, revealed little enthusiasm for the Jenckes bill. It was feared that a stronger infusion of Democrats would make the newly elected Forty-first Congress less inclined to reform than the Fortieth Congress, for civil service reform was still an exclusively Republican program. Julius Bing urged Jenckes to secure passage of his bill by the Fortieth Congress, then assembling for its lameduck session, since chances for victory would be greater. In addition, Bing reasoned that "the new appointments under Gen. Grant's administration could be made under its operation while in the case of a further procrastination, all the political patrons of the new appointees might coalesce in the 41st Congress with the intrinsic opponents of the bill to endanger its adoption." [18]

Patronage-mongers did not await the assembling of the Forty-first Congress to oppose the bill. Senator John A. "Black Jack" Logan, who previously had introduced a civil service reform bill, was the first to attack the Jenckes bill in the lameduck session of the Fortieth Congress. Evidently the prospect of Grant instead of Johnson in the White House gave Logan, a stalwart supporter of Grant's nomination, a new perspective on reform. Formerly an "out" he was now very much an "in." The system which he had espoused earlier he now denounced as unconstitutional, undemocratic, anti-republican, aristocratic, and monarchial. The new administration's civil service policy should be, Logan declared, "He who does not unite in its views is not to be intrusted with its employment." [19]

Despite Jenckes's spirited reply, Logan's speech had its effect. Two days later, Villard and Jenckes concluded that the prospects of the civil service bill were not good. The *Nation,* which had been confident of congressional support, reported on January 14, 1869, that leading politicians of both parties would oppose a bill curtailing their appointing power. Without pressure from the people, the

---

[18] Bing to Jenckes, no place, December 5, 1868, *ibid.*

[19] *Congressional Globe,* 40 Cong., 3 sess., 262–266. The quotation is found on p. 263. A year and a day earlier, Logan called for a bill creating a civil service bureau to examine candidates. The bill he envisioned reflected western resentment over civil service policy. It was to apply only to the District of Columbia and to insure apportionment of offices among states according to population. A few weeks later, Logan introduced his proposed bill, which was referred to committee and never heard from again except when Logan wished to pose as a reformer. *Ibid.,* 40 Cong., 2 sess., 366, 806; *Congressional Record,* 47 Cong., 2 sess., 650.

Nation predicted, the Jenckes bill would not pass and without it Grant's "reforming power" would be hampered.[20]

Logan's attack was seconded on January 30, 1869, by George W. Woodward, a Pennsylvania Democrat. Even Woodward had presumed before Logan's speech that passage of the reform bill was assured by its press support and by the favorable response to Bing's questionnaires. Woodward's speech was an echo of another era— the days of Jacksonian Democracy. To cure the country's ills he advocated not civil service reform but rotation in office, hard money, no excise taxes on industry, a revenue tariff, no government subsidies, retrenchment, and payment of the debt. Once this program was put into effect, Woodward insisted, public morality would improve and the spoils system would provide honest civil servants.[21]

A few days later—after consulting with New York reformers— Villard advised Jenckes not to press his bill until the next Congress. Even if Jenckes were successful in getting the bill through the House, Villard reasoned, there would be no time for its enactment by the Senate. Acknowledgment of defeat did not lessen reformers' resentment that the Jenckes bill "lay untouched on the Clerk's table" during the entire session. They insisted that "a decent self-respect should oblige Congress to show or feign some disposition to purge the civil service from the taint of political corruption." [22]

While the Jenckes bill was being sidetracked, congressmen led by Benjamin F. Butler hastened to repeal the Tenure of Office Act. Butler, a spoilsman from Massachusetts, had been an incompetent political general in the Civil War and was striving hard to make current services erase his past from Grant's memory. Butler successfully stifled debate in the House and the Tenure of Office Act was repealed by a bipartisan vote of 121 to 47. Conspicuous friends of reform, such as Jenckes, Horace Maynard of Tennessee, and three congressmen from Ohio—Robert Schenck, James A. Garfield, and Samuel Shellabarger—voted in the negative, and Curtis, writing in *Harper's Weekly,* claimed that repeal of the Tenure of Office Act by the House made passage of the Jenckes bill even more imperative.

[20] *Congressional Globe,* 40 Cong., 3 sess., 266–268; Villard to Fanny Villard, Washington, January 11, 1869, Villard Papers; *Nation,* VII, No. 185 (January 14, 1869), 23.

[21] *Congressional Globe,* 40 Cong., 3 sess., 747–751.

[22] Villard to Jenckes, Boston, February 5, 1869, Jenckes Papers; Henry Brooks Adams, "The Session," *North American Review* (Boston), CVIII, No. 223 (April, 1869), 618.

Other reformers, however, represented by the *Nation,* no longer regarded the Tenure of Office Act as a reform measure and favored repeal. Despite the action of the House, the Senate did not consider repeal until after the House repeated its vote in the next Congress. Even then, the Senate did not relinquish all of its power but struck a compromise with the House. The *Nation* immediately dubbed the resulting act "an office-seekers' measure." Senators opposing repeal, like representatives who opposed it, were generally highly regarded by reformers. Charles Sumner of Massachusetts, Lyman Trumbull of Illinois, George F. Edmunds of Vermont, and Carl Schurz of Missouri serve as examples.[23]

Schurz's early career reads like an Anthony Hope novel. A German revolutionary in 1849, Schurz narrowly escaped capture and possible execution by crawling through a sewer to safety. He then risked his dearly bought freedom by returning to Germany and rescuing from prison his beloved professor and fellow revolutionary, Gottfried Kinkel. After brief stays in France and in England, Schurz moved in 1852 to America, where he again interested himself in politics. By 1860, he was a vigorous campaigner and because of his influence with German-Americans a power in the Republican party. Schurz was also "an indefatigable office seeker" whom Lincoln rewarded with the Spanish mission. Chaffing in far off Madrid at his inactivity and lack of influence, Schurz returned to America, pushed emancipation, went off to war, but failed to add luster to the reputation of political generals. After the war he toured the South and pleased Radicals by advocating Negro suffrage as a condition for reconstructing the seceded states. Schurz was editing a St. Louis newspaper when he became a senator in 1869. In Congress he espoused civil service reform and made it one of the prime objectives of his career.[24]

Despite his dislike of the Tenure of Office Act, Schurz favored its suspension rather than its repeal. Suspension of the act, which "everybody" knew had to be amended, would keep civil service reform before the people and aid in producing "a pressure" on Con-

[23] "Money in Politics," *Harper's Weekly* (New York), XIII, No. 631 (January 30, 1869), 66; *Nation,* VIII, No. 185 (January 14, 1869), 21–22; *ibid.,* No. 197 (April 8, 1869), 266; *ibid.,* No. 194 (March 18, 1869), 201. See William D. Mallam, "The Grant-Butler Relationship," *Mississippi Valley Historical Review* (Cedar Rapids), XLI, No. 2 (September, 1954), 259–276.

[24] For details of Schurz's career, see Claude Moore Fuess, *Carl Schurz* (New York, 1932). On Schurz as an office seeker, see Harry J. Carman and Reinhard H. Luthin, *Lincoln and the Patronage* (New York, 1943), pp. 82–84.

gress. Repeal of the act would militate against bringing "the reform bill properly before the two houses. . . ." "I have talked with the most prominent friends of reform," he wrote, "and they are entirely of my opinion." Moreover, Schurz explained, he did not wish to join in "flinging down legislative powers at the feet of 'personal government.' " [25]

On April 5, 1869, a week after passage of the compromise Tenure of Office Act, Jenckes spoke again for his measure. With Johnson out of office a separate civil service department was no longer needed. The bill, accordingly, eliminated many constitutional objections by reverting to the presidential commission. Jenckes also reversed his earlier stand and attacked legislative usurpation of executive powers. With the change in White House tenants, Jenckes insisted that congressmen should not meddle with appointments and claimed that a screening board was needed. Jenckes's speech was well received by the press. George William Curtis, however, regretted that the reform bill did not include postmasters, diplomatic officers, and assessors and collectors of internal revenue. [26]

Grant's lesser appointments soon convinced reformers that the President, as well as Congress, was not meeting their expectations. When Schurz saw the President about the St. Louis Post Office, an appointment had already been made. To Schurz's gentle remonstrance, Grant replied, "Why, Mr. Schurz, I know Missouri a great deal better than you do." At first the President's uncooperative attitude fostered the belief that he had no conception of "political necessities." Schurz, who had resolved to specialize in civil service reform, was baffled by the administration's appointing policy. He wrote a Missouri friend: "I have certainly not forgotten Mr. Waldauer and am doing for him the best I can. But this is a lottery, and heaven knows upon what mysterious theory the distribution of prizes is made. . . . I have worked very hard for my friends. In some cases I have not succeeded at all, in others too much. . . . Some Missourians have been favored with consulates by a providential dispensation which an ordinary understanding cannot fathom, and which, I am sure, I did not control." Schurz's affinity for reform was no doubt heightened by this frustrating experience in the

[25] Schurz to William M. Grosvenor, Washington, March 29, 1869, in Frederic Bancroft, ed., *Speeches, Correspondence and Political Papers of Carl Schurz* (New York, 1913), I, 481–482.

[26] *Congressional Globe*, 41 Cong., 1 sess., 517–523; "Office-Seeking," *Harper's Weekly*, XIII, No. 645 (May 8, 1869), 291.

early days of his senatorial career. Complaining that office seekers "swarm about me like grasshoppers," Schurz insisted that being a senator was "the meanest drudgery a human imagination ever conceived." He maintained that the "utter absurdity" of the spoils system was convincing "even the dullest patriots" of the necessity for reform.[27]

Others began to question Grant's distribution of the patronage. The fear that he was ignoring political necessities through his independence proved short-lived. Grant soon paid, from the reformers' point of view, all too much attention to political claims. "I am, so far, somewhat disappointed," wrote Bing on April 8, "in the apparent disregard of the principle of intrinsic fitness & qualification in some of the Executive appointments. . . ." Although the *Nation* of the same date was still pleased with Grant and doubted "if so many respectable men have been put in government offices at once for many a long day," its satisfaction ceased after all Republican members of the Fortieth Congress who had failed re-election were neatly provided for in the civil service. When the entire Ohio delegation urged it, Grant even appointed as governor of Montana the notorious James M. Ashley, the "original impeacher" from Ohio with a weakness for corruption. Ashley's appointment was soon complemented by that of Daniel Sickles as minister to Spain. Although Sickles was from an old New York family and was among the first congressmen to hold competitive examinations for West Point nominees, his scandalous career of corruption, seduction, and murder did not make him a favorite with reformers. Sickles and Ashley became symbols of Grant's disreputable appointments. Grant, obviously, was not the man to help reformers capture the Republican party.[28]

Commenting in June on Grant's removals from office, the *Nation*

[27] Curtis to Norton, Staten Island, March 13, 1869, Curtis Papers; Schurz to Margaretha Meyer Schurz, Washington, March 20 and April 12, 1869, in Joseph Schafer, ed., *Intimate Letters of Carl Schurz, 1841–1869* (Madison, Wisconsin, 1928), pp. 475–476; Schurz to James Taussig, Washington, April 18, 1869, in Bancroft, *op. cit.*, I, 482–483.

[28] Bing to Jenckes, Washington, April 8, 1869, Jenckes Papers; *Nation*, VIII, No. 197 (April 8, 1869), 266; *ibid.*, No. 198 (April 15, 1869), 286; *ibid.*, No. 199 (April 22, 1869), 305; "The Governor's 'Fall,'" *ibid.*, No. 204 (May 27, 1869), 408. For the flamboyant aspects of Sickles' career, see W. A. Swanberg, *Sickles the Incredible* (New York, 1956), *passim*. John Hay, who served as first assistant to Sickles in Madrid, however, thought highly of him. See Hay to Dr. Charles Hay, January 28, 1870, and Hay to Robert Todd Lincoln, May 7, 1870, in Tyler Dennett, ed., *Lincoln and the Civil War* (New York, 1939), pp. 306, 320.

remarked that he himself provided a striking and unexpected illustration of the need for civil service reform. "Few people—few of his supporters certainly—were prepared for 'the clean sweep' which he has made. . . ." Even those who had expected extensive changes had not anticipated that they would be made by spoils methods. The resultant scandals, the *Nation* continued, "have been enormous, and have been deeply felt by the whole community. One has hardly time to get over the indignation excited by one story of fraud and abuse when he finds himself face to face with another." [29]

Reformers failed to re-establish themselves in their old stronghold, the diplomatic service. "You remember," exclaimed John Hay, "how all the flunkeys said when Seward went out and Fish in, that politics had left the State Department and respectability and culture were to have a chance. Look at the herd of swine Fish has commissioned. . . ." Charles Eliot Norton, who had been enraptured with Grant and had hoped for a foreign mission, was neither enraptured nor hopeful by July, 1869. He wrote Curtis, "Grant's surrender, partial though it may be, to the politicians was an unexpected disappointment, but a very instructive one. His other mistakes were what might have been expected,—what indeed we ought to have been prepared for. But some of his appointments are disgraceful,—personally discreditable to him. . . . The question seems to be now whether the politicians,—'the men inside politics,'—will ruin the country, or the country take summary vengeance, by means of Jenckes's bill, upon them." Locked out of the foreign service, reformers turned even more to the Jenckes bill. [30]

Henry Adams was a rare reformer who very quickly learned to expect nothing from Grant. "We here look," Adams wrote from Washington in February, "for a reign of western mediocrity, but one appreciates least the success of the steamer, when one lives in the engine-room." Two months later, Adams wrote with satisfaction—the Adams family never seemed genuinely happy unless it had just suffered defeat— "My hopes of the new Administration have all been disappointed; it is far inferior to the last. My friends have almost all lost ground instead of gaining it as I hoped. My family is buried politically beyond recovery for years. I am becoming more and more isolated so far as allies go. I even doubt whether I can find an in-

---

[29] "The Coming Question," *Nation*, VIII, No. 206 (June 10, 1869), 448.
[30] Hay to John Bigelow, May 9, 1870, in Dennett, *op. cit.*, p. 323; Norton to Curtis, Vevey, Switzerland, July 22, 1869, Norton Papers.

dependent organ to publish my articles, so strong is the current against us." A few days later, Henry wrote his brother Charles Francis, Jr., the treasurer of the Social Science Association, "I can't get you an office. The only members of this Government that I have met are mere acquaintances, not friends, and I fancy no request of mine would be likely to call out a gush of sympathy." Nor could Henry obtain anything for himself. The administration was presumptuous enough to ignore the Adams family.[31]

With their ambitions thwarted, the Adams brothers forsook the conventional methods of political advancement and espoused civil service reform. In February, Henry had recognized that the struggle against "*political* corruption" was more basic than free trade and would be more difficult than the antislavery crusade. By June he was engaged in writing an article on civil service reform, and described it as being "very bitter and abusive of the Administration" and, although he expected it to get him into "hot water," he felt that he had "nothing to lose." Henry and his brothers, Charles Francis, Jr., and John Quincy, were "up to the ears in politics and public affairs, and in time," Henry hoped, "we shall perhaps make our little mark." [32]

Other groups besides reformers were excluded from office. Editors as a class were not recognized by Grant in his appointments, although it was well known that Lincoln lavishly bestowed patronage upon the country's press. By April 15, Grant had given no important editor or publisher a post. Charles A. Dana, editor of the *New York Sun,* was finally offered the appraisership of New York, but he declined since his acceptance would have removed the efficient incumbent. The exclusion of editors from the patronage, together with the scramble for office and the spread of corruption, did much to direct "public attention to the necessity of a change in the system. The press of both parties," the *Nation* reported on April 22, "has within the last week or two spoken more strongly than ever in favor of the adoption of the Jenckes plan, or something like it." Editors, always a vital part of the civil service reform movement,

[31] Henry Adams to Charles Francis Adams, Jr., Washington, February 23 and April 29, 1869, and Henry Adams to Charles Milnes Gaskell, Washington, April 19 and June 20, 1869, in Worthington Chauncey Ford, ed., *Letters of Henry Adams (1858–1891)* (Boston, 1930), pp. 152, 156–157, 161–162.

[32] Henry Adams to Edward Atkinson, Washington, February 1, 1869, and Henry Adams to Gaskell, Quincy, August 27, 1869, *ibid.*, pp. 151, 165–166.

provided the driving force that eventually secured substantial legislation.[33]

III

Organized agitation for civil service reform grew steadily in the early days of the Grant administration. Jenckes suggested in March, 1869, that the American Social Science Association prepare a reform memorial addressed to the collectors of the ports of New York and Philadelphia. Twenty of the "first citizens of Boston" signed such a memorial and the association asked their New York committee to follow Boston's example. Another organization joined the fight for reform in April, when a Boston meeting of free traders founded a reform league whose objectives were not only free trade but also civil service reform and the speedy resumption of specie payments. In June, Villard arranged for the Social Science Association's fall meeting in New York and engaged George William Curtis to speak on civil service reform. From New York Villard pushed on to Philadelphia to establish a local organization there.[34]

The timing of Villard's visit to Philadelphia was excellent. The "leading citizens of all parties" were "thoroughly disgusted" with recent federal appointments. "Hundreds of the best citizens" signed a petition written by Henry C. Lea urging Philadelphia's congressmen to support the Jenckes bill or some similar measure. After seeing about fifty prominent Philadelphians, Villard organized a committee and made arrangements for a fall meeting. The nucleus of the Social Science Association in Philadelphia was composed of Joseph Rosengarten, Lea, and James Miller McKim, an abolitionist founder of the *Nation*.[35]

Upon his return to Boston in July, Villard met with the association's civil service reform committee, which had recently received

---

[33] Carman and Luthin, *op. cit.*, pp. 118–129; *Nation*, VIII, No. 198 (April 15, 1869), 286; *ibid.*, No. 199 (April 22, 1869), 306–307. There were still, however, a number of editors, not of the "respectable" press, who were uninterested in reform since they were sufficiently inside politics to get "their own hands and those of their friends into the public treasury." *Ibid.*, No. 200 (April 29, 1869), 325.

[34] James A. Barnard to Jenckes, Boston, March 29, 1869, and Villard to Jenckes, Boston, April 2, 1869, Jenckes Papers; *Nation*, VIII, No. 200 (April 29, 1869), 326; Villard to Fanny Villard, New York, June 17 and 29, 1869, Villard Papers.

[35] *Nation*, IX, No. 211 (July 15, 1869), 42; Villard to Jenckes, Boston, July 19, 1869, Jenckes Papers; Villard to McKim, Boston, December 1, 1869, James Miller McKim Maloney Memorial Collection, New York Public Library. McKim was the father-in-law of Wendell Phillips Garrison, Villard's brother-in-law.

a progress report from Washington. The report stated that Secretaries George S. Boutwell and Jacob D. Cox of the Treasury and Interior Departments "objected strongly" to the creation of an independent civil service commission by the Jenckes bill. "They insisted that there should be a separate board in each department under the control of its respective chief." Assured that the Treasury and Interior Departments would support the Jenckes bill if the commission idea were dropped, the committee instructed Villard to ask Jenckes whether he would either amend his bill or draw up a new one.[36] Even though this pressure was applied, Jenckes retained the commission.

During the summer of 1869, Curtis prepared for his fall address to the Social Science Association. Furnished by Villard with Jenckes's speeches and reports and other civil service documents, he studied a topic which had interested him for nearly two years. In late October, Curtis presented his paper to a well-attended association meeting in New York City. He sought "rather to call attention to the necessity of reform by exposing the present condition of the service, and the inevitable result of the existing system, than by considering the details of a method." Curtis did state, however, that "the basis of any good system must be some kind of competitive examination for which the bill introduced by Mr. Jenckes provides, and the value of which has been tested in other countries." Curtis asserted that "objections to the reform show rather a desire to oppose than reason in opposition." The *Nation* regarded this address as the most influential one delivered at the session and stated that it alone indebted the public to the Social Science Association. Additional comfort was derived from the knowledge that Curtis, one of the country's most popular lecturers, would keep reform agitation alive by repeating the lecture on the lyceum circuit.[37]

Also in October, 1869, Henry Adams published a hard-hitting article in the *North American Review*.[38] Adams charged that Grant, aided by the Grand Army of the Republic, carried rotation in office to a new extreme. The Grand Army cleared the public service

---

[36] Villard to Jenckes, Boston, July 26, 1869, Jenckes Papers.

[37] Villard to Jenckes, Boston, July 19, 1869, *ibid.;* "Social Science," *New York Times*, October 28, 1869, p. 2, c. 3; "The Social Science Meeting," *Nation*, IX, No. 227 (November 4, 1869), 381.

[38] Henry Brooks Adams, "Civil-Service Reform," *North American Review*, CIX, No. 225 (October, 1869), 443–475.

of alleged rebels. It organized an espionage system in the departments, investigated the pasts of the clerks, and denounced victims to the appropriate department head.[39] Adams further charged that more than any previous President, Grant allowed external dictation of executive powers, and that, since both Grant and the Republican party failed to reform the civil service, action independent of party was the remaining alternative. Adams, however, did not blame Grant for promising much and disappointing many. He blamed reformers who eschewed office yet failed to stand by Grant against the avalanche of office seekers, politicians, and personal friends.

Civil service reform to Adams did not mean saving $100,000,000 a year but rather wresting back the Executive's appointing power which Congress had usurped. Adams demanded that "Congress keep its hands off executive powers," and suggested that "novel legislation" like the Jenckes bill, despite its good intentions, was "wrong both in principle and in detail, calculated to aggravate rather than to check this evil." Arguing that the President had sufficient power to institute a system of competitive examination, Adams maintained that Congress should follow the course of the British Parliament, which advised and approved the competitive system but did not legislate upon it. Congress, for example, could legislate on matters within its own sphere by making solicitation of office by congressmen a penal offense. Adams' point of view obviously betrayed his seven-year residence in Great Britain, where civil service reform was being accomplished by executive order.

Adams was under no illusions concerning a speedy reform; there was work enough for a generation. His recipe for reform was to appeal "directly to the people." Whenever the public declared for reform, Adams believed, it would be accomplished. Public opinion was to be aroused by constant exposure of corruption. On the legislative level, Adams would set aside the Jenckes bill, since it was "too cumbrous for the weak reforming influence in Congress to put in motion." Instead, he advocated that Congress pass two resolutions; one recommending that the President extend competitive examinations to all branches of the civil service where he believed they were necessary; the second declaring that Congress should return to early governmental practice on removals from office.

Adams' article not only outlined a method of civil service reform

---

[39] Adams' view of the Grand Army is confirmed in Joseph A. Ware to Jenckes, Washington, November 17, 1869, Jenckes Papers.

but also revealed why many had become civil service reformers. Although the genteel element was genuinely interested in good government, its concern for reform, Adams showed, had resulted primarily from loss of political power. This underlying cause for the reform movement was illustrated by Adams when he contrasted Attorney General Hoar with Secretary of the Treasury Boutwell— a contrast that the *Nation* applauded.[40] Boutwell, Adams stated, was "the product of caucuses and party promotion" but Hoar was "by birth and by training a representative of the best New England school, holding his moral rules on the sole authority of his own conscience, indifferent to opposition whether in or out of his party, obstinate to excess, and keenly alive to the weaknesses in which he did not share. Judge Hoar belonged in fact to a class of men who had been gradually driven from politics, but whom it is the hope of reformers to restore. Mr. Boutwell belonged to the class which has excluded its rival, but which has failed to fill with equal dignity the place it has usurped." [41]

Henry Adams enlarged on his objections to the Jenckes bill in a letter to Secretary Cox, who earlier had expressed dissatisfaction with the commission device. Adams wrote, "I care little for the competitive theory, but I believe the very existence of our Government hangs on the permanence of tenure which is to bar partisan corruption. But this permanence must come from the President. Congress by creating an independent board with immense powers, is splitting up the Government. I am sure everyone who has had any administrative experience, will agree to this."

Although Adams and Jenckes were both striving to improve administration by ending congressional interference with appointments, their proposed methods differed. Jenckes believed that a commission would effectively achieve the desired separation, while Adams hoped that Grant's Cabinet, not Congress, would initiate reform. Despite opposition from some reformers, Jenckes clung to his measure, saw Grant, and reported that the President favored his bill. Adams, however, did not surrender his hope for executive leadership. "You," he wrote Cox, "are the reserve force, the silent

---

[40] "The North American Review for October," *Nation*, IX, No. 228 (November 11, 1869), 415.

[41] On the floor of the House, Representative Jacob Benton of New Hampshire regarded the Jenckes bill as a "cunningly devised" scheme to keep the administration's friends out of office "unless they belong to the particular, select favorite class." *Congressional Globe*, 41 Cong., 2 sess., 3258.

agency by which I hope this contest is to be decided, and your interference now seems to me to have become necessary." "Give the
country a lead!" cried Adams. "We are wallowing in the mire for
want of a leader. If the Administration will only frame a sound
policy of reform, we shall all gravitate towards it like iron filings
to a magnet." Although Cox in his report of 1869 called "forcibly
and manfully" for a reform of the civil service, no one else in the
administration followed his lead. Grant's first annual message to
Congress completely ignored civil service reform.[42]

Henry Adams, nevertheless, was pleased with the result of his
article and with himself as well. He wrote, "I am actually winding
myself up in a coil of political intrigue and getting the reputation
of a regular conspirator. My progress in a year has alarmed me, for
it is too rapid to be sound. I am already deeper in the confidence of
the present Government than I was with the last, although that was
friendly and this a little hostile. It seems a little strange that after
the violent attack I made on it . . . there should be no soreness,
but the fact is, nearly every member of the Cabinet is in perfect sympathy with me in abusing themselves. You see there is a line of division in the Cabinet, and I am on the side which has the strongest
men, and Reform is always a sure card." [43]

The strongest men, however, did not prove to be the most durable,
nor did Secretary of the Treasury Boutwell prove deserving of
Adams' severe criticism. From 1870 to 1872, he administered stringent
tests in the Treasury Department. Boutwell also appointed E. B.
Elliott, a friend of reform who later became a civil service commissioner, to the Treasury board of examiners. Elliott helped prepare
a guide for Treasury clerkship examinations designed to aid in
hiring competent workers. These examinations especially stressed
arithmetic, but also included weights, measures, bookkeeping, gram-
mar, spelling, geography, history, and law. According to Elliott, admission to the Treasury Department under Boutwell was "invariably" at the lowest level and written examinations were "invariably"
required for promotion. Elliott testified that enforcement of these
rules was "steady & regular & firm, the standard moderate but persistently enforced examination in no case merely formal." He also

---

[42] Adams to Cox, Washington, November 8, 1869, in Harold Dean Cater, ed.,
Henry Adams and His Friends (Boston, 1947), pp. 43–44; *Nation,* IX, No. 232 (December 9, 1869), 498.

[43] Adams to Gaskell, Washington, December 7, 1869, in Ford, *op. cit.,* pp. 173–174

stated that Boutwell's system, unlike competitive examinations, "took cognizance of special qualifications derived from experience in previous employment and of other special attainments." Finally, the first competitive examination in the United States civil service was held in Boutwell's department in 1870, when six third-class clerks were examined for vacancies in the next class. Although competitive, this examination was not open to all applicants.[44]

Inherent demands of the civil service necessitated reform in Boutwell's department. His connection with competitive and stringent pass examinations seems strange considering his opposition to civil service reformers and their intense dislike of him, but Boutwell had to administer a large office. Responsible officials recognized the need for skilled employees—a need which increased as government functions multiplied and became more complex. Boutwell, like reformers, desired efficient workers and was prepared to use examinations to obtain them, but unlike reformers, he wished to continue making political appointments. Whether Boutwell's actions were the product of the Treasury Department's personnel recruitment requirements or were based on a desire to "flank" reformers by giving them a species of reform can only be conjectured. It is clear, however, that historians relying mainly on such partisan sources as the *Nation* have overlooked Boutwell's reform activities. What was actually—from the standpoint of personnel administration—an enlightened regime has been renowned as a blatant example of the spoils system.

---

[44] "Civil Service Reform," I, 27, 31–35, 91–92; III, 558–559, Elliott Papers, Civil Service Commission Library, Washington, D. C.

V

LIMITED VICTORY
FOR REFORM

By shutting the door to public service on the "respectable and cultured" members of society, Grant unwittingly converted many of them to civil service reform. Had he admitted them to office their ardor for the Jenckes bill might have cooled. But Grant's actions prospered reform. The tighter he kept the door the more frustrated reformers became and the more frustrated they became the more concerted became their demand for civil service reform. Reform was their weapon—the battering ram that would splinter the shut door. But throughout early 1870 there was no break-through; Grant closed the door even tighter.

I

Grant's first annual message to Congress in December, 1869, and his ensuing actions disappointed reformers. His message conspicuously omitted any mention of civil service reform; this omission, the *Nation* said, "formed the great scandal of General Grant's administration." A second disappointment followed immediately. To fill vacancies in the Supreme Court, Grant nominated Attorney General Hoar and former Secretary of War Stanton. Hoar, an experienced judge from an old Concord family and to reformers an ideal political leader, was rejected by the Senate; while Stanton, whose temperament was anything but judicious, was immediately confirmed. Hoar, reformers believed, had been rejected because of his unpopularity with the Senate—an unpopularity which stemmed largely from his refusal to tolerate political appointments in the Justice Department.[1]

Discussion of reform bills by Congress helped reformers forget their disappointment in Grant. On December 7, 1869, Senator Lyman Trumbull, Republican of Illinois, gave a speech supporting his reform bill, which would make it a misdemeanor for congressmen to advise the President on appointments. This bill was designed to accomplish just what Henry Adams wished—the restoration of executive patronage to the President. Nevertheless, the split among reformers over methods led Carl Schurz to oppose Trumbull's bill and to question who would supply the President with information concerning applicants if congressmen were not allowed to do so.[2]

Schurz introduced his own reform bill on December 20. It was similar to the Jenckes bill in many respects, yet in others it diverged significantly. Like the Jenckes measure, it would have created a board to examine candidates for office, limited appointment to successful examinees, empowered the board to make rules necessary for its functioning, and endowed it with judicial powers respecting civil servants. The scope of the Schurz bill, however, was far more extensive. It included the entire civil service except the foreign service, the Cabinet, and certain presidential appointments in the judiciary department. Schurz's commission contained nine members who were to hold office for twelve years, while Jenckes's commission contained four members appointed for five years.

Yet certain features of Schurz's bill were compromising. The appointing power could ignore successful examinees by requesting examination of a new person, and Schurz provided that "mere inquiries concerning the character, antecedents, social standing, and general ability may be substituted for formal examinations." Schurz, like most reformers, placed a civil servant's antecedents and social standing on a par with character and general ability. While the Jenckes bill advocated tenure during good behavior, Schurz's bill bowed to the principle of rotation in office. An incumbent holding office when the bill passed was to remain in office for five years. Superiors, however, could remove incompetents by ordering them to be examined. All subsequent appointments were to be made for eight

---

[1] *Nation* (New York), IX, No. 232 (December 9, 1869), 498; "Why Judge Hoar Was Not Confirmed," *ibid.*, No. 235 (December 30, 1869), 582–583.

[2] *Congressional Globe*, 41 Cong., 2 sess., 17, 1078.

years, but the first year was to be one of probation during which the appointing power could make arbitrary removals.[3]

Despite rotation, the Schurz bill impressed reformers, but not Congress. Although the *New York Times* remarked, "civil service reform is not a Utopian dream, but an impending question for practical decision," Congress twice refused even to consider the bill and was, Curtis lamented, "sublimely unconscious" of the "great evil" that "the increase of political corruption" represented.[4]

Congress gave more attention to the Jenckes bill. A three-day debate started on May, 3, 1870, when Jenckes again reported a new version of his measure. This time the commission had been reduced to three members with five-year terms. To appease those advocating rotation of offices, the committee had added a new section making affected civil servants subject to re-examination every four years at the discretion of the commission. Jenckes stated that his primary object was to root out dishonesty and incompetence among the 20,000 officers who handled public money.

The arguments of Jenckes and his opponents followed familiar lines. The opposition charged that offices would be further removed from the people and that the machinery was impractical. Those opposing the bill also complained that it would interfere unconstitutionally with the appointing power and would undermine executive responsibility, since a department head would no longer choose his own officers. Opponents further argued that most abuses in the civil service were the product of human frailty, which no legislation could change. Jenckes asserted that offices would be brought closer to the people and that the system of examination was practical, for large groups could be examined at one time. He further declared that the bill was constitutional, since the legislative power creating the offices could certainly prescribe qualifications for the officers. Jenckes protested that the theory of administrative responsibility did not work in practice and warned that if it were indeed impossible to improve the civil service, particularly in the New York Customhouse, the United States government had better "abdicate its duties." Having expected opposition from those who would lose patronage if the

---

[3] *Ibid.*, pp. 236–238; "How Abuses Grow into Institutions," *Nation*, X, No. 237 (January 13, 1870), 20–21.

[4] "Mr. Schurz's Civil Service Bill," *New York Times*, January 14, 1870, p. 4, cc. 5–6; *Congressional Globe*, 41 Cong., 2 sess., 2953, 4309; Curtis to Norton, [Staten Island], May 3, 1870, Curtis Papers, Harvard University.

bill passed, Jenckes was not discouraged nor surprised by the House's reaction to his measure. Confident that millions of people were interested, he spoke of his plans to appeal directly to them if the House again spurned his bill. In conclusion, Jenckes expressed his faith that the spoils system would end and his desire "to live to hear its death-knell sounded." The "death-knell" was far from sounding during that session of Congress; in order to keep his bill alive, Jenckes moved that it be recommitted.[5]

This debate of May, 1870, like other congressional debates on civil service reform, generally ignored European experience. Supporters of reform, while fully cognizant of administrative developments abroad—particularly in England [6]—seldom cited them in support of their program. Reformers possibly reasoned that American isolationism and especially Anglophobia would make a reference to European success with competitive examinations more harmful to the movement than beneficial. Opponents of reform except for an occasional thrust at the "monarchical" origins of civil service reform also shunned Europe's example. They possibly feared a close examination of European administration would aid reformers. Consequently, congressmen tended to overlook the administrative experiments by European "laboratories."

Consideration of the Jenckes bill again provoked favorable comment. Papers already interested in reform, such as the *New York Times* and a good portion of the Philadelphia press, supported Jenckes. Even the *Philadelphia Morning Post,* which only a few months previously had severely berated Philadelphia's collector for not using the customhouse more thoroughly in the last election, endorsed civil service reform. One enthusiastic correspondent declared that a few more similar discussions would bring every "honest & honorable" man in the country into sympathy with Jenckes.[7]

Agitation for the Jenckes bill, while spirited, was not national. Gains in popular support were mostly in the Northeast and were not great enough to affect Congress. An Ohio professor wrote Jenckes that most western papers were "apathetic or opposed" to reform.

[5] *Congressional Globe,* 41 Cong., 2 sess., 3182–84, 3222–25, 3258–61.
[6] See, for example, Rosengarten to Jenckes, Philadelphia, July 6, 1870, Jenckes Papers, Library of Congress
[7] "A Blow at Political Patronage," *New York Times,* May 5, 1870, p. 4, c. 3; *Nation,* IX, No. 231 (December 2, 1869), 473–474; Edwin S. Hart to Jenckes, Philadelphia, May 5, 1870, Rosengarten to Jenckes, Philadelphia, May 6, 1870, and William A. Aiken to Jenckes, no place, May 7, 1870, Jenckes Papers.

Neither the western portion of the Social Science Association nor its great campaign for civil service reform had materialized. Furthermore, when most excise taxes were eliminated along with the machinery for their collection, business ardor for reform cooled. Even in the East, civil service reform agitation had not kept pace with its early activities. Although Curtis repeated his reform lecture on the lyceum circuit from Baltimore to Portland, Maine, and the *Nation,* the *New York Times,* and *Harper's Weekly* continued their agitation, many reformers, such as Henry Adams, were by early 1870 "in the middle of a battle over revenue reform, free trade and what not." Civil service reform during these months frequently fell into the "what not" category.[8]

During the summer of 1870, the administration's "strong" men became weaker. Hoar was the first to go. He was dismissed in June, 1870. Events leading to Hoar's dismissal were complicated. To further his scheme for the annexation of Santo Domingo, Grant rewarded several supporters with local federal patronage. With these offices, men like Roscoe Conkling of New York and Benjamin Butler of Massachusetts built political machines. Hoar, who ignored political claims in selecting personnel, was unpopular with this group to which Grant daily grew more attached. Butler, for one, hated Hoar and personally claimed credit for the Senate's rejecting his nomination to the Supreme Court. Hoar had weakened his position with Grant by opposing the Santo Domingo project, while support of it had ingratiated these men in the President's confidence. When senators informed Grant, at the very time that southern congressmen were demanding a Cabinet seat, that they would no longer visit the Justice Department while Hoar was Attorney General, Grant asked Hoar to resign. Hoar was completely surprised by Grant's letter, and his colleagues first learned of his resignation from the newspapers.[9]

Reformers were disappointed and baffled rather than outraged by Hoar's resignation, since he kept the circumstances secret. "In

---

[8] G. W. Shurtleff to Jenckes, Oberlin, January 28, 1870, *ibid.;* Curtis to Norton, Staten Island, May 3, 1870, Curtis Papers; Adams to Charles Milnes Gaskell, Washington, April 3, 1870, in Worthington Chauncey Ford, ed., *Letters of Henry Adams (1858–1891)* (Boston, 1930), p. 185.

[9] Ellis Paxson Oberholtzer, *A History of the United States Since the Civil War* (New York, 1917–37), II, 310–311. Jacob Dolson Cox, "How Judge Hoar Ceased to Be Attorney-General," *The Atlantic Monthly* (Boston), LXXVI, No. 454 (August, 1895), 162–173.

losing Hoar," Curtis lamented, "we lose by far the ablest man in the administration." Many were incensed by Hoar's replacement, Amos T. Akerman, a Georgia Confederate turned Republican, whose enemies described him as a "third-rate rebel and a fourth-rate lawyer." Added to Curtis' disappointment was his apprehension that the general course of the Republican party would bring it defeat in 1872. "It is unpardonable & it is perilous," he wrote Norton. "Think of the party that in 1864 was laughing at the destruction of the government coming to control it in 1872!" [10]

The Conkling-Fenton struggle in July for control of the New York Customhouse added to Curtis' fears. When Grant became President, he appointed as New York collector Moses H. Grinnell, a prominent businessman who belonged to neither the Reuben Fenton nor the Roscoe Conkling faction. This appointment occurred during Grant's brief period of relative independence. Despite his political activities, Grinnell filled his post to the satisfaction of reformers, but politicians felt that he failed in his duty to the party. Grant, siding with the Conkling forces, demoted Grinnell to naval officer, removed Edwin A. Merritt, the pro-Fenton incumbent of that post, and appointed Thomas Murphy collector. The *Nation* remarked, "in appointing Mr. Murphy, it may be fairly inferred that the President has cast aside all regard to the better aims and tendencies of the party, for Mr. Murphy is a politician of the politicians, has never been anywhere but 'inside politics,' is rich through Government contracts, and has that peculiar reputation which consists in being generally believed capable of participation in any job. . . ." [11]

Fenton was defeated in the senatorial struggle over Murphy's confirmation. The maneuvering in Washington was ludicrous. Lobbyists with "pockets full of affidavits" counteracted each other with wine in parlors and whisky at bars and fought each other with "claims" and "records." There was "button-holing . . . promising, and threatening." Murphy was denounced as a "traitor to the party and a swindling contractor," and bets were placed on both Murphy

---

[10] Curtis to Norton, West New Brighton, New York, June 26, 1870, Curtis Papers; *Nation*, X, No. 260 (June 23, 1870), 395.

[11] "'The Interests of the Party,'" *ibid.*, XI, No. 262 (July 7, 1870), 4. Merritt returned to the customhouse as collector under Hayes. There is some evidence that Murphy was Grant's choice rather than Conkling's and that the latter wisely supported Murphy and thereupon won Grant's gratitude. William J. Hartman, "Politics and Patronage" (Columbia University, 1952), p. 156.

and Fenton. Conkling managed Murphy's fight "with great skill and ferocity," and the *Nation* looked for the second clean sweep of the New York Customhouse in two years. Despite its contempt for Fenton and his followers, the *Nation* questioned whether Conklingites with Murphy at their head would be better.[12] Although Curtis favored Conkling over Fenton, the latter's defeat left him discouraged. "Fenton will," Curtis predicted, "henceforth work to defeat Grant and as the case now stands, New York is lost to the Republicans indefinitely." [13]

The dismissal of John Lothrop Motley, minister to England, followed the Conkling-Fenton confirmation struggle. Motley's appointment had seemed ideal to reformers. He was a scholar in politics, a distinguished historian, and a man of culture completely at home in London society. Furthermore, Motley was in line for a top diplomatic appointment: he had been mistreated by Johnson, had delivered an eloquent campaign address supporting Grant, and had aided Grant's biographer Adam Badeau with his work. Motley, however, was not an ideal diplomat; he was impetuous, passionate, and even hotheaded. At first, he represented his friend Charles Sumner, chairman of the Senate Foreign Relations Committee, as well as the State Department, and he even violated Secretary of State Fish's instructions. Grant wished to fire him immediately but retained him out of consideration for Sumner. After his initial mistakes (which were not publicized), Motley did a creditable job and through lavish entertaining made a favorable impression on English society. His dismissal smacked of revenge coming as it did after Sumner's opposition to Grant's scheme to annex Santo Domingo. The *Nation* moralized that Motley's dismissal had resulted from the current appointing system, which obligated the senator to secure offices for his friends and, in turn, obligated them to suffer for the senator's mistakes. "Motley's recall," wrote Norton, "is a very heavy blow to him, & if there is not some special reason for it not known to the public, the act is very discreditable to Grant, and damaging to our credit." [14]

---

[12] *Nation*, XI, No. 263 (July 14, 1870), 19. "Clean sweep" was a bit of an exaggeration on the part of the *Nation*. Actually, Grinnell merely removed all the Johnson men, while Murphy proceeded to kick out the Fenton adherents.

[13] "Party Orthodoxy," *Harper's Weekly* (New York), XIV, No. 709 (July 30, 1870), 482; Curtis to Norton, Ashfield, Massachusetts, July 24, 1870, Curtis Papers.

[14] Allan Nevins, *Hamilton Fish* (New York, 1937), pp. 156–383 *passim; Nation*, XI, No. 265 (July 28, 1870), 50; Norton to Godkin, Siena, Italy, July 24, 1870,

II

While the reform element was bemoaning the treatment of Motley, George William Curtis was roughly cuffed in another political fray. In September, 1870, the second act of the Conkling-Fenton feud took place at the New York State Republican Convention, where Curtis played a prominent role in Conkling's behalf. But before Curtis could come on stage, significant behind-the-scenes work had to be accomplished. Through threats of dismissal to those already in government employ and promises of office to those who were without it, Conkling and Murphy won over enough Fenton delegates to dominate the convention. These negotiations required time, and, to delay the convention's proceedings, a gang of Conklingites "broke into the hall" and started a "lively fight," which gave negotiators time to complete their task. To give the proceedings an air of morality, the Conkling men elected Curtis temporary chairman. After the defeat of the Fenton nominee by a wide margin, Curtis delivered an impressive address, which he hoped would stampede the convention into nominating him for governor. When William Orton, head of Western Union and one of Conkling's chief allies, approached him about the nomination, Curtis, feigning disinterest, replied, "If it is evidently the wish of the Convention I will not decline. But I don't want the office and I entrust my name to your honorable care." Professional politicians made short work of the Curtis candidacy. He was nominated by an efficient Conkling lieutenant, Charles Spencer, who later voted for another candidate thereby thoroughly confusing the Curtis men. "In one word, my dear boy," Curtis wrote Norton, "I was the undoubted choice of the Convention and I had been disgracefully 'slaughtered' by my friends!" Curtis attempted to convince himself he was "glad" that he would not have to run. "The only real harm the affair can do me," he confided to Norton, "is that my influence will decline with those who think I want office!!" [15]

If the Republican State Convention looked bad, the 1870 New York Democratic Convention at Rochester appeared infinitely worse in reformers' eyes. The Democratic Convention could boast no struggles; it was completely dominated by Boss William Marcy

Godkin Papers, Harvard University; Marjorie Frye Gutheim, "John Lothrop Motley" (Columbia University, 1955), pp. 280–288, 354–374.

[15] *Nation*, XI, No. 272 (September 15, 1870), 163; Curtis to Norton, Ashfield, September 17, 1870, Curtis Papers.

Tweed, who was then at the height of his power. Even so, Tweed distributed 2,000 free railroad tickets to the Tammany "boys" but had the foresight to preserve the peace at Rochester by putting them on a milk train rather than on an express. After twenty-one hours of eating, drinking, fighting, and stealing, the "boys" arrived only one hour before the convention and immediately went through Rochester's saloons and restaurants. Since they were not needed after all, only a select few attended, strategically placing themselves where they could best pick pockets. The *Nation* hoped Samuel Jones Tilden, a wealthy and respected New Yorker who opened the convention for Tweed, got an idea of the company he was keeping when his pocket was picked. Fearful of an evening with the "boys," Rochester officials insisted they leave town before dark. A fitting conclusion to the excursion occurred at Jersey City, where the local police "locked up large batches of them, including a Commissioner of Charities and Correction." When reformers compared the two parties, the Democrats were left invariably in the rear. "The administration," said the *Nation,* " 'retains in office unworthy men'— which is true, but what are the Democracy going to do about it? The Democrat is not alive, so far as we have heard, who favors a Civil Service bill. . . ." [16]

Besides retaining "unworthy men" in office, the administration seemed intent on ridding itself of the worthy ones. David A. Wells, the leader of revenue reform, was not reappointed, and even unofficial observers, such as Henry Adams, left Washington. Despite his dislike of Boston and his fondness for the Capital and its intrigues, Adams became a Harvard professor of medieval history and edited the *North American Review,* which he used as a forum for the reform movement. In October, 1870, he wrote, "On some accounts I am not sorry to have left Washington as things have taken a political turn there which is by no means favorable to me. All my friends have been or are on the point of being driven out of the government and I should have been left without any allies or sources of information. As it is, I only retire with the rest and leave our opponents to upset themselves. . . ." [17]

---

[16] *Nation,* XI, No. 274 (September 29, 1870), 199.

[17] For details of Wells's exit from public life, see Oberholtzer, *op. cit.,* II, 298–300; Adams to Gaskell, Washington, September 29, 1870, and Cambridge, October 25, 1870, in Ford, *op. cit.,* pp. 194, 196; Adams to Cox, Cambridge, October 31, 1870, in Harold Dean Cater, ed., *Henry Adams and His Friends* (Boston, 1947), pp. 45–46.

Jacob Dolson Cox was the next worthy man to "retire," following a concerted effort by spoilsmen to secure his removal. Politicians had many grievances against Cox. He had instituted genuine tests for appointees in the Interior Department, particularly in the Patent Office and in the Census Bureau, had kept spoilsmen out of the Indian Bureau (a prodigious feat), had published a letter attacking political assessments, and had refused clerks a second paid vacation to go home to vote in the fall elections. After Grant forced Cox to revoke his order regarding clerks' absences and spoilsman Senator Zachariah Chandler of Michigan boasted in the Interior Department offices that Cox would be removed, Cox resigned. "I saw symptoms," he later explained, "of lack of backing at headquarters. . . ." [18]

Cox's resignation was perfectly timed to affect fall elections and public opinion. One correspondent wrote Grant that the "men of character," the "reserve strength" of the Republican party, "recognize Gen. Cox's high character and the purity of his administration of affairs. Everywhere they regard his resignation as an ill omen. Don't let the Republican reserves lose confidence." Unlike Hoar, Cox did not remain silent. On congressman James A. Garfield's advice, he published correspondence relating to his resignation before the New York election, and publication had the desired effect. John Gorham Palfrey, historian and former postmaster of Boston, regarded Cox's opposition to the administration as "damaging" and decided not to vote in the coming election. He found it too difficult to choose "between the very vicious principles of the Democrats, & the very vicious practices of the Republicans" and suspected he was in a "crowd" of "good company." [19] Cox's opposition reflected the

---

[18] Cox to James A. Garfield, Washington, October 24, 1870, Garfield Papers, Library of Congress. "Mr. Cox's Resignation," *Nation*, XI, No. 277 (October 20, 1870), 252. Hesseltine disagrees with this account, since Grant's revocation of Cox's order was dated October 20—fifteen days after Cox resigned. William Best Hesseltine, *Ulysses S. Grant* (New York, 1935), pp. 217–218. Whatever date Grant's order bears, it was reported by the *Nation* of October 13, which went to press before Cox resigned. "Things Plain to Be Seen," *Nation*, XI, No. 276 (October 13, 1870), 232. Cox therefore must have been aware of Grant's intention to revoke his order before he resigned. For conflicting views on why Cox resigned, see Hesseltine, *loc. cit.*, and Nevins, *op. cit.*, pp. 465–467. Nevins argues that the fraudulent McGarrahan land claim, backed by Ben Butler, occasioned Cox's resignation. But whatever was the reason, reformers believed that civil service reform was the cause of Cox's resignation.

[19] M. F. Force to Grant, Cincinnati, October 18, 1870, Grant Papers, The Rutherford B. Hayes Library, Fremont, Ohio; Garfield to Cox, October 26, 1870, cited

growing discontent of many Republicans; the election of 1870 resulted in a severe setback for the administration. Thirty congressional seats were lost and with them the two-thirds Republican majority. New York and Indiana, key states in a presidential election, were carried by the Democrats; and in Missouri Liberal Republican insurgents, aided by Democrats, captured the governorship.

Even after the election, the Cox resignation continued to attract attention. A meeting held in New Haven, dominated by Yale professors and the "principal inhabitants of that city," sent a "warm letter of sympathy" to Cox and denounced the "condition of the civil service as the root of much of our political corruption." Harvard College was not outdone by Yale. A Republican "caucus" in Cambridge unanimously adopted resolutions sympathetic to Cox, and a group of young Harvard alumni contemplated forming a civil service reform club.[20]

The resignation of Cox brought out another evil of the spoils system—political assessments. Both parties had long required civil servants to give a percentage of their salaries for conducting local, state, and national campaigns. Despite denials that these payments were involuntary, it was assumed that civil servants were obligated to contribute to the party treasury. Since his letter informing Interior Department clerks that they need not contribute was an important circumstance leading to Cox's resignation, reformers saw this evil, which previously had escaped their notice.

The *Nation,* making up for past neglect, vigorously attacked political assessments. Besides discussing the topic in relation to Cox, it published the year-old correspondence between a former United States marshal, Francis Barlow (brother-in-law of Curtis' wife), and the New York Republican State Committee. The committee had assessed Barlow and his subordinates $1,000, although his salary could not honestly exceed $6,000. Since the assessment rate for 1869 was 2 per cent, Barlow sent the committee $120 but refused to collect anything from his subordinates. Barlow's check was returned,

by Theodore Clark Smith, *The Life and Letters of James Abram Garfield* (New Haven, 1925), I, 462; John G. Palfrey to Norton, Cambridge, November 7, 1870, Norton Papers, Harvard University

[20] *Nation*, XI, No. 280 (November 10, 1870), 307; Adams to Cox, Cambridge, November 11, 1870, in Cater, *op. cit.,* p. 47; W. L. Richardson to Jenckes, Boston, November 29, 1870, Jenckes Papers.

and he was informed that assessments were not based on salary "but upon the ascertained income" of the office. The *Nation* concluded that Barlow was assessed not by his salary "but by the supposed amount of his stealings." [21]

III

The election of 1870, with its publicity of compulsory assessments, however, was not entirely a triumph for reform. In the spring of that year—while pleading passionately for civil service reform—Jenckes himself was frantically campaigning to retain his seat in Congress. Added to his usual troubles with Senator William Sprague of Rhode Island was a squabble with Senator Henry B. Anthony of the same state. Jenckes was warned by a friend, Ezra D. Fogg, that "busy bodies" were using his proposed senatorial candidacy to upset Anthony. Anthony questioned the circumstances under which Jenckes had acquired some stock, and the editor of the *Providence Press* joined the fray to "abuse" Jenckes.[22]

Patronage apparently was the basis for both the *Press*'s hostility and Jenckes's difficulty. The *Press*'s "abuse," Providence gossip had it, was based on the supposition that Jenckes would endorse Joseph J. Manton for the collectorship of that port. Fogg reported "that such a nomination is a flagrant departure from all the spirit of your 'Civil Service' bill, because 'tis a 'nomination not fit to be made.'" Besides Manton there were two other candidates for the Providence collectorship. Jenckes was responsible for the appointment owing to a recent change in the rules governing patronage distribution in Rhode Island. No matter whom Jenckes chose, a majority would be disappointed. The abundance of advice, all conflicting, and the mounting opposition at home no doubt prompted Jenckes to write his office-seeking friend George Manchester. "Your note is received," answered Manchester, "in which you desire me to indicate confidentially what changes should be made and how you can be of service to me." Manchester's advice that did not deal with himself occupied precious little of the page. He did suggest conciliating Gov-

---

[21] "The 'Explanation' in Reply to Mr. Cox," *Nation*, XI, No. 281 (November 17, 1870), 324–325; "How the Thing Is Done," *ibid.*, 329–330; "The System," *ibid.*, 325.

[22] Ezra D. Fogg to Jenckes, Providence, February 24, 1870, Charles Adams to Jenckes, Providence, February 21, 1870, and A. Payne to Anthony, Providence, February 25, 1870, Jenckes Papers.

ernor Stevens, who was united with Senator Sprague in opposition
to Jenckes, by giving a position to his son.[23] Whatever Jenckes's
pretensions or beliefs, if he were to remain in Congress he had to
dispense patronage wisely.

Post offices had to be taken care of. "Stand by your Friends," Fogg
admonished Jenckes. "Give Mr. Lawton the Post Office at Valley
Falls.—Secure that 'Peg' on your side for next Fall." As usual, the
Valley Falls appointment—and Lawton did not receive it—served
but to anger different factions. To appease the Chace faction of
Rhode Island Republicans, Jenckes cleverly moved the site of the
Manville Post Office and appointed Jonathan Chace postmaster in
place of the incumbent, who technically was not removed but was
superseded by site.[24]

These last-minute attempts to create a Jenckes machine were not
successful. The Sprague forces prevented Jenckes's nomination, but
the deadlocked Republican district convention failed to nominate
anyone. During the acrimonious campaign in which five candidates
ran for Congress, Jenckes attacked Sprague for disgracing Rhode
Island with his one-man rule based on bribery and fraud and, with
"ample proof," accused him of trading money and munitions to the
Confederacy for cotton. Sprague's man was elected, but the *Providence Journal* claimed that great corruption attended the election
and that hundreds of votes were purchased at $5.00 a head.[25] When
Jenckes attempted to have the election investigated, one of his supporters informed him "many persons object to saying definitely that
there was bribery at the election, who would have been willing to
say they *thought* as much, but the names we have are all good and
perhaps there are enough of them to answer the purpose." The
supposition was wrong. The purpose was not answered; the election was not investigated.[26] Jenckes's defeat was final.

[23] Fogg to Jenckes, Providence, February 24, 1870, J. H. Coggeshall to Jenckes,
Providence, June 30, 1870, and Manchester to Jenckes, South Portsmouth, April
25, 1870, *ibid.*

[24] Fogg to Jenckes, Providence, April 19, 1870, Charles Adams to Jenckes, Providence, May 23, 1870, and J. W. Marshall, First Assistant Postmaster General, to
Jenckes, Washington, June 21, 1870, *ibid.*

[25] "Extraordinary Charge Against a Senator," *Harper's Weekly*, XIV, No. 726
(November 26, 1870), 755. Jenckes was correct. Sprague's wartime adventures in
cotton trading are fully discused in Thomas Graham Belden and Marva Robins
Belden, *So Fell the Angels* (Boston, 1956), pp. 251–258.

[26] William W. Douglas to Jenckes, Providence, December 10, 1870, and Ulysses
Mecur to Jenckes, Towanda, Pennsylvania, December 26, 1870, Jenckes Papers.

Insurgent reformers, nevertheless, posed a serious threat to the Grant administration in the fall of 1870. Failing to capture the Republican party, reformers contemplated forming a new party. In October, the *Nation* demanded a party that would insist on civil service reform, revenue reform, and minority representation of the "thoughtful, conscientious, and intelligent" part of the population, "which is now excluded from all direct share in the government." [27] Henry Adams late the same month asked Schurz to write an article for the *North American Review* emphasizing free trade and reform in the Liberal Republican revolt in Missouri. This revolt had started during the Missouri Republican Convention, when a large number of Liberal Republicans under the leadership of Schurz bolted the convention to protest the Radicals' disfranchisement of voters with Confederate leanings. The bolters nominated Benjamin Gratz Brown for governor, and Schurz publicly accused the Radicals of favoring disabilities in order to "monopolize the local offices." Although federal civil servants who supported Schurz were summarily dealt with, the election brought success on the state level for the Liberal Republican movement.[28]

In congratulating Schurz on the victory, officers of the American Free Trade League predicted that the time was "near at hand when a new political movement in favor of Revenue and Civil Service Reform may be started with success." They also proposed a conference to decide whether an attempt should "be made to control the organization of the new H° of Representatives by a union of Western Revenue Reform Republicans with Democrats." The Free Trade League was not alone in suggesting an alliance between reform elements and Democrats. From San Francisco a correspondent wrote Senator Lyman Trumbull of Illinois that there was a "strong current . . . in favor of Trumbull and Hancock for our next President and Vice President, on a conservative national platform em-

---

[27] "Things Plain to Be Seen," *Nation*, XI, No. 276 (October 13, 1870), 232. In addition, the author advocated that Cabinet officers be allowed on the floor of the House. He evidently had just read Gamaliel Bradford's article on "Congressional Reform," which advocated that Cabinet members be allowed to speak in Congress. *North American Review* (Boston), CXI, No. 229 (October, 1870), 330–351.

[28] Adams to Schurz, Cambridge, October 27, 1870, in Ford, *op. cit.*, p. 197; Frederic Bancroft, ed., *Speeches, Correspondence and Political Papers of Carl Schurz* (New York, 1913), I, 513. For an elaborate discussion of Liberal Republicanism in Missouri, see Thomas S. Barclay, *The Liberal Republican Movement in Missouri: 1865–1871* (Columbia, 1926), *passim*. For information on the Republican state convention in 1870, see *ibid.*, pp. 233–249.

bracing Civil Service Reform, a Revenue Tariff and the subordination of the military to the civil power." [29]

When invitations were issued for a New York conference sponsored by the Free Trade League, Schurz—still trying frantically but unsuccessfully to convince Grant that he was not hostile to him nor his party—declined, as did both Cox and Gratz Brown. The independent press, however, was well represented. Henry Adams of the *North American Review,* Charles Nordhoff and William Cullen Bryant of the New York *Evening Post,* Samuel Bowles of the *Springfield Republican,* Horace White of the *Chicago Tribune,* William Grosvenor of the *St. Louis Democrat,* and Godkin were all in attendance.[30]

The proposed new party did not materialize. James G. Blaine, the Republican Speaker of the House, told reformers privately "that public opinion and the composition of the House demanded a recognition" of their claims and promised them the important Ways and Means Committee and any other positions they might desire.[31] Blaine's offer went far beyond reformers' expectations and caused a debate, which split the conference. The officers of the Free Trade League favored a break with the Republican party, but the editors wished to await the actions of Congress, holding the new party as a "threat." The editors' opinion prevailed. Blaine's clever maneuver staved off an open revolt when feeling against the administration was particularly high.

The reformers' conference next debated the widening of its revenue reform platform. This debate, as reported by Henry Adams, revealed an increasing interest in civil service reform. Western delegates considered reforming the civil service a stronger issue than revenue reform, since in the West revenue reform—which mostly meant tight, hard money—was economically disadvantageous and politically unpopular. Civil service reform, they insisted, was more

---

[29] Mahlon Sands to Schurz, New York, November 10, 1870, Schurz Papers, Library of Congress; O. P. Fitzgerald to Trumbull, San Francisco, January 4, 1871, Trumbull Papers, Library of Congress. Hancock was General Winfield Scott Hancock, a Democrat who ran for the presidency in 1880.

[30] Hesseltine, *op. cit.,* p. 221. Schurz, however, did write Henry Adams an "excellent letter." For this and other details of the conference, see Adams to Cox, Cambridge, November 28, 1870, in Cater, *op. cit.,* pp. 49–51.

[31] James A. Garfield was to be chairman of the Ways and Means Committee Garfield to Cox, Washington, December 17–23, 1870, Cox Papers, Oberlin College, Oberlin, Ohio.

easily understood and less easily answered. Despite resistance from the Free Trade League, the conference endorsed both reforms.[32]

Not all Republican reform leaders threatened to forsake their party. George William Curtis maintained that "the Republican who asks whether a new party is not desirable, merely asks whether it is desirable that the Democratic party should be successful." John Murray Forbes, an old China merchant who became a railroad builder, emphatically agreed with Curtis. "Of course Grant makes mistakes . . . but our only chance is to stick by him, & make the best of him. To badger him & quarrel with him is only to play into the hands of the Rebs, & this is the worst of the Revenue Reform movement which all tend to strengthen the enemy." [33]

But none could doubt that the administration was losing supporters. Added to dissatisfaction over Grant's appointments and dismissals was the effect of election losses, the Missouri defection, Cox's resignation, and the outcry against assessments. The administration was further harassed by the plotting of party treason by some reformers and the publication of articles in the *Chicago Tribune* hinting at an alliance with the Democratic party.[34]

General unrest and dissatisfaction necessitated a change of tactics. "Always favoring practical reforms," Grant, in his December, 1870, annual message to Congress, called for a reform of the civil service that would "govern, not the tenure, but the manner of making all appointments." The distribution of patronage was not only embarrassing for the Executive but was also an "arduous and thankless labor imposed" on congressmen. In addition to these drawbacks, Grant complained, "The present system does not secure the best men, and often not even fit men, for public place." Reformers were elated by Grant's support of their cause. "It is . . . something to have got to the mark on Civil Service," commented Henry Adams to Cox, "and for this you are responsible. But I still see a long fight before us. . . ." [35]

---

[32] The Free Trade League was not actually opposed to civil service reform; it merely did not want its particular reform to be lost in the clamor for civil service reform. The question was one of emphasis.

[33] "The Parties," *Harper's Weekly*, XIV, No. 728 (December 10, 1870), 786; Forbes to Norton, Boston, December 16, 1870, Norton Papers.

[34] "The Political Situation," *Nation*, XI, No. 282 (November 24, 1870), 344–345.

[35] James D. Richardson, *A Compilation of the Messages and Papers of the Presidents 1789–1897* (Washington, 1896–99), VII, 109; Adams to Cox, Cambridge, December 8, 1870, in Cater, *op. cit.*, p. 52.

The lameduck session of the Forty-first Congress responded with four reform bills. Jenckes for the last time introduced his bill, which was again modified and again approved by Grant. Riding the crest of reform sentiment, Jenckes had enlarged the scope of his bill to match that of Schurz's—all officers of the government except judges and clerks of the United States courts, Cabinet members, and ministers abroad were to be selected by competitive examinations. In addition, the bill required the examination of all incumbents. Those adjudged incompetent were to be dismissed. But this session ignored the Jenckes bill.[36]

Congress, however, thoroughly debated the Trumbull bill, which made it a penal offense for congressmen to solicit, recommend, or advise the executive department on appointments. Senator Trumbull wished the President to be allowed to receive written recommendations from congressmen, but the committee—intent on cutting the thing out by the roots—emphatically disagreed. The wording prohibited all congressional recommendations. Trumbull gained an important convert to his bill—John Sherman of Ohio—who regarded it as an entering wedge of civil service reform but would not vote for the measure unless it were amended along the lines of Trumbull's original intention. Trumbull's measure was strongly opposed by Oliver P. Morton of Indiana, whom Grant had lavishly rewarded with spoils for his support of the Santo Domingo scheme. Morton protested that although he would be "glad to be relieved of this labor," he had no right to shirk his duties. The bill, he argued, was unconstitutional, based on false principles, and degrading to congressmen who would be the only ones declared unfit to recommend officers.[37]

Despite Grant's message advocating reform, Congress enacted neither the Jenckes nor the Trumbull bill and failed as well to enact bills introduced by Schurz and Henry Wilson.[38] It was ap-

---

[36] *Congressional Globe,* 41 Cong., 3 sess., 378; "The Beginning of Civil Service Reform," *Harper's Weekly,* XV, No. 743 (March 25, 1871), 258; *Nation,* XII, No. 290 (January 19, 1871), 34. The *Nation* joyfully anticipated the wholesale removals that would occur if the bill passed.

[37] *Congressional Globe,* 41 Cong., 3 sess., 292–294.

[38] Senator Wilson, a Massachusetts Republican, had introduced a civil service bill on January 19. In place of the civil service commission, it substituted boards of three examiners selected by the head of each department. All appointments were to be made for four years, including a probationary period, and were to be approved by the board. The *New York Times* declared that Wilson's bill was in many respects superior to the Jenckes bill (except for the four–year term). Its machinery

parent that unity was needed before results could be achieved. After consultation, congressional reform leaders agreed on a simple joint resolution empowering the President to appoint a commission which would prescribe rules for examining applicants. The draft, written by Representative William H. Armstrong of Pennsylvania, was approved by Grant. In the closing moments of the lameduck session, Trumbull moved the resolution as a "rider" to the civil appropriation bill. After a motion to table and effectively kill the rider was lost by one vote (26 to 25), the Senate approved it by a vote of 32 to 24.[39]

In the House, Henry L. Dawes of Massachusetts, in charge of the appropriation bill, recommended concurrence with all the Senate amendments, since the whole bill would be lost if a conference committee were required. Garfield and Armstrong spoke strongly for the rider, but John A. "Black Jack" Logan opposed it with fury. The civil service rider, he said, was "the most obnoxious bill" of that type to come before the House. Insuring the rider's passage by attaching it at the last minute to a necessary appropriation bill particularly galled Logan. "I will not call it a trick," he said, "but it has been put upon this bill at this time, although the House has uniformly voted down every bill of the kind that has come before it." Despite Logan's fulminations, the Senate amendments passed by a 90 to 20 vote, and trick or no trick, Congress declared itself in favor of civil service reform.[40] The reform press did not, as was its habit, moralize on the political condition of the day from the manner in which this legislation was pushed through. The shoe was on the other foot.

---

was simpler, and it guarded against two abuses that Jenckes's measure failed to touch—it forbade political activity by officeholders, and it prohibited the levying of political assessments on government employees. "Civil Service Reform," *New York Times*, January 23, 1871, p. 4, cc. 4–5.

[39] *Congressional Globe*, 41 Cong., 3 sess., 1935, 1997. Jenckes frequently has been credited with the authorship.

[40] *Ibid.*, pp. 1935–36; "The Beginning of Civil Service Reform," *Harper's Weekly*, XV, No. 743 (March 25, 1871), 258

VI

THE FIRST CIVIL SERVICE COMMISSION

By taking a new reform tack, Grant divided reformers. They had opposed his former course with varying degrees of intensity, but now the less intense supported Grant in his reform efforts, while the more extreme continued to oppose him. The fruits of their limited victory proved more harmful to the cause of civil service reformers than had their earlier defeats.

I

Reformers gave the limited victory a divided reception. George William Curtis, who usually magnified every half-baked crumb from the administration table into the oven-browned loaf of reform, rated the rider as "insignificant" until a letter from Jenckes informed him of its possibilities. Curtis then responded with a glowing editorial in *Harper's Weekly* praising everyone from Jenckes and those connected with the passage of the rider to Ulysses S. Grant and the Republican party. Though sometimes critical of the party, Curtis was typical of reformers who remained stanchly loyal to it. Even before he decided that the rider was a significant advance toward civil service reform, for which Grant should be given partial credit, Curtis privately advocated the President's renomination. Perhaps Curtis' continued support of Grant was not based entirely on abstract principle and party loyalty; in a recent letter, Curtis had mentioned—almost casually—that Grant planned to nominate him minister to England.[1]

[1] Curtis to Thomas A. Jenckes, New York, March 8, 1871, Jenckes Papers, Library of Congress; "The Beginning of Civil Service Reform," *Harper's Weekly* (New

Unlike Curtis, Godkin and Schurz worked to prevent Grant's renomination. Shelving Grant, Schurz reasoned, would remove the cohesive force that held the spoilsmen together and would allow leadership to return to the "liberal and vigorous element of the Republican party," who alone could "save its future usefulness." Schurz was encouraged in early 1871, when Jacob D. Cox organized the Central Republican Association of Hamilton County, Ohio. This association stood for civil service reform, tariff reduction, resumption of specie payments, and general amnesty for the South, but was not a third party. Schurz wrote Cox that he was "delighted" with the association and was certain that a majority of the Republican party agreed with its platform, which was essentially the same as that of the Missouri Liberal Republicans. "If we only succeed," Schurz continued, "in rallying those who think alike, the Republican organization will in truth be the *new party* of the future. Similar associations ought to be organized all over the country. . . ." Schurz urged the independent press to encourage these organizations, which, "when the preliminary movements of the next Presidential election come on . . . may be strong enough to represent a formidable balance of power." Reflecting the general optimism in the Liberal Republican camp, Schurz declared, "Unless I greatly mistake the signs of the times, the superstition that Grant is *the* necessary man, is rapidly giving way. The spell is broken, and we have only to push through the breach." [2]

Both the stop-Grant and the civil service reform movements received unwilling assistance from the New York Customhouse. Following an investigation, a congressional committee published an extremely hostile report on the customhouse's general-order business. While aiding the cause of reformers, the investigation sprang from the determination of Senator Reuben Fenton to strike back at Roscoe Conkling, who had gained control of the New York Customhouse. Fenton complained that his friends had been removed from the customhouse, but, when challenged by Conkling, refused

---

York), XV, No. 743 (March 25, 1871), 258; Curtis to Charles Eliot Norton, New York, March 4, 1871, Curtis Papers, Harvard University; *Nation* (New York), XII, No. 297 (March 9, 1871), 149, 156.

[2] *Ibid.*, No. 300 (March 30, 1871), 210; Schurz to E. L. Godkin, Washington, March 31, 1871, and Schurz to Cox, Washington, April 4, 1871, in Frederic Bancroft, ed., *Speeches, Correspondence and Political Papers of Carl Schurz* (New York, 1913), II, 253–255; H. W. Thomson to Schurz, Cincinnati, March 27, 1871, Schurz Papers, Library of Congress.

to name one. Conkling, who brazenly claimed to be a "disinterested and unbiased witness" of New York Customhouse affairs, insisted he had asked for no appointments or removals since Murphy took office (Murphy apparenty needed no advice), and denied that anyone had been dismissed because of friendship for Fenton. But Fenton thought otherwise. Out of power and cut off from spoils, he turned to reform. He instigated the special customhouse investigation which produced the scathing report, and also introduced a customhouse reform bill. Fenton's bill suggested a four-year term for all presidential appointees with removal only for cause determined by a fair trial. The administration ignored his proposal.[3]

Less than a month after the passage of the rider, Grant fired the respected Naval Officer Moses Grinnell and the competent Appraiser George W. Palmer. Both Grinnell and Palmer, while testifying before the recent investigation committee, had called for business principles in the customhouse. Palmer had further testified that removal of employees for their political beliefs injured the service. Their testimony contrasted with that of Collector Murphy, who—when asked how to remedy frauds—belittled such reorganization proposals with a sanctimonious allusion to the imperfectibility of man. Grinnell's removal especially came as a surprise, since he had "spent more money for Grant his friends & the party" than he had received in fees and perquisites at the customhouse. The *Nation* called these removals a shocking example of the administration's attitude toward reform and suggested that their suddenness was to keep officeholders "in a state of healthy apprehension and uneasiness, which makes them frisky, active, and wide-awake, like the application of pepper or turpentine which dealers make to tender parts of their horses before showing their paces." [4]

Criticism was soon allayed. In June, three months after the rider passed, Grant appointed the Civil Service Commission with George William Curtis as chairman. Other members were Joseph Medill, publisher of the *Chicago Tribune;* Alexander G. Cattell, a New Jersey banker who was secretly plundering the Navy Department;

[3] *Congressional Globe,* 41 Cong., 3 sess., 690, 724. The *Nation,* XII, No. 298 (March 16, 1871), 170, expressed "amazement" at this proposal from "such a quarter," and naively labeled it an example of the "rapid progress the cause of civil-service reform is making."

[4] *Ibid.,* No. 297 (March 9, 1871), 149; *ibid.,* No. 301 (April 6, 1871), 229; Francis C. Nye to Jenckes, New York, April 4, 1871, Jenckes Papers.

Dawson A. Walker, a Georgia judge; and E. B. Elliott, David C. Cox, and Joseph H. Blackfan of the Treasury, the Interior, and the Post Office Departments respectively. The very pleased *New York Times* said of the commission, "It affords a practical proof that the President is actively enlisted for a reform, and that he has the sense and courage to call to his aid men who are in earnest beyond suspicion. President Grant's Administration has settled the *Alabama* claims honorably; it has put the national credit where Pendletonian assaults will hardly touch it; if now it can compass Civil Service reform, its record will be more lastingly creditable than that of any since the days of Washington and Hamilton." [5]

The commission began work immediately. As soon as Curtis' appointment was announced, he asked Jenckes and Schurz for practical details of the systems they advocated. "What we want now," Curtis wrote Jenckes, "is a simple practicable method which will be likely to be adopted and the lessons of your experience and thought upon the subject would be very valuable." Three weeks later, Curtis sought Jenckes's help in dealing with two specific problems. The first problem was to distinguish between offices essentially political and those essentially nonpolitical. Curtis obviously intended a very broad coverage by the new system, since he wondered whether collectors of ports (presidential appointees confirmed by the Senate) should be included. Second, Curtis questioned whether regulation of tenure was necessary if appointments were determined by open-competitive examinations. Curtis reasoned that regulating appointments would eliminate the incentive to make removals and would reconcile administrative responsibility (requiring removal of incompetents without the inconvenience of a trial) with tenure during good behavior. Braving the summer heat, the Civil Service Commission met in Washington on June 28, 1871, as Curtis dramatically put it, to "wrestle with the Dragon that consumes our national

---

[5] "Civil Service Reform," *New York Times*, June 6, 1871, p. 4, cc. 5–6. The Treaty of Washington with Britain had just been ratified by the Senate, and the administration opposed George H. Pendleton's scheme of redeeming Civil War bonds with inflated greenbacks. The *Times* was once more an administration paper, having supplanted Greeley's pro-Fenton *Tribune*. Even the *Nation*, despite its desire to run down Grant, admitted a month later that the administration by overhauling its financial management and the civil service could "make itself indispensable." *Nation*, XIII, No. 314 (July 6, 1871), 1. On Cattell's corrupt activities, see Ellis Paxson Oberholtzer, *A History of the United States Since the Civil War* (New York, 1917–37), III, 180–182.

Health & honor." The commission determined that its function was advisory and that action should rest with the President.[6] Grant could do one of three things—reject the commission's future recommendations outright, pass them on to Congress, or enforce them on his own responsibility.

Although Curtis was deeply attached to the idea of reform through open-competitive examinations (an "axe at the root of patronage"), other commissioners were not. Cattell, who wished to preserve patronage, would only favor competitive examinations closed to Democrats. No matter what the commission attempted, he feared it would hurt the party. Since he was a personal friend of Grant's, Cattell reinforced his own viewpoint by stating that the President "was not a thorough believer in competitive examination" and firmly opposed any reduction in his power of removal. Curtis continued to struggle for open-competitive examinations, which had "revolutionized" the English civil service, but prepared himself for a setback. "I have reason to doubt," he wrote Jenckes, "whether the President quite meant what he said in regard to the abolition of patronage: and I think there is at present a feeling in the Commission favorable to competitive examination after nomination by the appointing power. This is a small step forward because it makes success through personal favor at least harder than it is now." [7]

Medill's criticism of competitive examinations proved even more formidable than Cattell's. He declared that the competitive system was unconstitutional since it annulled executive appointing power. Curtis suggested that the law creating the commission had already virtually negated department heads' right of selection by vesting inferior officers' appointments with the President. The commissioners asked for Attorney General Amos T. Akerman's opinion whether it was constitutional for them to designate persons eligible for ap-

---

[6] Curtis to Jenckes, West New Brighton, New York, June 5, 1871, and New York, June 24, 1871, Jenckes Papers; Curtis to Schurz, no place, June 5, 1871, Schurz Papers; Curtis to Parke Godwin, Washington, July 7, 1871, Bryant-Godwin Collection, New York Public Library; "Minutes of the Civil Service Commission," June 28, 1871, I, 6, Library of the United States Civil Service Commission, hereafter cited as "Minutes." For a detailed discussion of the Grant commission based on these "Minutes," see Lionel V. Murphy, "The First Federal Civil Service Commission: 1871-75 . . . ," *Public Personnel Review* (Chicago), III, Nos. 1, 3, 4 (January, July, October, 1942), 29–39, 218–231, 299–323.

[7] Curtis to Jenckes, New York, June 24, 1871, Washington, July 2, 1871, and Ashfield, Massachusetts, August 6, 1871, Jenckes Papers; "Minutes," June 29 and 30, 1871, I, 7–11.

pointment and whether the law creating the commission allowed the President to limit appointments made by department heads to persons passing an independently administered competitive examination. Pending the Attorney General's opinion, the commissioners adjourned. The fact that they voted themselves each $500 caused some derisive glee among the opposition, who could claim that hypocritical reformers began reforming the civil service "by lining their own pockets" at the rate of $50 a day.[8]

The prospects of Attorney General Akerman giving a favorable decision were not good. Curtis "found him inclined to sustain" the objection to the competitive system. "Of course," a somewhat discouraged Curtis wrote Schurz, "the competitive examination designates one person and not a class of persons and if it be unconstitutional nothing remains but a pass examination which can be controlled by patronage. My wish is to put the Civil Service beyond the poison of patronage." In a similar vein, Curtis complained to Jenckes, "if we can only have a pass examination we cannot really reach the evil. The pressure for the selection from the eligible class will be as furious as it is now, and the system will give away." [9]

Akerman, however, did not contemplate a system of farcical pass examinations. He had "a loose notion, not crystallized into an opinion" that the appointing power's field of selection could be limited to a class which passed a competitive examination. Akerman asked Jenckes's opinion of this idea, which essentially was a compromise. Jenckes, annoyed at the obstacle to his plan, stressed the constitutionality of the competitive system. The substance of the difficulty was whether Congress could "push its qualifying authority . . . to the point of paralyzing the appointing authority." Jenckes thought Congress could, and in one of the last of his prodigious accomplishments for civil service reform he dug up citations stretching back eighty years to prove that competitive examinations were constitutional. "Either the Constitution does not mean what its language apparently imports," Akerman replied to Jenckes, "or there has been a wide departure from it in practice. Your citations prove this." Having received Jenckes's opinion, Akerman proceeded "at

---

[8] *Ibid.*, July 1 and 10, 1871, pp. 13–15, 21; *Nation*, XIII, No. 316 (July 20, 1871), 33. Despite his criticisms, Curtis relied more on Medill than on any other member of the commission. Curtis to Jenckes, Ashfield, August 6, 1871, Jenckes Papers.

[9] Curtis to Schurz, Ashfield, July 20, 1871, Schurz Papers; Curtis to Jenckes, Ashfield, July 18, 1871, Jenckes Papers.

once to examine the subject and form conclusions." He delivered his opinion on August 31, which showed that his "loose notion" had "crystallized" despite the weight of Jenckes's citations. The appointing power, he decided, could not be restricted to one candidate but could be limited to a class selected competitively. Curtis, despite his former opposition, now bowed to the inevitable. "This brings it just where I told the President it lay, upon his shoulders," he commented almost cheerfully. "If he will make the reform it can be made. If not, not." [10]

The commissioners reassembled in October, 1871, to outline a reform system. "The difficulty," Curtis said, "is to arrange it without expense so as not to depend on Congress which is radically hostile." Despite the attitude of Congress, Curtis was encouraged; "every state Convention of both parties" had "demanded the reform," and New Jersey specified "that removals shall not be without cause." The Washington correspondent of the *New York Times* reported the commissioners' belief that after four years under Grant reform would be so deeply entrenched in the public mind that no subsequent administration would dare dispense with it.[11]

Not content to formulate their rules in an intellectual vacuum, the commissioners continued to solicit information and recommendations. Jenckes was consulted, but no longer in Congress and in poor health, he was only able to contribute to reform occasionally between the fall of 1871 and his death in 1875. Besides utilizing Jenckes, the commission frequently consulted editorials, letters, and civil service materials from other nations. As one would expect, its prime example and source of information was Great Britain. After a decade of using limited competitive examinations, the British had adopted open-competitive examinations in 1870. The secretary of the British Civil Service Commission, Benjamin Jowett, sent "the latest orders and directions of the commission . . . showing the working of the British System." [12] The example of Britain rein-

[10] Akerman to Jenckes, Washington, July 18 and August 5, 1871, *ibid.* Jenckes's letter to Akerman is discussed in Curtis to Jenckes, Ashfield, August 6, 1871, *ibid.*; Murphy, *op. cit.*, p. 38, n. 49; Curtis to Norton, Ashfield, September 10, 1871, Curtis Papers.

[11] *Ibid.* Many of these demands were ambiguously worded, leaving ample loopholes for politicians. "Civil-Service Reform in the Party Platforms," *Nation*, XIII, No. 327 (October 5, 1871), 220–221. For the *Times's* quote, see *ibid.*, No. 330 (October 26, 1871), 265.

[12] "Minutes," October 17, November 11, 14, and 23, 1871, I, 24, 43, 46, 57–58. "It is a matter of general information, that under President Grant a trial, begin-

forced Curtis' determination to establish as much competition as Akerman's decision allowed.

The commission forged ahead. Curtis succeeded in getting the competitive principle for promotions adopted, and this rule later was modified to require competitive examinations at the lowest grade of entry. On November 1, Curtis reported that Grant "approved generally of the rules" and ten days later that they were "favorably received" by the Cabinet. Unknown to Curtis, Grant and his Cabinet actually thought the rules "impracticable," but Grant nevertheless promised in his annual message to give them a "fair trial." With this assurance, the commission formally submitted its recommendations on December 18, 1871.[13]

The commission achieved results. Grant promulgated the rules as of January 1, 1872, and requested an appropriation. "A great triumph of a great reform," said the *Nation,* although it doubted Grant's good intentions. The rules provided that all appointees were to be United States citizens of adequate character, age, and health and able to speak, read, and write English. The commission, not wishing to ask a hostile Congress for new machinery, remained at the head of the system.[14] Part of its task was grouping departmental positions into uniform grades for purposes of examination and promotion. Since entrance into the service was in most cases allowed only at the lowest grade, and since those already holding office would not be tested, the administration was insured a predominantly Republican civil service for several years. Vacancies in the lowest grade were to be filled from a group of three individuals who achieved the highest grades on a "public competitive examination." Requirements of the appointing power were thus met (as they still are today) in letter if not in spirit. Vacancies occurring above the lowest grade were to be filled by competitively examining those already employed. If, however, no one within the service

---

ning January 1st, 1872, was made of the *merit system* in a limited way; the regulations, competitions and examinations being closely analogous to those so long in practice in Great Britain." Dorman B. Eaton, *Civil Service in Great Britain* (New York, 1880), p. 445.

[13] "Minutes," October 27, November 1 and 11, 1871, I, 33–34, 38, 43; Allan Nevins, *Hamilton Fish* (New York, 1937), p. 601; *Nation,* XIII, No. 336 (December 7, 1871), 361. The report and rules are reprinted in Charles Eliot Norton, ed., *Orations and Addresses of George William Curtis* (New York, 1894), II, 29–80, 81–85. Murphy, *op. cit.,* pp. 221–224, elaborately analyzes the rules.

[14] *Nation,* XIII, No. 338 (December 21, 1871), 393; Curtis to Jenckes, Washington, October 27, 1871, Jenckes Papers.

could competently fill a vacant position, a public competitive examination was to be held. A probationary period of six months was provided for all appointees whose superiors were in a position to judge their abilities.[15] In each department, there was to be a board of three examiners appointed by the President and supervised by the commissioners. The rules also prohibited an old abuse—the levying or paying of political assessments "under the form of voluntary contributions or otherwise." Even postmasters with an annual salary of less than $200 were included under this rule.

The new regulations applied to almost everyone in the civil service. Officers responsible for handling large sums of government money, however, were to be approved by superiors responsible for the funds, and a handful of the very highest officers were completely exempt from the rules.[16] This inclusion of nearly the whole civil service under a set of complicated regulations within two weeks of its publication proved impossible, since the civil service outside of Washington had never been systematically organized. Ten days after the new system supposedly went into effect it was temporarily suspended by a new rule approved by the board.[17]

II

While the commission struggled over reform procedure, the vocal debate over corruption grew louder and Republicans rapidly polarized into pro- and anti-Grant factions. In New York City, the Democratic and spectacularly corrupt Tweed ring was finally exposed and overthrown by the combined efforts of the *New York Times* and *Harper's Weekly*—both strong supporters of the Grant administration. The Tweed ring gave the "best citizens" an ex-

---

[15] Presidential appointees, persons appointed to positions abroad, and postmasters were exempt from the probationary period.

[16] Officers excluded were "the heads of departments, assistant secretaries of departments, assistant attorneys-general and first assistant postmaster-general, solicitor-general, solicitor of the Treasury, naval solicitor, solicitor of internal revenue, examiner of claims in the State Department, treasurer of the United States, register of the Treasury, first and second comptrollers of the Treasury, judges of the United States courts, district attorneys, private secretary of the President, ambassadors and other public ministers, superintendent of the coast survey, director of the Mint, governors of territories, special commissioners, special counsel, visiting and examining boards, persons appointed to positions without compensation for services, despatch agents, and bearers of despatches." Norton, *op. cit.*, II, 84–85. On April 16, 1872, all assistant postmasters-general were excluded from the application of the rules. *Ibid.*, II, 115.

[17] "Minutes," January 10, 1872, I, 98.

ample of the potential for corruption that existed in unreformed politics and of their own strength when aroused to action. To prevent a recurrence of ring rule in New York, the *Nation* recommended taking municipal affairs out of politics and urged that respectable Republicans stop regarding all Democrats as thieves and work with the better element of that party. One of these "better" Democrats, Deputy Controller Andrew H. Green, set about to undo some of the havoc wrought by Tweed's controller, "Slippery Dick" Connolly. Green told his municipal clerks that their sole duty was office duty and that incompetency would be the sole cause for removal. He also admonished them neither to take part in politics nor to pay political assessments.[18]

On the state level, the Conkling-Fenton feud continued to spread dissension in New York Republican ranks. On Fenton's side were the anti-Grant elements headed by Horace Greeley and a large number of Tammany Republicans. These Republicans were especially repellent to reformers, since, in exchange for patronage, they offered Tammany Hall only token resistance and prevented any real Republican opposition. Led by Conkling and Murphy, the administration or customhouse faction controlled the state's federal patronage and strongly favored Grant's renomination.

Conkling was anxious for harmony in the fall of 1871. Even though exposure of the Tweed ring had greatly increased Republican chances, unity seemed necessary to assure a Republican victory, and Conkling took steps to achieve it. He called attention to the corruption in New York City in a published letter in which he urged that the "best men in the Republican party" be nominated and elected to the state legislature and executive offices. Complaining that "men stand talking about federal patronage, and differences among leaders, and personal feeling between individuals, and the like," Conkling asked, "What have such things to do with the duty of this hour?" [19]

Despite Conkling's precautions, the New York Republican Convention of 1871 proved an exciting spectacle with the police taking almost as large a part in the proceedings as the delegates. Not only did the police break up a general free-for-all in which table legs

---

[18] "The Bottom of the Great City Difficulty," *Nation,* XIII, No. 323 (September 7, 1871), 159; *ibid.,* No. 333 (November 16, 1871), 314.

[19] Conkling to John A. Griswold, Utica, August 26, 1871, in Alfred R. Conkling, *The Life and Letters of Roscoe Conkling* (New York, 1889), pp. 336–337.

served as weapons, but they also restored order on the platform and defended it against a "storming-party from the body of the hall." Notwithstanding the violence, a conciliatory Conkling was in command. Remembering his success the preceding year with Curtis as chairman, he once again put respectability in the chair—this time in the person of Andrew D. White, president of Cornell University —and included an innocuous plank in the platform commending the administration for its "worthy efforts" to reform the civil service. Even though the Fentonites bolted the convention, they supported its platform and candidates.[20] The bitter party split, however, was portentous of later developments: the Fentonites, frustrated in their quest for spoils, moved rapidly toward Liberal Republicanism.

A by-product of the Conkling-Fenton feud was the assault of Greeley's *New York Tribune* on Collector Tom Murphy. The *Tribune* claimed that Murphy had only escaped apprehension for manufacturing "shoddy" hats during the war through fraud and also accused him of associating with the Tweed ring in real estate speculations. The *Nation* reprinted these forgotten details of Murphy's past, claiming Murphy and members of the Tweed ring were of "a class of greedy adventurers, without conscience, or honor, or shame, or decency, or patriotism, or fear of God or devil, or any strong spring of action, except love of money, and who go into politics and repeat the party war-cries for the same reason that other men pick locks and forge bills—to avoid honest labor, fill their bellies with rich food, and adorn their bodies with rich clothing. We hope the Republican press will see to it that the President gets no peace until this particular rascal is relegated to private life." [21] The Republican press fulfilled the *Nation*'s hope. Grant had "no peace"; Murphy was removed from his post in November, 1871.

What Tweed and Murphy were to New York reformers, Ben Butler was to Massachusetts reformers. By siding with Grant on the annexation of Santo Domingo and any other pet project, Butler had managed to seize the Republican party organization in his state and was renowned as a "low spoilsman and constant advocate of rascality, whatever its variety." Campaigning for the gubernatorial nomination, Butler espoused prohibition and received the

[20] *Nation*, XIII, No. 327 (October 5, 1871), 217; "Civil-Service Reform in the Party Platforms," *ibid.*, p. 220.
[21] *Ibid.*, No. 326 (September 28, 1871), 201.

support of a good many "respectable" people. Although he was defeated, he spread consternation through the ranks of the "party of morality." Confronted by the spectacle of Boss Tweed, Tom Murphy, and Ben Butler, the *Nation* found it difficult not to believe the country was on the "eve of a cataclysm." [22]

Charles Eliot Norton, writing from abroad, emphatically agreed. "The Nation & Harvard & Yale Colleges seem to me almost the only solid barriers against the invasion of modern barbarism & vulgarity. . . . The whole country is, like New York, in the hands of the 'Ring,'—willing to let things go, till they are so bad that it is a question whether they can be bettered without complete upturning of the very foundations of law & civil order." Observing Butler, Tweed, and rapacious capitalists like Jim Fisk made Norton feel that the core of the problem was essentially one of ethics. So great was his revulsion against the new capitalists that Norton questioned the further validity of the "systems of individualism & competiton. We have erected selfishness into a rule of conduct, & we applaud the man who 'gets on' no matter at what cost to other men." Although he was not an agitator like Wendell Phillips (who was now in league with Butler), Norton felt capital had an "unfair advantage over labour" and approved the recent attempt of the Paris Commune to redress its grievances by force. Norton basically shared the typical reformer's aversion to violence, especially violence that would overturn social order, but he advocated "occasional violent revolutionary action to remove deep seated evils." Norton's radical view, however, was a temporary romantic aberration rather than a permanent viewpoint. Close contact with John Ruskin, William Morris, and Charles Dickens was probably the reason for his revolutionary turn of mind. But it is significant that actions of repulsive politicians and capitalists convinced Norton even temporarily that violent revolution would make men "more conscious of their duties to society." [23] In America, the same forces drove many respectable people to oppose Grant and to espouse civil service reform, revenue reform, and hard money.

By the summer of 1871, forces opposing a second term for Grant

---

[22] Oberholtzer, *op. cit.*, II, 313; *Nation*, XIII, No. 326 (September 28, 1871), 202.

[23] Norton to Godkin, Dresden, Germany, November 3, 1871, Godkin Papers, Harvard University. For mention of Norton's contacts with Ruskin, Morris, and Dickens, see Sara Norton and Mark Anthony DeWolfe Howe, *Letters of Charles Eliot Norton with Biographical Comment* (Boston, 1913), I, 303–419, *passim*.

found themselves outside the Republican party. Grant's most conspicuous opponent, Carl Schurz, serves as an example. As late as May 22, 1871, he received form letters requesting his pleasure concerning Missouri post office appointments. After this date, however, indications are that Schurz was completely eliminated from administration patronage. By mid-August, Schurz announced that he would not support Grant's re-election. In a Chicago speech, which criticized the Republican party's use of patronage, he advocated the "one-term principle" as part of civil service reform. Schurz and his supporters reasoned that a one-term President would not attempt to weld the civil service into a political machine to secure renomination.[24]

A month later, in September, 1871, Schurz, speaking in Nashville on "The Need of Reform and a New Party," left no doubt about his future course. Opposition to Grant led Schurz to forsake completely his earlier radical views and to seek southern support. After dwelling on "abuses of the patronage" and "shameless corruption," he insisted that the civil service must be reformed. Schurz stressed the South's particular need for civil service reform because of the "large number of uneducated and inexperienced voters, easily led by designing men for mean, selfish purposes." The designing men were fed by patronage and would be eliminated by reform. Schurz also spoke against the "corporations of tremendous power" that exercised "an almost uncontrollable influence" in public affairs and demanded that the "donation of public lands to such monopolies, to the disadvantage of the laboring people," cease.[25]

Schurz's Nashville speech produced tangible results. The "best citizens" of that city, irrespective of party, joined the "stop-Grant" movement. Similar organizations were started in Texas, and Schurz received letters from Louisiana and Mississippi asking for help in establishing local "stop-Grant" associations. "If the matter is pushed with the necessary energy," Schurz wrote Cox with optimism, "we may see an association of this kind in every Congressional district of the South before next spring." Schurz then confided his plan for an organization in St. Louis with branches throughout Missouri

[24] James W. Marshall, First Assistant Postmaster General, to Schurz, Washington, May 22, 1871, Schurz Papers. After this date, the Schurz Papers contain no letters asking advice on postal appointments. The Chicago speech is discussed in Curtis to Schurz, Ashfield, August 19, 1871, *ibid.*

[25] Bancroft, *op. cit.,* II, 259, 260, 293.

and his hope that existing reform clubs in northern cities would admit "the progressive men of both parties." [26] Schurz and his companions were well on their way toward founding a new party, and civil service reform was one of their chief issues. The Liberal Republican Convention at Cincinnati in 1872 was the logical outcome of their labors.

III

The Congress which convened in December, 1871, was once again confronted with civil service reform despite the passage of the rider the preceding spring. On December 4, Senator George F. Edmunds, a Vermont Republican, reintroduced the Jenckes bill to make the Grant Commission rules effective beyond the current administration. The bill was referred to committee and not heard of again.[27]

Acrimonious debate, however, resulted when Senator Lyman Trumbull attempted to revive the Joint Committee on Retrenchment. His resolution called for investigation of the civil service to ascertain whether expenses could be cut. Furthermore, Trumbull wanted to consider the expediency of legislating civil service reform tenets into law. Supporters of Grant countered with a resolution to create a Senate Committee of Investigation and Retrenchment but, as was the Senate's custom with standing committees, did not include specific instructions. Both Trumbull and Schurz claimed that conditions in the New York Customhouse illustrated the need for further civil service investigation and legislation. Conkling, inspired to his best efforts when the New York Customhouse was under attack, opposed Trumbull's resolution with vigor, and Oliver P. Morton protested that the drift of the debate was to show "that there is corruption existing under this Administration." [28]

Opposition from the administration's special friends kept the Trumbull resolution from passing. Its support had come mainly from Democrats and insurgent Republicans such as Sumner, Schurz, Trumbull, and Fenton, although Logan, an administration wheel horse, voted for the measure lest the country believe that Grant feared an investigation. A moment after Trumbull's resolution failed, the resolution creating a Senate Committee of Investigation

---

[26] Schurz to Cox, St. Louis, October 14, 1871, *ibid.*, II, 314.
[27] *Congressional Globe,* 42 Cong., 2 sess., 2–3, 43.
[28] *Ibid.*, pp. 42, 51–53, 86–87, 92–99.

and Retrenchment was passed; it included no specific instructions.[29]

After a long debate, which "convulsed" the country, the Senate adopted the first part of Trumbull's original instructions, relating generally to cutting expenditures, but dropped the consideration of civil service reform legislation. Senators supporting the administration made the best of the investigation by dictating the committee's personnel. Instead of choosing the committee chairman by ballot, as was customary, all members were chosen by a resolution which neglected the old rule, "the child is not to be put to a nurse that cares not for it." Six of the seven committee members were hostile to Trumbull's resolution in its strongest form and neither Trumbull nor Schurz was on the committee.[30]

The *Nation,* expressing disappointment in the committee's composition, suggested that Conkling and Morton, from their own point of view, had handled the whole affair poorly. If they had supported Trumbull's resolution from the start and had appeared to want investigation, the *Nation* concluded, "they would have shielded the Administration just as effectively as now, and have avoided the terribly damaging debate of last week." As though acting on this advice, Conkling offered a resolution instructing the new committee to investigate the general-order business in the New York Customhouse. Later amendments, accepted by Conkling, broadened the committee's instructions to encompass a complete customhouse investigation. Frauds, inefficiencies, political assessments, and the use of patronage for political purposes were to be scrutinized. This resolution was passed on December 19, 1871; the same day Grant relayed to Congress the rules drawn up by the Civil Service Commission.[31] Lukewarm personnel did not prevent the committee from starting its investigation immediately. In January and February of 1872, scores of witnesses contributed three volumes of testimony. These hearings completely aired the general-order business and acquainted the public with the activities of two shadowy figures— George Leet and Wilbur T. Stocking.

Leet, a one-time chief clerk in a Chicago freight depot, enlisted as a Union private in 1862 and emerged from the Civil War a colo-

[29] Charles H. How to Logan, Chicago, January 22, 1872, Logan Papers, Library of Congress; *Congressional Globe,* 42 Cong., 2 sess., 132.

[30] *Ibid.,* pp. 160–194.

[31] *Nation,* XIII, No. 338 (December 21, 1871), 393; *Congressional Globe,* 42 Cong., 2 sess., 159–160, 208–209.

nel attached to Grant's staff. While still holding his army commission, he secured a War Department clerkship in 1868. When Leet informed President-elect Grant that he wished to settle in New York, Grant wrote a letter of recommendation to Moses Grinnell, at that time a prominent New York merchant. Leet knew that Grant intended to appoint Grinnell New York collector and informed Grinnell of that fact when he presented his letter. Overwhelmed by his good fortune and the coincidence that Leet brought both news of his appointment and a letter from Grant, Grinnell asked Leet what he wanted. Leet promptly demanded the general-order business,[32] from which he expected to clear $60,000 annually. Somewhat intimidated by this demanding friend of Grant, Grinnell gave Leet supervision over the general-order business which Cunard and North German Lloyds had formerly handled themselves. After farming out this share for $5,000 a year and half of all profits over $10,000, Leet returned to Washington and kept his general-order business under cover by using a New York agent. During the years 1869 and 1870, Leet resided in Washington, rooming and boarding with Grant's private secretaries—Generals Horace Porter and Orville Babcock—and maintaining an army commission as well as a post in the War Department, where he filed Grant's army papers. Even while drawing three salaries, Leet used his intimacy with Grant's official household to threaten Grinnell with dismissal unless he received a larger share of the general-order business. Grinnell's successor, Tom Murphy, gave Leet and his friend Wilbur T. Stocking, former army sutler, the whole North River general-order business. At this point, Leet moved to New York and openly took charge of his customhouse interests.[33]

Revelation of the circumstances under which Leet gained his

---

[32] The general-order warehouse system required merchants to pay duty on their goods and to take possession of them within forty-eight hours after a ship entered port. Goods remaining beyond this inadequate period were discharged from the vessel under a general order by the collector. Once in the custody of customhouse officials, general-order goods were sent to a specially designated warehouse where, besides cartage, a month's storage was charged even if the goods were removed immediately. Joint Select Committee on Retrenchment, "Report," *Senate Reports*, 41 Cong., 3 sess., No. 380, 1–2.

[33] *Nation*, XIV, No. 341 (January 11, 1872), 17. The best account of Leet and Stocking's activities is found in William J. Hartman, "Politics and Patronage" (Columbia University, 1952), pp. 165–172. For the report based upon the hearings, see Committee on Investigation and Retrenchment, "Report," *Senate Reports*, 42 Cong., 2 sess., IV (in 3 parts), No. 227.

"sinecure" compounded New York merchants' dissatisfaction with the general-order business. Their earlier testimony of the rise in rates accompanying Leet's monopoly had not achieved redress. Even when Grant told Murphy in May of 1871 to sever Leet's connection with the customhouse because of hostile criticism, Murphy successfully defended him by saying that the attack was engineered by the steamship companies. Publicity from the January, 1872, investigation, however, proved too much for Leet. He testified that in twenty months he and Stocking had netted only $55,000, but refused to corroborate his statements with his firm's books. The value of his plum will never be known, but a recent investigator, William Hartman, accepts as reasonably accurate the figure $172,000 estimated by the Democratic minority of the investigating committee. Even before the committee presented its report, public opinion forced Grant to instruct Murphy's successor, Collector Chester A. Arthur, to reform the general-order business. Storage rates were lowered by 35 to 40 per cent, and the public careers of Leet and Stocking ended.[34]

Investigation of the customhouse also publicized the moiety system. This system sought to make customhouse employees zealous detectors of fraud by giving one-third of the proceeds from confiscated goods to the government Treasury; one-third to the informer or detector; and one-third to the collector, naval officer, and surveyor of the port. Fraud on any item of a shipment led to confiscation of the whole consignment. Moieties amounted to much more than the salaries of customs officials in the larger ports, and their overstimulated zeal proved trying to importers. The existence of such a system was common knowledge, but many were "surprised, if not shocked" to learn that a customhouse official or a special agent could ransack the books and premises of a merchant accused of evasion not in search of designated proof, but rather to determine whether any proof existed at all. Naylor and Company, a large iron firm that took seriously the fourth amendment safeguard against "unreasonable searches or seizures," complained of this practice and suggested that specific search warrants be required.[35] General search warrants, like moieties, were not immediately done away with, and merchants were plagued a bit longer by these nineteenth century counterparts of the Writs of Assistance, against which James

---

[34] Hartman, *op. cit.*, pp. 169–172, 185; Oberholtzer, *op. cit.*, II, 598.
[35] *Nation*, XIV, No. 343 (January 25, 1872), 50.

Otis so eloquently protested in the era of the American Revolution.

Since the customhouse investigation was conducted with the coming election in view, the political activities of that institution received much attention. Murphy, who was accused of influencing New York State Republican conventions in Conkling's behalf, admitted that the deputy collector administered the nonpolitical business of the customhouse which left the collector free for political action. The levying of assessments was also found to be a common practice in the New York Customhouse. Assessment of customhouse workers the preceding November became newspaper copy early in 1872 when an employee sued Murphy for recovery of his $30. Publicity was all that this civil servant received; the defense successfully maintained that the payment was purely voluntary.[36] All in all, the New York Customhouse provided much campaign material for both civil service reformers and anti-Grant politicians.

IV

Although the Civil Service Commission's program received Grant's backing, his special friends in Congress conspicuously opposed it. On January 10, Senator Matthew Carpenter of Wisconsin offered a resolution that the "political delusion called 'civil service reform,' " which transferred "the patronage . . . to a board of schoolmasters," was unconstitutional. A few days later, Carpenter elaborated on his objections in a carefully prepared senatorial speech. He claimed the rules not only violated the Constitution, but were anti-republican and favored the sons of the rich, who could afford a liberal college education, instead of maimed soldiers. Both John Sherman of Ohio and Oliver Morton of Indiana supported a fair trial for the new rules, but labeled "many" of them "utterly impractical." In the House of Representatives, Henry Snapp of Illinois introduced and defended a resolution hostile to the Civil Service Commission regulations. Snapp contended that civil service reform was not only a "humbug" but a trap set by Democrats to wreck the Republican party. Two weeks later, Representative Elizur H. Prindle (a New York Republican), in a well-reasoned speech, attacked the new system.[37]

---

[36] Hartman, *op. cit.*, pp. 173–174; *Nation*, XIV, No. 343 (January 25, 1872), 50; *ibid.*, No. 344 (February 1, 1872), 66.

[37] *Congressional Globe*, 42 Cong., 2 sess., 333, 441–446, 453–458, 463–464, 810–812.

These attacks, particularly Carpenter's, had a disquieting effect on the commission. Grant, however, told Curtis that Carpenter had not disturbed him and further demonstrated his favorable attitude toward reform in a letter to Commissioner Joseph Medill. "It is my intention that Civil Service shall have a fair trial. The great defect in the past custom is that executive patronage had come to be regarded as the property of the party in power. The choice of Federal officers has been limited to those seeking office. A true reform will leave the office to seek the man." Whatever his spoils-minded friends or reform-minded enemies may have thought, Grant was in the reformers' camp in early 1872.[38]

Presidents, as E. E. Schattschneider has pointed out, tend to support civil service reform while legislators tend to oppose it. Most congressmen in the spring of 1872 adhered to this theory. They were distinctly cool if not openly hostile to reform. The commission's rules caused congressmen almost invariably to react in one of two ways—either to devise their own "better" reform system or to attack the regulations being promulgated. On March 2, Republican Representative John B. Hay of Illinois and William T. Clark of Texas joined George McCrary of Iowa in promoting a constitutional amendment to limit civil servants' tenure to four years and to make elective all officers whose duties were within one state. This amendment would prevent arbitrary removals from office but would also destroy what little career service existed outside of Washington. It would, of course, appeal to westerners by insuring a geographical distribution of offices. Thomas J. Speer, a Georgia Republican, was more direct in his attack. He repeated the old saw, " 'To the victor' and not the vanquished, 'belong the spoils,' " and later said, "I am not willing, under the guise of reforming the civil service, to saddle upon the country the expensive, impractical, anti-republican, and un-American scheme which the civil service commission has proposed." [39]

Despite veiled and open hostility, Congress remembered it was an election year and appropriated funds for the commission. In early March, 1872, the Senate provided for a $50,000 appropriation. Even though Grant's friends, Carpenter, Cameron, Chandler, and

[38] "Minutes," January 20, 1872, I, 104; Grant to Medill, February 1, 1872, quoted by William Best Hesseltine, *Ulysses S. Grant* (New York, 1935), p. 264, n. 46.

[39] E. E. Schattschneider, *Party Government* (New York, 1942), pp. 137–140; *Congressional Globe*, 42 Cong., 2 sess., 1354, Appendix, 127–130.

Logan, attempted to repeal the legislation forming the commission, one friend of Grant, Roscoe Conkling, insisted that he would vote for "as much as is necessary of appropriation or of power to enable a fair trial to be given to what is sometimes denominated civil service reform." Although admittedly not an admirer of "all that is said in the name of civil service reform," Conkling vigorously denied an accusation that he believed the experiment would fail. The vote, which cut across party lines, showed Republicans, who were in power, more opposed to the commission than Democrats. Geographically the vote, like previous votes on civil service reform, showed support strongest in the Northeast and progressively weaker further West and South.[40]

The $50,000 appropriation was whittled down by the House. A month after the appropriation for the commission was approved in the Senate, the hostile House cut it down to $10,000 by a vote of 115 to 59. Benjamin F. Butler moved to strike out the $10,000 but afterwards "repented." Once more the administration's friends were conspicuous in their opposition. Garfield wrote Medill in disgust, "If the House had desired to help the Cincinnati movement [the anti-Grant, Liberal Republican movement] they could hardly have found a more efficient way than they adopted yesterday." A conference committee under Garfield's influence later raised the appropriation to $25,000, which both houses approved on May 3. Thus the much-debated, much-opposed reform was sustained. The commission had an appropriation, though it was but one-fourth of the $100,000 originally proposed in committee.[41]

While the niggardly House aided the Cincinnati movement, the Civil Service Commission's program strengthened Grant's position. Even temporary suspension of the rules had not caused adverse comment; it was apparent that problems had to be solved before the regulations could be enforced. The whole civil service outside of Washington had to be classified into various grades, and specific rules of appointment had to be devised for posts defying simple classification. By March 12, 1872, the commission had completed the classification, which Curtis submitted to Grant along with supplementary regulations. Once again Grant approved by executive order

---

[40] *Ibid.*, pp. 1502–07, 1535–37, 1575.

[41] *Ibid.*, pp. 1535, 2398, 3020–21, 3053–55; Garfield to Medill, Washington, April 13, 1872, and Garfield to David A. Wells, Washington, April 22, 1872, Garfield Papers; *Nation*, XIV, No. 355 (April 18, 1872), 250.

the commission's recommendations with few minor changes. His order admitted that political activity had previously determined civil servants' tenure of office, and, although defending their right to be active politically, Grant declared that "honesty and efficiency, not political activity, will determine the tenure of office." [42]

The new regulations divided the civil service into roughly four classes. One class, primarily composed of clerks, was required to be examined competitively before appointment; while a second class, including consuls receiving salaries ranging from $1,000 to $3,000, was appointed on the strength of recommendation followed by a "pass" examination. A third class, including such posts as collectors of customs at major ports, was not required to take an examination but was chosen, if possible, from a subordinate post in the department where the vacancy occurred; and a small fourth class of the highest officers, such as Cabinet members, was to be appointed by traditional methods.

The supplementary regulations sought to eliminate problems encountered in testing and appointing applicants. Those taking a specific examination were limited to a practicable number—a provision reformers admitted "necessary," although they feared it might become a "loop-hole" allowing the spoils system to retain its position. Provision was also made for holding departmental examinations throughout the states.[43] To allay adverse criticism of their first report, which deprecated continued proscription of former Confederates, the board required that each appointee give "satisfactory evidence of his fidelity to the Union and the Constitution." [44]

The day after Grant ordered into effect the supplementary regulations, the Trumbull bill evoked a savage three-day debate in the House. This debate showed that the reform argument was shifting away from retrenchment toward the spoils system's effect on politics. The bill as reported by Representative Charles W. Willard, a Vermont Republican, forbade congressmen to advise the President or department heads on appointments unless requested in writing to do so. Willard's supporting speech stressed that a greater danger than

---

[42] "Minutes," January 10 and March 12, 1872, I, 98, 133. Grant's order, the report of the advisory board, and the additional regulations are reprinted in Norton, op. cit., II, 87–116.

[43] This regulation was one of Grant's few changes. The members of the advisory board had planned to determine when examinations should be nationwide.

[44] "The Civil-Service Regulations," Nation, XIV, No. 356 (April 25, 1872), 269–270.

the loss of millions of dollars menaced the country "through this debasement of politics and parties into organizations seeking the control of the Government for what can be made out of it." [45]

Ben Butler, as usual, supplied pyrotechnics for the occasion and once more provided reformers with disquieting evidence of hostility from the President's closest friends. "One of the most onerous, unpleasant, and troublesome duties that, as a member of Congress, I have to perform," Butler stated, "is to advise and be advised upon the questions of appointments to office," but for the good of party, constituents, and country, he would do his duty and oppose the Trumbull bill. Butler then argued that civil service reform was always strong among "the 'outs' and never with the 'ins' unless with those who have a strong expectation of soon going out." Butler equated opposition to Grant with civil service reform, which he called the stillborn babe of Cincinnati. Although Butler had punctuated his speech with remarks asserting Grant's hostility to civil service reform, Garfield forced him to admit that he was unauthorized to speak for the President. [46]

In a speech the following day, Garfield showed that friends as well as enemies of reform were doing their best to identify Grant with their particular view. He insisted that the President was "not only sincere, but deeply in earnest" on the subject of civil service reform, and privately labeled Butler "a beast . . . in debate." Despite Garfield's attempt "to impress the House with its unworthyness [sic] in the treatment this subject has received at its hands," the "beast" triumphed; "the bill was whistled down the wind, by a vote of 97 to 79. . . ." Analysis of the vote supports Butler's contention that the party out of power always favored civil service reform, for over twice as many Republicans opposed reform as favored it while a similar proportion of Democrats supported the Trumbull bill. Democratic congressmen—with nothing to lose—were perfectly happy to hamper their Republican colleagues' control of the patronage. The small number of supporting Republican votes came principally from New England, Ohio, New York (a minority of the state's Republicans), Illinois, Michigan, and Iowa. Republican opposition was strongest in states where political machines were powerful. Repub-

---

[45] *Congressional Globe,* 42 Cong., 2 sess., 1138, 2512–13. Although the Trumbull bill was reported by Willard, consideration was postponed until congressmen could consult the commission's supplementary rules. *Ibid.,* p. 1838.

[46] *Ibid.,* Appendix, pp. 267–269.

licans from Massachusetts, New York, Pennsylvania, Indiana, Wisconsin, and all southern states voted overwhelmingly against reform.[47] Reform had not gained ground in Congress.

---

[47] *Ibid.*, p. 2585; Garfield to Wells, Washington, April 22, 1872, and Garfield to Burke Aaron Hinsdale, Washington, April 22, 1872, Garfield Papers.

VII

GRANT'S UNCONDITIONAL SURRENDER

The actions of Grant and his friends confused and divided reformers. While the administration belatedly supported civil service reform, it was well known that the President's closest friends opposed reform. As the campaign of 1872 approached, many ardent reformers called for Grant's renomination in behalf of reform, but others equally ardent opposed it on the same grounds.

I

Amid this confusion, the Liberal Republican movement got off to an auspicious start in early 1872. A convention held in Jefferson City, Missouri, on January 24, 1872, formally promulgated a set of political principles—among which civil service reform was a cardinal tenet—and issued a call for a national convention of Liberal Republicans to meet in Cincinnati on May 1. Schurz's months of hard work organizing opposition to Grant and exposing administration blunders had achieved results. "Daily we see State Movements to support this come-outerism," wrote Wendell Phillips Garrison, of the *Nation*, "and I now think it more probable than not that the Convention will not only construct a platform but nominate candidates. Chas. Francis Adams's name is most prominent, & seems to me most available. I think the Democratic party would accept him, & if they did, Grant's chances would not be worth a rush." A host of leading newspapers gave the movement cordial support. Among them were the *New York Tribune,* the New York *Evening Post,* the *Nation,* the *Chicago Tribune,* the *Cincinnati Commercial,* the *Springfield Republican,* and the Louisville *Courier Journal.* Prominent individuals in all states followed the lead taken by newspapers. David A. Wells's statement, "The movement . . . is bound to win & is spreading every day," expressed the independent reformers' confidence on the eve of the Cincinnati convention.[1]

As the Liberal Republican movement accelerated, its original program was adulterated by the adhesion of various disgruntled elements. Conciliation of the South, civil service reform, and free trade were obscured. Supporters of the movement included Horace Greeley, America's leading protectionist, and John W. Forney, editor of the Philadelphia *Press* and former Philadelphia collector, who felt Grant had not rewarded him adequately and now praised instead of damned civil service reform in order to camp with Grant's enemies.[2] Another adherent was Senator Reuben E. Fenton, whose interest in reform seemed inversely proportioned to the amount of patronage he controlled. With these "supporters," the Liberal Republican movement very quickly came to stand for but one thing—opposition to Grant.

The Cincinnati gathering had its bizarre aspects, as do most third-party conventions.[3] Susan B. Anthony and a few friends conspicuously paraded about in the interest of women suffrage; and George Francis Train, the well-heeled eccentric who circled the globe in eighty days and sponsored everything from Fenianism to free love, was prominently present. Newspaper editors came in droves to join reformers and dissatisfied politicians in president-making. Four prominent newspapermen—Horace White of the *Chicago Tribune,* Samuel Bowles of the *Springfield Republican,* Murat Halstead of the

---

[1] Wendell Phillips Garrison to Henry Villard, New York, April 3, 1872, Villard Papers, Harvard University; Wells to Gordon L. Ford, Norwich, Connecticut, April 15, 1872, Miscellaneous Papers, New York Public Library.

[2] When Cox resigned, Forney castigated civil service reform as "ridiculous," but on January 20, 1872, he ran an editorial praising it. Quoted in *Nation* (New York), XIV, No. 345 (February 8, 1872), 82.

[3] The description of the Cincinnati convention was taken primarily from Earle Dudley Ross, *The Liberal Republican Movement* (New York, 1919), pp. 86–105; Ellis Paxson Oberholtzer, *A History of the United States Since the Civil War* (New York, 1917–37), III, 16–26. Other sources consulted include: George S. Merriam, *The Life and Times of Samuel Bowles* (New York, 1885), II, 184–188; Glyndon G. Van Deusen, *Horace Greeley* (Philadelphia, 1953), pp. 404–407; Royal Cortissoz, *The Life of Whitelaw Reid* (New York, 1921), I, 208–210; Joseph Frazier Wall, *Henry Watterson* (New York, 1956), pp. 99–107; Henry Watterson, *"Marse Henry"* (New York, 1919), I, 241–257. Watterson later was a strenuous opponent of civil service reform. Wall, *op. cit.,* p. 194, and Arthur Krock, ed., *The Editorials of Henry Watterson* (Louisville, Kentucky, 1923), pp. 66–69.

Cincinnati Commercial, and Henry Watterson of the Louisville *Courier Journal*—heroically styled themselves the Quadrilateral [4] and worked behind closed doors mapping out convention strategy with Carl Schurz, the permanent chairman.

One member of the Quadrilateral, Horace White, chairman of the platform committee, had the difficult task of harmonizing the convention's diverse interests. The resulting platform dismissed the tariff question as a local issue and castigated the spoils system as an "instrument of partisan tyranny and personal ambition." After stating "that honesty, capacity, and fidelity, constitute the only valid claims to public employment," the platform urged that offices become posts of "honor" rather than matters of "arbitrary favoritism and patronage." The only positive detail offered to secure these ends was the one-term principle. Neither the open-competitive system nor a commission to enforce it was mentioned.[5]

With only equivocal planks on civil service reform and the tariff question in the Liberal Republican party platform, the choice of a presidential candidate became vitally important to reformers. Although Charles Francis Adams was their favorite, his congenital frigidity proved detrimental to his nomination. When Adams' statement that he would not "peddle" with anyone "for power" nor be "negotiated for" was published, the chances of other candidates improved. Western reformers favored Senator Lyman Trumbull, and Senator Charles Sumner had a few followers. Chief Justice Salmon P. Chase once again threw his well-worn hat in the ring, and another Supreme Court Justice, David Davis, a millionaire who had just been nominated by the Labor Reform party on a poor man's ticket, caught the presidential fever. Other names mentioned for the nomination included Benjamin Gratz Brown of Missouri, Senator Reuben Fenton, Andrew G. Curtin, the former war governor of Pennsylvania whose feud with Simon Cameron had driven him into the Liberal Republican camp, and Horace Greeley.

Members of the Quadrilateral, supporting either Adams or Trumbull, did not fear Greeley and even took his lieutenant, Whitelaw Reid of the *New York Tribune*, into their confidence. Although they felt certain that Adams would be nominated since he was the

---

[4] The name was taken from the four points whose possession was the key to Austria's occupation of Lombardy-Venetia.

[5] For the Liberal Republican party platform, see Henry Steele Commager, ed., *Documents of American History* (New York, 1949), II, 70–71.

second choice of most state delegations pledged to favorite sons, a factional struggle among Missouri Liberal Republicans resulted in his defeat. Horace Greeley was nominated on the sixth ballot; and Gratz Brown was awarded the vice-presidential nomination for starting the Greeley trend.

The chagrin of reformers over the Cincinnati ticket was immeasurable. Not only was Greeley the foremost advocate of a protective tariff and a friend of the spoils system; he was also widely regarded as intrinsically unfit for the presidency. Godkin called him "a conceited, ignorant, half-cracked, obstinate old creature" and predicted that his "election . . . would be a National calamity of the first magnitude. . . . the triumph of quackery, charlatanry and recklessness." Schurz, who more than anyone else had originated and nurtured the Liberal Republican movement, was most disappointed. In a forthright manner, he wrote Greeley that "the first fruit of the great reform, so hopefully begun, was a successful piece of political hucksteri ng and that the whole movement had been captured by politicians of the old stamp." Schurz regretted that the reform movement itself illustrated the "demoralization" of political life. "Its management differs in nothing from the practices it professed to condemn. In its present shape it does no longer appeal to that higher moral sense which we hoped to have evoked in the hearts and minds of the people. Its freshness and flavor are gone and we have come down to the ordinary level of a campaign of politicians." Although Schurz's future course was uncertain, he urged Greeley to pledge the appointment of a civil service commission to handle his administration's patronage along reform lines.[6]

Schurz was not alone among Liberal Republicans in debating whom to support. Many reformers sought to avoid the dilemma of voting for Greeley or Grant. "Is there no way out of the wretched mess into which these Cincinnati nominations have plunged us?" asked Godkin. "If the matter be left as it stands, it will be impossible for any one to speak of 'reform,' during the next fifteen years, without causing shouts of laughter." Although Godkin's view was shared by others, plans to shelve Greeley did not succeed. A closed conference held at New York's Fifth Avenue Hotel on June 20, 1872, made no nominations, and Schurz with other notables stepped over

---

[6] Schurz to Greeley, Washington, May 6 and 11, 1872, and Godkin to Schurz, New York, May 19, 1872, in Frederic Bancroft, ed., *Speeches, Correspondence and Political Papers of Carl Schurz* (New York, 1913), II, 363–364, 368, 372, 376.

into the Greeley camp. Just seven weeks earlier in his opening address at Cincinnati, Schurz had spoken against the sentiment "anyone to defeat Grant." He now found himself supporting Greeley for this very reason.[7]

Reformers supporting Greeley rationalized their decision by repeating his promises concerning civil service reform and their hope that his election would break up both the old parties. Horace White assured Schurz that Greeley would "hold up both hands for" a law bringing the civil service "under the English or Prussian system *as to permanence*" and that his view on civil service reform is "satisfactory to me and would be so to you if you had, as I now have, the faculty of believing that he is a sincere man."[8]

Schurz followed White's lead and became "confident" that he could "make Greeley commit himself to certain *specific* reform-measures." To Schurz's query about his plans for reforming the civil service, Greeley replied, "Let it be settled that a President is not to be reëlected while in office, and civil service reform is no longer difficult." "As to the machinery of boards of examiners, etc. . . . I defer to the judgment of a Congress unperverted by the adulterous commerce in legislation and appointments, which I have already exposed and reprehended." Greeley further professed not to blame what he termed the unencouraging progress of the Civil Service Commission on the commissioners.[9] This answer could not have been all that Schurz wanted, but in his position he grasped at whatever he could.

---

[7] Godkin to Schurz, New York, May 19, 1872, and Schurz to Godkin, Washington, May 20, 1872, *ibid.*, II, 376, 378; *Nation*, XIV, No. 365 (June 27, 1872), 413. Roughly 200 invitations (signed by Schurz, William Cullen Bryant, Wells, Cox, Oswald Ottendorfer, and Jacob Brinkerhoff) were issued to this closed conference. Both Ottendorfer and Brinkerhoff were prominent German-Americans. Ottendorfer published the New York *Staats-Zeitung* and Brinkerhoff was from Ohio and had had an interesting antislavery career. Following the breakup of the closed conference twenty-five intensely anti-Greeley men met, drew up a set of ten resolutions, and nominated W. S. Groesbeck of Ohio and Frederick Law Olmsted, respectively, for President and Vice President. *Ibid.*

[8] Schurz to Parke Godwin, Washington, May 21, 1872, Bryant-Godwin Collection, New York Public Library; White to Schurz, New York, June 9, 1872, and Chicago, June 15, 1872, in Bancroft, *op. cit.*, II, 382, 383.

[9] Schurz to Godkin, Pittsburgh, June 23, 1872, Schurz to Greeley, St. Louis, June 26, 1872, and Greeley to Schurz, New York, July 8, 1872, *ibid.*, II, 385–386, 391–392. When the commission's rules first appeared, Greeley charged that they "allowed Grant to promote 'a vigorous factional proscription in his own Party.'" Quoted by Lionel V. Murphy, "The First Federal Civil Service Commission: 1871–75 . . . ," *Public Personnel Review* (Chicago), III, No. 4 (October, 1942), 299.

Godkin, however, harbored no illusions about Greeley. "What I seek," he wrote Schurz, "is not a sham break-up of parties, such as the Greeley movement promises, but a real break-up, involving something more than the construction of a new party machine out of the pieces of the old ones. But I see no hope of this from electing Greeley. Bowles, White and the rest are to me preaching the very doctrines now, against which we have been all thundering for three years. They are accepting blindly a grossly unfit candidate at the hands of a bellowing Convention and are going to support him solely because he is 'available'; not because they have the smallest reason to expect from him any support of their principles, but because he promises a change of officers, and they are denouncing as silly and dishonest all those who, having supported the Cincinnati Convention for better things, now refuse to 'fall into line,' as they call it. If this be not the old 'party tyranny,' pray what is it?" [10]

The campaign of 1872 split reformers into three factions. Schurz and Horace White represented the first faction, which was anti-Grant, pro–Liberal Republican, and disappointed by the Cincinnati Convention. It supported Greeley—but only as a lesser evil. The second faction, typified by Godkin and Charles Eliot Norton, was made up of reformers with Liberal Republican sentiments who crawled back into the Grant camp after Greeley's nomination.[11]

Members of the third faction, of whom George William Curtis is the prime example, were pro-Grant and anti–Liberal Republican from the start (without personal bitterness toward the originators of that movement) and after the Cincinnati fiasco were anti-Greeley with relish. Although they took Grant's reforming efforts seriously, they did not support him solely, or even primarily, because of his civil service policies. These men were more occupied with the issues growing out of the Civil War than Liberal Republicans were. "The contest," Curtis wrote, "will be Grant against the field: Grant with all his faults, and they are not great, against every element of every kind of Democratic, rebellious, Ku Klux, discontented, hopeful and unreasonable feeling." Greeley "excused secession, he tried to negotiate at Niagara—he tried to bully Mr. Lincoln into buying a peace, he bailed Jeff Davis, and the worst Northern Copperheads support

[10] Godkin to Schurz, Lenox, Massachusetts, June 28, 1872, in Bancroft, *op. cit.*, II, 388.

[11] Norton to Godkin, St. Germain, France, July 26, 1872, Godkin Papers, Harvard University.

him. That is eno' for the South. It ought to be eno' for the Country!"
Curtis ignored both the civil service and the tariff in praising Grant
and damning Greeley. He felt that the opposition's noblest sentiment was that both parties must be destroyed and electing Greeley
was the best means of achieving that end. "The argument," Curtis
skeptically observed, "seems to be, first chaos, then cosmos." [12]

Liberal Republicans, on the other hand, considered civil service
reform a real campaign issue. Senator Trumbull accused the Grant
regime of corruption and embarrassed Grant's supporters by quot-
ing the December, 1871, report of the Civil Service Commission.
This development particularly disturbed Senator Logan, whose
hatred of the commission was boundless. In August, he wrote Grant's
Secretary of War, William Worth Belknap (later remembered for
his corrupt sale of Indian trading-post positions), who *"at once"*
sought clarification of the report's damaging passages. When inquiry
was made, Curtis dashed off an explanatory editorial for *Harper's
Weekly* and later prepared a brief formal letter which the commissioners signed. [13]

The letter illustrated both the commission's tendency to exag-
gerate political corruption and its willingness to aid Grant's campaign. Trumbull had stated that one-fourth of the nation's revenue,
or $95,830,986.22, was lost each year and had implied that the Grant
administration was responsible for this loss. Curtis explained that
this estimate, originally made by Revenue Commissioner David A.
Wells, was designed to provide the "most forceable illustration of
the mischief of the system" and actually dated from "the administration of Andrew Johnson when the evils of the 'spoils' system cul-
minated." The loss was not money actually collected and then stolen,
as Trumbull had asserted, but money due the government and
never collected. The letter also claimed that during Grant's administration deficiencies and defalcations under the internal revenue
law had amounted to but one-seventh of those during Johnson's
term of office. "We regret," the commissioners concluded, "that in
our desire to divest our report of any partisan character whatever
and to make it as concise as possible, we failed to explain this state-

---

[12] Curtis to Norton, Ashfield, June 30, 1872, Curtis Papers, Harvard University.
[13] Belknap to Logan, Washington, August 15, 1872, Logan Papers, Library of
Congress; "Senator Trumbull and the Revenue," *Harper's Weekly* (New York),
XVI, No. 819 (September 7, 1872), 690; Curtis to Belknap, Ashfield, August 25, 1872,
Logan Papers.

ment, more in detail, & to show how ingenious and successful were the efforts of the administration to prevent the loss to which we alluded." [14] Logan could hardly have hoped for a better explanation.

Greeley, who looked less and less like a winner as the campaign progressed, suffered overwhelming defeat and died shortly thereafter. The effects of the campaign on the reform movement were almost as disastrous. Not only were the hopes of many reformers dashed by the Greeley nomination, but, in addition, reform factions distrusted one another. Those who had returned to Grant's standard were especially suspicious of those who had backed Greeley. Wendell Phillips Garrison, for instance, ascribed Horace White's support of Greeley to "selfish motives" and "expectations of political and other profit." [15] When the *Nation* blamed Schurz for the Cincinnati disaster, he admonished Godkin to "spare the slain and wounded after the fight, whose lot is by no means the most enviable. . . ." All reformers could have joined with Curtis in calling it "a very melancholy Campaign." [16]

Immediately after the election, Horace White began planning a December meeting to reunite reformers. Unfortunately for White's plans, neither Godkin nor any of the "old set" was interested. Godkin wrote, "I do not see that we could come to any conclusion about the future. The result of the Cincinnati movement has been so unfortunate, that there is at present a slight odor of ridicule hanging around everybody who had anything to do with getting it up. Moreover we do not yet know what the election meant exactly, beyond contempt for Greeley." Although Godkin agreed with White's reform sentiments and expressed hope that they would "be found side by side on the old ground," he advocated a policy of wait and see with a possible meeting in February, 1873.[17]

Postelection strategy posed no difficult problem for Schurz, who

---

[14] Curtis, Cattell *et al.* to Logan, September, no day, 1872, *ibid.* For another example of the exaggeration of statistics by reformers see *Congressional Globe,* 41 Cong., 3 sess., 400, 459–460, 666.

[15] Henry Villard disagreed. He endeavored to convince Garrison, his brother-in-law, that although White had been inconsistent, his main objective had been the noble one of breaking up both parties. Villard to Garrison, Baden-Baden, Germany, July 11, 1872, Villard Papers. White and Villard were old friends; they met as reporters covering the Lincoln-Douglas debates.

[16] Schurz to Godkin, St. Louis, November 23, 1872, Godkin Papers; Curtis to Norton, Ashfield, September 6, 1872, Curtis Papers.

[17] Godkin to White, New York, November 11, 1872, Schurz Papers, Library of Congress.

lacked Godkin's pessimistic strain. "We should continue to struggle for the realization of the ideas embodied in our original program," he wrote, "and be governed by no other consideration." Schurz wished to conciliate reformers and wrote Godkin requesting a personal conference on "certain things likely to come up in Congress this winter, especially the Civil Service matter, the postal-telegraph bill etc. I shall probably not be in a situation to do much of anything of importance this winter," Schurz continued, "but things may possibly take such a turn as to make it necessary for the defeated to take position and I should be very glad to act in concert with you." [18]

Other reformers considered a unified program necessary. John Murray Forbes wrote, "4 years hence there may be a chance for a real Reform Movement & it may then be a necessity & forecasting men ought to be preparing from today. The first *nucleus* ought to be a strong Daily at N Y or Washington devoted to supporting Grant in his Civil Service Reform professions, but ready to stand to its guns if his bad advisers manage to hold him back from effective reform—Congress is very strong against reform & nothing but positive expression & public opinion will drive them to it— Some of the President's advisers are at least lukewarm. It needs a Civil Service Reform League with a good organ." [19]

Forbes's program was sensible, but the effects of the election were not easily erased. The three reform factions were not immediately unified; neither was a civil service league formed nor a newspaper founded. With their ranks divided, reformers, who had thrived under abuse, were discouraged by ridicule. Liberal Republican reformers who had seceded from the Republican party were powerless; and reformers who had remained with the Republican party were too weak to retain the advances already gained. Demoralized and divided, reformers were easily conquered.

II

The conquest did not immediately follow the election. Grant himself proved a temporary rallying point for all reformers. Shortly

---

[18] Schurz to White, no place, no date [probably about November 15, 1872], in Bancroft, *op. cit.*, II, 444–445; Schurz to Godkin, St. Louis, November 23, 1872, Godkin Papers.

[19] Forbes to Norton, Boston, December 10, 1872, Norton Papers. In this letter, Forbes also gave ample evidence of his sound money position and of his laissez-faire conception of the functions of government.

after the election, a delegation of about thirty Pennsylvania politicians under Simon Cameron's leadership entrained at Philadelphia for Washington in a palace car well stocked with champagne and whisky. Upon their arrival the group marched (as best they could) to the White House, where they urged Grant to ignore civil service rules and appoint their man postmaster of Philadelphia. Grant told the delegation that he could not set aside the regulations in view of Republican party pledges. Leaving in disgust, the delegation retired to a hotel, where they regretted with profanity having "worked" for Grant.

Reformers rejoiced at the news of Grant's stanch stand. The *Nation,* praying that he would be strengthened, credited "his action to an honest wish for a reformed civil service." Even Schurz conceded, "Grant has made a good beginning, in which we most certainly support, and if our support is superfluous, applaud him. But the true test," Schurz added—no doubt thinking of Congress—"is still to come." Curtis also praised Grant for standing "nobly" against Cameron but expected little aid from either Congress or the Cabinet and even expressed doubts about Grant. He wrote Norton, "fortunately Grant is tenacious and resolved upon the *spirit* which should govern appointments. I suppose however that he may not see why *good* party men should not be taken." [20]

News from Washington quickly ended what optimism reformers dared to entertain. Western congressmen arriving in late November for the next session of Congress were outspokenly hostile and even claimed that in the West, especially in Illinois, the Republican victory was a mandate against civil service regulations. Soon after Congress convened, Representative Henry Snapp of Illinois, who a year previously had called civil service reform a "humbug," vehemently attacked the commission as "irresponsible" and "a cheat and a swindle." He dismissed the inclusion of civil service reform in the Republican party platform by saying that everyone knew the real issue was whether or not the rebels would gain control of the government.[21]

Having expected little from Congress, reformers were not disap-

---

[20] *Nation,* XV, No. 386 (November 21, 1872), 325; Schurz to Godkin, St. Louis, November 23, 1872, Godkin Papers; Curtis to Norton, Boston, December 2, 1872, Curtis Papers.

[21] *Nation,* XV, No. 388 (December 5, 1872), 358; *Congressional Globe,* 42 Cong., 3 sess., 194–199.

pointed. The real question, as they saw it, was how firm would Grant remain. His annual message, which stressed the necessity for congressional legislation binding future presidents to the civil service rules, pleased them. But a rumor soon circulated that the Cameron delegation's visit to Grant was merely a hoax to throw "dust in the eyes" of reformers since the man appointed under the rules was a Cameron protégé. In addition, when Logan's man—instead of the chief assistant—got the Chicago postmastership, the President was criticized for not maintaining the "spirit" of the rules.[22]

Reformers continued to find Grant's actions confusing. As United States district attorney in New York City he appointed George Bliss, a confidant and an adviser of Tom Murphy. Although this position was exempt from the rules, the *Nation* pointed out that it called for a "good and experienced lawyer"—and Bliss, chief manager of the customhouse party, was not a good lawyer. The administration also pardoned a Philadelphia supporter convicted of repeating his vote. The usual consultation with the local district attorney was omitted and although the pardon was given upon the recommendation of "prominent" Philadelphians, their names were kept secret. When Grant rejected an appeal from a local reform organization to reverse the decision, Henry C. Lea made the story public. The *Nation's* Washington correspondent commented in December, 1872, "the impression is gaining ground that the President's determination to carry out the new civil-service rules, however emphatically it may be expressed, does not mean much after all." [23]

Between spoils appointments Grant sandwiched in talks with the commissioners and seemed interested in reform problems. While conversing with Curtis in late January, 1873, Grant expressed concern over an undue proportion of applications from the Washington area. In order to alleviate pressure, he suggested that a system of nominations (probably meaning examination after nomination) be used. The President also "expressed pretty positive feeling that examinations be confined to lower positions." Shortly thereafter the commission met with Grant and his Cabinet. "The Civil Service

---

[22] James D. Richardson, *A Compilation of the Messages and Papers of the Presidents 1789–1897* (Washington, 1896–99), VII, 205; *Nation*, XV, No. 391 (December 26, 1872), 418.

[23] *Ibid.*, pp. 418–419; *ibid.*, XVI, No. 397 (February 6, 1873), 86–87; "Correspondence: The Undercurrent at Washington," *ibid.*, XV, No. 391 (December 26, 1872), 424.

Board are admitted," Hamilton Fish wrote, "& a long, long talk ensues—but all things have an end, & so at length had this—without much apparent result having been reached." The commissioners were not so bored. One of them reported that the interview was "prolonged and harmonious." [24]

Despite meetings with commissioners, Grant soon departed from their rules. When the New York surveyor, Alonzo Cornell, vacated his position, which was clearly under the rules, reformers viewed the nomination of his successor as a test case. Grant's hesitation produced apprehension, but after Curtis consulted with him he nominated Deputy Surveyor James I. Benedict in accordance with the rules. Although reformers tasted victory, they again grew apprehensive when, in early February, members of the Conkling machine bragged that Grant would withdraw the nomination. Two weeks later the nomination was withdrawn, but an announcement was made that reform methods would be used in selecting the new surveyor. A committee of three, including Curtis and Collector Chester A. Arthur, was to find the customhouse employee best fitted for the post. Once more reformers' suspicions were allayed. But spoilsmen were to be the final victors. Curtis' serious illness kept the committee from holding an examination or making a report. In mid-March, George H. Sharpe, an active politician and the local United States marshal, was appointed without the committee's knowledge. Sharpe's appointment goaded an ill and testy Curtis into action. Three days after it was announced, he published a letter in the *New York Tribune* emphasizing that Sharpe's appointment was made without his knowledge or consent and ominously added that "men do not willingly consent to be thus publicly snubbed." On March 18, 1873, Curtis resigned as chairman of Grant's Civil Service Commission.[25]

[24] Hamilton Fish, "Diary," January 28, 1873, III, 353, Fish Papers, Library of Congress; memorandum of a meeting of the advisory board, January 27, 1873, in "Civil Service Reform 1853–1883," I, 115A–116, 118, E. B. Elliot Papers, Library of the United States Civil Service Commission, hereafter cited as "Civil Service Reform." These papers in three volumes consist primarily of memoranda, along with some letters, mainly of E. B. Elliott, a commissioner and Treasury official, T. R. Deland, clerk to the Treasury board of examiners, and Charles Lyman, clerk to the Grant commission.

[25] *Nation*, XVI, No. 399 (February 20, 1873), 126–127; *ibid.*, No. 403 (March 20, 1873), 189. Curtis was so ill that complete rest for six months was prescribed. During this period, which began about February 12, 1873, he dictated all of his correspondence to his wife. Curtis to Norton, West New Brighton, New York, March

Curtis' resignation attracted wide attention. His successor, Dorman B. Eaton, considered Curtis' action "most conscientious" but precipitous and harmful to the cause of reform. The independent anti-Grant press disagreed. "Those who have the interests of reform at heart," reported the *Nation*, "will be glad to know that Mr. Curtis has resigned" and that he will no longer lend "the strength of his name to what cannot, under the present Administration, be anything more than a pretence." Curtis himself was more kindly disposed than his defenders. "As to the Civil Service," he wrote, "I think that the President means better than he does. But our views differed so that I could not remain." [26]

Grant's choice of Eaton as chairman of the commission proved that he had not abandoned reform completely. Eaton, like many civil service reformers, was a New Englander by birth and a resident of New York. A university-trained, erudite lawyer (who helped prepare a new edition of James Kent's *Commentaries*), Eaton was painfully aware of the unsavory nature of contemporary business and political life. While a counsel for the Erie Railroad, he was seriously injured by vicious assailants. In 1870, he gave up his law practice and spent the rest of his life fighting for municipal and civil service reform.

The President also filled the place of Commissioner Joseph Medill, who resigned when Curtis did, with a friend of reform, former Congressman Samuel Shellabarger. As if to show reformers that he had not changed ground, Grant, in answering Medill's resignation letter, reiterated a promise from his second inauguration address: "The spirit of the rules will be maintained." [27] Things of the spirit, however, have always been subject to manifold interpretations. Yet

---

12, 1873, Curtis Papers. The connection between Curtis' illness and the failure of the special commission to meet or act has apparently been overlooked. Edward Cary, *George William Curtis* (Boston, 1894), p. 233, states that Curtis had decided to resign before his illness. It seems obvious, however, that Sharpe's appointment caused Curtis' resignation, although his illness might have influenced his drastic action.

[26] Dorman B. Eaton, *The Experiment of Civil Service Reform in the United States*, May, 1875, p. 15; *Nation*, XVI, No. 405 (April 3, 1873), 229; Curtis to James Freeman Clarke, West New Brighton, April 9, 1873, Clarke Family Papers, Harvard University.

[27] Grant to Medill, April 9, 1873, quoted in William Best Hesseltine, *Ulysses S. Grant* (New York, 1935), p. 359. Hesseltine adds that Grant's actions belied his words since on March 24, only twenty days after his inauguration, he wrote concerning twenty-three appointments. *Ibid.* Hesseltine, however, assumes but does not give evidence that these twenty-three positions were under the rules.

both Curtis and Eaton, the men most intimately associated with Grant's civil service activities, regarded his efforts as sincere if sometimes misguided.

The *New York Times* also thought Grant's efforts genuine and tried to counter the effect of Curtis' resignation by frequently publicizing the progress of the civil service rules. The *Times,* however, merely demonstrated that the rules were in effect only in Washington and in the New York Customhouse. The Secretary of the Treasury had applied the rules to the customhouse on October 10, 1872, to "test the system thoroughly . . . before extending it elsewhere." This trial was successful according to an 1873 report by New York Deputy Naval Officer Silas W. Burt, chairman of the local supervisory board. Burt, an early adherent to Jenckes's ideas, probably had more experience with competitive examinations than any other civil servant. Two years previously, Burt had persuaded Naval Officer Grinnell to fill vacant posts by the merit system. Burt administered one of the first competitive examinations in the United States civil service on March 3, 1871; the very day Congress approved the civil service rider. Grinnell's dismissal, however, cut short these early examinations. Burt's 1873 report maintained that customhouse examinations under the new rules tested "not mere book learning but capacity to do work applied for" and showed that the six-month probationary period worked well as a final test. The new system was "not visionary." [28]

The competitive system also benefited the Treasury Department in Washington, where, for example, an examination was held in March, 1873, to select forty first-class clerks. E. O. Graves, the department's chief clerk, administered to 565 candidates, including thirty-five or forty women, nine separate six-hour examinations "conducted with great thoroughness" and "with entire impartiality." During the preceding ten months, twenty-eight examinations were held in the Treasury Department. Three-fourths of these examinations tested employees trying for promotion, while one-fourth tested candidates for admission. The questions dealt with arithmetic, history, government, geography, spelling, and English. The over-all

---

[28] "The Civil Service Experiment," *New York Times,* March 27, 1873, p. 4, cc. 2–3; "Report of the Treasury Examining Board," *ibid.,* March 20, 1873, p. 5, c. 2. Burt's report is reprinted in "Civil Service Reform: Its Working in the Custom-House—Report From an Official Engaged in Applying the Rules," *ibid.,* March 24, 1873, p. 8, cc. 1–2. For editorial comments, see *ibid.,* p. 4, cc. 1–2.

effect of these examinations was considered "highly encouraging." [29]

Curtis' resignation foreshadowed modification of the civil service
rules. On May 24, 1873, the Cabinet and the commission fully and
frankly exchanged views and decided that government employees
should be more evenly apportioned among the states and that examinations should take cognizance of fitness for special duties. Although the commission was confident of administration support,
Congress was hostile. With the election safely behind, congressmen
not only failed to enact the rules but also refused to give the commission additional funds. Only a last-minute amendment saved the
residue of funds appropriated before the election of 1872 for the
commission's future use.[30]

New civil service rules were suggested by the commission in June
and were made effective on August 5. Among other things, these
rules abolished personal solicitation, required that all recommendations to office (including those of congressmen) be made in writing,
forbade removal merely to make way for another, allowed examination of applicants for anticipated vacancies, and provided for
geographical distribution of offices by dividing the country into five
examination districts where semi-annual examinations were to be
given. The *Nation,* despite its anti-administration bent, found the
proposed regulations "useful, and calculated to give greater strength
and sincerity to the reform." The new rules, however, did not impress the fall party-conventions of 1873. "Last year," lamented
Curtis, "every Republican State Convention uttered a sonorous note
upon the necesssity of reform, and the National Convention gave no
uncertain sound. This year not one Convention, except that of last
week in Massachusetts, has alluded to the subject." [31]

Curtis was more aggressive when he returned to his editorial work
after six months of rest. Snubbed by the administration and unable
to realize his political ambitions,[32] he attacked Grant's civil service

---

[29] "Washington: Special Dispatch to the New-York Times: Civil Service Examinations," *ibid.,* March 27, 1873, p. 1, c. 3; "The Civil Service Experiment," *ibid.,*
p. 4, cc. 2–3.

[30] *Ibid.,* May 26, 1873, p. 1, c. 6; *Congressional Globe,* 42 Cong., 3 sess., 2036–37.

[31] "Civil Service Reform," I, 152, Elliott Papers; *Nation,* XVI, No. 417 (June 26,
1873), 425; "The New York Convention," *Harper's Weekly,* XVII, No. 874 (September 27, 1873), 843.

[32] Curtis veiled his political ambitions carefully, but an occasional remark like
the one that he had "less and less inclination to position" reveals that he was
politically ambitious. Curtis to Norton, Ashfield, September 6, 1872, Curtis Papers.

policy with especial vigor. Curtis relished his new independence and was proud when the anti-administration *Springfield Republican* called one of his articles "another Bomb Shell." He exploded in an editorial that "public disbelief of the reality and thoroughness of the reform" was not surprising. "The President forbids political assessments upon subordinates, and issues an executive order virtually reproving the political officiousness of officers of the service. But, in total contempt of his orders, they levy assessments, desert their posts of duty, assume the management of all party assemblies, and continue to use patronage as a party lever." Grant could have inspired confidence in his administration, Curtis contended, if he had fired his corrupt brother-in-law who was collector of New Orleans, dismissed the postmaster at St. Louis for levying political assessments, filled New York Customhouse posts in keeping with the spirit of the rules, and required civil servants to attend to their duties instead of their party's needs. "Until these things are done, constantly and consistently done," Curtis concluded, "the work of the Commission, faithful, able, and devoted as we know it to be, will be in vain, and the Republican party will have no right to claim that it has really reformed the civil service." [33]

The *New York Times* disagreed with Curtis. Although wishing that reform had progressed further, it stated that Grant "has done more for the reform than all other Presidents since John Adams" and contended that the rules were a complete success where applied —in the Treasury Department, for example, only one out of 115 probationary appointees had been dropped.[34]

Nevertheless, Curtis and other reformers interpreted Republican losses in the election of 1873 as a "rebuke" to Republican "recklessness." Signs of this recklessness enumerated and exaggerated by Curtis included the Salary Grab Act (which made a 50 per cent increase in congressmen's compensation retroactive for two years), unfit nominations, and "Contemptuous violations of the spirit and the letter of the civil service rules." Although the Salary Grab Act was a potent issue, it is doubtful if civil service reform greatly affected the off-year election; in the eyes of average citizens, the reform was already in operation. The absence of Grant's long

---

[33] Curtis to Norton, Ashfield, September 19, 1873, *ibid;* "The Prospects of Civil Service Reform," *Harper's Weekly,* XVII, No. 878 (October 25, 1873), 938.

[34] "The Prospects of Civil Service Reform," *New York Times,* October 28, 1873, p. 4, c. 3; "The Civil Service—Complete Success of the System so Far as Tried," *ibid.,* November 10, 1873, p. 5, c. 4.

coattails to ride on, local issues, and the beginning of the panic of 1873 probably affected many more votes than did civil service reform. As the panic spread, the public forgot civil service reform. The rise of inflationist sentiment forced even reformers—weak though they were—to devote their energies primarily to preserving sound money.[35]

A conspicuous reason for reformers' lack of strength was their lack of unity. Charles Francis Adams, Jr., was determined to get reformers together to work out a plan of action. In March, 1873, after consulting Schurz and Godkin, Adams suggested that the celebration of the *Nation*'s newly achieved circulation of 10,000 might be made, after the European fashion, the occasion for a political demonstration. Using this method "would give us a reason for meeting, and we could lay down the faith without undertaking to form a party." Godkin, however, did not wish to hold the "conciliabulum" before the fall. "We must," he insisted, "let Grant's *new* Administration show itself, & the Civil Service 'reform' work itself out a little more, before showing ourselves." [36] Yet the fall came and the proposed demonstration did not come off.

Undaunted, Adams attempted in November and December of 1873 to organize another consultation and public demonstration. "We cannot sit still and grumble," he wrote, "we must go forward to the country with something positive, or give up any pretense of directing public opinion." The demonstration, Adams felt, was especially needed to strengthen Schurz's position in the impending struggle against inflation. Adams asked David A. Wells to *"very quietly"* sound out a few of his friends. "We must not," Adams insisted, "have a town meeting for *discussion;*—not more than 8 or a dozen. That part must be very quiet & private. To the public demonstration we can let in all *except the political bummers;* every man of the stripe who ruined us at Cincinnati must be rigorously excluded." [37]

Difficulties soon arose to hamper plans for united action. Re-

---

[35] "The Lesson of the Autumn," *Harper's Weekly,* XVII, No. 881 (November 15, 1873), 110. Reformers' correspondence in the next few years showed very little interest in civil service reform and great concern over inflation. The Schurz Papers in 1874 particularly bear out this generalization.

[36] Adams to Schurz, Boston, March 17 and 25, 1873, and Godkin to Schurz, New York, March 26, 1873, Schurz Papers.

[37] Adams to Schurz, Boston, November 13, 1873, *ibid.;* Adams to Wells, Quincy, November 13, 1873, and Boston, December 1, 1873, Wells Papers, New York Public Library.

formers still clung to their old differences. Godkin and Horace
White were especially at odds. On top of their old quarrel growing
out of the campaign of 1872, they had newly disagreed over Granger
attempts to regulate railroads, with which White was so taken that
he had no time for other activities. Godkin seemed no more interested in the reformers' meeting than White. He would not alter
his plans requiring his absence from New York at the appointed
time. This turn of events forced Adams and Schurz to abandon the
meeting since one of its prime objectives was to end "bickering"
between Godkin and White. "Lack of concentration," Adams complained, "is now paralyzing our action." Reformers in 1874 continued traveling the diverse roads they had commenced during the
campaign of 1872, while Congress continued to starve the Civil
Service Commission.[38]

III

Grant's annual message of December, 1873, suggested forming a
special committee to help the Civil Service Commission devise en-
forceable rules. The House responded by organizing a committee
whose members the *Nation* described as "experienced whitewashers
who have already given ample proof of their proficiency in the
business." The *New York Times* defended the committee against
such "unmerited abuse" and asserted that a majority of its members
favored reform. Yet a civil service committee which had Ben Butler
as its leading figure and did not have the House's outstanding reform champion, James A. Garfield, as a member could hardly be
considered favorable to reform.[39]

The Forty-third Congress soon took other steps against reform.
Representative James S. Smart, a New York Republican, introduced
a bill designed to shelve the commission by requiring congressmen
to select civil service officers. Despite its appeal to the spoilsmen,
nothing came of this bill or a similar one introduced in the Senate.
But the House unanimously joined Ben Butler's attempt to cripple
the competitive system with a joint resolution giving preference to
disabled veterans and their dependents. A year elapsed, however,
before the Senate passed the resolution.[40]

---

[38] Adams to Schurz, Quincy, December 22, 1873, and Schurz to Adams, Washington, December 25, 1873, Schurz Papers.

[39] Richardson, *op. cit.*, VII, 255; "The Organization of Congress," *Nation*, XVII,
No. 441 (December 11, 1873), 383; *New York Times,* December 15, 1873, p. 4, c. 1.

[40] *Congressional Record,* 43 Cong., 1 sess., 766; "The Enemies of Civil Service

Under Eaton, the commission remained on excellent terms with Grant and proved ready both to conciliate Congress and to further reform with rule changes. Like Curtis, Eaton attempted to shield the President from the blows of impatient reformers. A thorough student of civil service reform who in 1874 corresponded with the English reformer John Bright on the subject, Eaton denounced certain rules as "incapable of execution, through faulty drawing," and freed the President "from all blame" for departing from them. Eaton particularly wished to amend the rules so that they would not apply to collectors and surveyors of ports. Although competition had not been extended to these offices, the Executive was required to fill vacated positions with subordinates whenever possible. This task was difficult since senatorial confirmation was required. It was over a departure from these rules that Curtis had resigned. Eaton later wrote, "the extension of rules in any form, in the first experiment to that class of officers, was at least of doubtful expediency." [41]

Eaton officially reported his criticisms of the rules to Grant, and at the same time wrote Curtis a conciliatory letter reminding him that their objectives were the same. Eaton's report, stressing the general success of the rules and the fact that both the President and his Cabinet favored them, was ridiculed for its frequent "exhortations" to "stand by" Grant and "not to lose faith in the soldier-statesman." The *Nation* concluded that "so far as the minor offices are concerned, the President and the heads of departments are really in favor of the reform, because it takes disagreeable work off their hands; while as to the more important offices, they are almost openly hostile to the spirit of the innovation, because it takes power away from them." Despite criticism from ardent reformers, the commissioners strategically retreated to a more defensible position which nearly all reformers would eventually occupy. [42]

Earlier congressional hostility appeared moderate when compared to the hostility aroused by the commission's annual struggle for an appropriation. Eaton feared that Grant's recent "decisive veto . . .

Reform," *New York Times*, February 28, 1874, p. 6, c. 3; "Members of Congress Appropriating Appointments," *ibid.*, May 7, 1874, p. 2, c. 5; "General Butler's Flank Attack," *Harper's Weekly*, XVIII, No. 896 (February 28, 1874), 190; *Congressional Record*, 43 Cong., 2 sess., 1521–23.

[41] Norton to Curtis, Cambridge, February 14, 1874, Norton Papers; Eaton, *op. cit.*, p. 14; Eaton to John Bright, Washington, May 21, 1874, Bright Papers, British Museum.

[42] Eaton to Curtis, Washington, April 16, 1874, Curtis Papers; *Nation*, XVIII, No. 460 (April 23, 1874), 260.

of the inflation scheme [designed to legalize a circulation increase
of $100,000,000] may call down retaliatory votes" on the commis-
sion's appropriation since the most zealous opponents of inflation
were the most zealous champions of civil service reform. The *New
York Times* insisted that a small appropriation "is absolutely necessary, and it cannot be refused unless Congress has made up its mind
to kill the reform outright." Inflationist Ben Butler had made up
his mind and knew that Congress would concur. When in June,
1874, Representative Stephen W. Kellogg, a Connecticut Republican
and chairman of the civil service committee, moved to appropriate
$25,000 for the commission, his motion was defeated 108 to 48.
The defeat of Kellogg's motion was not sufficient to satisfy Butler,
who moved to bring back into the Treasury the unspent balance of
funds previously appropriated for the commission. John A. Kasson
(who ironically would have charge of the Pendleton bill nine years
later) successfully sponsored an amendment to Butler's motion that
repealed the legislation creating the commission, although it stipulated that department heads were to retain rules stressing competence. The Senate, less hostile to civil service reform than the House,
actually appropriated $15,000 for the commission, but the House
refused to concur. The conference committee compromised by striking out both the Senate and House amendments leaving the commission intact but without additional funds.[43]

Despite their general disapproval of the Forty-third Congress,
civil service reformers applauded when it ended the moiety system.
This system divided forfeited property—not merely the duty in
question, but the entire consignment—among the government; the
informer; and the collector, naval officer, and surveyor of the port.
Moieties and perquisites of the three chief officers in the New York
Customhouse were estimated in 1872 at $50,000 annually—a sizable
sum when one considers that the President earned only half that
amount.[44] These officers contributed heavily to their party's treasury,
and for this reason were of great political significance as well as
for their control over lesser posts and political assessments.

Although the moiety system had been under periodic attack for

---

[43] Eaton to John Bright, Washington, May 21, 1874, Bright Papers; *New York
Times,* May 18, 1874, p. 4, c. 1; *Congressional Record,* 43 Cong., 1 sess., 4888–89,
4919, 4974–76, 4997.

[44] *Congressional Globe,* 42 Cong., 2 sess., 2558. The President's salary was soon
raised to $50,000 by the Salary Grab Act.

twenty years, it did not come under heavy fire until the exposure
and publication of the Phelps, Dodge case in early 1873. A disgruntled clerk, who had been fired for dishonesty, accused Phelps,
Dodge and Company of making certain undervaluations in shipments. A special Treasury agent investigated this charge (aided by
broad powers enabling him to search the company's books) and
concluded—or at least alleged—that it was true. According to law,
the whole shipment had to be forfeited. The undervaluations were
made on items in shipments totaling $1,750,000. The value of the
property on the invoices was $271,017. The undervaluation itself
came to $6,000, and the duties the company avoided paying
amounted to about $2,000. Phelps, Dodge and Company settled out
of court for $271,017. Merchants and reformers thought "knavish
politicians" searching for personal and party funds were at the bottom of the case. They complained that seizures of books and papers
were outrageous and that the moiety system drove Treasury agents
to excess. Attempts were made in Boston and in New York to repeat the Phelps, Dodge success. So great was the reaction that in
January, 1874, even Ben Butler, who probably shared in the moieties
from Phelps, Dodge and Company, introduced a bill to end the
moiety system.[45]

By June, 1874, a bill abolishing the moiety system and placing
restrictions upon the right of search became law. Although the bill
raised the official salaries of collectors, those in the larger ports,
particularly in New York, suffered a decline in income. New York
Collector Chester A. Arthur's salary dropped from approximately
$56,000 a year to $12,000. The office of collector was no longer the
political plum it had once been.[46] The ending of the moiety system—a significant step toward civil service reform—was achieved
largely through pressure applied by those reformers who were merchants. This important group of reformers had very practical reasons for supporting reform. They had constant contacts with custom-

---

[45] Richard Lowitt, *A Merchant Prince of the Nineteenth Century* (New York,
1954), pp. 275–283. See also an indignant but excellent article, "The Extraordinary
Element in the Case of Phelps, Dodge & Co.," *Nation*, XVI, No. 409 (May 1, 1873),
297–299. For other pertinent material, see *ibid.*, No. 408 (April 24, 1873), 278; *ibid.*,
XVII, No. 426 (August 28, 1873), 138; "Public Opinion and Treasury Seizures,"
ibid., XVIII, No. 445 (January 8, 1874), 21–22.

[46] See William J. Hartman, "Politics and Patronage" (Columbia University, 1952),
pp. 186–191, and Leonard D. White, *The Republican Era, 1869–1901* (New York,
1958), pp. 123–126, for excellent short discussions on the ending of moieties.

house employees, and reform would enable their businesses to function more smoothly.

While the moiety system was being killed, Grant's Civil Service Commission was falling upon bad times. Soon after the commission's rules were instituted in the New York Customhouse, they were ignored. Arthur barred Silas W. Burt, chairman of the supervisory board, from examinations given by the collector's office. Six years later, when Burt gained access to examination records, he discovered that applicants were limited to those Arthur wanted appointed. Arthur was not the only official breaking the rules. By 1874, administration of the merit system was unsatisfactory.[47]

Although its rules were flouted and the commission received no appropriation, it staged a brief rally in 1874. Rules for appointing and promoting lighthouse keepers were submitted to Grant in May and were later promulgated. In early April, E. O. Graves, the Treasury Department's chief examiner, logically arranged the sixty rules then in effect, and on May 28 the commission resolved to extend the New York rules to all the principal customhouses in spite of Eaton's objection that Congress should first appropriate funds to the commission. In September, Grant responded by extending the rules to federal offices in Boston. Paradoxically, Boston's collector was Butler's henchman, W. A. Simmons, who had recently been nominated and confirmed despite reformers' angry protests. This extension of the rules marked the last advance under the Grant commission.[48]

Shortly after rules were extended to Boston, the Republican party suffered defeat in the election of 1874. The Democrats won a major-

---

[47] Arthur was in the class ahead of Burt at Union College. Silas W. Burt, "Writings: Civil Service Reform 1886–1900" (Binder's title of a 158 page manuscript sketch of Arthur's political career), p. 76, also a memorandum in Burt's writing on the back of an envelope laid in the above. Burt Writings, New York Public Library; Eaton, *op. cit.*, p. 30.

[48] "Minutes of the Civil Service Commission," May 28, 1874, II, 49, 53–55, Library of the United States Civil Service Commission; Eaton, *op. cit.*, p. 30; "Civil Service Reform," I, 164, 231, Elliott Papers. Curiously Eaton's draft of the Boston order did not reach Grant the first time he mailed it. "I cannot understand how it could have miscarried nor where it is!" complained Eaton. "But Babcock [Grant's corrupt private secretary] says it never arrived." Eaton to E. B. Elliott, New York, September 7, 1874, *ibid.*, I, 233. On Simmons, see, for example, "What Are They Going to Do About It?," *Nation*, XVIII, No. 453 (March 5, 1874), 150–151; "The Boston Collectorship," *Harper's Weekly*, XVIII, No. 897 (March 7, 1874), 210. Simmons, however, agreed to give the regulations a fair trial. "Civil Service Reform in Boston," *New York Times*, November 3, 1874, p. 5, c. 1.

ity of seventy votes in the House and the Republican senatorial majority was reduced to a narrow margin. Reasons for the Republican defeat were apparent. Apart from the usual mid-term reaction, there were dislocations and hardships following the panic of 1873, which were matched by a series of corrupt and extravagant blunders. The Salary Grab Act, the Sanborn contract, and Boss Shepherd's activities in the District of Columbia led to revulsion against everything Republican.[49]

Although Grant's annual message in December, 1874, once again endorsed the civil service reform regulations, it stressed the impracticability of maintaining them without congressional support. Grant further threatened to abandon competitive examinations if Congress failed to act. And the lameduck session of the Forty-third Congress was only too glad to kill civil service reform through inaction. No appropriation was made, and on March 9, 1875, competitive examinations were discontinued. In addition, a congressional act providing that future Treasury Department appointments be apportioned according to population of the states went into effect.[50] Congressmen, having killed civil service reform, gave the spoils system new life by increasing their own influence in the selection of civil servants.

Grant's reasons for abandoning civil service reform are not clear. Despite its controversial nature, Grant had supported the commission thus far and had been especially lavish with his support after election defeats and before election victories. Perhaps the realization that he would not be running again, coupled with mounting official cares, made the whole experiment seem futile to him. The old military hero may have tired of his fight with Congress and found it less trying to revert to practices advocated by his friends and advisers. Moreover Grant's espousal of the commission was probably tempered by his belief that the President should follow the dictates of Congress and the people.[51] He may well have interpreted congressional refusals to appropriate funds as a mandate to drop reform. Whatever his reasons and the logic involved, reformers knew Grant had surrendered.

The individual best qualified to evaluate Grant's relation to civil

---

[49] Oberholtzer, op. cit., III, 137–143.

[50] Benjamin H. Bristow to Charles Lyman, Washington, March 9, 1875, in "Civil Service Reform," I, 251, Elliott Papers.

[51] Consult Hesseltine, op. cit., p. 159, on Grant's concept of the presidency.

service reform was Dorman B. Eaton, who did so in an address to the American Social Science Association two months after the experiment had ended. Although Eaton primarily blamed Congress and party managers for the "disaster," he charged Grant with partial responsibility. "To accomplish such a reform, he needed the zeal, the self denial, and the persistency of the true reformer," and these things Grant did not have. Unfortunately, Grant's "unenthusiastic nature failed to give the impression of his real earnestness in the cause . . . he never took it up with that stern resolution which its magnitude . . . demanded" and as a consequence "public confidence was withdrawn." For the past year, Grant was believed to be "wavering," and the administration of the rules was "of course, unsatisfactory." Nevertheless, continued Eaton, Grant "is entitled to justice, which will award him no small praise. He was the first President who had the moral courage and the disinterestedness to attempt the overthrow of the spoils system, and he was the last of the great forces of his party to leave the field." Grant "nobly withstood" most of the "pressure, the fatiguing solicitations, and the partisan menace" which he was subjected to. Although Eaton felt a "surrender" better than a "feeble existence of the rules, which would only bring, upon the reform and the President, public contempt," he also lamented that "history . . . must adjudge this so-called abandonment to have been a needless and unjustifiable surrender." [52]

---

[52] Eaton, *op. cit.,* pp. 27–31.

VIII

HAYES'S CAUTIOUS ADVANCE

The civil service reform movement reached its nadir in 1875. Reasons for its decline are evident. Politicians opposed reform because they needed patronage in order to continue in politics. Among businessmen, merchants supported reform but the more dominant industrialists still found it more rewarding to secure special favors from politicians than to increase the efficiency of the government service. Even passage of the reform rider led to the decline of the movement because its objective was apparently realized. The Grant commission, attempting too much in theory and accomplishing very little in practice, convinced many that reform had failed after a fair trial. The greatest factor in the decline of the early civil service reform movement, however, was the election of 1872. It split into three hostile factions the intellectuals who had become the mainspring of the movement. Still disorganized, divided, and bickering in 1875, reformers would have to compose their differences before effective agitation could again commence.

I

Grant's last two years in office were disastrous. Numerous earlier scandals in his administration were eclipsed when Secretary of the Treasury Benjamin H. Bristow uncovered a whisky ring which had defrauded the government of millions. Grant, who cried "Let no guilty man escape," proceeded to put his friends before principle and carefully made certain that his implicated private secretary, Orville E. Babcock, received no punishment. In 1876 when Bristow discovered that Secretary of War William Worth Belknap had sold Indian-post traderships, Grant accepted Belknap's resignation "with regret" and frustrated congressional plans for his impeachment.

Bristow, in turn, was plagued for discovering corruption and made so uncomfortable that he resigned in June, 1876.[1]

Grant's unconditional surrender to the enemies of civil service reform signalized the complete return to spoils practices. The abandonment of reform was illustrated in the fall of 1875 when Zachariah Chandler was appointed Secretary of the Interior. The selection of spoils-minded Chandler to clean up that department, especially the corrupt Indian Bureau, was ironic since he was largely responsible for reformer Jacob D. Cox's resignation from the same position five years previously. The *Nation* commented that the selection of Chandler for Cox's old position indicated "that the President has important work for him to do, and knows that he is the man to do it. Mr. George W. Curtis and civil-service reform will not serve his purpose this time, so he is going to try 'Old Zach.' and civil-service corruption." "Old Zach" did not keep reformers waiting. He regarded refusal to pay political assessments as "an offence against the Government" and a few weeks after taking office dismissed the experienced chief clerk of the Patent Office for refusing to pay an assessment.[2]

The triumph of spoilsmen led reformers to organize. When in February, 1875, Henry Adams called for a "consultation," his appeal won the cooperation of Godkin, Schurz, and Cox. A dinner honoring Schurz on his retirement from the Senate provided a suitable occasion for an "entirely informal and confidential" gathering. Cox wrote, "Let us strive to avoid the rock we split on before. We want a union of men who think alike on essential doctrines of finance, economy, & civil service reform, for the sake of infusing honesty into our political action; & for the same reason we want to avoid the union of incongruous elements for the purpose of an illusive success—I know you feel as I do, & regret the unhappy course things took in '72—Please God we shall do better next time." [3]

The reform demonstration occurred on April 27, 1875, and did

---

[1] Allan Nevins, *Hamilton Fish* (New York, 1937), pp. 762–837, covers the dismal last days of the Grant administration.

[2] *Nation* (New York), XXI, No. 539 (October 28, 1875), 269; *ibid.*, No. 543 (November 25, 1875), 331. The chief clerk was given the same treatment as were government employees dismissed for bad conduct: he was neither allowed to resign nor given the customary month's leave of absence.

[3] Jacob D. Cox to Carl Schurz, Toledo, February 23, 1875, and Schurz to Francis A. Walker, Washington, March 4, 1875, Schurz Papers, Library of Congress.

much to end the three years of indecision and division among reformers. The principal address made by William M. Evarts, the
presiding officer, expressed the hope and determination "that in
the next Presidential election the country shall not be forced to
choose 'the least of two evils,' " and also stated "profound indifference as to what party-name the candidate may bear, provided he be
fit for the office." [4]

Despite their April meeting, reformers were inactive during the
summer of 1875 even after Ohio Democrats renominated their incumbent governor, William Allen, on an inflationist platform. To
oppose Allen, the Republicans nominated Rutherford B. Hayes,
a sound money advocate. Henry and Charles Francis Adams, Jr.,
were not so complacent. To them, the significance of this election
clearly extended far beyond Ohio, for the success of the reform
movement, which stressed sound money as well as civil service reform, depended on Hayes's election. Reformers' scheme to hold the
balance of power demanded Hayes's victory.[5]

Although Schurz was not particularly alarmed over the situation
in late July, he later returned from Europe to campaign for Hayes.
Fully sensing the pivotal importance of the decision in Ohio, Henry
Adams predicted that his friends would "pretty surely control the
next presidential election" if Schurz were successful in swinging
the governorship to Hayes; but if Schurz were not, reformers would
be "smashed to flinders." Hayes won the election by 5,000 votes.
"Narrow enough," said Henry Adams, "but every man in that five
thousand is one of us. You will hear more of this next year. We will
play for high stakes and have nothing to lose. . . ." [6]

Equally heartening were other portents of the growing strength
of civil service reformers. The New York Republican Convention
of 1875 chose George William Curtis as its chairman and adopted
an anti–third-term resolution. Even the customhouse crowd gave
its support to "good" men in order to hold the party together. De-

---

[4] *Nation*, XX, No. 513 (April 29, 1875), 287.

[5] Adams to Charles Milnes Gaskell, Beverly Farms, Massachusetts, May 24, 1875,
in Harold Dean Cater, ed., *Henry Adams and His Friends* (Boston, 1947), p. 67;
Charles Francis Adams, Jr., to Schurz, Boston, June 28, 1875, Schurz Papers.

[6] Schurz to Charles Francis Adams, Jr., Thusis, Switzerland, July 22, 1875, in
Frederic Bancroft, ed., *Speeches, Correspondence and Political Papers of Carl
Schurz* (New York, 1913), III, 160; Adams to Gaskell, Beverly Farms, October 4
and 15, 1875, in Worthington Chauncey Ford, ed., *Letters of Henry Adams (1858–
1891)* (Boston, 1930), p. 272.

claring that the obvious reason for this rare "self-sacrifice" was the
Democratic victory in 1874, the *Nation* predicted that Republican
gestures toward reform would be too late to prevent their defeat in
New York. This prophesy was given added weight when the Democratic Convention nominated Samuel Jones Tilden for governor on
what reformers considered an excellent platform. Tilden was popular among reform agitators for assaulting Boss Tweed and the corrupt New York canal ring. Reformers were elated to be wooed by
both parties in New York State. So encouraged were Schurz and a
few colleagues by this shift that they secretly pushed their plans to
induce both parties to nominate Charles Francis Adams, Sr., for
the presidency. The name Adams, it was maintained, would be a
special asset during the centennial-year campaign of 1876. Reformers held their heads higher as the year 1875 drew to a close. They
had achieved unity among themselves, the Ohio election seemed to
indicate that they would hold the balance of power between Republicans and Democrats in 1876, and chances looked good for the
revival of their major objective—civil service reform. Horace White
spoke for all reformers when he said, "Unless we can reform the
Civil Service the country will go to the dogs." [7]

As the centennial year 1876 opened, Adams was no longer the
sole reform candidate. The "personal magnetism" of James G.
Blaine, the popular Republican leader from Maine, had captivated
certain reformers, but the candidate making the heaviest inroad
among Adams' supporters was Benjamin H. Bristow. Support for
Bristow's nomination continued to grow. Henry Adams even medi-
tated purchasing the New York *Evening Post* as an organ for Bristow
if he were nominated and Adams had Schurz slated as editor. Bristow
was popular not only among reformers but also in the party at
large. When Curtis asked the efficient Postmaster General Marshall
Jewell "whom the party—not the managers—would make the candidate . . . he answered instantly, Bristow." Efficiency and Bristow
proved too much—Jewell did not last out the summer in office.

[7] *Nation*, XXI, No. 533 (September 16, 1875), 173; *ibid.*, No. 534 (September
23, 1875), 189; Schurz to William Grosvenor, Thusis, July 16, 1875, and Schurz
to Charles Francis Adams, Jr., Thusis, July 22, 1875, in Bancroft, *op. cit.*, III,
156, 159; Schurz to Samuel Bowles, Boston, November 23, 1875, Henry Cabot
Lodge to Schurz, Boston, December 13, 1875, Schurz to Lodge, New York, December 25, 1875, and White to Schurz, no place, December 28, 1875, Schurz Papers.

Party regulars shed no tears over his removal. "Why, God damn him!" said one, "he ran the Post-Office as though it was a factory." [8]

The Fifth Avenue Hotel conference of reformers, held in New York on May 15, indicated their strength. It was "not confined to the Liberals of 1872," Schurz explained, and contained many "Republicans in good standing." He emphasized that it did not plan to make independent nominations before the Republican Convention and that it would remain friendly toward the party if reformers were nominated. Nearly all invited easterners were present, and many westerners, kept away by distance, sent "warm letters of adhesion." Prominent in attendance were what the *Nation* called the " 'moral element' . . . ministers, professors, and respectable persons who do not believe politics should be pursued as a trade." Speeches were short and stressed that "most of the prevailing abuses" had their roots in the condition of the civil service. The conference adopted a platform written by Schurz, which stated that two great questions must be settled in the centennial election—sound currency and civil service reform—and suggested that reforming candidates were needed rather than empty platform promises. Although the conference nominated no one, it enumerated presidential qualifications which would eliminate both those who opposed reform outright and those middle-of-the-road individuals who would alienate neither the "good" nor the "bad." It also warned Republicans that independent action could be expected if a reform candidate were not nominated.[9]

Pressure for reform and Bristow continued to mount within the Republican party organization after the New York conference. This pressure was apparent when Roscoe Conkling, a leading machine candidate for the nomination, failed to secure unanimous support from his own New York delegation. "Bristow Clubs" were founded

---

[8] Schurz to Bowles, New York, January 4, 1876, and Schurz to B. B. Cahoon, New York, March 3, 1876, in Bancroft, *op. cit.*, III, 218, 223; Henry Adams to Schurz, Boston, February 14, 1876, and no place, March 6, 1876, and Adams to Lodge, Boston, February 20, 1876, in Ford, *op. cit.*, pp. 273–277, 279; George William Curtis to Charles Eliot Norton, West New Brighton, New York, February 28, 1876, Curtis Papers, Harvard University; *Nation*, XXIII, No. 577 (July 20, 1876), 33.

[9] Schurz to L. A. Sherman, New York, April 15, 1876, in Bancroft, *op. cit.*, III, 230–231; *Nation*, XXII, No. 568 (May 18, 1876), 313. The "Address to the People" can be found in Bancroft, *op. cit.*, III, 240–248.

in Boston and Cincinnati, and a "Reform Club" was organized in New York by the "better part" of the Union League Club with Dorman B. Eaton as one of the leaders. The New York club demanded resumption of specie payments, civil service reform, retrenchment, and set forth qualifications for nominees that eliminated all serious contenders except Bristow. In June, a few days before the Republican Convention, the *New York Times* printed and supported a letter from Eaton urging a strong civil service reform plank as well as a reform candidate.[10]

When the Republican Convention met in Cincinnati on June 14, everybody wondered who would be nominated. James G. Blaine was in the lead, but his chances had recently been damaged by publication of the "Mulligan letters" revealing use of his congressional position to further certain railroad interests. Bristow was popular with reformers, but politicians had no desire to reward him for unearthing corruption by placing him in a position where he could unearth more. Senators Conkling and Morton were too obnoxious to Republican reformers to gain general support. Of the favorite sons, Governor Hayes of Ohio, who had alienated neither machine politicians nor reformers, appeared the most formidable. As early as February he had taken care to convince reformers of his sound views on civil service reform, currency, and the South, and had continued corresponding with them. Hayes was nominated over Blaine on the seventh ballot on a platform containing an innocuous civil service reform plank.[11]

Hayes's nomination was generally satisfactory to reformers, despite the Fifth Avenue conference's stated opposition to a middle-of-the-road individual. Schurz, the leading spirit of that conference, was pleased with Hayes and worked for his election. The meeting of the conference's executive committee called on June 30 to consider nominations of both parties took no further action. "The nomination has been well received," Hayes wrote in his diary. "The best people, many of them heretofore dissatisfied with the Republican

---

[10] *Nation*, XXII, No. 561 (March 30, 1876), 201; *ibid.*, No. 566 (May 4, 1876), 286; Eaton to Curtis, [New York], May 13, [1876], Curtis Papers; *New York Times*, June 7, 1876, p. 4, cc. 1–3, p. 6, c. 2; *ibid.*, June 10, 1876, p. 4, cc. 4–7.

[11] Frederic Bancroft and William A. Dunning, eds., *The Reminiscences of Carl Schurz* (New York, 1907–08), III, 368; Charles Richard Williams, *The Life of Rutherford Birchard Hayes* (Columbus, 1928), I, 434. For details of the Republican Convention of 1876, see Ellis Paxson Oberholtzer, *A History of the United States Since the Civil War* (New York, 1917–37), III, 263–269.

party, are especially hearty in my support. I must make it my constant effort to deserve this confidence." [12]

Prominent among the few reformers unhappy over Hayes's victory was Henry Adams. "We organized our party," he wrote, "and as usual have been beaten. After our utmost efforts we have only succeeded in barring the road to our opponents and forcing them to nominate as candidate for the Presidency one Hayes of Ohio, a third rate nonentity, whose only recommendation is that he is obnoxious to no one." [13] Three months later Adams still retained his views but placed the blame for the failure of the "Independent party" squarely on Schurz's shoulders. "Console yourself about politics," he wrote Henry Cabot Lodge. "You are indeed the one who has the best right to complain, for you had the most trouble in forming that rope of sand, the Independent party. I cannot help laughing to think how, after all our labor and after we had by main force created a party for Schurz to lead, he himself, without a word or a single effort to keep his party together, kicked us over in his haste to jump back to the Republicans. . . . I hope he will get his Cabinet office, and I hope he will forget that we ever worked to make him our leader, independent of party. He can hereafter buy power only by devotion to party, and further connection with us would not help us and would be fatal to him." Discouraged with the results of his Independent party and "satisfied that literature offers higher prizes than politics," Adams buried himself in the study of America's past.[14]

II

After Hayes's nomination, attention was centered on the Democratic National Convention at St. Louis. Despite reformers' long aversion to the Democratic party, it possessed certain elements of attraction in 1876. While the reformers' own party had been blackened by

---

[12] Schurz to Parke Godwin, New York, June 20, 1876, Bryant-Godwin Collection, New York Public Library; Williams, *Life of Hayes*, I, 456.

[13] Adams to Gaskell, Beverly Farms, June 14, 1876, in Ford, *op. cit.*, p. 288. Either the date of this letter is wrong or Adams completed the letter a few days after starting it. Hayes was nominated on June 16. The *Nation* was not enthusiastic about Hayes's nomination either. *Nation*, XXII, No. 573 (June 22, 1876), 390.

[14] Adams to Lodge, Beverly Farms, September 4, 1876, Adams to Gaskell, New York, April 14, 1877, and Washington, November 25, 1877, in Ford, *op. cit.*, pp. 299, 300, 302.

the last years of Grant's regime, certain Democrats were beginning
to sense the need for political reform. Senator John B. Gordon of
Georgia, influenced by the whisky frauds, delivered a strong speech
in March, 1876, demanding tenure during good behavior in the internal revenue service. Gordon wrote Manton Marble, editor of
the Democratic New York *World*, "I insist that no party should be
permitted to secure its continuance in power by such fatal tamper-
ing with our rev. agents. This is the paramount idea in my speech
& the Dem. party can well afford to stand upon such an issue &
forego the patronage which brings & will forever bring such dis-
repute upon our Republican Institutions. . . . Let us . . . convince the country that we mean *real reform*." [15] Gordon's espousal
of reform was understandable, for southern Democrats favored civil
service reform more when out of power during the Reconstruction
period than after it.[16] Reformers were additionally pleased when
the Democratic National Convention at St. Louis nominated Tilden,
their party's most conspicuous reformer.

After Tilden's nomination, reformers demanded a "frank and
vigorous pledge" from Hayes on civil service and currency reform.
Many practical politicians also recognized the power of the independent vote. "As to Civil Service Reform," Senator John Sherman
of Ohio wrote Hayes, "you cannot be too strong & clear." The legislation that created the Civil Service Commission, Sherman added,
"clearly declares the policy and your hearty approval of that policy
is not only politic but clearly right." Garfield agreed. He wrote
Hayes, "I hope you will not fail to make a pointed allusion to the
reform of the Civil Service in your letter of acceptance. . . . All
classes of Republicans are looking for your letter with great anx-
iety. . . ." [17]

---

[15] *Congressional Record*, 44 Cong., 1 sess., 1579–81; Gordon to Marble, Washington, March 12, 1876, Marble Papers, Library of Congress. Although Gordon's
speech was praised by reformers, both the Republican *New York Times* and the
independent *Nation* noted that no other Democrats had endorsed the speech
"The Democrats and the Civil Service," *New York Times*, April 6, 1876, p. 4,
cc. 3–4; "The Democrats and the Government," *Nation*, XXII, No. 561 (March
30, 1876), 204.

[16] One gains this impression from reading the Schurz Papers. After Hayes
restored "home rule" and improved the quality of federal appointees located in
the South, southern ardor for civil service reform—never very warm—noticeably
cooled.

[17] Schurz to Hayes, Fort Washington, Pennsylvania, June 21, 1876, in Bancroft,
op. cit., III, 250–251; Curtis to Hayes, West New Brighton, June 22, 1876, Sher-

Hayes, too, felt that civil service reform was *"the* issue" of the campaign. He consulted with both Curtis and Schurz, and his letter of acceptance, dated July 8, reflected their views. It called for the abolition of the spoils system and for a "thorough, radical and complete" reform of the civil service. If elected, Hayes promised that partisanship would not be expected of officers and that their tenure would be secure if their work were satisfactory. As assurance that patronage would not be prostituted to secure a second term, he promised to serve but one.[18] "Such words," Hayes wrote Curtis, "as 'bold,' 'ringing,' etc. do not apply, perhaps, to what I have said, but I have tried to hit the nail on the head, and to hit it pretty hard. The two parts, I took thought about, were the Civil Service, and the South." [19]

Most reformers and Independents agreed that Hayes had "hit the nail on the head." Curtis was most enthusiastic. He wrote Hayes, "The tone and grasp of the letter are alike most striking, for they show unmistakably that it is not the work of a politician but of a very different person. It is this conviction that will carry the letter home to the hearts of Mr. Lincoln's 'plain people,' and assure them that your election will be their triumph." Garfield was no less enthusiastic. "All our friends who believe in good government are rejoiced, and look upon your letter as a great reinforcement of our strength." [20]

---

man to Hayes, Washington, June 26, 1876, and Garfield to Hayes, Washington, July 1, 1876, Hayes Papers, The Rutherford B. Hayes Library. Citations from the Hayes Papers were obtained from copies of original letters. See also *Nation,* XXII, No. 573 (June 22, 1876), 387.

[18] Hayes to Curtis, Columbus, June 27, 1876, and Curtis to Hayes, West New Brighton, June 30, 1876, Hayes Papers; Hayes to Schurz, Columbus, June 27, 1876, and Schurz to Hayes, St. Louis, July 5, 1876, in Bancroft, *op. cit.,* III, 254–256; Hayes to Edward McPherson, William A. Howard *et al.,* Columbus, July 8, 1876, in Williams, *op. cit.,* I, 460–461. Fearing that he had offended the President, Hayes wrote Grant that his rejection of a second term was not meant as a reflection on him. Hayes to Grant, Columbus, July 14, 1876, Grant Papers, The Rutherford B. Hayes Library. Not all reformers favored the one-term principle: the *Nation* opposed it on grounds that reform such as Hayes promised could not be established in four years and that Hayes would be just as badly needed in 1881 as in 1877. "The One-Term Guarantee," *Nation,* XXIII, No. 579 (August 3, 1876), 68.

[19] Hayes to Curtis, Columbus, July 10, 1876, Hayes Papers. Privately Hayes pledged that, if elected, reform would have a fair trial. Hayes to Richard Henry Dana, Jr., Columbus, July 11, 1876, *ibid.*

[20] Curtis to Hayes, Ashfield, Massachusetts, July 13, 1876, and Garfield to Hayes, Washington, July 11, 1876, *ibid.* See also Dana to Hayes, Boston, July 10, 1876, *ibid.*

With part of their number supporting Tilden reformers were again divided in a presidential election, but the bitterness that marked their split in 1872 was not present in 1876. Those supporting Tilden included Oswald Ottendorfer, Parke Godwin, John Bigelow, David A. Wells, Charles Francis Adams, Jr., and his brother Henry, who could not turn his back on the man who led him to "triumph" over the Erie ring. Other reformers roundly denied that Tilden was a reformer. "He has been too much of a demagogue," wrote Schurz, "and is too much of a wirepuller and machine politician now to be depended upon as a man of principle." Eaton also called Tilden's reform claim "preposterous." "Gov Tilden is a cold, hard, selfish man—an intense partisan having neither the spirit nor the courage of reform—save where it is popular." Yet, despite their differences, reformers could agree with Schurz that "the cleansing of Government service from those officers who had disgraced it— seems to me in any event secured." The *Nation* in discussing the relative merits of Hayes and Tilden said, "Nothing is more remarkable or more cheering . . . than the position they both take up with regard to the reform of the civil service." [21]

The effect of Hayes's letter promising reform was partially offset when Secretary of the Interior "Zach" Chandler was elected Republican National Committee chairman. To choose Chandler to lead Hayes's campaign for civil service reform was indeed shocking. The *Nation* described Chandler as one of the "most disreputable, coarse, and unscrupulous" exponents of the spoils system, who had been one of "Grant's inner council of advisers" so "largely responsible for the scandals of his Administration." After predicting that Chandler's election meant political assessments, Schurz urged Hayes to write a public letter to the National Committee opposing such a move and suggested that "no effort should be spared" to remove Chandler.[22]

[21] Adams to Lodge, Beverly Farms, June 30, 1876, in Ford, *op. cit.*, p. 293; Schurz to Charles Francis Adams, Jr., Fort Washington, July 9, 1876, and Schurz to Ottendorfer, Fort Washington, July 22, 1876, in Bancroft, *op. cit.*, III, 259 277; Eaton to John Sherman, Narragansett Pier, Rhode Island, July 29, 1876, Hayes Papers; "The Democratic Letters," *Nation*, XXIII, No. 580 (August 10, 1876), 84. Mark D. Hirsch, "Samuel J. Tilden: The Story of a Lost Opportunity," *American Historical Review* (Washington), LVI, No. 4 (July, 1951), 788–802, agrees with Schurz and Eaton.

[22] "Things for Mr. Hayes's Consideration," *Nation*, XXIII, No. 577 (July 20, 1876), 36; Schurz to Hayes, Fort Washington, July 14, 1876, in Bancroft, *op. cit.*, III, 260–261.

Chandler was not removed, civil servants were assessed, and Hayes did not publicly protest. Schurz repeatedly called Hayes's attention to the levying of "voluntary contributions" and urged that it be stopped. Hayes did nothing until Schurz threatened to throw up all his speaking engagements. This threat caused Hayes to write the secretary of the Republican National Committee, in a letter marked "private," "that if assessments are made as charged it is a plain departure from correct principles and ought not to be allowed. I trust the committee will have nothing to do with it." This "private" letter and a personal note from Hayes promising that if elected, political assessments would "go up, 'hook, line and sinker' " were the only answers to Schurz's demands. The secretary, who claimed to know nothing about the collecting of assessments, had already told Schurz "that probably Mr. Chandler, who scarcely ever shows his face here and does not otherwise trouble himself about the management of the campaign, makes those operations at Washington his special business." Schurz was obviously too heavily committed to Hayes to withdraw his support so late in the campaign; he kept his speaking appointments.[23]

As time progressed, it became obvious not only that civil service reform was not *"the* issue" of the campaign but also that Hayes no longer intended it to be. "WE MUST CHOOSE OUR OWN TOPICS," he wrote Garfield. *"The danger of giving the Rebels the Government,* is the topic people are most interested in. Next *Tilden* and after that *Schools—one term—*etc. etc." Civil service reform, if indeed the one-term idea could be considered a part of it, was relegated to a poor fourth place behind the anti-Catholic public school issue. This defection from reform was not a temporary aberration. Hayes later reiterated to Garfield that the "true issue" with the masses was "shall the late rebels have the government?" and even wrote to Schurz in a similar vein.[24]

Reformers, however, refused to "wave the bloody shirt." Schurz admitted that "to the 'plain people' who think that a Democratic

---

[23] Schurz to Hayes, Fort Washington, August 14, 1876, *ibid.,* III, 285–286; Schurz to Hayes, Fort Washington, September 3, 1876, and New York, September 5, 1876, Hayes Papers; Hayes to R. C. McCormick, Columbus, September 8, 1876, *ibid.;* Hayes to Schurz, Columbus, September 15, 1876, in Bancroft, *op. cit.,* III, 339.

[24] Hayes to Garfield, Columbus, August 6 and 12, 1876, Garfield Papers, Library of Congress. These quotations were taken from copies in the Hayes Library. Hayes to Schurz, Columbus, August 9, 1876, in Bancroft, *op. cit.,* III, 284–285.

victory would bring the Rebellion into power no other argument need be addressed. But there are vast numbers of Republicans or men who used to vote the Republican ticket who have lost their fear of the return of the Rebellion to power. They want a *change,*" Schurz concluded, a change in the direction of reform. Curtis begged Hayes to show "sympathy with the sincere reform element" of the Republican party in their intra-party struggle with spoilsmen. Hayes assured Curtis that stressing the rebellion issue "does not mean that we are indifferent to Reform" and mentioned as evidence that all six new candidates for Congress from Ohio were his *"intimate* personal friends" and were in agreement with him regarding reform.[25]

The slighting of reform drew comment. When George Frisbie Hoar, a Republican congressman from Massachusetts, made a strong civil service reform speech, it attracted the *Nation's* attention as "almost the only one of the kind we have had during the campaign from any active Republican politician." The *New York Times* pointed out that the fundamental nature of civil service reform entitled it to be one of the campaign's chief issues, and Charles Eliot Norton found in Cambridge "less & less faith that Hayes & Reform are synonymous." [26]

A large number of northerners voted for Tilden despite the "bloody shirt" campaign. Yet, even with a 250,000 majority in the country at large, he did not become President because Republican-controlled returning boards in South Carolina, Florida, and Louisiana gave those states to Hayes. Louisiana, whose returning board threw out 13,000 Tilden votes, was by far the most corrupt, yet Hayes after conversing with Sherman and Garfield, who had visited Louisiana, had "no doubt that we are justly and legally entitled to the Presidency." [27]

---

[25] Schurz to Hayes, Fort Washington, August 14, 1876, *ibid.,* III, 286–287; Curtis to Hayes, Ashfield, August 31, 1876, and Hayes to Curtis, Columbus, September 4, 1876, Hayes Papers. Among the six were Joseph Warren Keifer, who later as Speaker of the House distinguished himself by his strong opposition to reform, and William McKinley, who as President restored to the spoils system a large number of civil servants whom Cleveland had added to the classified list. *Infra,* pp. 224, 264.

[26] *Nation,* XXIII, No. 587 (September 28, 1876), 187; "The Fundamental Reform," *New York Times,* September 30, 1876, p. 4, cc. 2–3; Norton to Curtis, Cambridge, October 3, 1876, Norton Papers, Harvard University.

[27] Hayes to Schurz, Columbus, December 6, 1876, in Bancroft, *op. cit.,* III, 346; Oberholtzer, *op. cit.,* III, 281–287; Harry Barnard, *Rutherford B. Hayes and His America* (Indianapolis, 1954), pp. 316–335. Recent historical scholarship concedes

Reformers were not so easily reassured by Republican "visiting statesmen," and did not like Hayes's policy of drift. Schurz complained, "The doings of the Louisiana returning-board are, to say the least, suspicious." He concluded that Louisiana and similar states would have gone Republican in a fair election, but added "such an assumption, however justifiable, is after all no solution of the question." Schurz was not alone in his feelings; he had received many letters "especially from New England, full of apprehension." [28]

Hayes, nevertheless, continued to drift right into the presidency. An understanding between southern Democrats of Whig extraction and northern Republicans very close to Hayes provided for his election in return for internal improvements for the South and a southerner in Hayes's Cabinet.[29] On March 4, 1877, by virtue of the "bloody shirt," fraud, and bargaining, Hayes was inaugurated into the presidency where he had promised in his letter of acceptance to devote himself to civil service reform.

III

Carl Schurz forgot his disappointment in the "bloody shirt" campaign and his doubts about the Louisiana election returns when Hayes asked for his opinion. Happy in his favorite role of adviser, Schurz warned Hayes that his doubtful title to the presidency would "for a time remain in the popular mind like a lingering cloud. . . . To clear away that cloud . . . your Administration must be . . . not only what would ordinarily be called a creditable one, it must be a *strikingly* good one, leaving a heritage of beneficent and lasting results behind it." Using this warning for leverage, Schurz advised Hayes not to retreat from his letter of acceptance and suggested a civil service paragraph for his inaugural address.[30]

Hayes did not retreat. His address was an amplification of his acceptance letter, which the *Nation* remarked must "have had the

---

South Carolina and Louisiana to Hayes but maintains that Florida voted for Tilden. The Democrats therefore were entitled to the presidency. C. Vann Woodward, *Reunion and Reaction* (Garden City, New York, 1956), p. 20.

[28] Schurz to Cox, St. Louis, December 28, 1876, in Bancroft, *op. cit.*, III, 352–354.

[29] The story is well told in Barnard, *op. cit.*, pp. 336–396, but he and other recent historians writing on the topic are indebted to Woodward, *op. cit., passim.*

[30] Bancroft and Dunning, *op cit.*, III, 373; Schurz to Hayes, St. Louis, January 25, 1877, in Bancroft, *op. cit.*, III, 367–374.

charm of novelty for the Republican managers, as none of them
during the canvass seemed to have any recollection of the letter or
its contents." Once again, Hayes called for "thorough, radical, and
complete" reform and this time gave details of a program, which
included nonpartisan appointments, discouragement of political
activity by officeholders, tenure during good behavior, and a constitutional amendment limiting presidents to one term of six years.[31]

Hayes's Cabinet pleased reformers. They regarded Schurz, who
had been appointed Secretary of the Interior, and Secretary of
State William M. Evarts, an anti-Conkling New York Republican,
as particularly strong men. The nomination viewed with the most
skepticism was that of John Sherman for Secretary of the Treasury.
Reformers had urged the reappointment of Bristow. Sherman, who
had not been openly friendly to civil service reform, favored a return to specie payments but had managed to remain on uncommonly
good terms with inflationists and had been mildly tinged with that
heresy in 1867. The *Nation,* in view of the obvious corruption in
Louisiana, thought it improper that a "Visiting Statesman" should
be appointed to a Cabinet post especially since he probably would
be "the ruling spirit of the new Administration." [32]

Despite minor criticism, reform enthusiasm for Hayes's administration continued. Four Cambridge scholars—Lowell, Longfellow,
Eliot, and Norton—telegraphed hearty approval of Hayes's course.
Reports circulated that a "clean sweep" was not imminent and that
Hayes was indifferent to political claims. "I am past hoping for
much in our time," Frederick Law Olmsted wrote Norton, "but I
agree with you as to appearances in Washington. The sky is brighter
than at any time since the election of Andrew Jackson." Tilden
supporters attending a dinner party given by Henry Adams were
"much pleased" with the opening of the Hayes administration and
gave Schurz "a large share of the credit." [33]

---

[31] James D. Richardson, *A Compilation of the Messages and Papers of the
Presidents 1789–1897* (Washington, 1896–99), VII, 444–445; *Nation,* XXIV, No.
610 (March 8, 1877), 139.

[32] Bancroft and Dunning, *op. cit.,* III, 374; *Nation,* XXIV, No. 611 (March 15,
1877), 153; *ibid.,* No. 610 (March 8, 1877), 139. Sherman in 1867 "strengthened"
Butler and Morton's "influence by bringing in a bill for the conversion of the
five-twenties into a five per cent. bond, and advising the bondholders, in an elaborate speech, to accept the reduction of interest without the option of being paid
off, lest the followers of Butler and Morton should become uncontrollable, and
a worse thing happen [to] them." *Ibid.*

[33] James Russell Lowell *et al.* to Hayes, Cambridge, March 9, 1877, Hayes

Hayes's inclination to leave the civil service intact soon met with opposition from reformers, who wished to see corrupt heads roll. John C. Hopper, secretary of the National Revenue Reform Association, asked Schurz to support his nomination as collector of New York in place of Conkling's lieutenant, Chester Arthur. Part of Hopper's program to achieve reform was a "clean sweep" of the whole customhouse crowd. A Boston reformer urged the removal of "the impersonation of dirty politics"—Ben Butler's henchman, Collector Simmons. A Philadelphia reformer also demanded the removal of both the Philadelphia collector and postmaster and concluded, "As long as Don Cameron's nominees continue in office, political reform will be impossible in this City and State." In a broad sense, reformers were not inconsistent in advocating removals and, in particularly corrupt places, "clean sweeps" since their main objective was an efficient nonpartisan civil service. A stable tenure of office was a means not an end in itself, and reformers never meant to apply it to undesirable civil servants as Hayes was doing.[34]

At Hayes's first Cabinet meeting, Evarts and Schurz were asked to formulate an urgently needed policy on appointments. The administration was scarcely three weeks old when the rules they devised were promulgated. Admission to the service was to be restricted to the lowest grade and to those who passed a standard, noncompetitive examination. Selection from the eligible class was not to be restricted except that "moral character will in all cases be considered, and preference will, other things being equal, be given to disabled soldiers." The *New York Times* was disappointed in the administration's attempt to pawn off "pass" examinations as civil service reform. These examinations had been written into law for over twenty years and had been no obstacle to spoilsmen. The only provision that the *Times* found "very important and very desirable" was the restriction of admissions to the lowest grade. The *Times*—now a strong reform paper rather than an administration organ—harped long on its disappointment and frequently alluded to the British civil service.[35]

Papers; *Nation*, XXIV, No. 611 (March 15, 1877), 153; Olmsted to Norton, New York, March 28, 1877, Norton Papers; E. B. Haskell to Schurz, Boston, March 20, 1877, Schurz Papers.

[34] John C. Hopper to Schurz, New York, March 14, 1877, William Endicott, Jr., to Schurz, Boston, March 22, 1877, and William Welsh to Schurz, Philadelphia, March 24, 1877, *ibid.*

[35] "Systematic Reform," *New York Times*, March 21, 1877, p. 4, cc. 3–4; "Civil

Hayes's popularity with reformers went up and down like a see-saw. His failure to sweep spoilsmen out of office and his timid civil service rules stopped reformers' early adulation of his administration. William Grosvenor, Schurz's former political lieutenant in Missouri now writing for the administration-supporting *New York Tribune,* complained on March 26, "I am afraid the President is making haste *too* slowly: the feeling is not as cordial as it was, & there is now doubt of his steadiness of purpose." Two weeks later a Philadelphian, after reading that Hayes had proposed as reform an eight-year term of office for civil servants, wrote Schurz in bitter disappointment, "the country has asked for bread & you have given them a stone." [36]

When Schurz established a three-member board of inquiry into appointments, promotions, and removals in the Interior Department, reformers' opinion of Hayes's administration once again shot up. This board was given "general powers of investigation and recommendation," but Schurz determined which cases would be examined and made all decisions subject to his approval. Schurz's determination to make "no dismissals without cause" earned him praise for striking the "key-note" of civil service reform. On April 10, only two weeks after Grosvenor had complained to Schurz, Horace White found public opinion in New York "very favorably disposed to the new Administration & especially towards civil service reform." A month later, New Haven reformer Francis A. Walker offered his "congratulations, as an Independent Republican, on the admirable tone and temper of the Administration, which is full of the true spirit of reform. The attempt of the hack politicians to bully the President, now, will only seem ludicrous when looked back upon next October." [37]

Service Reform in England," *ibid.,* March 22, 1877, p. 4, cc. 5–6; "Blackboard Examination," *ibid.,* March 26, 1877, p. 4, c. 3. Evarts' attitude toward civil service reform while in the State Department may be found in Chester Leonard Barrows, *William M. Evarts* (Chapel Hill, North Carolina, 1941), pp. 343–346.

[36] Grosvenor to Schurz, New York, March 26, 1877, and M. Ralph Thayer to Schurz, Philadelphia, April 11, 1877, Schurz Papers. Hayes had a tendency to re-appoint officers who had successfully completed one term but not those who had completed two. *Nation,* XXIV, No. 622 (May 31, 1877), 313. Schurz also proposed an eight-year term in a reform bill he introduced when in the Senate.

[37] "The Civil Service," *New York Times,* April 6, 1877, p. 1, c. 4; *Nation,* XXIV, No. 615 (April 12, 1877), 213; P. O. to editor, Washington, April 9, 1877, in *New York Times,* April 16, 1877, p. 2, cc. 4–5; White to Schurz, New York, April 10, 1877, and Walker to Schurz, New Haven, May 8, 1877, Schurz Papers.

Post Office appointments caused reformers again to grow apprehensive. Especially obnoxious was the naming of Benjamin Butler's
nephew, George H. Butler, as a special agent to establish postal
routes and offices in the Black Hills. George Butler had been Consul-
General of Egypt in 1869, where his activities included selling vice-
consulships, touring Egypt with dancing girls, public drunkenness
and disorder, and "a shooting affray in the streets of Alexandria."
Joseph R. Hawley, the Connecticut Republican leader, predicted
that Butler's nomination would "be regarded as indicating a possible
perpetuation of the mysterious power which Benjamin F. Butler
exerted over Gen. Grant's administration." Despite Schurz's repeated
urging, Hayes at first refused to revoke Butler's appointment and
only relented when newspapers loudly echoed the protests. "It
would be a joke," Whitelaw Reid of the *New York Tribune* wrote
Schurz, "if the fact should become public, that the Civil Service
Reform champion in the Cabinet was unable to secure the dismissal
of a person whose appointment compelled the friends of the Administration to hold their noses whenever its Civil Service reform was
mentioned, until *The Tribune* lost all patience, and openly denounced the shameful act." Perhaps this disillusionment with the
Hayes administration led Reid to open up his columns a few days
later to Gail Hamilton (Mary Abigail Dodge), Blaine's kinswoman
and a vitriolic opponent of civil service reform in general and of
Carl Schurz in particular.[38]

Hayes, however, gave the civil service his attention after conciliating the South by withdrawing federal troops from that area. On
April 22, 1877, he entered in his diary, "Now for civil service reform.
Legislation must be prepared and executive rules and maxims. We
must limit and narrow the area of patronage. We must diminish
the evils of office-seeking. We must stop interference of federal
officers with elections. We must be relieved of congressional dictation as to appointments." The next day, Secretary of the Treasury
Sherman, under the President's orders, appointed a commission
headed by a reform-minded New York aristocrat, John Jay, to investigate the New York Customhouse.[39]

---

[38] *Nation*, XXIV, No. 619 (May 10, 1877), 271; Hawley to Schurz, Hartford,
May 3, 1877, and Reid to Schurz, New York, June 10, 1877, Schurz Papers. The
Tribune remained opposed to reform until well after the passage of the Pendle-
ton Act in 1883. For irregularities in the Treasury Department, see the *New
York Times*, May 17, 1877, p. 4, c. 1.

[39] Charles Richard Williams, ed., *Diary and Letters of Rutherford Birchard*

The commission's first report on May 24 confirmed what reformers had been saying. It suggested that 20 per cent of the customhouse's employees could be immediately dispensed with and that subsequent reductions might be necessary. A general atmosphere of laxness was prevalent. The one rule strictly enforced was the paying of political assessments, which some clerks recouped by "exacting or accepting from . . . merchants unlawful gratuities." After making these charges, the Jay Commission recommended "the emancipation of the service from partisan control." [40]

Sherman approved the commission's minor recommendations but asked for the President's opinion on "that part relating to the appointments upon political influence without due regard to efficiency" since matters of general policy were involved. Hayes's reply virtually repeated the commission's recommendations. "It is my wish that the collection of the revenues should be free from partisan control, and organized on a strictly business basis. . . . Party leaders should have no more influence in appointments than other equally respectable citizens. No assessment for political purposes, on officers or subordinates, should be allowed. No useless officer or employee should be retained. No officer should be required or permitted to take part in the management of political organizations, caucuses, conventions, or election campaigns." [41]

In his instructions to Arthur, Sherman considerably watered down the President's letter. While demanding that Arthur cut down his force within a month, Sherman suggested, "in a government like ours, other things being equal, those [officers] will be preferred who sympathize with the party in power; but persons in office ought not to be expected to serve their party to the neglect of official duty. . . ." Sherman's letter did not mention political assessments, and Hayes, in fact, had not prohibited them in the guise of "voluntary contributions." Finally, instead of removing Collector Arthur, as reformers had expected, Sherman commended him for his ap-

---

Hayes (Columbus, 1924), III, 430. Sherman could hardly have been considered a reformer; a month earlier he had wanted to appoint a friend as customhouse auditor, but Collector Arthur had refused to displace the incumbent, a career officer who had held the post thirty-five years. William J. Hartman, "Politics and Patronage" (Columbia University, 1952), p. 202.

[40] "Commissions to Examine Certain Custom-Houses of the United States," House Executive Documents, 45 Cong., 1 sess., I, No. 8, 14–16.

[41] Sherman to Hayes, Washington, May 26, 1877, Hayes Papers; Hayes to Sherman, Washington, May 26, 1877, in Williams, Life of Hayes, II, 77.

proval of the Jay Commission's preliminary report. Curtis cleverly paraphrased Sherman's letter to Arthur: "Mr. Collector, the President wishes the Custom-house to be taken out of politics. You will please do it in your own way, only—you will, of course, leave politics in." [42]

Reformers' disappointment in Hayes continued. "Godkin does not think the administration is distinguishing itself in the line of civil service reform," Horace White reported. "He is in fact dissatisfied & discouraged, though not ready as yet to make any public declaration to that effect." White continued by summarizing the reform viewpoint: "At the beginning there should have been some heavy & decisive blows at the old system—for instance, the removal of the Collectors at Boston, N. Y. & Phila. followed by appointments of friends of reform. Known to the country as such, & fostered by unequivocal instructions for all officers & their subordinates. Perhaps it is not too late for such a course now, but if it or something like it, is not taken I shall expect to see the Administration battered in pieces from without & within & the cause of civil service reform put off for years. For if our enemies can say that, with an Administration of our kind & with a President who didn't want to be reelected, we could still do nothing, will they not convince the country that reform is simply impracticable & that time should not be wasted upon it? Gen. Boynton thinks that John Sherman is deliberately seeking to kill civil service reform by seeking to enforce a spurious reform. Perhaps he doesn't know the difference between the two. If so, so much the worse." [43]

Striving to please everybody, Hayes moved to satisfy reformers. On June 22, 1877, he issued an order forbidding federal officeholders "to take part in the management of political organizations, caucuses, conventions, or election campaigns," and prohibiting political assessments. The President was again popular with reformers, and again politicians were disgruntled. The *Nation* called Hayes's order the "best thing he has yet done for politics" after ridding the

---

[42] Sherman to Arthur, Washington, May 28, 1877, in "Commissions to Examine Certain Custom-Houses," pp. 18–20; "The Prospects of Reform," *Harper's Weekly* (New York), XXI, No. 1071 (July 7, 1877), 518. By July, 1877, Arthur had successfully completed the difficult task of cutting his force. Hartman, *op. cit.*, p. 206.

[43] White to Schurz, New York, June 14, 1877, Schurz Papers. Henry V. Boynton was the Washington correspondent of the *Cincinnati Gazette* and a very close friend of Benjamin H. Bristow. See also Lodge to Schurz, Nahant, Massachusetts, June 6, 1877, and Samuel Bowles to Schurz, Springfield, June 13, 1877, *ibid.*

South of carpetbaggers, but warned Hayes not to compromise for the support of spoilsmen, who it was rumored were turning toward Grant for 1880. Compromise would only strengthen the hope that reform was a temporary interlude before the return of the old regime. If reform were to be achieved, the President's order had to be enforced persistently.[44]

Samuel Bowles felt that the administration had at last irrevocably committed itself. "The theory of civil service reform at Washington is beautiful," he wrote Schurz, "but the practice is often pretty bad. But the comfort is that it seems to me you have gone so far that you cannot go back—that you must go through and find still waters beyond." [45]

---

[44] Richardson, *op. cit.*, VII, 450–451; *Nation*, XXIV, No. 626 (June 28, 1877), 373; "The Hopes of the Office-Holders," *ibid.*, pp. 376–377. Other pleased reformers were Eaton and David A. Welles. See Eaton to Schurz, New York, July 8, 1877, Schurz Papers.

[45] Bowles to Schurz, Springfield, July 3, 1877, in Bancroft, *op. cit.*, III, 414.

IX

BATTLE FOR THE
NEW YORK CUSTOMHOUSE

Hayes's vacillating course actually kept reformers united. They had been unified by the magnitude of their defeat during Grant's administration, and with every three-step advance under Hayes followed by a two-step retreat, reformers could not enjoy the luxury of faction. Having won no clear-cut victory, they remained united and vigilant. Even Hayes's attack on Roscoe Conkling, while in many respects pleasing to reformers, reflects his ambivalent reform policy.

I

Under Hayes, the New York Customhouse became a battleground. Grant had given control of its patronage to Roscoe Conkling, but Hayes moved to displace him. In the long struggle that followed Hayes was identified with reform and Conkling with spoils. This oversimplification was not fair to Conkling and obscured the administration's complex reasons for breaking up the Conkling machine.

While Conkling had never been an advocate of civil service reform, he had not been its strongest enemy. In fact, among Grant's spoilsmen friends Conkling had been the least conspicuous opponent of reform. Butler, Logan, "Zach" Chandler, and the Camerons had all been outspokenly hostile to the Civil Service Commission, while Conkling had favored an appropriation to give it a fair trial. Furthermore, not all reformers disliked Conkling—President Andrew Dickson White of Cornell University, for example, was his lifelong political supporter. Conkling had given reformers less reason for complaint than most political bosses, for he had usually kept in mind the commonweal as well as his machine when making appointments. Nevertheless, after Hayes's election reformers vociferously demanded the scalps of the collectors of New York, Boston, and Philadelphia to cripple the Conkling, Butler, and Cameron machines. The first of these machines which Hayes attacked was Conkling's relatively respectable organization.[1]

Hayes had political reasons for attacking Conkling, who had crossed him repeatedly. Conkling had opposed Hayes's nomination; he had been conspicuously silent during the campaign; he had failed to carry New York for Hayes; he had hindered the Republican effort to "count " Hayes in; and, after Hayes's inauguration, he had referred to him as "Rutherfraud." Apparently Conkling's main objective was to discredit the reform wing of the New York Republican party led by Secretary of State Evarts. On the other hand, Evarts, who wished to create an administration party from the remains of the old Fenton machine, enlisted Hayes's support. The administration stood to gain doubly by attacking Conkling—not only would reformers be pleased, but also a hostile faction that had failed to deliver the vote in 1876 would be eliminated.[2]

There was also another reason for Hayes's attack. In December, 1877, Hayes's close friend and confidant, William Henry Smith,

---

[1] White Papers, Cornell University, *passim*. White tried unsuccessfully to enlist Conkling in support of civil service reform. Andrew Dickson White, *Autobiography* (New York, 1905), I, 171. Chester Arthur was Conkling's personal choice for collector of New York; within the limits of the spoils system he proved himself an able administrator and brought a measure of efficiency into the New York Customhouse. George Frederick Howe, *Chester A. Arthur* (New York, 1934), pp. 48–49.

[2] John Sherman later wrote Hayes, "I have always felt that Mr. Evarts unkindly involved you in the N. Y. quarrel which might have been avoided or postponed, and that when we were in it he displayed great weakness." Sherman to Hayes, Washington, March 8, 1881, Hayes Papers, The Rutherford B. Hayes Library, Fremont, Ohio. Hayes's biographers ascribe his attack on Conkling to higher motives. Eckenrode's disappointing biography claims that Hayes attacked "because of his patriotism, his determination to do his best for the country." H. J. Eckenrode, *Rutherford B. Hayes* (New York, 1930), p. 272. Barnard says that Hayes had to choose between "his desire to be conciliatory and fair" and "his desire to strike an unmistakable blow for reform." Prodded by irregularities uncovered by the Jay Committee, he decided on the latter course. "But Hayes conducted no crusade. It was not his objective to overthrow the party organizations. He merely wanted them to conform to principles which, he felt, would strengthen them." Harry Barnard, *Rutherford B. Hayes and His America* (Indianapolis, 1954), pp. 452, 456–457.

collector of Chicago and manager of the Western Associated Press, complained to Hayes of frauds and discrimination by New York Customhouse officials. Smith later charged that these officials allowed local merchants excessive damages and consistent undervaluations on their imports, making it impossible for western merchants to compete successfully with New York importers. Outraged Chicago businessmen complained that the New York ring aimed at their destruction, and Smith claimed that it perpetrated frauds greater than those of the Tweed ring and the whisky ring combined. Hayes agreed that there was fraud and discrimination and added that this view was generally held in Boston and other cities. He concluded that "this with other reasons, all legitimate," necessitated the removal of Collector Arthur and Naval Officer Cornell of New York.[3]

Contrary to what might have been expected, Secretary of the Treasury Sherman, who hoped to succeed Hayes in 1880, did not wish the administration to attack Conkling. As early as December, 1876, Sherman attempted to bring about an understanding between Hayes and Conkling. During the next six months, Sherman's attitude underwent no change despite the fact that he had left the Senate and had become Secretary of the Treasury. On July 5, 1877, he wrote Hayes, "After full conversation with Collector Arthur and others, I think it would be well to let him know, in anyway you think advisable, that he will not be disturbed during the continuance of his present office. As to Gen. Sharpe [the New York surveyor], it is a matter of indifference, and, perhaps, it would be as well to nominate someone agreeable to Mr. Evarts to take his place."[4] By retaining Arthur and giving an appointment to Evarts, Sherman hoped to strike an equilibrium in New York politics.

But reformers wanted no equilibrium. They continued to demand the removal of both Arthur and Cornell and the replacement of Surveyor Sharpe, whose term had expired. William Grosvenor wrote bitterly to Schurz in July concerning the recent paring of the customhouse staff. "You do not hear the row that I do about the outrageous

---

[3] Smith to Hayes, Chicago, December 13, 1877, and Hayes to Smith, Washington, December 16, 1877, in Charles Richard Williams, ed., *Diary and Letters of Rutherford Birchard Hayes* (Columbus, 1924), III, 454–456; Charles Richard Williams, *The Life of Rutherford Birchard Hayes* (Columbus, 1928), II, 91, n. 1; Smith to Sherman, Chicago, March 23, 1878, Hayes Papers.

[4] Sherman to Hayes, Washington, December 12, 1876, and New York, July 5, 1877, Hayes Papers; Hayes to Sherman, Columbus, December 17, 1876, Sherman Papers, Library of Congress, copy in Hayes Library.

partiality & knavery of the recent selections of persons to be removed. It was, and everybody here knows it, a most impudent
avenging of Conkling & his crew, by ousting the men who had become distasteful. And Cornell, Sharpe, Arthur & the rest, are not
in politics—Oh! no. If that is civil service reform, let us take a rest
as a reformer." Despite continued urging from reformers, Hayes
did not move until after the Jay Commission had made its final
report on August 31 and after Naval Officer Cornell had openly
defied his authority.[5]

Cornell, a member of the Republican National Committee as
well as a federal official, ignored Hayes's order forbidding officeholders to engage in political activities. Hayes considered excusing
national committeemen from his order, but the resulting outcry
from reformers caused him to drop the idea.[6] Cornell's refusal to
resign began to assume the proportions of a "national scandal" and
a "test case." The contest would be between the administration and
the spoils senators led by Conkling. The *Nation* said that Cornell
"must" be removed, for if he could defy the President with impunity
the civil service policy would be broken. "I think," David A. Wells
wrote Schurz, "there is a feeling that on civil service reform there
is hesitation—perhaps timidity to go forward in the path commenced. I hope there will be no hesitation in meeting the defiance
apparently shown by Cornell at New York." Hayes side-stepped
Cornell's challenge. He did not fire him outright, but announced
on September 6 that both Cornell and Arthur were being replaced
in a customhouse "reorganization." The *Nation* grumbled about
Hayes's lack of "pluck," but it and virtually all reformers supported
the President.[7]

[5] Grosvenor to Schurz, no place, [July 15, 1877], Schurz Papers, Library of
Congress. Arthur claimed, however, in a letter to the Jay Commission that
he tried to base his removals on evidence it had gathered. Arthur to Jay
Commission, June 12, 1877, Arthur Letterbook, New York Historical Society,
cited by William J. Hartman, "Politics and Patronage" (Columbia University,
1952), p. 206. Charles Eliot Norton to Hayes, Ashfield, Massachusetts, July 22,
1877, Norton Papers, Harvard University.

[6] *Nation* (New York), XXV, No. 629 (July 19, 1877), 33; E. L. Godkin to
Schurz, New York, July 15, 1877, Charles Nordhoff to Schurz, New York, July
16, 1877, and Schurz to Grosvenor, Washington, July 17, 1877, Schurz Papers.

[7] *Nation*, XXV, No. 636 (September 6, 1877), 143; Wells to Schurz, Norwich,
Connecticut, September 1, 1877, Schurz Papers; *Nation*, XXV, No. 637 (September 13, 1877), 159; Horace White, "New York Custom-House Changes," *ibid.*,
p. 162.

Shortly after his lieutenants were removed from the customhouse, Conkling launched a savage counterattack at the New York State Republican Convention in Rochester. His obscure henchman Representative Thomas C. Platt, as temporary chairman, made a "violent and abusive attack on the Administration." Conkling wrote the convention's platform, which completely ignored the Hayes administration and piously called for an ideal civil service. Stalwart domination of the convention was threatened however when George William Curtis offered an amendment to the platform "eulogizing the President and his course in the strongest manner" and supported it with "a powerful speech calling on the Convention to support him both in his civil-service policy and in his treatment of the South." [8]

Conkling responded vehemently. While maintaining that New York Republicans had the right to criticize Hayes, he argued inconsistently that a state convention was not called upon to approve or commend the administration. His speech was most memorable, however, for its vilification of Curtis, who had opposed Conkling's presidential nomination in 1876, had worked for the removal of Arthur and Cornell, and was now a stanch Hayes supporter. Conkling questioned Curtis' manhood and ridiculed reforming "soothsayers and phrasemongers" for their ignorance of the realities of party organization. Conkling questioned rhetorically, "Who are these men who, in newspapers and elsewhere, are cracking their whips over Republicans and playing school-master to the Republican party and its conscience and convictions? They are of various sorts and conditions. Some of them are the man-milliners, the dilettanti and carpet knights of politics men whose efforts have been expended in denouncing and ridiculing and accusing honest men. . . ." Again capitalizing on Curtis' connection with the fashion magazine *Harper's Bazaar*,[9] Conkling continued, "They forget that parties are not built up by deportment, or by ladies' magazines, or gush." Conkling sneered, "Some of these worthies masquerade as

---

[8] *Ibid.*, No. 640 (October 4, 1877), 203. The term Stalwart was first used by Blaine in 1877 to designate Republicans unwilling to give up hostility and distrust of the South as a political motive and was later appropriated by Conkling's followers to mean "a man who votes for Conkling or Platt, 'first, last, and all the time'. . . ." *Ibid.*, XXXII, No. 833 (June 16, 1881), 415.

[9] From November 2, 1867, to March 15, 1873, Curtis had written a column called "Manners Upon the Road" for *Harper's Bazaar*. Gordon Milne, *George William Curtis & the Genteel Tradition* (Bloomington, 1956), pp. 139–140, 267

reformers. Their vocation and ministry is to lament the sins of other people. Their stock in trade is rancid, canting self-righteousness. They are wolves in sheep's clothing. Their real object is office and plunder. When Dr. Johnson defined patriotism as the last refuge of a scoundrel, he was unconscious of the then undeveloped capabilities and uses of the word 'Reform.' " [10]

Conkling's speech and manner of delivery made a profound impression on all present. "It was the saddest sight I ever knew," Curtis wrote, "that man glaring at me in a fury of hate, and storming his foolish blackguardism. I was all pity. I had not thought him great, but I had not suspected how small he was. His friends—the best—were confounded. One of them said to me next day, 'it was not amazement that I felt, but consternation.' " Conkling carefully wrote his speech for the press, Curtis continued, "and therefore you do not get all the venom and no one can imagine the Mephistophelean leer and spite." [11]

The reform group was thoroughly offended by the convention proceedings, particularly by Conkling's performance,[12] but they admitted that the slate of candidates nominated was a good one. Again, reformers were in a dilemma. Should they condemn the proceedings by failing to vote and thus allow a Democratic machine to triumph, or should they support the ticket and thereby approve the convention that selected it? But even while debating their immediate course, reformers agreed that Conkling had "put himself frankly at the head of the malcontents" and despite his temporary triumph had sealed his fate.[13]

When the Senate's special session convened in October, 1877, Hayes submitted his New York Customhouse nominations. Theodore Roosevelt, Sr., was nominated for collector, L. Bradford Prince

[10] Conkling's full speech except for one deletion is found in Alfred R. Conkling, *The Life and Letters of Roscoe Conkling* (New York, 1889), pp. 538–549. The missing words "man-milliners" are found in Donald Barr Chidsey, *The Gentleman from New York* (New Haven, 1935), p. 246.

[11] Curtis to Norton, Ashfield, September 30, 1877, Curtis Papers, Harvard University.

[12] See, for example, Ellis H. Roberts to Curtis, Utica, September 27, 1877, and John Y. Foster to Curtis, Newark, September 28, 1877, Curtis Collection, The Rutherford B. Hayes Library. Hereafter, as in this footnote, the location of the Curtis Collection will be given to avoid confusion. The Curtis Papers located at Harvard University will continue to be cited without their location in each citation.

[13] *Nation*, XXV, No. 640 (October 4, 1877), 203.

for naval officer, and Edwin A. Merritt, who years earlier had been a Fentonite naval officer, for surveyor. These appointments revealed clearly that the Hayes-Conkling struggle was not one of reform versus the spoils system but rather a struggle between two Republican factions. The nominations did not reflect reformers' preferences. Several prominent reform spokesmen had suggested David A. Wells as collector and Curtis, an administration consultant on New York patronage matters, had persistently urged the promotion of Deputy Surveyor James I. Benedict to the surveyorship. This recommendation had special significance for Curtis, who four years previously had resigned as chairman of the Civil Service Commission when Grant failed to make Benedict surveyor. Furthermore, reformers supported the promotion of Deputy Naval Officer Silas W. Burt. Not only was the advancement of qualified subordinates a reform principle, but Burt, a prominent reformer, could be counted on to institute the merit system. Curtis strongly opposed Prince, who, it was said, had received financial help from Boss Tweed and had consequently been friendly to Tweed legislation. Nevertheless, reformers acquiesced in the New York nominations. "The position of the President is, for many reasons, very difficult," Curtis explained to Burt. "He cannot do all that he would. There must be many inconsistencies and many mistakes; but I think that we should not despair so long as the general tendencies of the administration are right." [14]

The question was whether Hayes's nominees would be confirmed. The Senate appeared hostile. A caucus of eighteen Republican congressmen gathered at Secretary Sherman's house in late October to determine party action on a Democratic resolution commending Hayes's policy. Most of those present "appeared to feel that the President had 'gone back on them,' " and only two, Jacob D. Cox of Ohio and William Crapo of Massachusetts, indicated that they would vote for the resolution. On November 15, Conkling, as chair-

---

[14] Charles Nordhoff to Schurz, New York, July 6, 1877, Dorman B. Eaton to Schurz, New York, July 8, 1877, and Wells to Schurz, Norwich, Connecticut, July 9, 1877, Schurz Papers; Curtis to Hayes, West New Brighton, New York, March 14 and October 25, 1877, and Curtis to Hayes, no place, August 2, 1877, abstracts in "Letters Received by the President of the United States, 1877–1881," II, 180, Hayes Papers; Curtis to Burt, West New Brighton, October 22, 1877, Burt Collection, New York Historical Society; Evarts to Curtis, Washington, October 24, 1877, Curtis Papers. Curtis requested Evarts to destroy his letters on Prince but saved Evarts' letter reporting their destruction.

man of the Senate Committee on Commerce, requested Sherman to explain why customhouse changes were necessary. Sherman's reply stressed that Collector Arthur's opposition to the program contemplated by the administration after receiving the Jay Commission's report necessitated his removal.[15]

Arthur did not take his impending dismissal in silence. On November 23, he attacked the Jay Commission and argued that he had practiced civil service reform all along by removing only for cause and by promoting efficient workers. Jay responded with an abstract of his commission's report which aptly illustrated "the character & extent of the abuses & the corruption" with quotations from Cornell and Sharpe.[16]

On November 30, 1877, Conkling won his first victory; the Commerce Committee unanimously voted (with three Democratic abstentions) to reject Hayes's nominations. Schurz complained, "The political situation seems extremely confused. The struggle for mastery in the Senate has re-inflamed party feeling to such an extent that men, who some time ago talked and acted very sensibly, are entirely off their balance. The administration, I am happy to say, takes things with great coolness, and I have no doubt, the real questions of the day will soon resume their place in the foreground again." [17]

Conkling triumphed again in December when Hayes resubmitted his nominations to the Senate. Conkling based his defense of Arthur and Cornell on reform grounds by arguing that their terms had not expired and that they did not merit dismissal. The crucial vote was taken in executive session on December 12, 1877. On that day Conkling dropped the pretense of reform and "won his victory mainly by representing the nominations as an attack on 'the courtesy of the Senate' and as an attempt to degrade him personally." A struggle between two Republican factions had evolved into a battle between the President and the Senate over the power of appointment. Only six Republicans (two of them from Massachusetts) joined with nineteen Democrats to support the President, while twenty-eight

---

[15] *Nation*, XXV, No. 643 (October 25, 1877), 247; Conkling to Sherman, Washington, November 15, 1877, Hayes Papers; *Nation*, XXV, No. 647 (November 22, 1877), 309.

[16] Hartman, *op. cit.*, pp. 211–212; Jay to Sherman, New York, November 26, 1877, Hayes Papers.

[17] Schurz to Henry Cabot Lodge, Washington, December 1, 1877, Schurz Papers.

Republicans and three Democrats sided with Conkling. The Senate's struggle to retain its spoils reunited temporarily even Blaine and Conkling, who had been enemies for twelve years. "The Senate," lamented one reformer, "is the citadel of the Spoils System." [18]

II

Discouraged reformers blamed the President for Conkling's victory. If Hayes's "hands were clean," said Horace White, Conkling would have been defeated. "The *natural* friends of the administration are lukewarm," wrote Edward L. Pierce from Massachusetts, "and the defeat of Roosevelt has added discouragement to discontent. Some things have gone wrong in Civil Service." Even Curtis, despite his closeness to the administration, felt that Conkling had defeated it "with weapons which its own inconsistency had furnished." "We are somewhat adrift," summed up Henry Cabot Lodge, "as to what civil service reform means in the Presidential mind & the reform element is sadly dispirited." [19]

Other actions of the administration disheartened reformers. A few months earlier, Attorney General Charles Devens carefully explained to officeholders that Hayes's order forbidding their political activity extended to caucuses and conventions but did not prohibit their participation in the campaign. This explanation had been provoked by Collector Simmons of Boston, who took Hayes's order more seriously than the administration had intended and kept himself and the customhouse out of the election of 1877. The "reform" administration evidently felt it needed the help of Simmons and the customhouse crowd to carry Massachusetts. Hayes's attempt to regain control of the nominating power—which was the core of the struggle with Conkling—appeared ludicrous when Secretary of State Evarts asked the Pennsylvania and Illinois congressional delegations to nominate ministers to England and Germany. Both delegations made unsuitable nominations. Pennsylvania named Boss Simon Cameron, whom Lincoln had sent to Russia because of

[18] *Nation*, XXV, No. 650 (December 13, 1877), 357; *ibid.*, No. 651 (December 20, 1877), 373; Richard Henry Dana, Jr., to Hayes, Boston, December 14, 1877, Hayes Papers.
[19] Horace White, "The Civil-Service Issue in the Senate," *Nation*, XXV, No. 651 (December 20, 1877), 376; Pierce to Schurz, Boston, December 27, 1877, Schurz Papers; "The New Year in Politics," *Harper's Weekly* (New York), XXII, No. 1098 (January 12, 1878), 26; Lodge to Schurz, no place, January 20, 1878, Schurz Papers.

his corrupt activities as Secretary of War, and Illinois suggested Colonel Robert Ingersoll, the enthusiastic supporter of James G. Blaine. The situation left everyone angry. Politicians were disappointed when their men were not nominated, and reformers were peeved that spoilsmen had been consulted.[20]

Reformers also voiced other complaints. They felt that Hayes's annual message of December, 1877, advocating executive dictation of appointments, calling mildly for systematizing subordinate appointments, and asking for an appropriation for the Civil Service Commission, was conciliatory and a retreat from his earlier declarations on civil service reform.[21] They opposed awarding appointments to Louisiana Returning Board members (who in the recent election saved that state for Hayes by throwing out enough Democratic ballots), keeping Grant's corrupt secretary, Orville Babcock, on the public payroll, offering Collector Arthur the Paris consulate if he would resign, and retaining Collector Simmons of Boston when his removal was as justified as Arthur's.

Exasperated reformers exerted increasing pressure on the administration in early 1878. Curtis urged Hayes to practice his civil service principles and sent him a confidential printed circular from the Republican Civil Service Club in Boston (an organization which grew out of the Bristow movement). The Civil Service Club lamented its long wait for the President to carry out "his oft-repeated promises" and called for united pressure on Hayes and congressmen to adopt reform methods. Although Schurz cheered reformers by crushing the corrupt Indian ring—exposing himself to "most savage attacks" by spoilsmen—Hayes did nothing for reform in early 1878.[22]

---

[20] *Nation*, XXV, No. 645 (November 8, 1877), 278; Edwin Lawrence Godkin, "The President and the Republican Party," *ibid.*, No. 644 (November 1, 1877), 264–266; *ibid.*, p. 261; *ibid.*, No. 648 (November 29, 1877), 324. Six years later, Hayes claimed that the majority of the Pennsylvania delegation approached him privately and said they had backed Simon Cameron under duress, and that he was not Pennsylvania's choice. Williams, *Diary and Letters*, III, 514–515.

[21] "The President's Present Position as Described by Himself," *Nation*, XXV, No. 649 (December 6, 1877), 342; James D. Richardson, *A Compilation of the Messages and Papers of the Presidents 1789–1897* (Washington, 1896–99), VII, 465–466.

[22] Curtis to Hayes, West New Brighton, January 9, 1878, Curtis Collection, The Staten Island Institute of Arts and Sciences, copy in Hayes Library; J. F. Dorsey, secretary of the Republican Civil Service Reform Club of Boston, to Curtis, no date, enclosed in Curtis to Hayes, West New Brighton, January 2, 1878, Hayes Papers; *Nation*, XXVI, No. 654 (January 10, 1878), 18; *ibid.*, No. 655 (January 17, 1878), 34; Ellis Paxson Oberholtzer, *A History of the United States Since the Civil War* (New York, 1917–37), III, 356–359.

Reformers continued to badger the President and so did politicians. Congressmen longed for restoration of party harmony. Even senators who voted to sustain Hayes in his struggle with Conkling were affected by this desire. Senator Henry L. Dawes of Massachusetts, for example, felt that "civil-service reform, holy and noble as it was, must be postponed in order to resist the Solid South and the silver movement, and restore Harmony in the Party." Hayes's January nominations indicated that he too wanted "harmony." The New York officers were not included in his list of customs officials. The President had given up his struggle with Conkling for the present. Also, Hayes reappointed the Washington, D.C., postmaster, who had completed two terms of office and had connections with the local machine. Even though the *Nation* was glad to see Hayes abandon his "queer notion" that an eight-year term was all any officeholder deserved in a reformed system, it thought there had "been worthier occasions . . . for a return to sounder doctrine." [23]

Hayes, however, was not conciliatory enough for spoilsmen. In late March, 1878, Senator Timothy O. Howe of Wisconsin, having failed to secure an appointment to the Supreme Court, exploded with a virulent speech attacking the administration. Godkin called it a "trial-balloon" sent up by spoilsmen to test public reaction. Blaine also joined Howe's attack, but the results were disappointing to spoilsmen. Schurz, who was flooded with complimentary letters following these speeches, commented, "If such men as Howe and Blaine would only go on a little while longer, they would succeed in making the administration positively popular." Having had their lesson, spoilsmen showed "remarkable" self-restraint. A Republican caucus held in April refrained from attacking the administration.[24]

Everyone was dissatisfied with Hayes in the spring of 1878. Jacob Dolson Cox, a friend of the President, said that Hayes "had utterly failed to accomplish anything in the way of Civil Service reform— and that he had pursued no system that could be defended by any class of politicians." Garfield agreed: "The impression is deepening that he [Hayes] is not large enough for the place he holds." In writing to Hayes, Garfield urged him to "abandon some of his notions

---

[23] "The Republican Senators and 'Harmony,'" *Nation*, XXVI, No. 654 (January 10, 1878), 20; *ibid.*, No. 655 (January 17, 1878), 34.

[24] Edwin Lawrence Godkin, "The Senatorial Attack on the Administration," *ibid.*, No. 666 (April 4, 1878), 222; Williams, *Diary and Letters*, III, 471 (March 25, 1878); Schurz to Lodge, Washington, April 6, 1878, Schurz Papers; *Nation*, XXVI, No. 668 (April 18, 1878), 253.

of Civil Service" if he wanted to hold any influence. Wayne Mac-
Veagh, a Philadelphia reformer who later became Garfield's Attorney General, wrote Norton that Hayes "is genuinely noble and
true-hearted,—only slow and patient and half-blind. But why should
we complain of him when Mr. Evarts saddens everybody but his
enemies day by day. It is enough to make ones heart break when he
reflects what possibility of great glory was before us and to what
distant future it seems to have receded." [25]

Glory for reformers receded even further when the approaching
election of 1878 brought an additional retreat from Hayes's civil
service order. The portion of that order which particularly troubled
Republican campaign managers—since Attorney General Devens
had already pointed out that it did not prohibit civil servants from
campaigning—was the section prohibiting political assessments.
Assessments were a vital source of revenue and were thought by
party regulars to be essential to victory. A modification of Hayes's
order seemed necessary. The President carefully explained that he
saw no objection to federal officers making political contributions
and intended to contribute himself but that any federal employee
refusing to contribute would not be removed. Hayes wrote Curtis
insisting that "the order issued last June stands without alteration,"
but Curtis agreed with Cox that Hayes "has broken up one system
without establishing another. This leaves him open to the charge
of a peculiarly personal administration." [26]

It was obvious that the administration had retreated. By the end
of May, the Republican Congressional Campaign Committee issued
its printed circular to federal officeholders stipulating the amount
they were to contribute, and assuring "those who happen to be in
Federal employ that there will be no objection in any official quarter
to such voluntary contribution." Although Schurz later drew up a
circular, which Hayes adopted as a guide for executive departments,
emphasizing that noncontributing clerks would retain their positions, it was generally feared that only Interior Department employees would take this circular seriously. "You and I have seen some

    [25] Theodore Clarke Smith, *The Life and Letters of James Abram Garfield*
(New Haven, 1925), II, 664; MacVeagh to Norton, Philadelphia, April 13, 1878,
Norton Papers.
    [26] *Nation*, XXVI, No. 670 (May 2, 1878), 285; Hayes to Curtis, Washington,
May 2, 1878, Curtis Papers; Curtis to Cox, West New Brighton, May 3, 1878,
Cox Papers, Oberlin College, Oberlin, Ohio.

stormy & dark times in politics," Norton wrote Curtis in late May, "but I don't think we have ever known the barometer [to] sink much more rapidly than in the last three months. . . ."[27]

Reformers' tempers were not improved by revelations of the Clarkson N. Potter Committee investigating the election frauds of 1876. Even though there was no evidence that Hayes had attempted to influence the count, use of patronage to reward the counters was not the "thorough, radical, and complete" civil service reform that reformers had anticipated. Ben Butler exposed "the bastard character of Mr. Hayes' pretended reform" by his cross-examination of witnesses before the committee. He forced the former appointment clerk of the Treasury Department, a personal friend of Hayes who had recently been appointed to an army paymastership, to admit that "he had never made, or observed, or even heard of, an appointment for other than political reason."[28]

III

When Congress was safely adjourned, Hayes revived the flagging spirit of reformers by removing Collector Arthur and Naval Officer Cornell from the New York Customhouse. Reformers celebrating the victory could not foresee that it would make Arthur President and Cornell Governor of New York. Astute Thurlow Weed, ancient New York wirepuller, however, warned Secretary of State Evarts that, in removing these men before some good reason for their dismissal could be given, he "was preparing crowns for his victims." Arthur was replaced by Surveyor Edwin A. Merritt and Cornell by Deputy Naval Officer Silas W. Burt. "This action," Norton wrote, "puts a new face on affairs."[29]

---

[27] George C. Gorham to an unknown party, Washington, May 27, 1878, Curtis Collection, Hayes Library; Schurz to an unknown party, Washington, June 12, 1878, in Frederic Bancroft, ed., *Speeches, Correspondence and Political Papers of Carl Schurz* (New York, 1913), III, 420–421; *Nation*, XXVI, No. 678 (June 27, 1878), 412; Norton to Curtis, Cambridge, May 21, 1878, Norton Papers.

[28] "The Democratic Designs," *Nation*, XXVII, No. 679 (July 4, 1878), 4–5; "Illustrations of 'Reform,'" *New York Times*, July 8, 1878, p. 4, cc. 3–4. The former appointment clerk was General T. C. H. Smith. Hayes reported that Butler and Conkling "were generally regarded as at the bottom of the Potter investigation." Williams, *Diary and Letters*, III, 491 (July 27, 1878). Hayes insisted, however, that his customhouse policy was not motivated by revenge. Hayes to James Tanner, no place, July 26, 1878, *ibid.*

[29] Thurlow Weed to Henry L. Dawes, New York, December 12, 1881, Dawes Papers, Library of Congress; Norton to Curtis, Cambridge, July, no day, 1878, Norton Papers.

Many people failed to see reform in the New York changes. One reformer even called the removals "a foul blow" to Conkling—a point of view which Curtis called "mere craziness." It was generally thought that Merritt's appointment was part of Hayes's plan to defeat Conkling's re-election in 1880 by reorganizing the New York party around the old Fenton wing. The New York daily press disapproved of Hayes's action. The *Tribune,* hostile to reform, pronounced it dangerous policy to change collectors with an election approaching. The pro-reform but anti-Hayes *Times* referred to the removals as "mingled imbecility and meanness." Even the friendly San Francisco *Bulletin* saw in Arthur's removal and Merritt's appointment the abandonment of civil service reform. Curtis hoped that Hayes would be neither "amazed nor disheartened by the outcry." [30]

Hayes's action seemed to confirm that he removed Arthur and Cornell to build an administration machine out of Fenton supporters. Even though Curtis again urged the appointment of Benedict for the surveyorship Merritt vacated, Hayes appointed General Charles K. Graham. Graham was a Union veteran, a civil engineer, and a Fenton Republican who had connections with neither the customs service nor reform. Despite his disappointment, Curtis continued his efforts to influence the President. He warned Hayes "that certain appointments, such as I have seen mentioned as probable, would be so apparently conclusive proof that the change is merely of one faction for another, that the result could only be disastrous." After speaking highly of Burt's appointment (the only genuine reform appointment), Curtis asked why the same policy could not have been followed with the new surveyor. "Why name a politician from the outside? . . . The selection of gentlemen, for instance, known only as 'Fenton politicians' would be fatal to all possibility of explanation and defense." [31]

Hayes was rankled by the reform outcry that followed each of his appointments. He had previously written Curtis, "we have only a per cent on our side—not enough to quarrel, or sulk about things.

[30] Curtis to George Edward Hall, Ashfield, July 17, 1878, Hayes Papers; *Nation,* XXVII, No. 681 (July 18, 1878), 33; William Henry Smith to Hayes, no place, August 5, 1878, in Williams, *Diary and Letters,* III, 497; Curtis to Hayes, Ashfield, July 17, 1878, Hayes Papers.

[31] Curtis to Hall, Ashfield, July 25, 1878, and Curtis to Hayes, Ashfield, August 20, 1878, *ibid.*

Let us get together. The harshest blows many crotchety reformers strike are against each other. Many of the blows are in sheer ignorance of facts." This time, Hayes parried Curtis by agreeing that one set of workers should not replace another and added that he did not wish to "proscribe people who have been active in politics." Hayes had no intention of removing New York's Conklingite postmaster, Thomas L. James, who had won the support of reformers and businessmen for efficiency and nonpartisan management of his office. "I believe he is a capital officer," Hayes commented. "I believe he does *not* use his office in politics. If so he can't be set aside merely for his opinions." [32]

But with Merritt as collector, the New York Customhouse was still very much in politics. Congressman Anson G. McCook of New York wrote Sherman a few days after the election of 1878 requesting the permanent suspension of an order to cut down customhouse personnel. This order was promulgated before the election but had been suspended during October and November. McCook complained that the order would "seriously affect several of my best friends, who stood by me in the late campaign in which I was elected by over 5000 majority." Sherman forwarded this letter to Hayes with the comment that it "presents fairly the claim of our Friend McCook that we must govern the N. Y. Customs House so as to keep in those who help him whether their services are needed or not. The Collector [Merritt] recommends the restorations proposed or [*sic*] I know no reason for declining except what is here stated. I dont [*sic*] want to embarrass you with this but send it for your information." [33]

Republicans lost the election of 1878, but Hayes thought his policies had been vindicated. Even though Democrats gained control of Congress, he regarded the election as a decision in favor of sound money and reform and opposed "to all revolutionary schemes which would destroy the stability of our Government." Yet his annual message maintained a "dead silence about civil-service reform, which only two short years" before formed "a very prominent feature in his programme." [34]

[32] Hayes to Curtis, Washington, July 31, 1878, Curtis Papers; Hayes to Curtis, Washington, August 22, 1878, Hayes Papers.

[33] Anson G. McCook to Sherman, New York, November 14, 1878, *ibid*.

[34] Williams, *Diary and Letters*, III, 508–509 (November 6, 1878); *Nation*, XXVII, No. 701 (December 5, 1878), 341.

Hayes, however, had not forgotten reform. "Now for the civil service," he again entered in his diary on December 8, 1878, "in case the New York appointments are confirmed. The first step in any adequate and permanent reform is the divorce of the legislature from the nominating power. With this, reform can and will successfully proceed. Without it, reform is impossible." [35] Hayes wrote Curtis that the "great majority" of senators did not want Conkling to oppose the nominations even though they would not cross him. "In no event," Hayes concluded, "will the old incumbents be allowed to return to their former places, if I have power to prevent it, and as to that I am not in doubt." Curtis was cheered by Hayes's determination and did what he could to bring victory by writing and lecturing.[36]

But the Conkling machine once more demonstrated its vitality. The Republican caucus in the New York legislature unanimously nominated Conkling for a third senatorial term. His election by the Republican majority followed, and current eulogies made him the peer of Webster, Clay, and Calhoun. The *Nation* commented that administration supporters could "hardly have supposed that it was for this they 'harmonized' last summer." Their support of the Republican ticket in New York had amounted to support for Conkling. Republican victories in other states also spelled trouble for Hayes. Such Stalwart supporters of Grant as John A. Logan of Illinois, Matthew Carpenter of Wisconsin, and Zachariah Chandler of Michigan, who had been retired two years previously, were again elected to the Senate.[37]

Hayes took the offensive despite New York's endorsement of Conkling. He submitted a letter to the Senate stating reasons for his New York appointments. The New York Customhouse which collected two-thirds of the nation's revenue, Hayes maintained, was of national rather than local significance, yet Arthur and Cornell "made the custom-house a center of partisan political management. The custom-house should be a business office. It should be conducted on

---

[35] Williams, *Diary and Letters,* III, 513. A few days later, however, Hayes complained how difficult it was to get the requisite information to appoint postmasters without consulting Congress. *Ibid.,* III, 515–516 (December 17, 1878).

[36] Hayes to Curtis, no place, December 16, 1878, and Curtis to Hayes, West New Brighton, December 18, 1878, Hayes Papers; "Civil Service Reform," *New York Times,* January 31, 1879, p. 5, c. 4.

[37] *Nation,* XXVIII, No. 708 (January 23, 1879), 60; Horace White, "Reform Within the Party," *ibid.,* No. 709 (January 30, 1879), 78.

business principles." Hayes had no hope that Arthur and Cornell would manage the customhouse as a business.[38]

On February 3, 1879, Conkling was finally defeated—Merritt and Burt's appointments were confirmed. Most Republicans opposed the administration, but—thanks to Sherman's "extraordinary personal efforts"—a minority combined with southern Democrats and supported it. The civil service reform movement had little influence on this vote. Administration support centered among senators from the South, where reform had no foothold.

Although reformers were gratified by Conkling's reliance in debate "on the principle that efficiency and fidelity . . . constitute the sole title to retention in the public service," their joy was modified by his exposure of the administration's inconsistency. Conkling showed that Hayes and his Cabinet had insisted on political appointments in the customhouse. For example, Supreme Court Justice Joseph P. Bradley, who cast the deciding vote on the electoral commission that elected Hayes, had a son provided for in the New York Customhouse for "manifest reasons," and J. Q. Howard, author of Hayes's campaign biography, was forced upon Arthur as deputy collector. While feeling "genuine pain" over these revelations, reformers regarded Conkling's defeat as a "great gain for the country —so great," the *Nation* added, "that we can well afford to disregard the motives of the disputants." [39]

Whatever use Hayes had previously made of the customhouse, he now wished to make it a showcase for reform. "My desire," he wrote Merritt, "is that your office shall be conducted on strictly business principles, and according to the rules which were adopted on the recommendation of the civil service commission by the administration of General Grant. In making appointments and removals of subordinates you should be perfectly independent of mere influence. Neither my recommendation, nor Secretary Sherman's, nor that of any member of Congress, or other influential persons should be specially regarded. . . . Let no man be put out merely because he

---

[38] Hayes to the Senate of the United States, Washington, January 31, 1879, in Richardson, *op. cit.*, VII, 511–512.

[39] *Journal of the Executive Proceedings of the Senate of the United States of America* (Washington, 1828–1948), XXI, 501–504; John Sherman, *Recollections* (Chicago, 1895), II, 683–684; *New York Times*, February 4, 1879, p. 2, c. 1; *Nation*, XXVIII, No. 710 (February 6, 1879), 93; "Who Is Responsible for the Custom-House?" *ibid.*, pp. 96–97. Oberholtzer, *op. cit.*, III, 306, states that Bradley cast his vote "at some cost to his conscience," but Bradley made no such admission.

is Mr. Arthur's friend, and no man put in merely because he is our friend." Hayes also directed Naval Officer Burt, Collector Merritt, and Surveyor Graham to devise regulations based upon the Grant rules with which Burt had had experience.[40]

Publication of Hayes's letter to Merritt brought praise from reformers, and this praise grew louder when the new rules were published. These rules applied to all New York Customhouse and subtreasury appointees with the exception of those to a few offices of special trust. Appointments were made from the three candidates with highest standing on a competitive examination, which was administered by one of three boards of examiners and observed by "well-known citizens." New appointees could enter only at the lowest grade; higher vacancies were filled by promotion within the customhouse.[41]

Naval Officer Silas W. Burt, an early and ardent civil service reformer, was the dynamic force behind the New York Customhouse rules. Although not opposed to competitive examinations, Collector Merritt believed the experiment would be short-lived and asked Burt to enforce the rules. "If you can revive this corpse you are entitled to all the glory," Merritt assured Burt. It was Burt's idea to invite prominent citizens, particularly editors, to observe examinations—an idea that Curtis enthusiastically approved. Twelve citizens were invited to each examination, and Curtis attended them all to explain the proceedings. "The editors who attended," Burt later recalled, "were specially interested and their impressions, always favorable, were reflected in their papers. . . ." Editors favoring the spoils system, however, invariably declined invitations.[42]

Reformers were pleased with Merritt's administration of the customhouse, despite a few indiscretions and despite his lukewarm attitude toward the competitive system.[43] Even the highly critical

---

[40] Hayes to Merritt, Washington, February 4, 1879, Hayes Papers; Hayes to Burt, Washington, February 6, 1879, in Williams, *Diary and Letters*, III, 520–521.

[41] *Nation*, XXVIII, No. 712 (February 20, 1879), 127; *ibid.*, No. 715 (March 13, 1879), 174.

[42] Silas Wright Burt, "A Brief History of the Civil Service Reform Movement in the United States," pp. K–L, Burt Writings, New York Public Library. Internal evidence suggests that his manuscript was written in 1906 and revised in 1908.

[43] For Merritt's lukewarm attitude see, Merritt to Curtis, New York, June 13, 1879, Curtis Collection, Staten Island Institute of Arts and Sciences; Curtis to Hayes, Staten Island, June 28, 1879, Hayes Papers.

New York Times admitted in July that "after four months' experience, it is simple justice to say that the reform has been applied there [the New York Customhouse] in good faith, and with a degree of pertinacity, a patient attempt to make it successful, and an enlightened appreciation of its nature and its scope, which have been an agreeable disappointment to the doubters." Dorman B. Eaton later reported to Hayes that Merritt's administration of open-competitive examinations in the New York Customhouse was highly successful. Never before, according to Eaton, had so much time been given to proper work and so little to partisan politics. Economy, efficiency, promptness, and high morale characterized the service. Even though political activity had not been entirely eliminated, Eaton was encouraged by its decline. Reformers felt, and rightly so, that Burt was responsible for the success of the President's experimental model.[44]

In April, 1879, Hayes forwarded the New York Customhouse rules to collectors of other ports for examination, modification, and adoption. This application of rules to customhouses outside of New York was not generally successful, for collectors proceeded to modify the rules out of existence. Before Hayes's term expired, however, serious reform experiments were attempted in both Boston and Philadelphia.[45]

Under Thomas L. James, a Conkling Republican, reform in the New York Post Office was in certain respects even more advanced than in the customhouse. When James was appointed in March, 1873, "incompetency, neglect, confusion, and drunkenness" that staggered "credulity" prevailed in the post office. James found 400 to 600 neglected bags of mail scattered throughout the building, and on one occasion a book clearly addressed to Vice President Schuyler Colfax was delayed for months. James replaced this chaos with system. He dismissed drunkards and incompetents but conducted no partisan proscription. He set up examinations and despite political pressure refused to hire unworthy applicants. By May, 1879, he decided that "pass" examinations were not adequate and instituted

---

[44] "The Civil Service Reform in the Custom-House," *New York Times,* July 9, 1879, p. 4, c. 3; Dorman B. Eaton, "Civil Service Reform in the New York City Post-Office and Custom-House," *House Executive Documents,* 46 Cong., 3 sess., XXVIII, No. 94, 35–37; Curtis to Burt, Ashfield, August 18, 1879, Burt Collection

[45] T. B. Shannon to Sherman, San Francisco, November 26, 1879, Hayes Papers; Eaton, "Civil Service Reform," p. 3.

open-competitive examinations a few weeks after they were established in the New York Customhouse. Eaton and New York businessmen were proud of their post office. In 1880, the volume of mail had increased one-third over 1875, yet the mails were delivered for $20,000 less, and collections and deliveries had been increased.

Ideal working conditions were not synonymous with reform. Efficiency was achieved by frequently working postal officials ten and eleven hours a day. In addition to overworking his officers, James kept them in a state of nervous apprehension by adjusting their salaries according to performance on periodic examinations. Aware that vast increases in mail volume made new workers necessary, James hoped to secure the services of boys so that the civil service would reap the blessings resulting from child labor. Henry G. Pearson, who succeeded James as New York postmaster, continued his policies and also gave periodic exams to adjust salaries as did Schurz in the Pension Office. Every three months, Schurz inspected the efficiency reports and promoted and demoted accordingly. He called this system a "powerful stimulant" and noted that everyone in the Pension Office was doing his "utmost." [46]

IV

With the approach of the election of 1879, the administration again wavered. In August, Curtis demanded the removal of a New York federal marshal for his "flagrant and contemptuous defiance" of Hayes's June, 1877, order. Evarts, who handled the administration's New York patronage, replied, "I have no doubt all what you say about him and his proper treatment is entirely correct, but - - - (the rest is better said than written.)" Despite its minor errors, in August the administration was still popular with reformers, who were pleased over accomplishments in the New York Customhouse.[47]

After a show of Conkling's power, reformers ceased to be satisfied with the administration. The Republican Convention at Saratoga was again dominated by Roscoe Conkling, and at his behest the deposed Naval Officer Alonzo B. Cornell was nominated for governor.

[46] *Ibid.,* pp. 39–43; Committee on Civil Service and Retrenchment, "Report [to accompany Bill S. 133]," *Senate Reports,* 47 Cong., 1 sess., III, No. 576, 57; Schurz to Godkin, Washington, December 7, 1879, Schurz Papers.

[47] Curtis to Hayes, Ashfield, August 8, 1879, Hayes Papers; Evarts to Curtis, Windsor, Vermont, August 12, 1879, Curtis Papers; Curtis to Burt, Ashfield, August 18, 1879, Burt Collection.

Conkling demonstrated that neither loss of the customhouse nor recent personal scandal had destroyed his influence in New York.[48] While admitting that Hayes had improved the civil service, reformers recalled that by awarding offices to those who "counted him in" he had strengthened the spoils system. The expectation of regaining the customhouse—which Hayes's policies nurtured—kept the Conkling machine in running order. Curtis pointed out to the President that Conkling had carried the convention by using officeholders in deliberate disregard of Hayes's June, 1877, order and demanded the removal of these offenders. Heads of offices, Curtis insisted, must see that their subordinates obeyed the order. "If Mr. Burt was the head of the whole Custom House, for instance, every subordinate would know that he erred at his peril. . . . I mean no reflection upon General Merritt. But as you also know, he acquiesces where Mr. Burt believes." [49]

The nomination of Cornell for governor and Howard Soule, an experienced corruptionist, for state engineer galvanized reformers into action. An Independent Republican Committee was formed, which called upon Republicans to "scratch" the names of Cornell and Soule. Curtis, who had cast the one ballot against making Cornell's nomination unanimous, regarded a Stalwart ascendency in the next administration fatal to customhouse reform. When he carried *Harper's Weekly* into the "scratchers' " ranks, many protest letters resulted. *"Stop my Harper's Weekly!!"* read a typical letter to the publisher. "I'll have nothing to do with a paper edited by such a *devilish sentimental ass as Geo. Wm. Curtis,* with his proposition to scratch, and his readiness to risk the triumph of the republican party, to defeat Conkling and the Republican candidates for the state of New York." [50]

While the President's strongest New York supporters were organ-

[48] *Nation,* XXIX, No. 739 (August 28, 1879), 136. Conkling's "magnificent torso" that lady reporters continually ballyhooed finally got him into trouble. A few days before the convention former Senator Sprague ran Conkling off his property with a shotgun for the extremely marked attention paid his wife, Kate Chase Sprague. Ishbel Ross, *Proud Kate* (New York, 1953), pp. 246–249; Thomas Graham Belden and Marva Robins Belden, *So Fell the Angels* (Boston, 1956), pp. 306–308.

[49] "The New York Machine Triumph," *Nation,* XXIX, No. 741 (September 11, 1879), 168; Curtis to Hayes, Ashfield, September 5, 1879, Hayes Papers.

[50] *Nation,* XXIX, No. 742 (September 18, 1879), 183; Curtis to Burt, Ashfield, September 30, 1879, Burt Collection; Edmund Edmonisser to Harper & Brothers, Washington, October 9, 1879, Curtis Collection, Hayes Library.

izing to "scratch" Cornell, the administration threw its support behind the regular nominees. John Sherman allowed customhouse employees to stump New York for Cornell at public expense and also said he would not object to their making political contributions. The campaign was made ludicrous when Sherman journeyed to New York to speak for Cornell, whom he had earlier accused of neglecting the duties of his office, and when Evarts and even President Hayes approved the Cornell ticket.[51]

The election encouraged Independents but also embittered their feelings toward the administration. Cornell won the governorship, but only because "Honest" John Kelly and Tammany Hall bolted the Democratic party. Curtis claimed that the election had delivered mortal wounds to Conkling and Sherman, and described Evarts' course as "unspeakable." The election also showed that New York would be a doubtful state in the forthcoming presidential election with Independents holding the balance of power. "Scratchers" proudly claimed to have cost Cornell 20,000 votes. Reformers felt the worst effect of the New York campaign was that the administration gave civil service reform the "air of humbug" and destroyed the hope of further reform under it. "I have little or no patience with Mr. Hayes," wrote Edward Cary, the editor of the *New York Times.* "He is a victim of 'goody' rather than good intentions & his contributions to the pavement of the road to the infernal regions are vast & various." [52]

With the election over, the Hayes administration moved again to conciliate reformers. John Jay, who had headed the customhouse investigation, wrote Schurz urging that the President stress reform in his annual message. Such an approach would have a "most happy" effect upon the Republican party in the campaign of 1880, while a repetition of the "folly exhibited at Saratoga may be fatal." The President's annual message did devote more space to civil service reform than to any other topic. He called attention to a forthcoming report by Eaton on the British civil service, attacked the spoils

---

[51] *Nation,* XXIX, No. 746 (October 16, 1879), 249; "The Administration and the New York Election," *ibid.,* No. 747 (October 23, 1879), 271; *ibid.,* No. 748 (October 30, 1879), 283.

[52] Curtis to Norton, West New Brighton, November 6, 1879, Curtis Papers; "National Significance of the New York Election," *Nation,* XXIX, No. 750 (November 13, 1879), 320; Wendell Phillips Garrison, "Disappearance of the Reform Administration," *ibid.,* No. 751 (November 20, 1879), 339–340; Edward Cary to Burt, New York, December 3, 1879, Burt Collection.

system, defended political activities of Cabinet officers but condemned such activity by subordinate civil servants, testified that competitive examinations had improved the public service, asked again for an appropriation to revive the Civil Service Commission, and condemned political assessments.[53]

Publication of Eaton's report on the British civil service came after the election of 1879, when Hayes especially needed aid in bolstering reform support. Eaton had long studied the British system and had given it special attention during a year's stay in England. When Hayes became President, he requested that Eaton, who was still chairman of the American Civil Service Commission, prepare a report on the British civil service. Eaton gladly complied and returned to England at his own expense to study reform more thoroughly. "I am astonished," he wrote Hayes, "at the immense length the English have distanced us, in the great cause of honest & efficient administration; and I assure you our partisan & venal ways —our frauds our intrigues & our inefficiency—will show a sad contrast with their regular & upright methods." [54]

Eaton's report was an elaborate history of Great Britain's civil service emphasizing the introduction and increased usage of competitive examinations in making appointments and promotions. His conclusion, stressing the virtues obtained through the English merit system, sounded like a fulfillment of the promises found in Jenckes's old speeches: abuses were abolished, education was stimulated, adminstration became efficient, and "the character and social standing of those who execute the laws" was elevated. Eaton's final chapter showed the bearing of English example upon the United States and argued cogently and with fervor that the merit system was highly adaptable to American conditions. Eaton not only identified the merit system with virtue, unselfishness, and patriotism, but also styled competition as a general law of progress. The real question, he stressed, was whether America was virtuous enough to espouse this system. Eaton's report was a boon to reformers, for it documented the successful application of the merit system in England —their intellectual mother country.[55]

[53] John Jay to Schurz, New York, November 7, 1879, Schurz Papers; Richardson, *op. cit.*, VII, 561–566.

[54] Dorman B. Eaton, *Civil Service in Great Britain* (New York, 1880), p. i; Eaton to Hayes, New York, January 10, 1878, Hayes Papers.

[55] Eaton, *Civil Service in Great Britain*, pp. 356, 361–428.

The reception of his report gratified Eaton. The *New York Times* called it "the most important contribution that has yet been made to the reform of the civil service in this country." "The book has attracted more attention than I anticipated," Eaton proudly reported, "& strange enough, I have not, as I have seen, got abused. Several papers have come to me from Texas, even, containing complimentary notices—some of them—perhaps all—democratic." Eaton was pleased that the hostile *New York Tribune* chose scholarly George Ripley instead of vitriolic Gail Hamilton to review his book. "That the Tribune should so feel its mistake & the tendency of public opinion as to substitute Ripley for Gail & soberness for ridicule, is certainly significant." The *Tribune*'s sobriety was of short duration; nevertheless, it indicated the growing power of reform.[56]

---

[56] "New Publications," *New York Times*, December 29, 1879, p. 2, cc. 2–3; Eaton to Curtis, New York, no date [1880], Curtis Papers.

X

REFORMERS ORGANIZE

Hayes's support of reform, while wavering and inconsistent, en-
forces E. E. Schattschneider's contention that Presidents favor civil
service reform. Schattschneider's hypothesis is that power in American political parties is lodged in local political bosses who control
Congress. The ultimate source of this power is patronage. Presidents,
however, attempt to concentrate political authority in themselves
by breaking the bosses' power through civil service reform. Grant,
although he eventually capitulated, long backed reform despite
congressional opposition, and Hayes used reform to attack Conkling
not because he was the most corrupt spoilsman, but because he was
the most powerful. Hayes wished to neutralize Conkling's power
derived from New York Customhouse patronage. By 1880, however,
it seemed that a distinct enemy of reform might be nominated for
the presidency. It was further evident that even a relatively friendly
President supported by unorganized individual reformers could not
institute full-scale civil service reform. Effective organization to apply the concerted weight of reformers was necessary to achieve reform.

I

The choice of a presidential candidate for 1880 perplexed reformers. The future of civil service reform in the Interior Department
and in both the New York Customhouse and Post Office depended
upon Hayes's successor. Despite his inconsistencies, reformers preferred Hayes to any other candidate, but his one-term declaration
precluded his being considered. With Hayes out of the running,
reformers divided their support among Elihu Washburne, Grant's
minister to France, Congressman James A. Garfield, and John Sher-

man, Hayes's Secretary of the Treasury, but united in opposition to both the Grant and Blaine "booms" for the nomination.[1]

Sherman was the strongest of reformers' candidates, but their opinion of him was divided. While Carl Schurz favored Sherman, who had pleased reformers by his recent handling of national finances during the difficult period when specie payments were resumed, Henry C. Lea of Philadelphia had no confidence in him. Lea thought Sherman was "a machine politician." "He is," Lea added, "perhaps a shade better than Conkling or Blaine, but I would greatly prefer to him Gen[l] Grant, who is a man with the courage of his opinions, though a coarse-grained man not over nice in the choice of his friends." Lea was "exceedingly disappointed" to note the support Sherman received from New York Independents, who were "apparently under the pressure of 'anything to beat Conkling.'"[2]

Lea was also disappointed by reports that Sherman was the administration's candidate and as such was "wielding all the power of the machine in the old way to secure the succession." Lea's contention was confirmed by newspaper reports that Sherman was busy employing patronage, particularly in the South, to build up his strength for the coming national convention. Sherman's denials were unconvincingly faint, and understandably so, since he was strengthening his position in various customhouses. On February 9, 1880, for example, Collector William Henry Smith of Chicago, who was acting as a special Treasury agent, reported to Sherman on the situation in the New Orleans Customhouse. He enumerated the "reliable Sherman men in Govt. service," advocated replacing the current collector with a Sherman man, and suggested assigning a special

---

[1] Henry C. Lea to Carl Schurz, Philadelphia, December, no day, 1879, Schurz Papers, Library of Congress; Lea to Edwin L. Godkin, Philadelphia, January 8, 1880, and Harry I. Sheldon to Godkin, Chicago, February 17, 1880, Godkin Papers, Harvard University.

[2] For supporters of Sherman, see Henry Cabot Lodge to Schurz, no place, January 1, 1880, and Franklin MacVeagh to Schurz, Chicago, February 4, 1880, Schurz Papers. Henry Adams thought Sherman should be supported upon the condition that he not "sell us out to Grant" but also thought seriously of "manoeuvring for a renomination of Hayes." Adams to Lodge, London, February 22, 1880, in Worthington Chauncey Ford, ed., *Letters of Henry Adams (1858–1891)* (Boston, 1930), p. 320. For opponents of Sherman, see Lea to Schurz, Philadelphia, December 8, 1879, Schurz Papers; Lea to Godkin, Philadelphia, January 8, 1880, Godkin Papers; E. Dunbar Lockwood to Schurz, Philadelphia, January 19, 1880, Schurz Papers.

Treasury agent to the customhouse to enable the collector to attend the Republican Convention at Chicago. Another supporter urged Sherman to make certain changes in personnel at the Buffalo Customhouse and warned him that any help from the collector there would be damaging since he was "looked upon as a pimp." These letters were forwarded to the President for his consideration.[3]

Despite disagreement over a candidate, Independents took steps to organize. As early as December, 1879, Schurz asked Curtis whether the New York "scratchers" were prepared to demonstrate against Grant's nomination. By February, New York and Philadelphia "Independent Republicans" were organized and the latter had warned their state convention that the nomination of Grant, Conkling, or Blaine would alienate a great many Republicans. New Yorkers adopted resolutions attacking both Grant and Blaine and planned a lecture series in which even so stanch a Republican as Curtis participated. In March, Massachusetts "Young Republicans" also made plans to stop Grant and Blaine. With all this organization under way, the *Nation,* remembering past blunders, issued a warning: "It would be very injudicious for the Independents at this stage in their history to start 'a boom' of any kind. Their aim ought to be to get a good candidate from the Republican Convention, and the best way to do it is to mention outright now the candidates whom they will not support. In 1872 and 1876 this threat would have been treated with ridicule and contempt; this year it will not be." [4]

While eastern reformers were carefully studying and planning their moves, anti-Grant men in St. Louis called for a mass meeting of Republicans to influence Chicago nominations. To prevent its failure, Lea and other reformers supported the St. Louis convention.

---

[3] Lea to Godkin, Philadelphia, January 8, 1880, Godkin Papers; *Nation* (New York), XXX, No. 763 (February 12, 1880), 105; William Henry Smith to Sherman, New Orleans, February 9, 1880, and C. Hamilton to Sherman, Buffalo, February 2, 1880, Hayes Papers, The Rutherford B. Hayes Library, Fremont, Ohio. These letters and subsequent citations from this collection were taken from copies of originals at the Hayes Library.

[4] Schurz to Curtis, Washington, December 29, 1879, in Frederic Bancroft, ed., *Speeches, Correspondence and Political Papers of Carl Schurz* (New York, 1913), III, 495; *Nation,* XXX, No. 762 (February 5, 1880), 87; Curtis to Silas W. Burt, West New Brighton, New York, May 19, 1880, Burt Collection, New York Historical Society; Horace White to Schurz, New York, March 20, April 10 and 23, 1880, Schurz Papers; *Nation,* XXX, No. 767 (March 11, 1880), 185–186. Schurz had previously expressed the *Nation's* viewpoint. Schurz to Lodge, Washington, January 3, 1880, in Bancroft, *op. cit.,* III, 495–496.

It failed to stop Grant, however, who despite his repudiation by reformers appeared to be moving irresistibly toward his third nomination. On May 23, his nomination looked "probable . . . but by no means certain" to Carl Schurz, who urged that the Edmunds, Sherman, and Blaine delegates unite to defeat and eliminate Grant.[5]

The Republican Convention which met in Chicago on June 2, 1880, was not friendly to civil service reform. The Committee on Resolutions refused to recommend a reform plank, and it became part of the platform only after a Massachusetts delegate demanded it from the floor. In the resulting debate, Webster Flanagan of Texas expressed the convention's sentiments and achieved immortality by shouting, "What are we here for except for the offices?" The convention in the end included a reform plank even more innocuous than that of 1876.[6]

Although the platform was disappointing to reformers, the presidential nomination was not. The convention was deadlocked over Grant and Blaine on June 7, and tension mounted higher the next day. "It looks alarmingly like Grant this morning because when Blaine breaks, I fear that enough of him will go to Grant to nominate him," Curtis reported. "Bad as B. may be, he is only a doubtful person while G. is a dangerous principle. God send us a good deliverance!" The deliverance came that same day when the anti-Grant forces combined to nominate James A. Garfield. "No third term, a party without a master, a candidate without a stain. We have met our enemies and they are ours," telegraphed an enthusiastic reformer to Schurz. Murat Halstead, editor of the *Cincinnati Commercial,* jubilantly wired Schurz, "John Logan said they could eat his nose if Grant was not nominated. It should be dressed as a boar's nose and eaten at a public banquet. Should the table be set in Washington?" Senator Henry L. Dawes of Massachusetts, however, expressed reservations concerning the nomination. "Garfield, good, glorious,

---

[5] Lea to Charles Eliot Norton, Philadelphia, April 7, 1880, Norton Papers, Harvard University; "The St. Louis Convention," *Nation,* XXX, No. 776 (May 13, 1880), 362; Schurz to Lodge, Washington, May 23, 1880, in Bancroft, *op. cit.,* III, 506. Senator George F. Edmunds of Vermont was unpopular with reformers in 1880, but four years later they thought more highly of him. Adams to Lodge, London, May 13, 1880, in Ford, *op. cit.,* p. 323; Ellis Paxson Oberholtzer, *A History of the United States Since the Civil War* (New York, 1917–37), IV, 170–171.

[6] *Nation,* XXX, No. 780 (June 10, 1880), 427; "The Republican Convention," *ibid.,* p. 430. Flanagan was appointed collector of customs at El Paso, Texas, in 1891. *Civil Service Record* (Boston), XI, No. 4 (October, 1891), 23.

and yet— It is an escape. Garfield is a grand, noble fellow, but fickle, unstable, more brains, but no such will as Sherman, brilliant like Blaine but timid and hesitating." Yet Dawes, who had strongly opposed the third term, was on the whole pleased with the nomination.[7]

The vice-presidential candidate proved hard for many to accept. Upon hearing of Garfield's nomination, Sherman telegraphed his lieutenants, "Now give us some first class man for Vice-President," but instead to conciliate Conkling they "rushed" to the New York delegation and secured Chester A. Arthur. Charles Eliot Norton called Arthur's nomination a "miserable farce," but William N. Grosvenor remarked, "every kite needs a tail, the only virtue of which is its weight." Grosvenor pointed out that "Arthur was a necessity" since "Conkling & Co. were half-ready to knife the candidate, relying upon 1884 for Grant. Arthur is the Chairman of the Republican State Committee, & won't commit *hari kari* even for Grant. Many pleasanter things, but not many wiser, have been done." The *Nation* reassured its readers that even though they could not "scratch" Arthur, the vice presidency was unimportant. After admitting that "General Garfield, if elected, may die during his term of office," it dismissed this as "too unlikely a contingency to be worth making extraordinary provision for." [8]

Reformers wanted Garfield to unequivocally support civil service reform in his acceptance letter. Garfield, however, shied away from reform despite warnings that Hayes's attempts to conciliate the "bosses" had failed.[9] His letter placed reform last among campaign issues and vaguely recommended legislation to regulate the appointment and tenure of civil servants without curtailing the executive

---

[7] Curtis to Burt, West New Brighton, June 8, 1880, Burt Collection; Lockwood to Schurz, Philadelphia, June 8, 1880, and Halstead to Schurz, Cincinnati, June 8, 1880, Schurz Papers; Dawes to Electa Sanderson Dawes, Washington, June 9, 1880, Dawes Papers, Library of Congress.

[8] Oberholtzer, *op. cit.*, IV, 76–77; Norton to Frederick Law Olmsted, Ashfield, June 13, 1880, Norton Papers; Grosvenor to Schurz, New York, June 9, 1880, Schurz Papers; *Nation*, XXX, No. 781 (June 17, 1880), 445.

[9] Edward Cary to Burt, New York, June 10, 1880, Burt Collection; Henry Mills Alden to Garfield, New York, July, no day, 1880, copy enclosed in Alden to Curtis, New York, July 12, 1880, Curtis Papers, Harvard University; "The Republican Nominations," *Nation*, XXX, No. 781 (June 17, 1880), 448. "In fact, Mr. Hayes's attitude towards civil-service reform furnishes an excellent illustration of one sense in which the French saying that 'small reforms are the worst enemies of great reforms' is profoundly true." *Ibid.*

department's discretion. Garfield also repudiated both Hayes's order removing officeholders from politics and his stand against congressional dictation of executive appointments. "The Executive," Garfield wrote, "should . . . seek and receive the information and assistance of those whose knowledge of the communities in which the duties are to be performed best qualifies them to aid in making the wisest choice." Despite disappointment, reformers supported Garfield rather than the Democratic nominee, Civil War general Winfield Scott Hancock. Curtis, however, feared that if Garfield were elected no firm civil service policy would be followed since his "fibre" was not "steel." [10]

With the reform vote still safe, Garfield took another step to conciliate Conkling. He wrote Hayes that upon the unanimous request of the Republican National Committee he was reluctantly going to New York on the condition that Sherman "& leading men of all shades of republicanism shall be invited." Garfield added, "If any part of the purpose of this meeting is to secure any concessions to the N. Y. men who are sulking—they will find no help in me beyond what I would give to any Republican. . . ." Although Conkling conspicuously absented himself from the meeting, several of his lieutenants attended and later claimed that Garfield had promised them the spoils of New York. Under these conditions, Conkling ceased his sulking, took to the stump, and later visited Garfield in Ohio. Garfield, doubtful about the New York meeting, confided to Hayes, "If I finished the N. Y. trip without mistakes, I shall be glad. I think some good was done." [11]

Many reformers, however, thought no good had been done. "Poor Garfield!" lamented Norton, "compelled to seek the sulky Achilles of New York in his tents; and with Marshall Jewell for his Nestor!" Schurz, without doubt, expressed the dominant sentiment among reformers when he wrote Garfield that his trip was a "mistake, for

[10] *Ibid.*, XXXI, No. 785 (July 15, 1880), 37; Horace White to Schurz, Long Branch, New Jersey, July 14, 1880, Schurz Papers. Schurz forwarded this letter to Garfield. Schurz to Garfield, Indianapolis, July 20, 1880, in Bancroft, *op. cit.*, IV, 5. Charles Richard Williams, ed., *Diary and Letters of Rutherford Birchard Hayes* (Columbus, 1924), III, 614 (July 19, 1880); Norton to Frederick Law Olmsted, Ashfield, July 22, 1880, Norton Papers; Curtis to Burt, Ashfield, July 22, 1880, Burt Collection.
[11] Garfield to Hayes, Mentor, Ohio, July 31 and August 18, 1880, William Henry Smith Papers, Indiana Historical Society, copies in the Hayes Library; Oberholtzer, *op. cit.*, IV, 96.

it was certain that under existing circumstances you could not make it without giving color to rumors of concession, surrender, promises etc., impairing the strength of your legislative record." Curtis, however, did not think the effects of Garfield's trip too harmful. "I had an exceedingly interesting talk with G. in New York," he wrote Hayes, "and I was very glad to know that, if elected, he will come in perfectly independent." Garfield was all things to all men.[12]

Behind the scenes, Garfield and Hayes were alive to the political value of the civil service. Garfield immediately after his nomination began to forward Hayes certain letters advising patronage changes. Hayes, despite the fact that he saw but a fraction of the proposed changes, understood Garfield's position. "I am doing nothing to hurt the cause if I can avoid it," he assured him. "You will of course be appealed to by all sorts of people and will be perfectly free to make known to me whatever you wish me to know. My purpose is to allow no danger to come through me." Hayes later urged Garfield not to "hesitate to refer communications, or make requests." [13]

Garfield's ardor for reform cooled as the presidential race grew warmer. Far from stopping political assessments, he even concerned himself with them. "Please say to Brady," Garfield wrote, "that I hope he will give us all the assistance he can. I think he can help effectually. Please tell me how the Depts. generally are doing." Thomas W. Brady, Hayes's Second Assistant Postmaster General, was not only busily engaged in assessing officeholders, but also, unknown to Garfield, in defrauding the Post Office of large sums of money. Assessments were systematically levied during the campaign, and if an officeholder failed to "contribute voluntarily" he was sent a reminder. In Pennsylvania, recalcitrant officeholders were warned by a third notice: "At the close of the campaign we shall place a list of those who have not paid in the hands of the Department you are in." [14]

[12] Norton to William Dean Howells, Ashfield, August 4, 1880, Norton Papers; Schurz to Garfield, Washington, September 22, 1880, in Bancroft, *op. cit.*, IV, 48; Curtis to Hayes, Ashfield, August 15, 1880, Hayes Papers.

[13] E. L. Applegate to Garfield, Portland, Oregon, June 16, 1880, and Garfield to Hayes, Mentor, June 30, 1880, *ibid.*; Garfield to Hayes, Mentor, July 5 and 19, 1880, Smith Papers, copies in Hayes Library; Hayes to Garfield, Washington, July 8 and 23, 1880, Garfield Papers, Library of Congress, copies in Hayes Library.

[14] Garfield to Jay Hubbell, Mentor, August 22, 1880, Garfield Papers; Edw. M. Johnson to S. B. Curtis, New York, October 23, 1880, George William Curtis Col-

Garfield's tactics proved successful. Although Republicans expected defeat after the September election in Maine and some reformers rationalized that a Democratic triumph would be no calamity, Garfield's victory was predicted after Indiana rallied for him in October. When victory followed, reformers congratulated themselves on the results of the Independent movement, which had stopped both Grant and Blaine, and wrote Garfield words of commendation and advice. "Your real troubles will now begin," Schurz warned him, but added that if President Garfield acted upon the teachings of Congressman Garfield his administration would be "most wholesome." " 'One thing thou lackest yet,' " John Hay frankly told Garfield, "and that is a slight ossification of the heart. I woefully fear that you will try too hard to make everybody happy —an office which is outside of your constitutional powers." Another prophesied better than he realized that Garfield would "disappoint the reformers at first more than Hayes—but not at *last*." [15]

II

The campaign of 1880 resulted in more than just the election of Garfield; at its height civil service reformers created an effective and permanent organization. A letter published in the August 5, 1880, *Nation* advocated agitating the masses by imitating the Loyal Publication Society which had profoundly influenced public opinion during the Civil War by distributing propaganda tracts—particularly to newspapers. Two weeks later, Frederick William Holls of Mount Vernon, New York, suggested that Independent Republicans organize a society to counteract "amazing ignorance, prejudice, and indifference" concerning civil service reform with "education and enlightenment . . . accomplished by agitation, political, social, and even religious." Holls desired to use abolitionist methods to destroy

lection, Hayes Library. Johnson was secretary of the New York State Republican Committee and S. B. Curtis was a customhouse employee. John Cessna to [officeholder], Philadelphia, October 25, 1880, copy *ibid*. Cessna was chairman of the Pennsylvania State Republican Committee.

[15] George Putnam to James Russell Lowell, Boston, September 29, 1880, Lowell Papers, Harvard University; Richard Watson Gilder to Lowell, New York, October 28, 1880, Rantoul Collection of Lowell Papers, Harvard University; Lea to Norton, Philadelphia, November 4, 1880, Norton Papers; Schurz to Garfield, Washington, November 3, 1880, in Bancroft, *op. cit.*, IV, 50; Hay to Garfield, no place, December 31, 1880, in John Hay, *Letters and Extracts from the Diary . . .* (Washington, 1908), II, 60; Curtis to Burt, West New Brighton, November 7, 1880, Burt Collection.

the spoils system by putting the argument entirely on the basis of "abstract moral *right*" and suggested that the proposed society sponsor a publication and issue tracts. Holls concluded by asking Independent Republican leaders to call for a preliminary meeting and by requesting letters from those interested.[16]

Holls's proposition inspired some fifty letters, many of which the *Nation* printed. Most replies were from the Northeast, but the Midwest, the South, and the Far West also responded. Curtis expressed pleasure at the "marked" interest in reform. He felt that it was "time that the vague and wobbling talk upon the Subject were brought to a focus" and suggested that the moribund New York Civil Service Reform Association "be revived and made the nucleus of an efficient organization." [17]

The New York association to which Curtis referred had been organized in May, 1877, with Dorman B. Eaton playing a leading part. Henry W. Bellows, wartime head of the United States Sanitary Commission and an outstanding Unitarian minister, was named president of the association. Its constitution allowed endorsement of a political candidate only by a three-fourths majority vote and provided for limitation of membership to 200 persons, annual dues of $10, and quarterly meetings. The constitution defined the association's objectives as the "promotion of reforms to remove the evils of patronage, favoritism and partisan coercion from the civil service, and cause appointments, promotions and removals to be made with due reference to character, capacity and economy." At Eaton's suggestion, the word "merit" was later substituted for "capacity" to back competitive examinations more directly. To achieve these objectives, the association proposed to hold meetings, raise funds, procure addresses, publish papers, and "generally, contribute to the development of a sound public opinion concerning the Civil Service." [18]

---

[16] *Nation*, XXXI, No. 788 (August 5, 1880), 93; "Civil-Service Reform Agitation," *ibid.*, No. 790 (August 19, 1880), 134–135.

[17] *Ibid.*, Nos. 791–803 (August 26–November 18, 1880), 153, 170–171, 184–185, 203, 221, 236, 252, 272–273, 290, 307, 323–324, 340, 357; Curtis to Burt, Ashfield, September 10, 1880, Burt Collection.

[18] "Minutes of the Executive Committee of the New York Civil Service Reform Association," May 11, 16, 23, 29, and December 20, 1877, Papers of the National Civil Service League, New York. Hereafter referred to as "Minutes." For a good biographical sketch of Bellows, see William Quentin Maxwell, *Lincoln's Fifth Wheel* (New York, 1956), pp. 319–326.

The association got off to a vigorous start. Nearly 300 people attended the first public meeting held on October 18, 1877. Bellows' inaugural address on "The Aspects and Needs of Civil Service Reform" revealed that he was no radical reformer. Among equally fit candidates, he did not object to preferring administration supporters and favored geographical distribution of offices. According to Bellows, civil service evils merely reflected private business morals. The New York press carefully covered this first association meeting. The *Journal of Commerce,* the *Tribune,* and the *Evening Post* were favorably inclined; the *World* and the *Times* were noncommittal, while the *Herald,* the *Express,* and the *Commercial* were hostile.[19]

Despite its auspicious start, the association rapidly failed. A second meeting was held in December, 1877, but when other gatherings did not muster a quorum the association adjourned in April, 1878, sine die subject to the call of its officers; the executive committee similarly adjourned in May subject to the call of the chair. After being dormant for over a year, the association advocated "scratching" Republican Alonzo Cornell in the 1879 New York gubernatorial race.[20] It then resumed its torpor for another year until the avalanche of letters to the *Nation* reawakened interest in a reform association.

Rapid steps were taken to reorganize. On September 17, 1880, members of the association met with interested persons and formed a committee to revive the organization. The association accepted motions recommended by this committee and unanimously elected to membership all who had written the *Nation* concerning formation of a society. A revised constitution was adopted and over 3,000 copies of it were distributed to newspapermen and members of Congress. The association's objectives and its nonpartisan character remained constant. Profiting from earlier experience, the constitution required but one meeting annually at which only ten members were necessary for a quorum; provision was also made for the calling of special meetings. The association was controlled by an executive

---

[19] "Minutes," October 18, 1877, including New York newspaper clippings dated October 19, 1877.

[20] *Ibid.,* December 20, 1877, February 22, March 1, April 4 and 18, May 2, 1878, and October 8, 1879. The association also resolved not to support Democrat Allen C. Beach for secretary of state and Republican Howard Soule for state engineer. *Ibid.,* October 8, 1879.

committee, which met monthly, disbursed funds, elected new members, and created and appointed committees.[21]

Further reorganization came in October when President Henry W. Bellows resigned. George William Curtis, an untiring worker for reform, was then elected president and held that position until his death twelve years later. Curtis in place of Bellows signalized the eclipse of clerical leadership by the more dynamic editors. A new nonpartisan executive committee was also chosen. One of its Democratic members, Everett P. Wheeler, was later elected chairman. Although dominated by professional men, the new executive committee reflected business interest in reform.[22]

The association began a full program of activities. Committees on legislation and publication, headed by Eaton and Godkin respectively, were formed and set to work. Not only were plans made to organize auxiliary associations throughout the United States, especially in educational institutions, but these plans were carried out. New associations were quickly established. Even before the parent association had planned to organize affiliated societies, steps had been taken to form a Brooklyn association with a constitution modeled on that of the New York association. The object of this new organization was to strengthen local reform sentiment. By May 5, 1881—five months after the New York association had started forming auxiliaries—associations modeled on New York's had been organized in Boston, Cambridge and West Newton in Massachusetts, Cincinnati, Milwaukee, Philadelphia, Providence, and San Francisco, and were being formed in Buffalo, New Orleans, Worcester and Pittsfield in Massachusetts, St. Paul, St. Louis, and Baltimore. Early beginnings were also apparent in fourteen other localities.[23]

By May 5, 1881, the publication committee had issued five pamphlets—a statement of the purposes of the association, an excerpt from Parton's *Life of Jackson* describing the "introduction" of the spoils system in federal offices, and three government documents. These publications were widely circulated. Out of the 10,000 printed

---

[21] *Ibid.*, September 17 and 28, October 6, November 18, and December 13, 1880.
[22] *Ibid.*, November 11 and December 6, 1880.
[23] *Ibid.*, December 13, 20, and 27, 1880, January 31, February 9, and May 5, 1881; "Minutes of the Executive Committee of the Brooklyn Civil Service Reform Association," November 26 and 29, December 6 and 17, 1880, Papers of the National Civil Service League.

copies of the statement of purposes 650 were distributed to members, 450 to affiliated societies, 3,000 were furnished to the press, 200 were gratuitously distributed, and 4,454 were sold. Reformers resourcefully distributed 10,000 of the 15,000 copies of Parton's pamphlet among the crowds gathered at Washington for Garfield's inauguration.[24]

Reformers also started their own long-talked-of periodical in May, 1881. It was called the *Civil Service Record* and was published monthly by the Boston and Cambridge associations. The *Record* apprised reformers of their movement by printing articles, speeches, notes, and pertinent quotations on civil service reform from newspapers, magazines, and books.

The organization of reformers into pressure groups helps the historian analyze the vanguard of the civil service reform movement. In connection with this work, four studies of association members have been made. The first and most elaborate is based on the forty-five members of the executive committee of the New York association from 1877 to 1883 who were interested enough in reform to attend committee meetings. The second and third studies analyze the occupations of the membership of both the Brooklyn and Boston Associations in 1882 and reveal the type of residential area in which reformers lived. A fourth study deals with the occupations of members of the California association in 1885.

Members of the New York association's executive committee are especially important since they were the driving force behind the civil service reform movement.[25] The average member of this committee was born in 1832 and was forty-eight years old in 1880. Two-

---

[24] "Minutes," May 5, 1881.

[25] The names were found in "Minutes," 1877–83, and the biographical information came from the following sources: Allen Johnson and Dumas Malone, eds., *Dictionary of American Biography* (New York, 1928–36); *The National Cyclopaedia of American Biography* (New York, 1892–1955); James Grant Wilson and John Fiske, eds., *Appletons' Cyclopaedia of American Biography* (New York, 1888–89); John Howard Brown, ed., *Lamb's Biographical Dictionary of the United States* (Boston, 1900–03); *New York City Directory,* 1877–83; *Who Was Who in America* (Chicago, 1942); *Who's Who in New York City and State* (New York, 1904, 1907); Charles Morris, ed., *Makers of New York* (Philadelphia, 1895); William J. Hartman, "Pioneer in Civil Service Reform," *New York Historical Society Quarterly,* XXXIX, No. 4 (October, 1955), 369–379; *Evening Post* (New York); *New York Times; New York Tribune; Harvard University Quinquennial Catalogue* (Cambridge, 1930); *Obituary Record of the Graduates of Bowdoin College* (Brunswick, 1890), pp. 279–342; and finally the newspaper "morgue' located in Columbia University's Journalism Library.

thirds of the committee were born within ten years of 1832 and matured in a period that was characterized by the rise of an industrial system, the fruition of democracy, the ferment of reform (particularly abolitionism), the fire of the Civil War, and the War's melancholy aftermath. Of the forty-five executive committeemen who attended meetings, twenty-one were lawyers.[26] Nine editors, including both the association's president and the chairman of the publication committee, and one journalist were among these leaders and assured the civil service reform movement of publicity. Intellectual interests were represented on the committee by three college professors, and five clergymen were attracted by and contributed to the moral tone of the movement. After 1880, clergymen, whose influence had been predominant, were overshadowed by editors. Five committeemen were statesmen;[27] a civil servant, a physician, and a social investigator[28] were also included. The fifteen businessmen on the committee included four bankers, three merchants, two insurance men, a manufacturer, a broker, a secretary,[29] a publisher, and a railroad financier and builder. Only two of these were on the committee before November 20, 1880; businessmen were latecomers to the reform movement.

Despite increasing business representation, professional men dominated the association's executive committee, and few committee businessmen represented the all-powerful industrial capitalism of the day. Better represented were merchants and bankers, but none of these were especially distinguished by wealth and economic power.

Available information on the leaders' religious affiliations shows them to have been overwhelmingly Protestant; they belonged to

---

[26] Although the percentage of lawyers was high, it was not inordinate for this type of movement, especially since many of them were not actively practicing law. It is difficult to assess the interests they represented; it is possible that some of these lawyers were corporation lawyers who shared their employers' attitudes. There is some duplication of occupations. For example, a man who was both a lawyer and a statesman was counted as both.

[27] They were Benjamin H. Bristow (Secretary of the Treasury), John Jay (diplomat), Orlando B. Potter (congressman), William Cary Sanger (Assistant Secretary of War), and Carl Schurz (Secretary of the Interior and senator).

[28] Richard Louis Dugdale, who is well known for his book, *The Jukes: A Study in Crime, Pauperism, Disease and Heredity*.

[29] The position of "secretary" in 1882 was of more importance and carried different responsibilities than does a secretarial position in the mid-twentieth century.

churches not only noted for an intellectual approach but for social position as well. Of the sixteen whose religious preferences are known, six were Episcopalian, five were Unitarian, two were Presbyterian, and one was interested in Eastern religions and Hindu literature; knowledge of the other two is merely negative—one left the Baptist church and the other was anti-Catholic.

These reform leaders came from similar backgrounds; their roots were primarily in New England and New York. Sixteen of the thirty known birthplaces were in New England, seven in New York, four abroad, and one each in Kentucky, Pennsylvania, and Ohio. Little data is available concerning the occupations of the fathers of these leaders, and most of the information found defies classification. But many of their fathers were publicly active as lawyers, bankers, politicians, and judges.[30] These committeemen could boast of New England, English, Dutch, or Huguenot ancestors. Silas W. Burt serves as an example. He traced his ancestry and discovered that forty-six of his male ancestors came to America from England before 1640. An Anglophile, like most reformers, Burt gave his genealogy as a reason why "England is dear to me. . . ."[31] England served as the reformers' model in other things as well as in civil service reform. As they grew older, their admiration for things English grew more pronounced.

Executive committeemen of the New York association were exceptionally well educated. Almost all attended and graduated from college, and many secured advanced degrees. Even the few who failed to receive a college education developed their intellectual faculties either by traveling abroad or in unconventional ways. Harvard University was the alma mater of the greatest number of these men: nine attended Harvard College, seven Harvard Law School, one its medical school and another its divinity school, and one took a Master of Arts degree there. Amherst and Bowdoin Colleges each claimed three of the New York leaders as alumni. Columbia and City College each instructed two, and three more studied law at Columbia. Eleven other schools were each attended by one member of the New York executive committee.[32]

The typical New York reform leader was formidably entrenched

---

[30] One of the fathers was a military hero: the only available information about Augustus R. Macdonough was that his father was Thomas Macdonough, the hero of the Lake Champlain battle in 1814.

[31] Burt to Godkin, no place, October 29, 1901, Godkin Papers.

[32] These schools were Yale; University of Vermont; Jefferson College at Canons-

in society. He married well, was a club man—the Union League, Century, University, and Harvard clubs were special favorites— and although his reform ardor was principally directed toward civil service reform he sympathized with and occasionally supported other movements. Several of these leaders had earlier been antislavery men but had usually been free-soilers rather than abolitionists. After the Civil War, some committeemen showed interest in the freedman, sound money, women's suffrage,[33] free trade, peace, anti-imperialism, and social settlement work. The majority, however, worked primarily for the civil service reform movement. In politics, the typical reform committeeman was a pre–Civil War Whig with free-soil proclivities. He was an early but independent member of the Republican party who supported Fremont in 1856, Lincoln in 1860 and in 1864, Grant in 1868, but he may have crossed party lines to vote for Greeley in 1872. In 1876, he more than likely voted for Hayes instead of Tilden and definitely supported Garfield in 1880. Four years later he deserted to the Democrats to support Cleveland, whom he continued to support in two succeeding elections. In 1896, the reformer returned to the Republican party to vote for McKinley.

Professional men may have led the civil service reform movement, but half of the followers were businessmen. Of 351 listed members of the Brooklyn association in 1882,[34] the occupations of 230 have been ascertained—117 were businessmen and 112 were professional men. Fifty-three or almost half of the businessmen could be classed as merchants, twenty were brokers,[35] five were insurance men, and three were bankers. Twenty-nine businessmen were listed by title rather than by business. The impressive titles included ten presidents, seven secretaries, and three treasurers. Few industrialists were connected with the Brooklyn association. Among Brooklyn's professional men, fifty-four lawyers, twenty-eight doctors, thirteen clergy-

---

burg, Pennsylvania; Union College at Schenectady, New York; Miami College in Ohio; Williams, Massachusetts; Beloit, Wisconsin; Queens College in Belfast, Ireland; University of Heidelberg, Germany; and Andover and Princeton theological seminaries.

[33] At least one member, Everett P. Wheeler, however, was actively opposed to women's suffrage.

[34] The names and addresses were secured from *List of Members of the Civil-Service Reform Association of Brooklyn,* February 16, 1882. Data on occupations was found in the *Brooklyn Directory,* 1882–83.

[35] A good many of these were probably customhouse brokers, whose occupation brought them into frequent contact with the civil service.

men, seven journalists, four civil servants, and two professors belonged to the association.

The Boston Civil Service Reform Association in 1882 [36] contained a larger proportion of businessmen than did the Brooklyn association. Of its 314 members whose occupations are known (total membership numbered 425), 180 were businessmen and 130 were professional men. Once again the merchants, sixty-four in number, dominated the businessmen, but in Boston more manufacturers, thirty-five in all, joined the association than did in Brooklyn. Among the professions there was little difference between the Brooklyn and the Boston associations. Lawyers, doctors, and clergymen once again predominated.

The personnel of the movement did not differ markedly from the Atlantic to the Pacific coast. In San Francisco, the California Civil Service Reform Association in 1885 contained 159 members, 151 of whose occupations are known. Listed among these members were eighty-four businessmen, sixty-four professional men, and one farmer. Eleven of the businessmen were "capitalists," nine followed mercantile pursuits, eight were manufacturers, four were insurance men, and four were bankers. Among the professional men were twenty-eight lawyers, thirteen were teachers and students (mostly from Berkeley), eight were in the medical professions, six were newspapermen, and four were engineers. On the Pacific coast those connected with the academic life had usurped the clergy's place, but there does not seem to have been any radical departure from eastern patterns.[37]

Both Boston and Brooklyn reformers clustered in certain neighborhoods—usually old and very fashionable ones. Boston reformers had the Common extremely well surrounded, many had addresses on Boylston, Tremont, and Beacon streets, and others lived in the Back Bay area. Brooklyn reformers concentrated in the fashionable Columbia Heights section near the East River.

---

[36] The names were secured from *List of Officers and Members of the Civil Service Reform Association of Boston,* 1882, and their occupations and addresses were found in the *Boston Directory,* 1882–83. Classification was at times difficult. For example, it was impossible to determine whether an individual with the term "Paper" written after his name was engaged in manufacturing or merchandising that product. Consequently the figures given are not mathematically exact, but the emerging picture is reasonably accurate.

[37] Civil Service Reform Association of California, *Secretary's Annual Report and List of Members, April 6, 1885* (San Francisco, 1885), pp. 8–11. This list of members also supplied the occupations.

Businessmen by the early 1880's were more interested in reform than they previously had been. The analysis of New York leaders bears out this generalization and contemporaries made similar observations. "Until very recently," the *New York Times* commented in September, 1881, "businessmen have not taken a very strong interest in the reform. Journalists, professional men, men more or less connected with public affairs, have from time to time joined in the effort to bring the reform to public attention, and to show what might be expected from it; but it is only lately that businessmen in considerable numbers have been drawn toward it." It was also obvious to contemporaries that commerce and finance were more compatible with reform than manufacturing. Since importers dealt with customhouse employees more than other businessmen did, merchants maintained a stronger interest in reform. A Philadelphia manufacturer, who was working hard to establish a civil service reform association in his city, complained to a New Yorker, "We do not seem to possess in this manufacturing town, the proportion of thinkers, writers or speakers of ability, which your great commercial & financial metropolis constantly draws to itself." [38]

Reformers also were hostile toward "monopolies." Godkin argued that as long as the civil service remained unreformed, legislation to curb the monopolists would be ineffective since they could buy key civil service positions with campaign contributions. The Anti-Monopoly League, he contended, should first work for civil service reform to assure enforcement of proposed anti-monopoly legislation. A short time later, the *Nation* insisted that political assessments were not the only source of party funds. "The truth is, and it is now a notorious truth, that the greatest danger to which all free countries are now exposed, arises from the facility with which money for electoral campaigns can be obtained." This money was supplied by a new and large class of extremely wealthy business and professional men. Obtaining money from this source was considered as dangerous as obtaining it from assessments. [39]

These studies on reform association membership lead one to question the validity of Matthew Josephson's explanation of the civil service reform movement in his book *The Politicos.* Josephson

[38] "The Business Side of Reform," *New York Times,* September 9, 1881, p. 4, c. 2; I. J. Wistar to Burt, Philadelphia, February 28, 1881, Burt Collection.

[39] Edwin Lawrence Godkin, "The 'Monopolists' and the Civil Service," *Nation,* XXXII, No. 835 (June 30, 1881), 452; *ibid.,* XXXIII, No. 855 (November 17, 1881), 389.

provocatively interprets the post–Civil War era in terms of the rise of industrial and later financial capitalism. As part of his over-all pattern, he stresses that the civil service reform movement was essentially a businessman's movement to render powerless the politician by depriving him of political assessments and plunder derived from the civil service. Reform, Josephson argues, would force political parties to obtain funds from businessmen whose point of view, in turn, the party would have to reflect. After 1880 and 1881 Josephson claims that even the industrial capitalist clamored for civil service reform.[40]

The movement for civil service reform did not originate "among a minority of intelligent capitalists and petty bourgeoise," as Josephson states, nor did businessmen, who were members in 1882, supply its driving force. Businessmen interested in reform were primarily merchants rather than industrialists, latecomers rather than originators of the movement, and followers rather than leaders. Certain businessmen and business organizations had supported Jenckes's early efforts but had coupled that support with a demand for the reform of the internal revenue system. Around 1870, after most excise taxes had been eliminated along with the machinery for their collection, business support for civil service reform fell off. Leadership of the reform movement was actually left to a group of professional men almost as hostile to the grasping capitalist as to the dominant spoilsman. Mercantile capitalists in the organization were inclined to be as outspoken as professional men in condemning the rapacious character of industrialism. Business ideals, however, pervaded the thinking of all reformers, even those who had no connection with businessmen, and reformers frequently called for "business" methods in government service. The civil service reform movement did eventually make politicians more dependent upon businessmen and subservient to their interests, but Josephson ascribes to businessmen a clairvoyance they did not possess when he assumes that they originally supported reform to attain what eventually resulted.

The reformer was actually out of step with the rest of society. The main tenet of his philosophy, laissez-faire, was rendered obsolete by the post–Civil War industrial transformation of the United States. His ideas were largely ignored. He favored free trade in an

---

[40] Matthew Josephson, *The Politicos, 1865–1896* (New York, 1938), pp. 276–277, 319–323.

age of growing protectionism. He demanded hard money when cries for currency expansion grew louder. He hated monopoly and rapacious capitalism when big business swept all before it. He disliked unions, strikes, and radicals, but these all became more common.[41] He was engulfed in the city of his fathers by an increasing flood of immigrants from eastern and southern Europe. He opposed imperialism, but in the twilight of his career witnessed America's most hypernationalistic war. The reformer stood for little government in a period when the civil service proportionately grew faster than the population, and he called for civil service reform while the blatant spoilsman reached his zenith. The reformer was an outsider, philosophically as well as politically.

Like its members, the civil service reform movement was essentially conservative. Its leaders were not interested in revolutionizing anything or even in recognizing the fundamental alteration industrialism had made in American society. The members were prosperous and to some extent were leaders, but their expectations were much higher than their achievements. Without sacrificing material gains, reformers wished to return to the attitudes of the good old days before Jacksonian democracy and the industrial revolution—days when men with their background, status, and education were the unquestioned leaders of society. In their frustration, reformers attacked the hated spoilsman's conspicuous source of strength in the civil service. The similar attack on monopolists awaited the Progressive era.[42]

---

[41] Ruth McMurry Berens, "Blueprint for Reform: Curtis, Eaton, and Schurz" (University of Chicago, 1943), p. 265, concludes that Curtis, Eaton, and Schurz "by birth and disposition . . . found themselves outside and very largely between the plutocracy rising on the one hand and the proletariat assuming menacing proportions on the other. . . ." This work is based upon an exhaustive study of the published writings of Curtis, Eaton, and Schurz.

[42] Both abolitionists and progressives have been analyzed along similar lines. David Donald, *Lincoln Reconsidered* (New York, 1956), pp. 19–36; George E. Mowry, "The California Progressive and His Rationale: A Study in Middle-Class Politics," *The Mississippi Valley Historical Review* (Cedar Rapids), XXXVI, No. 2 (September, 1949), 239–250; Richard Hofstadter, *The Age of Reform* (New York, 1955), pp. 131–173. Although Berens, *op. cit.*, pp. 265–269, clearly demonstrates that Curtis, Eaton, and Schurz were disappointed in their expectations during the post–Civil War period, she concludes that reformers were motivated by their ethical concepts, which were drawn from Christian concepts of morality. *Ibid.*, pp. 259–274. These conclusions are accepted by Paul P. Van Riper, *History of the United States Civil Service* (Evanston, Illinois, 1958), pp. 78–86.

XI

GARFIELD'S ASSASSINATION

Civil service reformers had reason for both concern and confidence in 1881. After his nomination, Garfield—whose backbone was anything but stiff—looked less and less like a reformer. The small advances reform had made under Hayes were obviously in jeopardy. On the other hand, the new associations changed reformers from unorganized individuals into a powerful pressure group, and the election of 1880 made certain Democrats conscious of the need for reform.

I

After Garfield's election many Democrats began to advocate civil service reform. The Democratic press called for reform legislation in the next session of Congress, and the Democratic lower house of the South Carolina legislature urged its senators and representatives to support reform. Respectable Democrats in New York met at Abram Hewitt's house after the election "to talk over the situation & see what to do." They appointed a committee of ten to make recommendations. It is safe to surmise that this committee was partial to reform since it included two members of the executive committee of the New York Civil Service Reform Association as well as Hewitt, who later championed reform in Congress. Although some reformers watched "the Democratic outburst of virtue & sound principles with amused interest but without sanguine expectation," others were hopeful of tangible results.[1]

---

[1] "Democrats and Civil Service Reform," *New York Times*, November 17, 1880, p. 4, c. 2; *Nation* (New York), XXXI, No. 804 (November 25, 1880), 370; *ibid.*, No. 807 (December 16, 1880), 420; William C. Whitney to Charles Stebbins Fairchild, New York, November 21, 1880, and Franklin Edson to Fairchild, New

Democratic endeavors for civil service reform before 1880 had either been isolated—like those of John B. Gordon of Georgia—or had been clearly partisan in their objectives. When Democrats, before the election of 1876, attached to an appropriation bill a provision preventing political assessments, Samuel J. Randall, the Democratic leader from Pennsylvania, humorously told the Republican side of the House, "We want to protect your clerks from being levied on." [2]

The sudden Democratic interest in reform after losing an election caused mirth among Republicans. Obviously, the Democratic party stood to benefit by advocating a reform that would attract Independents and would also curtail Republican exploitation of the civil service. Garfield's victorious campaign, Godkin generously estimated, had been financed by a 5 per cent assessment on the $20,000,000 aggregate salaries of federal officeholders. One hundred per cent compliance would have meant a staggering $1,000,000 for the Republican fund. Democrats, on the other hand, had to rely on voluntary contributions. It is puzzling why Democrats, who had lost elections since 1860, had not supported reform earlier. Perhaps their idealogical commitment to the spoils system was so strong that only repeated defeat convinced them of their urgent need for reform.[3]

Democrats were but a part of the swelling chorus demanding reform. Prominent individuals, like President James McCosh of Princeton, endorsed reform, as did the newly founded associations. President Hayes remembered reform in his final message to Con-

---

York, December 11, 1880, Fairchild Papers, New York Historical Society; George William Curtis to Rutherford B. Hayes, West New Brighton, New York, December 1, 1880, Hayes Papers, The Rutherford B. Hayes Library, Fremont, Ohio.

[2] *Congressional Record*, 44 Cong., 1 sess., 2808. The Republican Senate succeeded in qualifying the measure; in its final form it prohibited civil servants levying, collecting, and paying political assessments on, from, and to other civil servants. Schurz to Hayes, Fort Washington, Pennsylvania, August 14, 1876, in Frederic Bancroft, ed., *Speeches, Correspondence and Political Papers of Carl Schurz* (New York, 1913), III, 286. This prohibition was circumvented by simply putting individuals not in government employ on assessment committees. Another example of an isolated Democratic attempt at reform was that of Americus V. Rice of Ohio. For information on Rice and his excellent bill, which included a retirement plan, see *Congressional Record*, 44 Cong., 2 sess., 810; *ibid.*, 45 Cong., 1 sess., 179; William H. Doherty to Schurz, Washington, March 19, 1877, Schurz Papers, Library of Congress; "A Wise Measure," *New York Times*, February 5, 1877, p. 4, c. 3.

[3] Edwin Lawrence Godkin, "The Democrats and Civil-Service Reform," *Nation*, XXXI, No. 805 (December 2, 1880), 388.

gress. He spoke of "the dangers of patronage"; called for a uniform method of appointment, promotion, and removal; praised the competitive system, particularly its application in New York City; damned congressional interference with executive appointments; and requested a $25,000 appropriation to revive the Civil Service Commission. Hayes's remarks on the civil service were referred to committee upon the suggestion of Senator George Hunt Pendleton, an Ohio Democrat. A few days later on December 15, 1880, Pendleton introduced bills to reform the civil service and to prevent political assessments.[4]

During a long public career, Pendleton had previously shown little interest in civil service reform. Although he had advocated the improvement of governmental machinery by giving Cabinet officers a seat and a voice in Congress,[5] he also had been connected with both events and ideas abhorrent to reformers. Pendleton had run with General George B. McClellan on the Democratic ticket in 1864, when virtually all reformers supported Lincoln and the Civil War; later he was the leading exponent of the "Ohio Idea" to pay the national debt with inflated greenbacks. His name had been linked briefly with corruption when he had pressed and collected a previously disallowed claim of $148,000 against the government by the Kentucky Central Railroad, of which he was president, and had pocketed half the amount for his services. Pendleton, who was intimately acquainted with Mrs. William W. Belknap, shrewdly pressed this claim while her corrupt husband headed the War Department.[6]

Yet there was an air of sincerity surrounding Pendleton and his bill. He invited the veteran reformer Silas W. Burt to criticize his measure. It was, Pendleton wrote, "framed after much consideration, and a thorough examination of the civil service in Great Britain and the methods already tried in our own country, and whilst I am not wedded to it, as it stands, I desire extremely to see the ideas embodied in it, carried out."[7]

---

[4] *New York Times,* December 13, 1880, p. 4, c. 1; James D. Richardson, *A Compilation of the Messages and Papers of the Presidents 1789–1897* (Washington, 1896–99), VII, 603–605; *Congressional Record,* 46 Cong., 3 sess., 49, 144.

[5] *Nation,* XXVIII, No. 727 (June 5, 1879), 377. As early as 1865, Pendleton advocated this idea. Pendleton to Hayes, Cincinnati, April 2, 1876, Hayes Papers.

[6] *Nation,* XXII, No. 560 (March 23, 1876), 186. Edwin M. Stanton had earlier rejected the Kentucky Central Railroad's claim.

[7] Pendleton to Burt, Washington, December 22, 1880, Burt Collection, New York Historical Society.

The *Nation* regarded Pendleton's civil service bill as fundamentally well conceived. It stated, "[It] establishes a Civil-Service Examination Board of five, to hold office during good behavior, and to prescribe the necessary regulations and superintend examinations; admits women equally with men to examinations, and, with a few natural exceptions, to appointments; directs the division of the country into five examination districts, and empowers the Board to regulate suspension and dismissal for misconduct or inefficiency." Eaton wrote, "For a man who has not technical familiarity, he has done well—exceedingly well," but he added that the bill was both unconstitutional and impractical.[8]

Ardent Republicans were worried by this latest Democratic maneuver. Jane Grey Swisshelm, whose vitriolic pen had long been enlisted in such causes as abolition, temperance, and particularly women's rights, was among those disturbed. She wrote the Stalwart "Black Jack" Logan, "I hope you will see the propriety of letting Republicans carry out their own reforms & not join with George William [Curtis] in calling on a Confederate Congress to aid you in compelling a victorious party to surrender to the enemy & shackle the hands of a Republican President. If Gen. Garfield aided by the advice of Republican Congressmen cannot fill the offices wisely he is not likely to be helped by George Pendleton & his rebel Brigadiers & George Curtis & sentimental hosts of perfectionists. For God's sake stand your ground like a man & do not hand our President over bound hand & foot to a Board of Dictators." [9]

Curtis, despite Jane Swisshelm's letter to the contrary, was unhappy with Pendleton and his bill. "It is this crude and hasty and palpably unconstitutional kind of scheming which constantly discredits the cause," he complained. His fears, however, proved unfounded. After consulting with Eaton, Pendleton magnanimously scrapped his own bill and substituted the bill written by the legislative committee of the New York Civil Service Reform Association. This new bill was substantially Eaton's creation.[10]

---

[8] *Nation*, XXXI, No. 808 (December 23, 1880), 433; Dorman B. Eaton to Hayes, New York, Wednesday, no date, Hayes Papers.

[9] Jane Swisshelm to John A. Logan, Hyde Park, Illinois, January 7, 1881, Logan Papers, Library of Congress.

[10] Curtis to Charles Eliot Norton, West New Brighton, December 21, 1880, Curtis Papers, Harvard University; *Congressional Record*, 46 Cong., 3 sess., 477; "Origin New York C. S. Reform Association & of the Civil Service Bill," [1881], Memorandum in Schurz Papers. The legislative committee of Eaton, Everett P Wheeler, and Peter B. Olney had been appointed on November 30, 1880, and it

Differences between the two bills were not great since both drew heavily on the earlier Jenckes bill. Both provided for a commission and competitive examinations, but the association's bill did not infringe upon the executive's right of removal and also limited the bill's application outside of Washington to post offices and customhouses employing over fifty men. The new Pendleton bill was favorably reported from committee on February 16, 1881. Despite numerous petitions, Congress ignored both the Pendleton bill and the association's bill to prevent political assessments, which had been introduced by and named after Democratic Representative Albert S. Willis of Kentucky.[11]

While Democrats were espousing reform, the problem of Cabinet appointments plagued Garfield and worried reformers. It was widely and correctly thought that James G. Blaine would be Secretary of State. Although Hayes claimed that this arrangement was generally acceptable, reformers were not pleased. "If Garfield makes Blaine Secretary of State," Norton wrote, "he will show a curious lack of perception of the real sentiment that made him President. There could hardly be a recovery from such a misstep,—for it would indicate the lack of moral discrimination, which was the gist of the campaign charges." [12]

With Blaine's appointment certain, both Conklingites and Independents had to be appeased. When Conkling's candidate for the Treasury Department, the Wall Street banker Levi P. Morton, was not appointed, Garfield tried to conciliate the New York "boss" by offering him a Cabinet position, but Conkling rejected the offer. Although Thomas L. James, who was appointed Postmaster General, was a Conkling supporter, James's espousal of civil service reform and his brilliant administration of the New York Post Office made

reported its bill to the executive committee on December 30, 1880. "Minutes of the Executive Committee of the New York Civil Service Reform Association," November 30, and December 30, 1880, Papers of the National Civil Service League, New York. Hereafter referred to as "Minutes."

[11] Select Committee to Examine the Several Branches of the Civil Service, "The Regulation and Improvement of the Civil Service," *Senate Reports*, 46 Cong., 3 sess., I, No. 872, 1–46, *passim; Congressional Record*, 46 Cong., 3 sess., 491. For petitions, see *ibid.*, 899, 1089, 1279–80, 1332, 1539. These petitions were inspired by the newly founded civil service reform association. "Minutes," December 20, 1880, and January 19, 1881.

[12] Hayes to James A. Garfield, Washington, December 4, 1880, Garfield Papers, Library of Congress, copy in Hayes Library; Norton to Curtis, Cambridge, January 21, 1881, Norton Papers, Harvard University.

him a far greater hero among reformers than among Conklingites. The Treasury was given to William Windom of Minnesota, an international bimetallist. As the Independents' representative in the Cabinet, Garfield cleverly appointed Wayne MacVeagh, who not only belonged to the anti-Cameron faction in Pennsylvania but also was Simon Cameron's son-in-law. For Schurz's place, Garfield selected Samuel J. Kirkwood, the old war governor of Iowa, who promptly dismayed reformers by doing away with civil service reform in the Interior Department.[13] Garfield completed his Cabinet with William H. Hunt, a native Republican of Louisiana, as Secretary of the Navy, and Robert Todd Lincoln, whose only distinction was that he was his father's son, as Secretary of War. Considering the diverse elements in the Republican party, Garfield had assembled his Cabinet with skill.

Even though Blaine's ascendancy was obvious, reformers were reasonably content with James and MacVeagh in the Cabinet. No one was more pleased than Hayes, who wrote his successor: "Your cabinet is simply perfect. It could not be better. It removes all sinister doubts, and assures us an able and happy Administration. I told Mrs. Garfield . . . that all troubles would be over in three weeks. *They are all over now."* [14]

Garfield's civil service policy, however, caused reformers much apprehension, and his inaugural address realized their fears. Instead of either espousing the Pendleton bill or a similar measure, the President proposed reforming the civil service by limiting tenure to a specific number of years. Godkin observed that such a policy of rotation in office would appeal only to the dregs of the labor market who could not command steady employment. "I fully share your disappointment at the apparent back sliding of Mr. Garfield," wrote a reformer to Burt. *"He knows better* & therefore I can only interpret his heretical proposition to fix on terms of office by law,

---

[13] *Nation,* XXXII, No. 825 (April 21, 1881), 269; *ibid.,* No. 827 (May 5, 1881), 307–308; *ibid.,* No. 828 (May 12, 1881), 326. Although one employee of the Interior Department informed Schurz that all was going well, the enforced resignation of Schurz's Commissioner of Pensions imperiled the reform initiated in his office and severely jolted the older clerks, who had expected to continue in office upon the basis of merit alone. E. P. Hanna to Schurz, no place, June 13, 1881, and J. A. Bentley to Schurz, Washington, June 17, 1881, Schurz Papers.

[14] *Nation,* XXXII, No. 820 (March 17, 1881), 177–178; *ibid.,* No. 819 (March 10, 1881), 159; Hayes to Garfield, Altoona, Pennsylvania, March 6, 1881, Garfield Papers, copy in Hayes Library.

as an adroit measure to defeat the whole scheme without openly opposing it." [15]

Although reformers rejoiced when New York City's Assistant Postmaster Henry G. Pearson was promoted to fill the place vacated by James, the President's other New York appointments were unpopular. When Garfield's first batch of minor officers pleased Conkling, it was feared that Garfield had surrendered to him. These "harmonious" appointments were soon followed by a bombshell which blasted the hopes of both Stalwarts and reformers and negated Garfield's own promises of secure tenure during the term of appointment. Edwin A. Merritt, collector of the Port of New York, was removed, and in his place Garfield nominated William H. Robertson, a state senator who had defiantly opposed Conkling. In addition, Garfield appointed Blaine's lieutenant, William E. Chandler, Solicitor General without even consulting Attorney General MacVeagh. Appointment of Half-Breeds (followers of Blaine and opponents of Conkling) to prominent posts served notice that Blaine controlled the administration. The *Nation* viewed the New York nominations "with alarm," but pointed out that Garfield's letter and inaugural address left little else to be expected.[16]

Conkling's anger was boundless. With his lieutenants, he immediately protested Robertson's appointment with especial vigor, since only two days previously Garfield had promised no change would be made. The Republican senatorial caucus, in an effort to patch up differences, appointed a committee headed by Henry L. Dawes. "Conkling raged and roared like a bull of Bashan for three mortal hours," Dawes reported. "It is an awful condition of things and, as yet I see no solution of it. For a great man I think our President has some of the weakest, and Conkling some of the ugliest

---

[15] Curtis to Burt, West New Brighton, February 5, 1881, Burt Collection; Curtis to Norton, West New Brighton, February 25, 1881, Curtis Papers; Richardson, *op. cit.*, VIII, 11–12; "The President's Plan of Civil-Service Reform," *Nation*, XXXII, No. 820 (March 17, 1881), 180–181; I. J. Wistar to Burt, Philadelphia, March 12, 1881, Burt Collection.

[16] "Minutes," March 16, 1881; Curtis to Burt, West New Brighton, March 23, 1881, Burt Collection; *Nation*, XXXII, No. 822 (March 31, 1881), 213–214; "The President's New York Appointments," *ibid.*, pp. 216–217; Edwin Lawrence Godkin, "The Robertson Nomination," *ibid.*, No. 825 (April 21, 1881), 272–273. Merritt was appointed Consul General at London, and the Senate did not confirm Chandler's nomination. Ellis Paxson Oberholtzer, *A History of the United States Since the Civil War* (New York, 1917–37), IV, 109–115, provides a good discussion of New York patronage problems.

streaks I have ever seen developed in human nature— The one wants to be watched like a child, the other like an assassin." [17]

While Conkling raged about senatorial courtesy, the Republican party received another shock when frauds in the Post Office Star Route system were exposed. These routes, primarily in the West, depended upon "stagecoach, buckboard and saddle horse" for transportation, and Indians as well as climatic elements made them dangerous. There were 9,225 such routes (some of them handling only three letters a week) for which $5,900,000 was appropriated in 1878. Between 1878 and 1880, Second Assistant Postmaster General Thomas J. Brady and accomplices furnished sham petitions requesting that service be "expedited" on ninety-three routes. Service was "expedited" on these particular routes which raised the cost from $727,119 to $2,802,214 and left only $3,097,786 for the 9,132 other routes. Although suspicion was aroused when Congress made up a deficit in 1880, Brady not only temporarily avoided exposure but got the money besides. When exposure did come, it was through the efforts of Postmaster General James, Attorney General MacVeagh, and the *New York Times*.[18]

Disclosures of Star Route frauds illuminated the mysterious New York dinner of the previous February honoring Stephen W. Dorsey and pushing him for the New York collectorship. Dorsey, formerly a carpetbag senator from Arkansas, was secretary of the Republican National Committee and ran Garfield's campaign in 1880. The Dorsey dinner was presided over by General Grant and the Reverend Henry Ward Beecher. The most revealing episode of the evening was Chester Arthur's little speech, doubtlessly inspired by wine, "Indiana was really, I suppose, a Democratic State. It had been put down on the books always as a State that might be carried by close and perfect organization and a great deal of—(laughter). I see the reporters are present, therefore I will simply say that everybody showed a great deal of interest in the occasion and distributed tracts and political documents all through the State." The question of where Dorsey got the money for the Indiana campaign, for it obviously was money that Arthur referred to, was answered by the

---

[17] William J. Hartman, "Politics and Patronage" (Columbia University, 1952) p. 238. Dawes to Electa Sanderson Dawes, Washington, April 30, 1881, Dawes Papers, Library of Congress.

[18] *Nation*, XXXII, No. 826 (April 28, 1881), 287; Oberholtzer, *op. cit.*, IV, 116-117.

exposure of Star Route frauds. Among Star Route contractors were Dorsey's brother, his brother-in-law, and a former partner. These three men controlled twenty-four contracts that originally had been worth $55,246 but had been increased to $501,072 leaving $445,826 for private and political uses.[19]

The situation had John Sherman worried. "We are now in serious embarrassment," he wrote Hayes, "much more serious than any you encountered but the subject is too broad for a letter. The Star route business looks bad. At best there was a criminal abuse of discretionary power by Brady." [20]

II

Against the background of Star Route exposures, the struggle for the New York Customhouse continued. Garfield refused to give way to Conkling. On May 5, 1881, he withdrew New York nominations favorable to Conkling but left Robertson's name before the Senate. Republicans were greatly confused and excited. Conkling urged senators to persuade Garfield to withdraw Robertson's name, but Garfield remained adamant: "Robertson may be carried out of the Senate head first or feet first. . . . I shall never withdraw him." John Sherman reluctantly agreed to lead the administration's forces against Conkling. "We are here," he wrote Hayes, "in the old trouble again. I do not like the removal of Merritt. It [the appointment of Merritt] was the one point in which I was justified against Conkling [sic] and I feel chagrined that the attack [on Merritt] came from Garfield or rather from Blaine." Realizing that he could not prevent Robertson's confirmation, since he had failed to prevent Merritt's two years earlier in the prime of his strength, Conkling decided to resign from the Senate so that an inevitable triumphant re-election would return him to that body in a stronger position. Thomas C. "Me Too" Platt, New York's other senator and Conkling's lieutenant, followed suit.[21]

---

[19] *Nation*, XXXII, No. 817 (February 24, 1881), 122; *ibid.*, No. 826 (April 28, 1881), 287.

[20] Sherman to Hayes, Washington, May 5, 1881, Hayes Papers.

[21] Dawes to Electa Dawes, Washington, May 5, 1881, Dawes Papers; Royal Cortissoz, *The Life of Whitelaw Reid* (New York, 1921), II, 61; Sherman to Hayes, Washington, May 12, 1881, Hayes Papers. Senator Dawes called Conkling "A great big baby boohooing because he can't have all the cake and refusing to play any longer [who] runs home to his mother." Dawes to Electa Dawes, Washington, May 16, 1881, Dawes Papers. Platt's significant career is discussed by Harold F. Gosnell, *Boss Platt and His New York Machine* (Chicago, 1924).

After resigning, Conkling and Platt hurried to Albany to lobby for the offices they had just given up. The situation was made more fantastic when Vice President Arthur and Postmaster James joined them to lobby against the administration of which they were part. Despite this lobbying, Garfield's prediction that Conkling had committed political suicide proved correct. To the delight of reformers and Half-Breeds, Conkling and Platt were not re-elected, despite the hold Conkling had had over the legislature only a short time before. When Conkling's enemies failed to unite on candidates, he and Platt hung on through the month of June hoping for an opportunity to return to the Senate. Platt, however, withdrew in early July after a Half-Breed delegation mounted a stepladder, peeped through an open transom, and witnessed him in the arms of a woman who definitely was not Mrs. Platt. A bit later Conkling's support gave way and he retired to private life.[22]

Conkling's loss of power was caused by his failure to regain patronage which he had lost when Arthur was removed from the New York collectorship. As long as Conkling had patronage he was all-powerful, and his machine even remained loyal during the lean years under Hayes in hopes of returning to power. Conkling's tactics after Robertson's nomination, however, amounted to a confession that he had no influence with Garfield and caused his support to give way. Stalwarts did not propose to starve for four additional years under Garfield. Conkling's colossal conceit had caused him to believe that his personal magnetism, rather than the offices he had available for patronage purposes, was responsible for his following.[23]

Despite the spectacle at Albany and the Star Route exposures, Garfield's administration continued to eradicate reform commenced under Hayes. The merit system was dispensed with in the Department of the Interior, and moves were made to discontinue it in the New York Customhouse. The administration proposed adopting "pass" examinations in place of competitive examinations and extending this system to all customhouses. Curtis emphatically opposed such a plan as "betraying reform." "It is simply impossible,"

---

[22] Garfield to Hayes, no place, May 22, 1881, Garfield Papers, copy in Hayes Library; Oberholtzer, *op. cit.*, IV, 125; Matthew Josephson, *The Politicos, 1865–1896* (New York, 1938), pp. 314–315.

[23] This analysis of Conkling's loss of power follows closely that of the author of "The Meaning of Mr. Conkling's 'Mistake,'" *Nation*, XXXII, No. 831 (June 2, 1881), 383.

he wrote Burt, "that we should gain more under this administration than under the last, if we should yield the principle of competition, because that was the gain. An extension of the minimum [pass examinations] to every Custom House in the country would not be so serviceable as the present competition in the New York Custom House alone." [24]

The administration began to backtrack a few days later. On June 11, MacVeagh invited Burt to a Washington meeting of collectors and promised him "more support than you have expected." Two weeks later, Burt received a letter from Secretary of the Treasury William Windom which bore marks of the administration's exhausting experience with office seekers. "I have seen no reason," he wrote, "to change my opinion of the civil service rules in force in your office and hope to find time to more thoroughly examine them. My experience in this Department has convinced me of the necessity for the enforcement of some such rules throughout the service." [25]

Hearing of the administration's problems with office seekers revived reformers' hope. After lamenting that Garfield was "sinning against the light . . . with the swing and *verve* which is characteristic of backsliders," the *Nation* remarked that he was "an impressionable man" who "takes his opinions and practices greatly from the company he keeps. Should his Cabinet officers be won over to the truth, there is hardly a doubt that he would himself come back to it. The only absolutely hopeless case among his companions, we fear, is Mr. Blaine." MacVeagh hopefully reported to Schurz, who was now co-editor of the New York *Evening Post,* that Garfield "dreads '*patronage*' more and more" and added "he is so good and true at heart, he is sure to learn. But it is awful to think he should need to learn so much. Keep hammering away very strongly on spoils, spoils, spoils, for every day a dozen Senators and Congressmen,—candidates for governor,—State Committeemen,—all forms of evil beset him every hour of every day." On the whole, MacVeagh thought, the "tide" was turning "toward decent permanency of tenure." [26]

---

[24] Curtis to Burt, West New Brighton, June 5, 1881, Burt Collection.

[25] MacVeagh to Burt, Washington, June 11, 1881, *ibid.;* Windom to Burt, Washington, June 21, 1881, *ibid.*

[26] *Nation,* XXXII, No. 385 (June 30, 1881), 449; MacVeagh to Schurz, Washington, June 30, 1881, Schurz Papers. Theodore Clarke Smith, *The Life and Letters of James Abram Garfield* (New Haven, 1925), II, 1154, is certain that Garfield would have pressed enactment of a genuine civil service reform law at the first session of Congress.

Garfield never had the opportunity to demonstrate his ability to learn. On the morning of July 2, 1881, accompanied by Blaine and other Cabinet members, he left the White House to attend the commencement exercises of his alma mater, Williams College. As the presidential party entered the Baltimore and Potomac railroad station in Washington, Charles Guiteau, who for weeks had been haunting the Capital looking for an office, stepped from the shadows, shot Garfield twice, and shouted words to the effect that he was a "Stalwart" and that "Arthur was President now." The first bullet merely inflicted a flesh wound but the second entered Garfield's back near the hip and lodged in his body. The first impression was that Garfield was fatally wounded, but when he did not immediately die it was thought that he would recover and that the country would be spared Arthur as President.[27]

Guiteau's bullet advanced the civil service reform movement. "We do not think," editorialized the *Nation*, "we have taken up a newspaper during the last ten days which has not in some manner made the crime the product of 'the spoils system.' There has hardly been an allusion to it in the pulpit which has not pointed to the spoils system as the *fons et origo mali*. In fact, the crime seems to have acted on public opinion very like a spark on a powder-magazine. It has fallen on a mass of popular indignation all ready to explode."

When Garfield's recovery seemed certain, the president of the

---

[27] Oberholtzer, *op. cit.*, IV, 119–120; *Nation*, XXXIII, No. 836 (July 7, 1881), 1. Guiteau was obviously insane. Before shooting Garfield he had a long and fantastic career as a member of the Oneida Community, a lawyer, an insurance salesman, and an evangelist. He rarely made a living at these vocations but got along in life by swindling innumerable hotels, railroads, and haberdashers. After plunging into politics to support Greeley in 1872, he neglected that pursuit until 1880. He wrote an incoherent speech, which was never delivered in full, favoring Garfield for the presidency, and became convinced that this speech was responsible for Garfield's election. He attempted to get the Austrian mission but soon decided to settle for consul at Paris. He plagued both Blaine and Garfield for weeks and provoked the former and was barred from the White House by the latter. Rebuffed, Guiteau began brooding over the way the Republican party was split between Conkling and Garfield. A few days later he received his first inspiration that he was God's agent to kill Garfield. This impression continued to grow until he shot Garfield. See Robert J. Donovan, *The Assassins* (New York, 1955), pp. 14–62, for a fascinating account of Guiteau. For hostility toward Arthur, see Norton to Curtis, no place, July 4, 1881, Norton Papers; Sherman to Hayes, Mansfield, Ohio, July 8, 1881, and Schurz to Hayes, New York, July 24, 1881, Hayes Papers; Curtis to Burt, Ashfield, July 24, 1881, Burt Collection; Isaac Lea to Henry C. Lea, Long Branch, New Jersey, August 16, 1881, Lea Papers, University of Pennsylvania.

Missouri Civil Service Reform Association even rejoiced over the attempted assassination which assured the success of reform. "The important point now," Burt noted, "is to show that the method of open competitive examination is the only feasible remedy that is satisfactory." In view of the excited state of the national mind, Burt suggested issuing propaganda along these lines.[28]

Yet the way of the reformer was not easy. While Garfield lay fighting for his life, Postmaster General James, hoping to improve his relations with Congress, suggested giving congressmen control of patronage but requiring their appointees to take competitive examinations. "We have been making such progress in every direction that this obstacle is peculiarly grievous," Burt complained, especially "coming from one who is popularly considered a 'reformer.'" Burt was fearful that Blaine and Windom would espouse James's point of view. The James plan, however, did not get beyond the "feeler" stage. Not only did Schurz oppose it, but also Senator Dawes published a letter in the *Springfield Republican* labeling congressional dictation of appointments the "worse phase of the evil." Dawes himself soon distressed reformers by advocating a genuine executive control of appointments. Dawes's plan called for selection of appointees by those immediately responsible. Although this chain of responsibility looked good on paper, the *Nation* protested that his plan would not work and suggested that Dawes should support the Pendleton bill, whose principles had already been proved in the New York Customhouse. Congressmen would still impose their influence by making threats to bureau chiefs rather than to Cabinet members.[29]

Despite counterplans, the competitive system prospered while Garfield's condition declined. On August 1, Robertson took over the New York Customhouse and promised, as did Secretary of the Treasury Windom, to maintain the civil service rules in force. By September the *New York Times* reported that the entire Cabinet, excepting Secretary of the Interior Kirkwood, took a "very strong interest in the reform, have become convinced of its utility, and

---

[28] "The Moral of It," *Nation*, XXXIII, No. 837 (July 14, 1881), 26; Henry Hitchcock to Schurz, Newport, July 21, 1881, and Burt to Schurz, New York, July 12, 1881, Schurz Papers.

[29] Burt to Schurz, New York, July 20 and 22, 1881, *ibid.*; "Defining Reform," *New York Times*, July 22, 1881, p. 4, c. 2; *ibid.*, July 30, 1881, p. 4, c. 1; "The Dawes Plan," *Nation*, XXXIII, No. 840 (August 4, 1881), 86.

that it is practicable." Some Cabinet members, the report continued, have even taken "important steps to carry it into effect."[30]

Reformers continued their energetic work and moved to perfect their organization. During the summer of 1881, the New York Civil Service Reform Association issued circulars to the press and distributed thousands of documents. On July 29, it invited other associations to a conference at Newport, Rhode Island, which had been planned even before Garfield was shot. It was hoped "that an interchange of views, as to measures and methods," would "do much to promote the movement now happily so well advanced." The leading items which Curtis wished to consider, besides organization, were pushing the Pendleton bill and arriving at a "common understanding on the question of tenure—the latter being the issue upon which perhaps there is much danger of a tangential escapade on the part of the administration, of Congress and of the people."[31]

Fifty-eight delegates assembled at Newport on August 11, 1881, representing the associations of Baltimore, Boston, Brooklyn, Buffalo, Cambridge, Cincinnati, New York, Philadelphia, Pittsburgh, Providence, St. Louis, Springfield, and West Newton. The conference resolved to "use every honorable means, in the press, on the platform, and by petition, to secure" passage of the Pendleton and Willis bills. This talk was not idle; a member from the Boston association proudly reported its plan to blanket Massachusetts with 100,000 copies of the Pendleton bill. To facilitate united action, the conference resolved to establish a National Civil Service Reform League. The executive committee of the New York association was to act as a provisional central committee. The conference also resolved to establish an association in each congressional district to lead or to drive congressmen into action on civil service reform.

Methods of reform were considered. The conference adopted

[30] *Ibid.*, p. 81; Windom to Burt, Washington, July 27, 1881, Burt Collection; "The Progress of Reform," *New York Times,* September 14, 1881, p. 4, c. 2. A week later, the *Nation* reported that Windom was "decapitating" federal officers who refused to work with William Mahone and his Virginia "Readjusters." *Nation,* XXXIII, No. 847 (September 22, 1881), 223.

[31] "Minutes," September 14, 1881; Curtis to Burt, Ashfield, July 2, 1881, Burt Collection; "Record of Conference," p. 3, in "Minutes," September 14, 1881; William Potts to Schurz, Chesterfield, Massachusetts, August 3, 1881, Schurz Papers. Potts was secretary of the New York Civil Service Reform Association, and he had conferred with Curtis about the coming conference.

Eaton's resolution insisting that a national civil service commission, as provided for in the Pendleton bill, should supervise local examination boards throughout the country. Eaton feared that a bill might be passed providing for competitive examinations to be administered locally, which would do away with uniformity and overall supervision. As Curtis anticipated, the conference disagreed on the question of tenure, but it went on record as "uncompromisingly opposed to arbitrary removals from office, as well as to all interference by members of Congress with the exercise of the appointing power." [32]

Reformers continued throughout the summer to exploit Garfield's weakening condition to further their cause. On September 16, the New York association distributed throughout the country a letter signed by numerous prominent men, from Peter Cooper to Rutherford B. Hayes, which connected the "recent murderous attack" on Garfield with the need for civil service reform. It urged that public protest meetings be held and that reform resolutions be adopted. This appeal became more effective when Garfield died three days later.[33]

Garfield dead proved more valuable to reformers than Garfield alive. In their loud and long lamentations for him and his lost opportunities, reformers quickly transformed their concept of Garfield from a weak, spineless tool of Blaine's to a fearless crusader for civil service reform. Garfield's earlier articles and speeches favoring reform were quoted at length, while his sorry record as President was ignored. "The cynical impudence," wrote Henry Adams, "with which the reformers have tried to manufacture an ideal statesman out of the late shady politician beats anything in novel-writing. They are making popular capital. They lie and manoeuvre just like candidates for office. The independents and reformers are as bad as the late lamented, and for the same reason. It pays." [34]

---

[32] "Record of Conference," pp. 4–10, in "Minutes," September 14, 1881. Perhaps the most interesting name listed among the delegates was Joseph George Rosengarten of Philadelphia, who was one of Jenckes's earliest supporters and had not given up working for reform.

[33] *Nation*, XXXIII, No. 845 (September 8, 1881), 183; Peter Cooper *et al.* to an unknown party, New York, September 16, 1881, Papers of the National Civil Service League. Frederick Law Olmsted suggested the idea, and Curtis, aided by Everett P. Wheeler and William Potts, drew up the circular. Potts to Hayes, New York, September 18, 1881, Hayes Papers.

[34] Adams to Godkin, Beverly Farms, Massachusetts, September 26, 1881, in Harold Dean Cater, ed., *Henry Adams and His Friends* (Boston, 1947), p. 115.

Civil service reform associations moved to take advantage of the situation. "I think we have a fine field before us," Edward Cary of the *New York Times* wrote Burt, "but, also, a desperate fight, & I am anxious to have the ass[n] go into it actively & in detail as promptly & vigorously as possible. We want more—much more—money; more publicity in a greater variety of forms, & more definiteness of action." The money was provided by Orlando B. Potter, who donated to the New York association $2,000 toward a memorial-publication fund for Garfield. This example of Potter, a Democrat and a businessman (who manufactured sewing machines), illustrates the recently awakened interest of both these groups in reform. Believing that a "reformed civil service would be the most fitting monument" over Garfield's grave, Potter proposed that the money be spent in publishing the late President's "opinions and utterances upon the importance and necessity of reform in the civil service of the country, with such facts in connection with his death as now emphasize and enforce them." [35]

A typical Garfield-memorial publication was a striking poster exhibited in every post office throughout the country. It pictured a monument with an epitaph proclaiming that Garfield "died . . . a martyr to the fierceness of factional politics and the victim of that accursed greed for spoils of office which was the bane of his brief conscious existence as President, and is the gravest peril that threatens the future of his country." The monument was surrounded by quotations from Garfield on civil service reform.[36]

New reform associations were rapidly organized during this time of great emotion. In October, 1881, the *New York Times* commented that "centres of discussion and agitation are now found in many of the principal States of the Union, from Massachusetts to California, and there is no doubt that their influence will be felt at the next session of Congress." [37]

---

[35] Cary to Burt, New York, September 29, 1881, Burt Collection; Potter to Curtis and Wheeler, New York, September 29, 1881, printed copy in the Papers of the National Civil Service League. By the end of the year, only $108 remained in the fund. "Minutes," January 4, 1882.

[36] This poster had originally been published in the *Buffalo Express* of September 20, 1881, copy in Papers of the National Civil Service League. Silas Wright Burt, "A Brief History of the Civil Service Reform Movement in the United States," [1906, revised in 1908], Burt Writings, New York Public Library, pp. N–O.

[37] *New York Times*, October 26, 1881, p. 4, c. 1.

As the end of the year approached, the big question was Arthur and his future policy. "Luckily," Henry Adams thought, "it will be hard for Arthur to begin worse than Garfield did, although he can but try." Wayne MacVeagh's resignation, after failing to get Arthur to commit himself definitely against the Star Route thieves, was a bad omen. "The new administration," Adams now predicted, "will be the centre for every element of corruption, south and north. The outlook is very discouraging." A week later, Adams reported that Washington was emptied of reformers: "all that swarm have vanished like smoke, and even I have ceased to lisp the word . . . and, like the rest of the world, am throwing up my cap for Mr. Arthur whose social charms we now understand to be most extraordinary, although only last spring we were assured by the same people that he was a vulgar and dull animal. To be in fashion is the first law of nature. My mouth is shut on reform politics for at least two years to come; I have not the physical strength to cry like St. John in the wilderness." [38]

_____

[38] *Nation*, XXXIII, No. 851 (October 20, 1881), 301; Adams to Henry Cabot Lodge, Washington, October 29, November 15 and 21, 1881, in Worthington Chauncey Ford, ed., *Letters of Henry Adams (1858–1891)* (Boston, 1930), pp. 330–332; MacVeagh to Godkin, Philadelphia, October 31, 1881, Godkin Papers, Harvard University.

XII

STALEMATE UNDER ARTHUR

Garfield's assassination gave reformers a simple, emotion-packed illustration which the previously uninterested masses could easily understand. The spoils system equaled murder. But politicians obtusely and obstinately refused to alter their behavior during most of 1881 and 1882.

I

Chester Arthur, Stalwart lieutenant of Roscoe Conkling, was President of the United States. One of his first actions was to use spoils to cement the coalition of Republicans and General William Mahone's Readjusters in Virginia.[1] Clearly reformers could expect little from this man who had been removed from the collectorship of the port of New York supposedly in a move to further civil service reform. Their only hope was Arthur's letter written when he accepted the nomination for Vice President. This letter, although revealing little faith in competitive examinations, had demanded that civil service management conform to the "conduct of successful private business." His plan included appointments based on "ascertained fitness," stable tenure of office, filling responsible positions by promotion as much as practicable, and prompt, thorough investigation of complaints and punishment of misconduct. Reformers wondered whether President Arthur would remember what candidate Arthur had said.

The President's first message, delivered in December, 1881, re-

---

[1] On Mahone's alliance with Arthur, see Nelson Morehouse Blake, *William Mahone of Virginia* (Richmond, 1935), pp. 223, 226; *Congressional Record*, 47 Cong., 1 sess., 85; *Nation* (New York), XXXIII, No. 855 (November 17, 1881), 383; George Frederick Howe, *Chester A. Arthur* (New York, 1934), pp. 215, 216.

ferred to this letter and maintained that its views would guide his administration. The troublesome question, he frankly admitted, was how to ascertain fitness for office. Arthur expressed the usual Stalwart suspicion that competitive examinations tested "mere intellectual attainments," and he raised the specter of immature college youth monopolizing appointments. But his observations, he insisted, were not offered in a "spirit of opposition." He suggested that certain nominations be submitted to a central examining board that would, "without resort to the competitive test," ascertain qualifications of candidates. This board, Arthur thought (no one else seemed in agreement with him), would put an end to the present mischief. While cautiously suggesting the need for further inquiry before legislation, he pledged himself to enforce "earnestly" any bill that Congress might pass which included the essential features of the British system. If no legislation were forthcoming, he urged the appropriation of $25,000 to reactivate the Civil Service Commission. The President concluded with a tribute to the great majority of civil servants who, he insisted, were not indolent, inefficient, or corrupt.[2]

Almost everyone from reformers to Half-Breeds took hope from the message. To the Half-Breed *New York Tribune,* Arthur seemed disposed to "submit" as little as possible to the program of civil service reformers, and Denver's *Rocky Mountain News* concluded that amateur statesmen of the George William Curtis stripe could not gather much comfort from the message. Both the *San Francisco Chronicle* and the *Atlanta Constitution* (isolated from reform pressure) failed to notice editorially the civil service section of the President's message. The Democratic New York *World*—which had jumped on the reform band wagon after defeat in 1880—attacked Arthur for criticizing competitive examinations and for not stressing the major Democratic reason for reform—the need for removing the civil service from politics. The reform-minded New York *Evening Post* was encouraged by the message, and concluded that Arthur's remarks indicated the subject's firm hold on the people. The *Philadelphia Inquirer* hoped that Arthur would "become as practical a civil service reformer as was his distinguished and patriotic predecessor." At headquarters of the National Civil Service

---

[2] James D. Richardson, *A Compilation of the Messages and Papers of the Presidents 1789–1897* (Washington, 1896–99), VIII, 60–63. The message quotes Arthur's letter of acceptance.

Reform League in New York, there was general satisfaction. Having expected little from Arthur, reformers were gratified by his message of qualified support. Even his advice to delay action did not dismay them.[3]

Competitive examinations as the method of personnel recruitment were not postponed so easily. On the day that Arthur's message was delivered to Congress, Pendleton again introduced his bill, which provided for a presidential commission of five members to devise civil service rules and to suggest action. Competitive examinations were to be given to all applicants for positions on a classified list, which could be expanded. Those ranking among the highest on examinations were to be appointed to vacancies; original entrance into the service was to be only at the lowest grade and after a period of probation. Promotion to higher grades was provided for on the basis of merit and competition. Officeholders were to be under no obligation to contribute time or money for political purposes. The commission was to report annually on its progress to the President.[4]

In a supporting speech, Pendleton argued that reform would eliminate from the civil service the twin evils of political corruption and business inefficiency.[5] After reproaching the spoils system with Garfield's delirious cry, "Do tell that crowd of office-seekers I cannot see them to-day—I am so sick," Pendleton laid the blame for Garfield's assassination on the appointing system. As a good Democrat, he castigated the prostitution of the present civil service for political ends, and used the New York Customhouse to illustrate government inefficiency. Customhouse removals in the five years preceding 1871

---

[3] "The Press on the Message," *Evening Post* (New York), December 7, 1881, p. 2, cc. 2–3, 5; "The President's Message," *Rocky Mountain News* (Denver), December 7, 1881, p. 4, c. 2; "The President's Message," *San Francisco Chronicle*, December 7, 1881, p. 4, c. 2; *Atlanta Constitution*, December 7, 1881, p. 4, c. 1; *World* (New York), December 7, 1881, p. 4, c. 2; *Philadelphia Inquirer*, December 7, 1881, p. 4, c. 2; George P. Briggs to Henry L. Dawes, Pittsfield, December 19, 1881, Dawes Papers, Library of Congress. At least one reformer, feeling that Arthur would "not surrender the system of *personal* politics," was disappointed rather than pleased by the message. J. A. Bentley to Carl Schurz, Denver, December 8, 1881, Schurz Papers, Library of Congress.

[4] *Congressional Record*, 47 Cong., 1 sess., 20. The Pendleton bill is printed in the *Civil Service Record* (Boston), I, No. 5 (September 19, 1881). Pendleton also introduced a bill to prevent political assessments. *Congressional Record*, 47 Cong., 1 sess., 20. Albert S. Willis, a Democrat of Kentucky, introduced both these bills in the House. *Ibid.*, p. 105.

[5] See *ibid.*, pp. 79–85, for Pendleton's speech.

had numbered 1,678—the equivalent of twice the entire force or more than one per secular day for five years. Daily collections of $480,000—making New York the world leader in business volume—and the intricacies of tariff legislation required a sensitive business organization, which the customhouse did not have. The cost of collecting revenue in the United States in 1874 was three, four, and five times that of France, Germany, and Britain respectively. The merit system, Pendleton maintained, would supply urgently needed business capacity and principles. He pointed to the success of this method in Great Britain, in the New York Post Office, in the Interior Department under Carl Schurz, and in the Census Bureau under General Francis A. Walker.

Pendleton also could have used the New York Customhouse to illustrate the efficiency of the merit system. Competitive examinations had been in operation there for nearly four years. Pendleton's customhouse statistics, giving a vivid picture of the evils of the spoils system, did not represent current civil service policy. His figures came from the bygone era of Johnson and Grant.[6]

In his speech Pendleton explained his—or more properly Eaton's —solution of the civil service problem. The bill applied to departments in Washington and to all other offices employing fifty or more workers. Obviously misunderstanding the provisions of his bill, Pendleton estimated that it applied to 100,000 employees, whose salaries aggregated $100,000,000 per annum, when it actually applied to only 10,000 officers. Appointments and promotions were to be made by competitive examinations designed to test the fitness of applicants for specific positions, not to test abstract or unrelated subjects. The bill did not deal with removals from office; it was hoped that controlled appointments would eliminate the motive for dismissal. Tenure of office was also avoided since reformers disagreed over the virtue of a fixed term, or tenure during good behavior.

It was "an excellent speech," wrote Republican Senator Henry L. Dawes of Massachusetts. The New York press echoed his enthusiasm —even the *Tribune* regarded Pendleton as sincere. The *San Francisco Chronicle* and the *Atlanta Constitution*, however, again re-

---

[6] Dorman B. Eaton, "Civil Service Reform in the New York City Post-Office and Custom-House," *House Executive Documents,* 46 Cong., 3 sess., XXVIII, No. 94, *passim.*

flected their readers' lack of interest by neglecting to comment editorially.[7]

In the Senate, Benjamin Hill, Democrat of Georgia, attacked the proposed bill. That effective orator doubted whether a remedy could be found in legislation. Lambasting hypocritical northern reformers for supporting Arthur in the election of 1880, Hill argued that reform must come from the people, who he felt had little interest in it. He advocated frequent changes of administration because a party in power for twenty years (whether Republican or Democratic) was bound to be corrupt. To turn the Republicans out was the conclusion reached by Hill and by other Democratic exponents of this rotation-in-office argument. Although Hill's opposition was silenced by a cancerous tongue—he died within the year—the Georgia delegation kept his lack of faith in reform.[8]

Other congressmen, though lacking Hill's directness, shared his fear that the Pendleton bill would overturn the system to which they owed their position. Thus in opposition they stalled the current bill while offering a host of rival solutions. Early in 1882 the Pendleton bill was ordered to be printed and referred to committee. Although the bill itself was reported on March 29, the committee's report, containing testimony, was presented too late for consideration during that session. Meanwhile, Congress suggested almost as many reform plans as it had members. A favorite western solution was the direct election of officers located outside of Washington. One of these direct-election bills was introduced by Senator Pendleton himself. This action casts doubt upon his reform motives, since to veteran civil service agitators the long ballot was a chief prop of corruption, especially in large cities. Other measures were proposed to fix civil servants' term of office. Foreshadowing his presidential attitude toward civil service reform, William McKinley introduced a bill prohibiting rules discriminating against Union veterans. This

---

[7] Dawes's high opinion of Pendleton's speech was, no doubt, enhanced by the attention—"in the main, very complimentary"—which Pendleton had paid his articles on civil service reform. Dawes to Electa Sanderson Dawes, Washington, December 13, 1881, Dawes Papers; *New York Tribune*, December 14, 1881, p. 4, c. 2.

[8] *Congressional Record*, 47 Cong., 1 sess., 85. In 1877, Hill had been regarded as a friend of reform. Charles Richard Williams, ed., *Diary and Letters of Rutherford Birchard Hayes* (Columbus, 1924), III, 448; "The Appointing Power," *New York Times*, April 19, 1877, p. 2, c. 4.

bill would have nullified the effects of reform measures. Andrew Gregg Curtin, Democrat of Pennsylvania, fathered another congressional plan of "reform" that would insure patronage to both parties and to all members of Congress. All positions in the executive departments were to be apportioned among congressional districts with senators and representatives making the nominations.[9]

Authors of plans labeled "reform" but actually designed to retain the spoils system were found outside as well as inside the halls of Congress. President Arthur himself advocated a four-year term for civil servants. William W. Dudley, the Commissioner of Pensions, originated one of the most ingenious plans. Already unpopular with reformers, since Garfield made room for him by removing the efficient previous incumbent of his post, Dudley made himself even more disliked. Faced with the problem of hiring a large additional force, he advised that a board of three examiners recommend applicants to the Secretary of the Interior. The appointees, however, were to be apportioned according to the Republican vote of the states and territories. Regularly voting Republicans, who were mature veterans with qualities impossible to measure by competitive examinations, were to be preferred. Dudley's genius was squandered; the Arthur administration made appointments by time-honored methods. The largest share of the plums went to Stalwart senators.[10]

Senator Dawes also introduced a rival measure. Although he had never lost his reputation for respectability, Dawes cleverly dispensed patronage and was not above cooperating with the master spoilsman—Ben Butler. To remain in politics, one had to be a politician.

---

[9] *Congressional Record*, 47 Cong., 1 sess., 85, 94, 96, 100, 471, 930, 1093, 1697, 2099, 2357, 3925; Edwin Lawrence Godkin, "Reformers Who Do Not Wish to Reform," *Nation*, XXXIV, No. 885 (June 15, 1882), 496. Curiously, the *Nation* briefly favored the direct election of postmasters in 1871. *Ibid.*, XIII, No. 330 (October 26, 1871), 265.

[10] Edwin Lawrence Godkin, "Mr. Blaine as a Reformer," *ibid.*, XXXV, No. 898 (September 14, 1882), 214. On Dudley, see H. Meiser to Schurz, East Saginaw, Michigan, June 20, 1881, Schurz Papers, and Carl Schurz, "Performance and Evasion," *Nation*, XXXIV, No. 875 (April 6, 1882), 288. All politicians and congressmen, however, were not hostile to improvements demanded by the service itself. The Senate directed its civil service committee to investigate the advisability of fixed salaries for certain officeholders rather than allowed fees. Fixed salaries were suggested for the offices of district attorney, assistant district attorney, collector of customs, collector of internal revenue, deputy collector, and United States commissioner. *Congressional Record*, 47 Cong., 1 sess., 226.

As late as the summer of 1881, while Garfield lay wounded, Dawes had denied that further reform legislation was necessary. "But presto, what a change!" commented the hostile Greenfield (Massachusetts) *Gazette*. "Our chameleon Senator has prepared a Civil Service Reform bill and introduced it for the consideration of the Senate! He has concluded that more legislation is necessary. He snuffs it in the air. He sees it in the public prints. He learns it from petitions." Dawes testified that years of handling patronage problems had convinced him that the spoils system was wrong. Office seekers, he contended, took too much executive and congressional time, political considerations were paramount in making appointments, offices were regarded as charities for the needy, and the appointing power was overtaxed. All these conditions bred corruption. A Massachusetts senator no longer could ignore the mushrooming civil service reform associations' demand for legislation.[11]

The Dawes bill provided for competitive examinations—a long step for a congressman to take—but eliminated the machinery of a central commission. In Dawes's plan each department was to have its own board of examiners and would be responsible for its own appointments. No new officer and no new independent power would be created. The lack of direct responsibility, Dawes felt, was the chief vice of the current system. His plan, he pointed out, would actually put the New York Post Office system into effect throughout the whole civil service. Although Pendleton defended the commission as necessary for uniformity, he acknowledged that one feature of the Dawes bill was superior to his own. This feature specified appointment from the three examinees scoring highest on an examination, rather than from among the highest, and would make it even more difficult for an appointing officer to find a political lieutenant among eligible candidates. There was, Pendleton concluded, no substantial difference between Dawes's bill and his own.[12]

But the actual author of the Pendleton bill, Dorman B. Eaton, thought differently. "I am compelled to believe," he wrote Dawes, that the enactment of the bill "would seriously jeopardize the cause of reform." Eaton also opposed Dawes's plan in a series of

[11] *Ibid.*, pp. 579, 1083; "Senator Dawes," *Civil Service Record*, I, No. 8 (January, 1882), 9. The Greenfield *Gazette* clipping is enclosed in C. L. Fisk, Jr., to Dawes, Greenfield, January 30, 1882, Dawes Papers.
[12] *Congressional Record*, 47 Cong., 1 sess., 1085–86.

letters to the *Boston Advertiser*. The commission, he stated, was
designed to create uniformity in the system and could not be dispensed with. Other reformers—such as George William Curtis and
Carl Schurz—did not share Eaton's aversion to the Dawes bill and
thought his attack too strenuous. Curtis feared that Eaton's tactics
would precipitate a struggle among the few reformers in Congress
and begged Dawes and the others not to fight but to agree. "If *we*
fight, nothing will be done." [13]

II

The first session of the Forty-seventh Congress was bombarded with
petitions favoring everything from women's suffrage and prohibition
to competitive examinations for civil servants. Blanks printed and
circulated by civil service reform associations had resulted in more
than fifty petitions. Most of these came from urban areas and from
districts where reformers were elaborately organized. Over 10,000
Bostonians signed one petition, and thousands from Chicago signed
another; New York City, Philadelphia, Baltimore, and Cincinnati
also sent Congress long lists of petitioners. These petitions boasted
distinguished as well as numerous signatures. A single petition was
signed by Charles W. Eliot, Henry W. Longfellow, William James,
Charles Eliot Norton, Thomas Wentworth Higginson, and Brooks
Adams. Congressmen time and again commented that the signers
were intelligent, influential, and highly educated individuals. Professional classes were especially attracted by these petitions. Conspicuous among those who signed them were college professors and
students, clergymen, lawyers, and businessmen. Signatures running
into the thousands did create pressure, but this pressure affected only

---

[13] Eaton to Dawes, New York, March 18, 1882, Dawes Papers. Eaton's letters
to the *Boston Advertiser* are reprinted in the *Civil Service Record*, I, Nos. 9 and
10 (February and March, 1882), 22–23, 27–32. Curtis' disgust with Eaton for insisting on his bill with a commission rather than Dawes's bill without a commission reveals inconsistency on Curtis' part and perhaps some jealousy of Eaton.
Two years previously Curtis wrote Silas W. Burt, who shared Curtis' dislike of
Eaton: "I have felt with you about the board you mention. But now that Mr.
Eaton's book is finished, why not make him act as a *real* chairman, and tell him
what [he] ought officially to propose to the President? A single board is, under
the circumstances, essential." Curtis to Burt, West New Brighton, New York,
November 25, 1879, Burt Collection, New York Historical Society. On Curtis'
fear of Eaton's tactics, see Curtis to Charles Eliot Norton, West New Brighton,
March 7, 1882, Curtis Papers, Harvard University; Curtis to Dawes, West New
Brighton, March 8, 1882, Dawes Papers; Curtis to Schurz, New York, October 26,
1882, Schurz Papers.

those congressmen from centers of reform activity. Congress on the whole remained adamant against reform.[14]

Petitions were not the only omen of strong reform sentiment. A significant portion of the nation's metropolitan press, always in favor of civil service reform, clamored more insistently for action after Garfield's assassination. This clamor was kept up throughout the first half of 1882 when Congress was in session. Magazines were filled with reform articles. The *Century*, for example, ran articles on civil service reform in its January, February, and June issues. There was some dissent, especially among western and southern newspapers. The *Kansas City Times,* the *Madison* (Wisconsin) *Democrat,* and Denver's *Rocky Mountain News* all opposed reform; the *Atlanta Constitution* ignored it. But in large eastern cities, papers opposing reform—such as the *New York Tribune*—were exceptional. And letters like those of the octogenarian "wirepuller" Thurlow Weed, calling civil service reform "the first, if not the worst," of "the bad elements" with which "the atmosphere is charged," had about them the musty air of a bygone age that caused the irreverent to laugh. The congressional mind, however, seemed more akin to Thurlow Weed than to the reform press.[15]

Congress not only followed Arthur's recommendation of caution and passed no reform legislation during that session; it also rejected his plea for a $25,000 appropriation to re-activate the Civil Service Commission. An attempt was made in the House to pass the requested appropriation, but Joseph Cannon of Illinois and Henry Neal of Ohio, both Republicans, conspicuously opposed it because school children would take jobs from mature men who "bared their breasts to the leaden storm." Both parties showed contempt for their numerous platform declarations by voting down the appropriation. An attempt for a $24,000 appropriation and a third move to appropriate $15,000 also met ignominious defeat. Only five Republicans favored this inadequate appropriation. Later the eyes of the majority were opened somewhat by the unfavorable press comment their action had prompted. With a vote equal to its previous

---

[14] *Congressional Record,* 47 Cong., 1 sess., *passim;* Papers of the Senate Committee on Civil Service and Retrenchment, 47 Cong., 1 sess., National Archives, Washington, D. C.

[15] John Howard Thatcher, "Public Discussion of Civil Service Reform, 1864–1883" (Cornell University, 1943), pp. 214–215; *Nation,* XXXV, No. 906 (November 9, 1882), 392.

rejection, the House appropriated $15,000 in a bill which spent over $25,000,000. A few congressmen spoke in favor of responding to the President's wishes, but Roswell G. Horr of Michigan was outspoken in his opposition. The House laughed and applauded when he shouted, "If Jonah was one of these modern civil-service reformers my sympathies are all with the whale." Horr berated the commission as the greatest "humbug" in the country and claimed that it would result in the poorest possible selections. Referring to the bizarre method—a flip of the coin—by which Albert S. Willis, Kentucky Democrat and sponsor of the civil service reform bills in the House, had won his nomination, Horr advocated the Willis system, which selected candidates either by "draw-poker or by throwing coppers." Horr favored dividing the whole clerical force of the country among the congressional districts and making each congressman responsible for his appointments—an end which the Curtin bill would have brought about. Thus the paltry appropriation was not passed by the House without the blatant advocacy of the most extreme spoils position—complete congressional exercise of the appointing power.[16]

The personnel of the House Select Committee on Civil Service Reform illustrated both Speaker Joseph Warren Keifer's perverted sense of humor and congressional hostility to reform. Horr was named a member of this committee. Some of his equally distinguished colleagues were chairman Godlove S. Orth of Indiana, a signer of assessment circulars; Benjamin F. Butterworth of Ohio, a congressman elected through the efforts of an ex-convict and ex-Democratic boss; and Jay A. Hubbell of Michigan, a famous collector of "voluntary contributions." In response to the urgent demand for civil service reform, these men with seven other committeemen produced after six month's labor "a bill to enlarge the powers and duties of the Department of Agriculture." [17]

While Congress ridiculed reform, the nation's press continued to expose the evils of the spoils system. "Voluntary contributions" were prominently publicized in 1882. Assessments generally came to 2 per cent of the officeholder's annual salary, but in many cases the officeholder's income was tapped by a state as well as by a congressional campaign committee. Some individuals were assessed up

---

[16] *Ibid.*, No. 889 (July 13, 1882), 22; *ibid.*, No. 890 (July 20, 1882), 41; *Congressional Record*, 47 Cong., 1 sess., 6013–16.

[17] The description of this committee is drawn from an attack on it by Willis in a speech before the House. *Ibid.*, pp. 5810–12.

to 7 per cent. Republican officeholders were not the only government employees to be assessed. Despite their sanctimonious attacks on Republican assessment of federal employees, Democrats assessed whenever and wherever they were able. New York City employees in 1881 were asked to contribute "voluntarily" 2½ per cent of their annual salaries to the Democratic party.[18]

It is difficult to ascertain how much revenue assessments produced. A Democratic congressman calculated that the Republican Congressional Campaign Committee would raise $2,000,000 in 1882, but the fulfillment of this estimate would have meant universal compliance. A Republican senator defending assessments claimed that only one-tenth of the civil service (11,514 out of 100,000) paid their assessment in 1880. The total amount raised by the 1878 circular, according to Republicans, was a bit over $106,000. To this figure, however, one must add the revenue collected by the more successful and less considerate state and local committees. A Virginia postmaster who paid his assessment to General William Mahone with a $20 Confederate note was not saved from removal by his sense of humor. When his neighbors sympathized with him, the post office was discontinued. Such methods inspired greater generosity on the state level. When in 1881 only about one-third of the New York Customhouse employees contributed to the state Republican executive committee, Republicans covered up their attempt at compulsory assessments by falsely stressing that contributions had been voluntary (assessment circulars had been printed) and correctly stressing the small response.[19]

Waning revenue from political assessments forced spoilsmen to scrape the bottom of the barrel. The assessment of navy yard laborers (evidently for the first time) in 1882, rather than indicating the

---

[18] In 1882, Mahone assessed federal officeholders from Virginia 5 per cent in addition to their regular 2 per cent assessment by the Republican Congressional Campaign Committee. *Nation*, XXXV, No. 896 (August 31, 1882), 165. Republicans claimed that almost all New York City employees contributed, but such unanimity is doubtful. Since the tenure of city employees in New York State was secured by statute as interpreted by the Court of Appeals, employees could refuse to contribute without fear of dismissal. Edwin Lawrence Godkin, "Which Raised Most Money for the Canvass," *ibid.*, XXXIII, No. 854 (November 10, 1881), 369.

[19] *Congressional Record*, 47 Cong., 1 sess., 5332–33, 5378, 5812; *Nation*, XXXV, No. 904 (October 26, 1882), 346; Edwin Lawrence Godkin, "Which Raised Most Money for the Canvass," *ibid.*, XXXIII, No. 854 (November 10, 1881), 369; *New York Tribune*, November 8, 1881, p. 1, c. 1.

audacity and growing power of the spoilsmen,[20] is more likely evidence that shrinking returns made it necessary to mail circulars to all possible donors. Civil servants were beginning to take at face value the protests that no one would be dismissed for refusing to contribute.

Taking advantage of the growing feeling against assessments, the New York Civil Service Reform Association set about to secure enforcement of the anti-assessment statute of 1876. This law prohibited government officers who were not appointed by the President and confirmed by the Senate from demanding or receiving money or property for political purposes. General Newton M. Curtis, a special Treasury Department agent, received such funds. In December, 1881, the New York association called this violation to the attention of Secretary of the Treasury Charles J. Folger, who sidestepped the issue by having Curtis resign and then turned the case over to the United States District Attorney. To the surprise and gratification of reformers, the federal government decided to prosecute the case; but the first indictment was quashed on the grounds that the defendant's given name was Newton, not "Nehemiah" as the copy clerk had indicated.[21]

Reformers blamed the President himself for the fiasco. One Julia Sand, self-appointed conscience to Arthur, questioned him, "Who is responsible for that mean little trick about 'Nehemiah M. Curtis'? But why should I ask, when I know, as well as you do, that you are? The thing would not have been done without your approval. But, if the blunder was a trick, it is equally true that the trick was a blunder, for everybody sees through it. . . . If you wish the public to believe that that blunder was really a mistake, there is only one way to do it—order your oily District Attorney to rectify the mistake & continue the prosecution."[22] The New York association also

---

[20] *Nation*, XXXIV, No. 885 (June 15, 1882), 491.

[21] "Address of Mr. Curtis Before the National League," *Civil Service Record*, II, No. 3 (August, 1882), 19. According to Burt, Newton M. Curtis was actually quite friendly to reform. Silas Wright Burt, "A Brief History of the Civil Service Reform Movement in the United States," [1906, revised in 1908], p. P, Burt Writings, New York Public Library.

[22] Julia I. Sand to Arthur, Saratoga, April, no day, 1882, Arthur Papers, Library of Congress. Some of the most interesting letters in the Arthur Papers are those from Julia Sand. These letters plying the President with advice—such as to stay clear of his old New York political friends—betray a real motherly fondness for Arthur and the hope that, like England's Henry V, he would break with his past now that he had come into power. Arthur seemed to have genuinely appreci-

goaded the government, which was ready to drop the case, into making a second effort. In the trial which followed, Curtis was convicted. Arthur's old and ardent friend, Edwin D. Morgan, former governor of and senator from New York, urged him to pardon Curtis for doing what "most of us have ourselves done," but Julia Sand's sentiments prevailed. When his application for a new trial was rejected, Curtis was fined $500, which, along with his expenses, was paid by the New York State Republican Committee. The conviction and the constitutionality of the statute of 1876 were later sustained by the Supreme Court.[23]

Oblivious to public sentiment following Garfield's death, Jay Hubbell, chairman of the Republican Congressional Campaign Committee, mailed the familiar assessment letter to officeholders in May, 1882. After carefully stipulating the amount expected, the letter explained that the committee was "authorized to state that such voluntary contributions from persons employed in the service of the United States will not be objected to in any official quarter." It was important that these contributions should seem to be voluntary; compulsory assessments were no longer in vogue after President Hayes's celebrated civil service order prohibiting them. Baldly favoring assessments was now as politically indiscreet as favoring free love—or even more so. Great care was taken in composing a letter asking for voluntary contributions in a compulsory manner. Chairman Hubbell's letter admirably suited this purpose, as it well might since President Hayes himself had aided the drafting of a similar letter to circumvent his own civil service order.

Assessments—whatever their real value—were regarded by Republican politicians as an indispensable source of revenue, while Democrats saw in them an inexhaustible "slush fund." To stop assessments—at least until they were in power—was a Democratic objective. In Congress moves were made to prevent assessments through amendments to appropriation bills, but these efforts were invaria-

---

ated Julia Sand's interest and on at least one occasion complied with her request and visited her while in New York.

[23] "Address of Mr. Curtis Before the National League," *Civil Service Record,* II, No. 3 (August, 1882), 19; Morgan to Arthur, New York, June 9, 1882, Arthur Papers; *Documents Relating to the Removal from Office of General N. M. Curtis* . . . (New York, 1882), *passim;* "The United States Against Newton M. Curtis," *Civil Service Record,* II, No. 3 (August, 1882), 23; "Decision of the United States Supreme Court in the Curtis Case," *ibid.,* II, No. 8 (January, 1883), 65–67.

bly voted down. Republicans remained unshaken by Democratic accusations of carrying Indiana in 1880 not only with Star Route graft but with "bread or blood money" extorted from civil servants.[24]

Vigorous protests greeted the stereotyped assessment circular issued in 1882. Jay Hubbell had miscalculated the emotional temper of the people. The northeastern press protested,[25] and the New York Civil Service Reform Association—still gloating over its recent court victory—promptly warned officeholders that response to the circular would render them liable to prosecution. The association's action was criticized by the *Philadelphia Record,* a strongly anti-assessment paper, which said it was absurd to place officeholders "between the upper grindstone of dismissal and the lower one of prosecution" and suggested there was "something paltry in squeezing the little sinners while all the big ones go untouched." [26]

One "big sinner," however, felt touched. Hubbell answered the association's warning to officeholders with an indignant letter to its president, George William Curtis, insisting that the assessment circular had been misrepresented and demanding an immediate settlement of differences. Ignoring Hubbell's demand, the counsel of the New York association informed Attorney General Benjamin Harris Brewster that he was expected to enforce the statute of 1876, and Brewster promised to look into the matter. An enraged Hubbell resorted to the "bloody shirt" for a fantastic defense of assessments, which somehow prevented southern outrages. Curtis in opposing this noble work was a "most efficient ally of the Southern Bulldozer." [27]

Despite the Hubbell-Curtis correspondence, assessments were paid. Occasionally a southern postmaster refused to contribute, but, on the other hand, laborers in the navy yards were extremely prompt

---

[24] *Congressional Record,* 47 Cong., 1 sess., 4854–60, 4909–12, 5329–33, 5335–44, 5377–78, 5663–65, 5813, 5923.

[25] "Stand and Deliver," *Harper's Weekly* (New York), XXXVI, No. 1329 (June 10, 1882), 355; *Philadelphia Record,* June 25, 1882, p. 2, c. 1. The circular was defended, however, by the *San Francisco Chronicle,* June 1, 1882, p. 2, c. 1; *ibid.,* July 10, 1882, p. 2, c. 1.

[26] Printed letter to federal officeholders from George William Curtis, Everett P. Wheeler, and William Potts for the New York Civil Service Reform Association, New York, June 17, 1882, Papers of the National Civil Service League, New York; *Philadelphia Record,* June 23, 1882, p. 2, c. 2.

[27] This correspondence is reprinted in "Assessment Circulars," *Civil Service Record,* II, No. 2 (July, 1882), 11–14.

to respond. Payments were aided by Attorney General Brewster's mid-July opinion that the statute of 1876 did not apply to congress-men. Spoilsmen received further aid from administration politicians. A. A. Freeman, the Assistant Attorney General for the Post Office, called the anti-assessment statute unconstitutional and claimed that it interfered with man's natural right to spend his money as he chooses. Secretary of the Treasury Folger kindly assured a Treasury employee, who longed to pay his assessment but was intimidated by threats of reformers, that it was perfectly safe to contribute.[28] Spoilsmen did not give up campaign funds easily. Inertia prevented them from seeing that assessments had become a political liability.

III

Throughout the first half of 1882 other issues as well as assessments occupied the political scene. Arthur's appointments held the center of the stage against an ominous backdrop created by the Star Route trials. In Pennsylvania an Independent Republican revolt, originat-ing in a squabble over spoils, was under way against Cameron fol-lowers and the Stalwart administration. Its repercussions were na-tional. Massachusetts was alienated when Arthur appointed Roland Worthington, editor of Boston's one Stalwart newspaper, Boston collector. In a protest letter, a plain-spoken acquaintance of Worth-ington called him a liar, cheat, and swindler. This appointment, ig-noring senatorial courtesy as much as had Hayes's removal of Arthur from the New York Customhouse, was made in defiance of the state's senators, the Republican merchants, and the press. It was not the only instance of Arthur's use of patronage for Stalwart ends. After a particularly flagrant case of replacing a Half-Breed incum-bent with a Stalwart, the Half-Breed *Tribune*—a firm supporter of the spoils system, which it called practical politics—winced, pro-tested, but did not recant its faith. Arthur, however, removed few individuals, but by refusing to reappoint nearly half the officers whose terms had expired he was able to appoint many Stalwarts. John Hay, a respected Half-Breed, accurately characterized Arthur's

---

[28] *Nation*, XXXV, No. 889 (July 13, 1882), 24; *ibid.*, No. 891 (July 27, 1882), 61; *ibid.*, No. 892 (August 3, 1882), 81. Brewster's action notified district attorneys throughout the country not to indict anyone under the act. Reformers were in need of a judicial construction of the act, but with Brewster's opinion the chance of obtaining one was nil unless a grand jury somewhere found an indictment.

policy—to "gobble all the vacancies for his particular friends and talk reform at every gobble." [29]

Legislation and the collecting of political assessments made reformers as displeased with Congress as with the President. "How disgustingly Congress has behaved!" commented Julia Sand, after the passage in August of an immense pork barrel River and Harbor Act over Arthur's veto. Democrats and Republicans had joined forces to drain the Treasury of $18,000,000. Following this act came Jay Hubbell's second letter requesting "voluntary" assessments. Hubbell expressed surprise that some civil servants had not responded, but concluded that pressing cares were responsible. This time a reply by return mail was requested. In Washington, agents of Hubbell's committee appeared in the departments armed with marked lists of employees. Those who had not as yet "voluntarily" contributed were approached personally. Cash on the barrel or the promise of it on the next payday was expected.[30]

Already under fire for its unanimous support of the River and Harbor Act, the Massachusetts delegation began to recognize the dominant opinion in its state against political assessments. George Frisbie Hoar announced that he regarded Hubbell's first circular as "unfortunate" and the second one containing a veiled threat "doubly so." Hoar thought it improper for senators and representatives to ask for political donations, since they were largely responsible for the nomination of civil servants. His opinion would have had more moral weight if it had come three months earlier when Hubbell issued his first circular. But even if tardy, a Massachusetts senator had to get on the right side of the question.[31]

In August, in an atmosphere of intense reaction against political assessments and Stalwart appointments, the National Civil Service

[29] Henry Hitchcock to Schurz, St. Louis, May 30, 1882, Schurz Papers; *Atlanta Constitution*, June 1, 1882, p. 4, c. 1; *San Francisco Chronicle*, May 26, 1882, p. 2, c. 2; Albert G. Browne to Dawes, Salem, April 13, 1882, Dawes Papers; *Nation*, XXXIV, No. 876 (April 13, 1882), 303; Edwin Lawrence Godkin, "The True Course for Independents and 'Half-Breeds,'" *ibid.*, No. 883 (June 1, 1882), 456; Howe, *op. cit.*, p. 207; John Hay to Albert Rhodes, Cleveland, February 14, 1883, in John Hay, *Letters and Extracts from the Diary* . . . (Washington, 1908), II, 90.

[30] Julia I. Sand to Arthur, New York, August 3, 1882, Arthur Papers; *Nation*, XXXV, No. 893 (August 10, 1882), 101; *ibid.*, No. 896 (August 31, 1882), 168.

[31] Representatives William W. Crapo and William A. Russell also spoke out for reform. *Ibid.*, No. 898 (September 14, 1882), 209.

Reform League held its second annual meeting at Newport, Rhode Island. George William Curtis, the league's president, attacked Arthur for his appointments and Hubbell for his assessments and warned the major parties that if the Pennsylvania reform movement were not heeded, a new party built on reform principles would result. The league was not content with mere denunciations. Angered by the derision with which Congress had treated civil service reform, it decided to become more active politically to secure a friendlier Congress. The *New York Times* enthusiastically reported the league's plan for questioning candidates on specific civil service reform measures and publishing their replies. If neither major candidate favored their cause, reformers planned to run their own man. It was agreed to prepare a general address to all voters and a specific one to the very receptive audience of clergymen, professors, and friends of education. The challenge of the spoilsmen was accepted, and this time the odds were with reformers.[32]

Almost all state party conventions held in 1882 favored civil service reform, and many politicians announced their "conversion." Everyone, including Greenbackers, Prohibitionists, and Anti-Monopolists, was for civil service reform, but few specifically demanded open-competitive examinations. Democratic conventions tended to damn political assessments and to soft-pedal competitive examinations. Southern and western conventions were less concerned with civil service reform than those in the North and East.[33]

When the Blaine-controlled Maine Republican Convention opposed civil service reform, Independent Republicans supported an insurgent ticket demanding reform. After this revolt, Blaine forgot the "bloody shirt," finances, and protection, and remembered civil service reform. Years before, in a letter to Jenckes, Blaine inferred his support of reform. Now he favored a species of reform—a seven-year term of office similar to the four-year term recently advocated

---

[32] "Questioning Candidates," *New York Times*, August 18, 1882, p. 4, cc. 3–4; *Proceedings at the Annual Meeting of the National Civil-Service Reform League Held at Newport, Rhode Island, August 2, 1882, with the Address of the President Hon. George William Curtis* (New York, 1882), pp. 5–35.

[33] "Resolutions of Conventions," *Civil Service Record*, II, No. 5 (October, 1882), 38; *Nation*, XXXV, No. 896 (August 31, 1882), 168; *ibid.*, No. 899 (September 21, 1882), 232. Both New York conventions and the Massachusetts Republican Convention supported competitive examinations. *Ibid.*, No. 900 (September 28, 1882), 252.

by President Arthur. Reformers did not take Blaine's declaration at face value; they could not forget that just a year previously he had "wallowed" in spoils like a "rhinoceros in an African pool." Carl Schurz accurately predicted that "in spite of 'booms' and 'plumes' and reform professions" Blaine would never be elected President.[34]

Blaine was joined in October by Benjamin F. Butler—the most fantastic "convert" of them all. Perennially seeking the governorship of Massachusetts from any party, Butler received the Democratic nomination in 1882 and posed as the reformer par excellence who advocated competitive examinations for even the "highest" offices. Apparently Butler was willing to take a competitive examination for the governorship—something the most zealous reformer had never advocated. The blatant spoilsman went on to say: "Integrity, capability, and efficiency in the incumbent have always seemed to me to insure to the occupant the best tenure of office. This in a public life of more than a score of years . . . has always been my guide. So that I can assert that I have never asked an officer so qualified to give way to any appointee of my recommendation. Indeed, upon the desirability of this tenure I can hardly believe that there is not a substantial agreement in the minds of all good men." [35] Although reformers did not take Ben Butler seriously, he found it necessary to take reform seriously.

Republican candidates failed to match their party platforms. Spoilsmen of that party continued to blunder. Dominated by the administration faction, the New York Republican Convention nominated Secretary of the Treasury Charles J. Folger for governor. As chairman of the Republican State Committee, the convention elected John F. Smyth, an expert at fixing primaries, who as former state superintendent of insurance had been impeached and narrowly escaped conviction. Theodore Roosevelt, who was running for the New York Assembly, regarded the election of Smyth as "an insult

---

[34] *Ibid.*, No. 896 (August 31, 1882), 168; *ibid.*, No. 898 (September 14, 1882), 210; Edwin Lawrence Godkin, "Mr. Blaine as a Reformer," *ibid.*, p. 214; Blaine to Thomas A. Jenckes, Augusta, November 7, 1868, Jenckes Papers, Library of Congress; Schurz to Joseph Medill, New York, September 21, 1882, in Frederic Bancroft, ed., *Speeches, Correspondence and Political Papers of Carl Schurz* (New York, 1913), IV, 155–156.

[35] *Nation*, XXXV, No. 902 (October 12, 1882), 298; Edwin Lawrence Godkin, "General Butler's Acceptance," *ibid.*, p. 300.

to honest men." [36] This opinion was shared by thousands. The Democrats, on the other hand, shrewdly nominated for governor the reforming mayor of Buffalo, Grover Cleveland. Immediately the chief Republican paper in Buffalo came out for Cleveland, and Independent Republicans such as Henry Ward Beecher and George William Curtis advocated "scratching" Folger's name to vote for Cleveland. [37]

Republicans elsewhere were also having troubles, as Jay Hubbell illustrated in Michigan. Earlier in the summer Hubbell had hoped to take Senator Thomas W. Ferry's place, but in September he even failed renomination to Congress. Although his defeat may have been caused by his local struggle with Ferry, it was attributed to political assessments. Two weeks after his defeat, Hubbell's campaign textbook (issued by the Republican Congressional Campaign Committee) appeared. The sections on civil service reform and political assessments were hysterically vituperative. George William Curtis, the epitome of decency, was especially singled out by Hubbell. He was called everything from "bogus reformer" to "partisan of ballot-box stuffers." This book only supplied more grist for the reformers' mill. [38]

Spoilsmen were still on the defensive when the campaign reached its last month. Local civil service reform associations carried out their league's recommendations and solicited and published candidates' views on specific reform measures. [39] When Republicans lost the October Ohio election, the press blamed the temperance issue

[36] *Ibid.*, No. 900 (September 28, 1882), 251; *ibid.*, No. 901 (October 5, 1882), 275; Roosevelt to William Thomas O'Neil, New York, November 12, 1882, in Elting E. Morison, John M. Blum, and John J. Buckley, eds., *The Letters of Theodore Roosevelt* (Cambridge, 1951–54), I, 58–59.

[37] Curtis' action nearly led to a shake-up in the editorial office of *Harper's Weekly*. His article on the nomination of Folger was edited to support Folger, and in view of his previous writings made Curtis look ridiculous. Deeply hurt, Curtis resigned, but the Harpers made amends by reassuring his independence and publishing in the next issue a letter clarifying his anti-Folger position. Curtis to Norton, Ashfield, Massachusetts, September 27, 1882, and New York, October 4, 1882, Curtis Papers.

[38] *Nation*, XXXV, No. 891 (July 27, 1882), 61; *ibid.*, No. 899 (September 21, 1882), 231; *The Republican Campaign Text Book for 1882* (Washington, 1882), pp. 99–103, 113–114.

[39] See, for example, "Reform in California," *New York Times*, September 17, 1882, p. 8, c. 1; Henry Hitchcock to Burt, St. Louis, October 2, 1882, Burt Collection; *Civil Service Record*, II, Nos. 3–6 (August–November, 1882), 23–24, 26–28, 39–40, 46.

and the resulting defection of Republican Germans. Ohio Republicans had interfered with the German's "Sunday recreation." Many Germans did switch, but Carl Schurz noted that the remaining Republican vote also fell off in strong temperance areas. Republicans had been chastised for civil service abuses such as the Jay Hubbel¹ assessment circular and the appointment of Stalwarts in the martyred Garfield's home state. As former President Rutherford B. Hayes said, the defeat was caused by "dissatisfaction with the boss system." [40]

The election in November proved the early Ohio election an accurate barometer. Republicans were defeated by huge majorities in many states. New York, Pennsylvania, Indiana, Connecticut, New Jersey, and even Massachusetts registered Republican setbacks. Cleveland was elected governor by what was then the largest majority in New York history. One hundred thousand Republicans did not support the Cameron ticket in Pennsylvania, and in Massachusetts thousands of others stayed home to let Ben Butler have the governorship.[41] Though Butler's election was a blow to reformers, two Massachusetts congressmen conspicuous for their contempt of civil service reform were defeated. One was beaten by an Independent Republican, Theodore Lyman, who entered the race solely on civil service reform grounds.[42] Reformers blamed the broad Democratic victory on the failure of Republicans to take reform seriously. Indeed, many of the local issues were over spoils practices: the New York Republicans were angered over administration appointments of Stalwarts and the scandal of the recent Republican Convention, and Pennsylvania was thoroughly sick of the Cameron dictatorship.

[40] Carl Schurz, "The Political Situation," *Nation*, XXXV, No 903 (October 19, 1882), 324. John Sherman, however, agreed with the press. John Sherman, *Recollections* (Chicago, 1895), II, 847. For complaints of Arthur's appointments in Ohio, see John Sherman to Hayes, Washington, July 2, 1882, and Hayes to Sherman, Fremont, July 5, 1882, Hayes Papers, The Rutherford B. Hayes Library, Fremont, Ohio; Hayes to Schurz, Fremont, October 12, 1882, Schurz Papers.

[41] Senator Hoar thought the civil service reform forces had allied with Butler. Hoar to Dawes, Worcester, November 8, 1882, Dawes Papers.

[42] The defeated incumbents were Selwyn Z. Bowman and John W. Candler. One month before the election, reformers despaired of the Massachusetts Independent movement since they had been unable to unite and "pull together as the machine men do." Success therefore had been doubly gratifying and indicated the tremendous strength of the Independents. Thomas Wentworth Higginson to Schurz, Cambridge, October 11, 1882, and Schurz to Higginson, New York, October 13, 1882, Schurz Papers.

The defeat was brought about, said the *Nation,* "not by this or that local trouble, but by a trouble that prevails in a greater or less degree everywhere." [43]

---

[43] *Nation,* XXXV, No. 906 (November 9, 1882), 389. This same viewpoint is expressed in the *Philadelphia Inquirer,* November 8, 1882, p. 4, c. 2, and the *San Francisco Chronicle,* November 8, 1882, p. 4, c. 2.

XIII

CONGRESSIONAL ACTION

"Congress is like a pack of whipped boys this winter," wrote Mrs. Henry Adams of the lameduck session in 1883. The same Congress that first rejected then reluctantly approved an inadequate appropriation for the Civil Service Commission now moved with haste to consider the Pendleton bill. Led by members of Jay Hubbell's campaign committee, congressmen moved with equal rapidity to end political assessments. A conversion had taken place under the stimulus of the election of 1882. The rejection of the Republican party at the polls hit many conspicuously identified with the spoils system. Political assessments had proved a liability. Abuses of officeholders still made good newspaper copy to a people grieving over their President's assassination by a disappointed office seeker.[1]

I

The outlook for the Republican party in 1884 was not promising; members of that party were filled with apprehension and the Democrats with anticipation. The "outs" were nearly in and the "ins" were nearly out. Yet the lameduck session of the Forty-seventh Congress had been elected in 1880 and was very much Republican. The

---

[1] Marian Hooper Adams to Robert William Hooper, Washington, January 7, 1883, in Ward Thoron, ed., *The Letters of Mrs. Henry Adams, 1865–1883* (Boston, 1936), p. 414. Eugene Hale, author of a powerful speech in defense of political assessments which Hubbell had printed as a campaign document, asked on the floor of the Senate "with a virtuous flush on his cheeks, 'Do you suppose anybody here would vote against a proposition to strengthen the law prohibiting political assessments?'" William B. Allison, another member of Hubbell's committee, promised to "go as far as any Senator to prohibit the soliciting of them [political assessments]." *Nation* (New York), XXXV, No. 911 (December 14, 1882), 495.

congressional "outs," or at least those who very shortly would be "outs," were in a majority and controlled the presidency. It would be advantageous for Republicans to make permanent the tenure of their office-holding friends while supporting the reform their constituents so obviously desired. Accordingly, the Republican senators met in caucus to discuss the Pendleton bill. Pending amendments were considered, and those offered by Republicans were generally approved. No vote was taken and nothing was done to bind senators to a particular course, but it was understood that all Republican senators with one or two exceptions would vote for the Pendleton bill.[2] Republicans supported the bill for two reasons: they could pose as reformers in 1884 and win back lost support, and they could "freeze" Republicans in office behind civil service rules if the Democrats would win the election.

The Democrats, on the other hand, were in a dilemma. Should they support reform, thus keeping the Independent vote while losing a share of the spoils, or should they oppose reform, risking the election without the Independent vote in a gamble to capture all the booty?[3] Democrats were, of course, strongly opposed to political assessments, which could hurt them during the next presidential campaign. The Congress that met in December, 1882, was thinking of 1884.

President Arthur, too, had been "converted" by the election of 1882. His message to Congress called for passage of the Pendleton bill, since the people desired prompt and definite action. After years of listening to the importunities of office seekers, Arthur, like other converts, now viewed patronage as an onerous burden rather than as a sacred trust. The President's attitude toward political assessments had also been transformed. He could now see that so-called voluntary contributions were at times obtained solely through fear

---

[2] *Ibid.*, No. 912 (December 21, 1882), 522.

[3] This same question was posed by the *Philadelphia Inquirer*, December 7, 1882, p. 4, c. 3, after contrasting the change in the political scene since the Pendleton bill was introduced at the last session. "Will they [Democrats] be so eager now, when, if passed, Senator Pendleton's bill would clip their wings and prevent a Democratic President from removing a single one of the present one hundred thousand Republican officeholders except for cause? . . . They have an excellent opportunity to prove their zeal for civil service reform. Should they prove it by passing the Pendleton Act then will the political millennium be near at hand." The Pendleton bill applied to about 10,000 officers, not 100,000 as the *Inquirer* stated.

of dismissal. A bill to prevent their collection, he stated, would receive his signature.[4] "Chet" Arthur had traveled a long way from the New York Customhouse.

Pendleton defended his bill before the Senate on December 12, 1882. His speech largely reiterated ideas he had presented a year previously. The efficiency of the Republican-controlled civil service as a political army and its inefficiency as an office force was again developed to the chagrin of Republicans. The same cure, competitive examinations, was recommended. Pendleton's speech further endeavored to answer two common objections to competitive examinations. He argued that they were not aristocratic, since all were eligible to compete. In answer to the western and southern fear that the examinations would be geared to the college student, Pendleton quoted New York Naval Officer Silas W. Burt to show that mature men without college training secured the best marks on New York Customhouse examinations.

Pendleton's strong stand for reform caused disaffection among Ohio Democrats and ultimately cost him his senatorial career. He rejected a suggestion by fellow party members that action be delayed until after the 1884 election, when Democrats instead of Republicans would be frozen in the departments. Pendleton pointed out that if Democrats did not pass the reform bill before the next election, there would not be a Democrat in the White House. The Independents had placed them on probation.[5]

Although the shift in senatorial attitudes seemed truly remarkable, the speeches and the actions of many supporters of the bill betrayed a fundamental opposition to the civil service reform movement. The undertone was one of expediency rather than of sympathy, and the spirit of compromise was not dead. A Washington officeholder, who complained to Schurz that congressional reform efforts were spasmodic, doubted "very much . . . the sincerity of any move in that quarter." Dorman B. Eaton, lobbying for the Pendleton bill, was alarmed by Congressman John A. Kasson's effort to push a compromise measure, which Republicans had hastily

---

[4] James D. Richardson, *A Compilation of the Messages and Papers of the Presidents 1789–1897* (Washington, 1896–99), VIII, 145–147. For a discussion of Arthur and civil service reform, see George Frederick Howe, *Chester A. Arthur* (New York, 1934), pp. 204–217.

[5] For Pendleton's speech and the provisions of his bill, see *Congressional Record*, 47 Cong., 2 sess., 204–208.

drafted in committee to head off the Democratic Pendleton bill. Reformers were particularly hostile to Kasson's measure, for it did not require competitive examinations and invited rotation by providing for a fixed period of tenure. Senator Henry L. Dawes's activities in behalf of his rival bill also alarmed Eaton, who promptly sent to New York for copies of his pamphlet attacking Dawes's measure. Republican Senator John Sherman desired a limited tenure of office and Senator James Z. George, a Mississippi Democrat, posed a "real" solution—a constitutional amendment providing for the local election of all federal officers.[6] In a situation not of their own choosing, congressmen followed the command of public opinion but tried, by linking their names and support to rival reform measures, to get maximum credit for doing as little as possible. It was apparent, however, that a reform-demanding public could not be satisfied by these compromise measures, and Kasson, Dawes, Sherman, and George eventually voted for the Pendleton bill.

Many congressmen found themselves in ludicrous positions. Most ludicrous of all was that friend of the Union veteran, Senator John A. Logan, Republican from Illinois. An intimate adviser to General Grant, Logan had long been a Stalwart's Stalwart and since the days of Thomas A. Jenckes a most conspicuous opponent of civil service reform. The election of 1882 coupled with personal presidential ambitions for 1884 no doubt converted Logan. He insisted that he had not contributed money to political campaigns for several years and, although he did not "claim to be a reformer," boasted that he had introduced a bill in 1868 "almost exactly like the bill now before the Senate." Logan justified his previous opposition to reform by demanding that the bill stipulate the precise duties of the commission instead of repeating the mistake of 1871, which resulted in failure. Logan tried hard to make it appear that vagueness, rather than his own and others' opposition, had killed Grant's Civil Service Commission. Less than a year before civil service reform had been a jest to politicians—now the tables were

---

[6] George W. Lockwood to Carl Schurz, Washington, December 15, 1882, Schurz Papers, Library of Congress; Edward Younger, *John A. Kasson* (Iowa City, 1955), p. 316; "Boston Civil Service Work," *New York Times*, December 15, 1882, p. 2, cc. 6–7; George William Curtis to Silas W. Burt, West New Brighton, New York, December 25, 1882, Burt Collection, New York Historical Society; Everett Pepperrell Wheeler to Schurz, New York, December 12, 1882, Schurz Papers; *Congressional Record*, 47 Cong., 2 sess., 319–321.

turned. "Civil Service reform," Mrs. Henry Adams—conscious of
actress Lily Langtry's impact on Washington coiffures—shrewdy observed, "is as fashionable as a 'Langtry bang.' " [7]

A few senators seemed genuinely happy to give the Pendleton
measure their wholehearted support. Two of these were George
Frisbie Hoar of Massachusetts and Warner Miller of New York—
both Republicans representing strong centers of reform. Hoar congratulated the country that this session would mark the time when
both parties "under the spur and excitement of an aroused public
opinion" were willing to give up the weapon of spoils. He favored
the bill because it had the support of the civil service reformers
who had studied the subject most thoroughly and to whom existing
public sentiment was largely due. Warner Miller, who had replaced
Thomas C. Platt, favored the Pendleton bill as it came from committee without amendment "in obedience . . . to the wishes of
many of my constituents, expressed to me in letters which I have
received from several prominent citizens of New York who have
carefully investigated and studied this question." Miller also approved the next big objective of the civil service reform movement
—repealing the law limiting the terms of certain officers to four
years. Miller, however, was a true party man; he boasted of civil
service efficiency after twenty-one years of Republican control with
very few removals. He ignored the dismissals spawned by intra-
party factional strife even though he owed his own senatorial seat
to the most spectacular of such struggles staged by Conkling and
Platt.[8]

A few stanch supporters of the spoils system were not caught up
in the reform avalanche. Senator Joseph E. Brown of Georgia was
the most conspicuous member of this small group. A true chameleon,
Brown had dexterously managed to keep in the forefront of Georgia
politics. Beginning as a prewar Democrat, he continued as the war
governor of Georgia, later became a scalawag, and then a post-
Reconstruction Democrat. Renowned for obstructing the Confederate war effort more effectively than many Union generals, Brown
was also the chief obstruction to the passage of the Pendleton bill.
He warned Democrats that, after twenty-two lean years, victory and

[7] *Ibid.*, pp. 246–247, 650; Marian Adams to Hooper, Washington, December
17, 1882, in Thoron, *op. cit.*, p. 408. For Logan's bill, see *supra*, p. 57, n. 19.
[8] *Congressional Record*, 47 Cong., 2 sess., 273–275, 282–284, 316–319.

power would be theirs in two years if they did not blunder. He reminded them that the bill would cause them to go before the country "handicapped" and force them to tell the people "that all the offices that amount to anything . . . are already disposed of" by the Pendleton bill. Brown insisted that parties fight for office as well as for principle and argued that Democrats would not work with the same zeal if offices were not held out to them. Contradicting his earlier warning that if victorious the bill would leave Democrats with only the lowest positions as plunder, Brown claimed that the Pendleton bill would be impossible to enforce and called it "humbug . . . deception and nonsense." What Brown wanted was his party in office. He was even willing to favor competitive examination for all offices if Democrats would be chosen until each party controlled half of the civil service. Mrs. Adams fancied that Brown "was only a little more outspoken than his colleagues in saying . . . 'It's all a humbug,' and maintaining that each party as it came to power must take the spoils." [9]

Although the portion of Brown's speech which boldly defended the spoils system met with mixed reception from Democrats, they unanimously supported his opposition to limiting civil service entrance to the lowest grade. Democrats favored admission to all civil service grades; this policy would shorten the time it would take for an equal distribution of offices to be reached. The question before congressmen was not what would be best for the civil service, but what would be best for their party. John Tyler Morgan, Alabama Democrat, provided a needed rationale. Certain offices, notably the Patent Office, required the highly developed skills of law, science, and art. Since these skills were not developed by working up from the lowest position, he argued that all grades should be open to competitive examinations. Democrats in this instance were successful; the Senate adopted their view. This concession, however, was the only one they would receive.[10]

---

[9] Marian Adams to Hooper, Washington, December 17, 1882, in Thoron, *op. cit.*, p. 408. For details of Brown's early career, see Louise Biles Hill, *Joseph E. Brown and the Confederacy* (Chapel Hill, 1939), *passim. Congressional Record,* 47 Cong., 2 sess., 276–279; *Nation,* XXXV, No. 911 (December 14, 1882), 495. The *Atlanta Constitution,* December 14, 1882, p. 4, c. 1, applauded Brown for courageously asserting what many Democrats thought about keeping Republicans in office, but added "many democrats will swallow it [Democratic loss of offices] rather than go on record against a reform that is greatly needed."

[10] *Congressional Record,* 47 Cong., 2 sess., 468–470, 600–610, 620–621.

Emboldened by success, Democrats made further moves to capture departments affected by the bill. An amendment proposed by James L. Pugh of Alabama would have required all affected officers to take open-competitive examinations. Appointed or reappointed officers would be apportioned among the states and territories according to population. This provision had two great advantages to Pugh: it would give his party an equal share of offices, and it would give his state and section an equal share of patronage. The uneven distribution of patronage was a source of annoyance to both the South and the West. Reformers pointed out that the Pugh amendment, an extreme application of the merit system to achieve partisan ends, could result only in chaos.

Whatever reformers thought, Congress was more interested in offices than in civil service reform. Logan was immediately on his feet to defend the crippled veterans, widows, and orphans whom this amendment would turn out of office. It would eliminate from the Treasury Department 293 of the 300 clerks charged to the District of Columbia—many of whom, according to Logan, were by-products of the Civil War. That these individuals were all Republicans, no doubt increased Logan's passion for anything connected with the Grand Army of the Republic. Pugh altered the wording of his amendment to leave crippled veterans, widows, and orphans in their sheltered posts, but this changed neither Logan's attitude nor the unanimous disapproval of the Republican side of the Senate. This unanimity had but one exception—Preston Plumb of Kansas. A firm believer of rotation in office, Plumb had no sympathy for the Pendleton bill. In addition, since he felt Kansas was not getting her share of offices, Plumb threatened to vote for Pugh's amendment. Obviously Plumb cared more for appointments from his locale, whether Republican or Democratic, than for entrenching Republican partisans. When the final vote was taken, however, Plumb's brave declaration of independence was forgotten. He wheeled into line and voted with the solid Republican delegation to oppose the amendment.

On the Democratic side, Thomas F. Bayard of Delaware, a consistent supporter of reform regardless of party politics, and Charles W. Jones of Florida conspicuously opposed Pugh's amendment. Pendleton was prominent among supporters of this amendment to his bill, which, reformers thought, would have caused more chaos than the spoils system. The final votes defeating both Pugh's amendment and Brown's similar amendment (designed to divide patronage equally between the parties) were strictly partisan with the exception of Bayard's vote, which was cast with Republicans against both amendments. The party struggle over these amendments in the latter part of 1882 indicated that concern over the Pendleton bill's effects on the civil service itself played second place to its calculated effects on either party.[11]

Zebulon B. Vance, a Democrat of North Carolina, further demonstrated the partisan character of the Senate. This man, who after the Democratic success in 1884 would move repeal of the Pendleton Act, introduced an amendment to add internal revenue offices with more than fifty employees to the scope of the bill. All Democrats, whether friends or enemies of reform, supported the measure, while all Republicans, except one, opposed it. This lone Republican supporter was Charles H. Van Wyck of Nebraska, a conspicuous opponent of civil service reform, who would soon leave Republicanism for the Populist party. Although the voting alignment on this measure looks strange at first, party reasoning soon becomes apparent. Employees of local federal offices were the backbone of Republican political machines, while employees of the Washington departments were not vital to party organization. To placate public opinion, Republican politicians were willing to sacrifice the Washington offices and even the very useful large customhouses and post offices, but nothing else. Logan, spokesman for Republican politicians, "utterly opposed" applying the merit system to all government employees. Most Democrats supported the Vance amendment not because they really favored it, but to maneuver Republicans into opposing the extension of reform. Senator James B. Beck of Kentucky self-righteously lamented: "The men in the great customhouses at New York and elsewhere, the men in the Internal-Revenue Department, the men all over the country in the post-offices are the principal political emissaries; and they are not affected by the civil-service reform contained in this bill; and when the Senator from North Carolina [Vance] moved to include them his motion was voted down by the Republican party, and these political emissaries

---

[11] *Ibid.*, 566–568, 570–571, 586, 591–594, 602, 651–652. Jones of Florida was absent when these final votes were taken. *Nation*, XXV, No. 913 (December 28, 1882), 541. For evidence of Bayard's consistent support of reform, see Charles Callan Tansill, *The Congressional Career of Thomas Francis Bayard, 1869–1885* (Washington, D.C., 1946), pp. 215–216.

will pay and work as they do now." Despite his ignorance of the
Pendleton bill, which already provided for customhouses and post
offices with over fifty employees, Senator Beck's appreciation for the
political importance of local offices was important. His statement
emphasized that the scope of the bill was determined not by the
needs of the civil service, but by the political potential of the offices
themselves. Although public opinion necessitated placing officeholders in large customhouses and post offices on a classified list to secure
them against political pressure, Republicans saved internal revenue
offices for their own partisan use by voting down the Vance amendment.[12]

Lack of bipartisanship was not limited solely to debate over the
Pendleton bill's scope. Votes on adjournment were largely party
affairs. Democrats, in no hurry to pass the bill, favored early adjournment, while Republicans opposed it. Compensation of the commission was also a partisan question. Led by Plumb, who although a
Republican exceeded all in zealous parsimony, Democrats favored
cutting down salaries, while Republicans were more generous. After
reducing the chief examiner's salary to $3,000 and unsuccessfully
attempting to cut it to $2,500, Plumb tried to eliminate the chief
examiner altogether. After all, he argued, the chief examiner would
do the commissioners' work while they loafed and drew pay. His
argument again proved unsuccessful. Despite his desire to cripple
the commission and his obvious antipathy to reform, Plumb eventually voted for the bill. Neither his final vote nor those of many
of his colleagues indicated sympathy with the reform objectives of
the bill.[13]

II

Not all senatorial disagreements were based on political differences.
Sectionalism determined senators' views on distribution of offices
on the basis of state population. The West and South, already underrepresented, expected even more inequality from civil service
reform. They feared that areas with the greatest number of educated
individuals would receive the most appointments. To allay these

[12] Charles Eliot Norton, ed., *Orations and Addresses of George William Curtis*
(New York, 1894), II, 308, 356; *Congressional Record*, 47 Cong., 2 sess., 565, 616–
617, 637.
[13] *Ibid.*, pp. 368–372, 505–528, 559, 561–562, 657–658, 660–661.

fears, the Senate passed Pendleton's amendment distributing offices "as nearly as practicable" according to state population. Charles Van Wyck, however, was certain the amendment would not be heeded if the qualification were left in. Speaking in terms that westerners and southerners understood, Van Wyck said: "Gentlemen coming from States that are not only full of civil-service reformers, but whose quota is more than full in the different Departments of this Government, very readily cast the sneer upon our asking for justice in the distribution of Federal patronage and the employment of persons in the Government service; but I want this bill based on some substantial principle in that regard."

Another westerner said that "some little rotation which would let in somebody west of the Mississippi would be a good thing. . . ." Western Republicans were joined by southern Democrats who also were underrepresented in the civil service. On the other hand, Joseph Hawley of Connecticut and George Edmunds of Vermont either were opposed completely to geographical distribution, or would tolerate it only with the qualifying phrase retained. When Van Wyck moved to strike out the phrase "as nearly as practicable" the noes had it 19 to 16. Cries of "no quorum" and a call for the yeas and nays ensued. Logan, however, claimed that with the qualifying phrase in the bill department heads would do as they pleased, for the Treasury Department had virtually ignored a similarly worded statute of 1875. The law must compel. Logan's power of persuasion, or perhaps just power, was so great that the Senate reversed its vote. The amendment passed on the second tally. Westerners and southerners were content as one more principle of reform was sacrificed.[14]

Sectional alignment bowed to party alignments over assessments. Although legislation aiming at competitive examinations and the ending of political assessments originally had been separated, the Senate's Committee on Civil Service and Retrenchment had combined the two. Joseph Hawley, the chairman of this committee, offered an amendment to the Pendleton bill which would end political assessments but not voluntary contributions. This amendment strictly forbade soliciting or receiving assessments by government officers from any government employee and soliciting by anyone

---

[14] *Ibid.*, pp. 505, 555, 595, 604, 610–611.

on government property. Democrats immediately moved to prevent voluntary contributions by officeholders. They claimed that no statute would be effective with this provision allowed.

The extreme "reform" position taken by Democrats was strenuously opposed by "reform" Republicans. Obviously they were not prepared to dispense entirely with the financial help received from the departments. Officeholders, according to a Republican defense of assessments, had both a constitutional and a natural right to contribute. This view prevailed when a vote was taken on a Democratic amendment to prevent voluntary contributions—the tally was strictly by party. Other Democratic attempts also failed. The prevention of voluntary contributions was at this time impossible. Democrats and Republicans, however, did unanimously approve Hawley's amendment designed to end assessments by congressional campaign committees.[15]

In the matter of assessments, both parties had reason for satisfaction. Democrats had done everything in their power to dam up their rivals' source of revenue, while Republicans seemingly had satisfied a reform-demanding public with a minimum of action. Just as with the Pendleton bill itself, the real struggle in passing Hawley's amendment occurred over the amendments to it. All congressmen had their own ideas about reform legislation. These ideas stemmed from their party and their geographical location and were tempered by public opinion. Most senators realized the necessity of meeting the demand for reform legislation. Senatorial ideas were tested in the numerous struggles over amendments, and within a month a common definition was reached.

The final Senate vote on the Pendleton bill was perfunctory. Thirty-eight senators from both parties supported it, 5 Democrats voted against it, and 7 more went on record in opposition to the measure. Thirty Republicans and 15 Democrats either voted for or declared themselves in favor of the bill. No Republican opposed the bill in the Senate's final vote. Even William Pitt Kellogg, head of the corrupt carpetbag machine of Louisiana, voted for the measure as did Don Cameron, the boss of Pennsylvania. Daniel W. Voorhees of Indiana and John R. McPherson of New Jersey were

---

[15] *Ibid.*, pp. 621–630, 642–645. Bayard refrained from voting on all of these measures. Presumably he feared that a firm stand for reform on these issues might jeopardize passage of the bill.

the only nonsouthern opponents of reform, while Pendleton of Ohio was conspicuous as the only Democratic exponent of his bill outside of the South.[16] The four other nonsouthern Democrats, all from the Far West, did not vote. Even in the South itself, 14 Democrats voted for the bill, while 10 opposed it; thus both Democratic opposition and support were found in the South. This southern vote can be explained neither by the existence of strong civil service reform associations nor by strong reform sentiment. Missouri and Maryland, it is true, both had strong associations and their Democratic senators voted for the bill, yet the senators from Mississippi and Arkansas, states without a reform movement, also unanimously voted for reform. Kentucky senators opposed the bill despite the existence of an association.

The decision made by most Democratic senators did not concern the bill's relation to the civil service, but rather the bill's relation to the election of 1884. Democrats voting against the bill did not wish to curtail Democratic patronage with the election "in the bag," while Democratic proponents of the measure felt that only good behavior would bring victory in 1884. Passage of the Pendleton bill, these Democratic supporters reasoned, would influence Independent voters in key states. After the final vote, Joseph Brown of Georgia roused the Senate to laughter by moving that the measure be called "a bill to perpetuate in office the Republicans who now control the patronage of the Government." Opposition to the Pendleton bill died hard.[17]

The House did not move at the Senate's leisurely pace, thanks to Abram S. Hewitt. Realizing that if the Pendleton bill were "debated and amended it would fail," Hewitt conceived a plan that was successfully executed. His Democratic colleague from New York City, S. S. "Sunset" Cox, called for immediate passage of the Pendleton bill without debate. Two Democrats from Illinois and Missouri attempted to delay the bill by having it considered by the Committee of the Whole, since it created new government offices and necessitated an appropriation. The chair, however, ruled that the House could deal immediately with the question. After the bill was read, cries of "Vote! Vote!" forced the speaker to call the House to order.

---

[16] "South" as here used includes the states where slavery was established before the Civil War.

[17] *Ibid.*, pp. 660–661.

John A. Kasson successfully moved the previous question, which meant that under the rules of the House the measure could be debated for only thirty minutes, this time to be equally divided between the exponents and opponents of the bill. John Reagan, Democrat from Texas and former Confederate Postmaster General, headed the opposition, whose task it was to change the mind of an extremely disorderly House in fifteen minutes. Little could be said in that time, and all that was said virtually repeated sentiments previously expressed in the Senate. Reagan's accusation that both parties were cheating the country and that the Republican party knew it was cheating the Democratic party caused appreciative laughter. Even though ordering the previous question had made amendments impossible, William E. Robinson of New York proposed an amendment that would have postponed the beginning of the bill's operation until July 1, 1885, thus giving Democrats, if victorious, a few months to make vacancies for their partisans.[18]

Having consumed their fifteen minutes in small doses, the opponents gave way to those favoring the bill. Albert S. Willis, Democrat from Kentucky, supported the Pendleton bill, but wished it adequately strengthened to prevent political assessments. This weakness, Willis argued, was the basis of Democratic opposition. John Kasson, outwardly peaceful, inwardly raging, closed debate by reviewing the progress of civil service reform. He attributed the potential success of the bill to the rightful judgment of Congress, inspired by the honest and earnest recommendations of the President and the civil service reform associations. "The young men of the country," he concluded, "and the active, intellectual, and nonpolitical forces, have largely contributed to this result." [19]

Little Phil Thompson, Democrat from Kentucky—whose fame rested on having killed his wife's lover rather than on his legislative ability—moved to recommit the bill with instructions to amend it to prevent all political contributions by officeholders. The yeas and

---

[18] Hewitt to James F. Colby, Washington, January 8, 1883, Civil Service Reform Association Papers, Collection of Regional History, Cornell University; *Congressional Record,* 47 Cong., 2 sess., 860–862.

[19] *Ibid.,* pp. 864–866. The Willis bill, written and endorsed by reformers, would have eliminated entirely political assessments. It had proved too strong medicine for Republicans. Kasson was angry because "he and his bill, on which he doubtless had visions of floating into the White House in 1884, were as dead as Moses and his bulrushes." Marian Adams to Hooper, Washington, January 7, 1883, in Thoron, *op. cit.,* p. 414.

nays resulted in defeat for this motion 113 to 85. The vote was, as one would expect, along party lines. The Democrats supported and the Republicans opposed this motion, which would have curtailed Republican political activity. Only one full-fledged Republican voted with the Democrats, but a few Republican Greenbackers supported the motion. Six Democrats voted with the Republicans. Some of these, like Abram S. Hewitt, no doubt, wished to have the bill passed as it was without further delay. Others who voted against this motion later voted against passage of the Pendleton bill as well, wanting nothing to do with it in any form.[20]

The final vote on the Pendleton bill in the House was 155 to 47. Added to this number the declared views of nonvoters made the total 162 to 48. Republicans from all sections supported the bill except for a few deviations in the Old Northwest and the South. The Democratic vote was far more indicative of the geographical strength of reform; the bill was not a Democratic party measure, and Democrats were free to follow the dictates of either their convictions or their constituents. Democrats who supported the measure were from the states of Massachusetts, Connecticut, New York, Pennsylvania, Maryland, Indiana, Illinois, Wisconsin, California, Nevada, Missouri, North Carolina, and Arkansas. Many of these states had strong reform movements. Democratic opposition was conspicuous in New Jersey, Ohio (Pendleton's own state), West Virginia, Kentucky, Tennessee, Virginia, South Carolina, Georgia, Alabama, and Texas. Generally speaking, opposition to the measure was limited to Democrats centered in the South and Old Northwest.[21]

Not a negative vote was cast from New England. The two Democrats from this section represented the strong reform centers of Boston and New Haven. Democrats—Archibald M. Bliss, a Brooklyn bank and railroad director, and two congressmen from New Jersey, also men of business—cast the 3 negative votes from New York and New Jersey. There were no local civil service reform associations to apply pressure on New Jersey Democrats. On the other hand, Baltimore, home of a lively civil service reform association, was

---

[20] *Congressional Record*, 47 Cong., 2 sess., 866–867. Allan Nevins, *Abram S. Hewitt* (New York, 1935), does not mention Hewitt's participation in debate over the Pendleton bill but gives an interesting account of his career.

[21] Analysis of this vote was computed from the *Congressional Record*, 47 Cong., 2 sess., 867.

represented by 2 Democrats voting in the affirmative. A third Democrat representing the area north of Baltimore also voted for the bill, while his fellow partisans from the rural Eastern Shore and the area south of Baltimore did not vote on the measure.

Ohio Democrats were conspicuous for their opposition to Pendleton's bill—the entire delegation except 1 paired member voted against it. Most Democratic politicians and newspapermen in Ohio were bitterly hostile to Pendleton and his measure; they very likely opposed the bill because it was Pendleton's and they were "jealous of the prestige he might acquire as its advocate." [22] On the other hand, Benjamin Butterworth, an ardent Republican foe of reform at the last session, joined other Ohio Republicans in voting for the bill. The entire Democratic Indiana delegation supported the bill except for 1 nonvoting member. Republicans, although supplying more affirmative votes than Democrats, provided the 1 negative vote cast by this state. Illinois cast 1 Democratic and 2 Republican nays, but the majority of both parties favored the bill. Republican Chicago supported the measure, but it was opposed in the southern and western portions of the state. Michigan, which was entirely Republican, supported the Pendleton bill, although Jay Hubbell was conspicuously absent.[23] The entire Wisconsin delegation—including 2 Democrats who represented the Milwaukee area where a civil service reform association was thriving—voted for the measure. In the Far West, the bill was supported by the 2 Democrats from California, 1 of whom represented San Francisco—the home of one of the three reform associations west of the Mississippi. Republicans from California did not vote on the reform measure.

The rough pattern of urban support continued in the border states, especially where civil service reform associations existed. The West Virginia Democratic affirmative vote came from the district including Wheeling and sections along the Ohio River. In Kentucky, which largely opposed the measure, 2 of the 3 yeas came from districts on the Ohio River including Louisville, which had a reform

---

[22] *Nation*, XXXVI, No. 916 (January 18, 1883), 48; *Philadelphia Record*, January 11, 1883, p. 2, c. 1.

[23] Hubbell was paired on political questions, but his partner, not regarding this vote as a party one, voted for the bill. One cannot say how Hubbell would have voted had he been present, for others as ardently opposed to reform as he outwardly favored the Pendleton bill in the final reckoning. The *Atlanta Constitution*, December 16, 1882, p. 4, c. 3, possibly using its imagination, reported that Hubbell had come out in favor of civil service reform.

association, and Covington. In Tennessee, however, William R. Moore, a Republican representing Memphis, voted against the bill. Moore had been a conspicuous opponent of reform in the previous congressional session and was one of the few Republicans who consistently maintained his principles. He had gained considerable notoriety for turning out a widowed postmistress because she was a Democrat and even more for seeking the removal of a Republican widow to install his brother-in-law as Memphis postmaster.[24] The only support the measure received in Tennessee was from Republicans in the eastern part of the state. Missouri, a state with a strong civil service reform association, strongly favored the measure: 1 Missouri Democrat voted in the negative, while 5 others voted yea. In the rural and Democratic South, where the civil service reform movement was nonexistent, congressmen felt no direct pressure for reform. Consequently many members either voting against the Pendleton bill or not voting at all were concentrated in that region. In the states that comprised the Confederacy, excluding Tennessee, only 14 representatives favored the measure while 22 opposed the bill and 26 were absent. The southern congressman was free to use his own judgment, and did. No doubt his vote, like that of his senatorial colleagues, was determined by his prognostication of the election of 1884.

Most congressmen, even those responsible for making it a law, did not like the Pendleton bill. "We are not legislating on this subject in response to our own judgment . . . but in response to some sort of judgment which has been expressed outside," Senator Plumb had cried out during the debate. Indeed, every member of Congress had received a letter from the National Civil Service Reform League urging the passage of the Pendleton and Willis bills, and local associations had applied additional pressure on their representatives. These letters may have helped enact the merit system, but they did not convert hostile congressmen into friends of reform. Members of Congress reluctantly supported the bill, and Democrats ridiculed the Republican reversal from swearing at "them d——d literary fellows" who knew nothing of practical politics to making their bill a party measure. The sudden reaction in favor of reform had started the night of the recent election: the decisive

---

[24] Edwin Lawrence Godkin, "Moore, of Tennessee, on the Civil Service," *Nation*, XXXIV, No. 882 (May 25, 1882), 439–440.

catalytic agent had been reformer Cleveland's overwhelming defeat of machinist Folger.[25]

The evening the Pendleton bill passed the House, Henry Adams was "immensely pleased to tumble over Kasson," who, despite the calm exterior he had maintained during the congressional debate, was in a savage mood because the House had passed the *"Boston* bill." Adams fancied that the "gentle Hale," a member of Hubbell's committee and author of a published speech favoring political assessments, was "equally pleased to please" reformers. "All the half-breeds, stalwarts and jelly-fish should set up a party founded on the glorious principle of contempt for reformers," Adams advised, after stating that the average congressman was "chiefly occupied in swearing at professional reformers and voting for their bills." [26]

---

[25] *Congressional Record*, 47 Cong., 2 sess., 594, 863; National Civil Service Reform League to Dawes, New York, December 18, 1882, and Executive Committee of the Massachusetts Civil Service Reform League to Dawes, Boston, December 4, 1882, Dawes Papers, Library of Congress.

[26] Adams to John Hay, Washington, January 7, 1883, in Worthington Chauncey Ford, ed., *Letters of Henry Adams (1858–1891)* (Boston, 1930), p. 345. Hale's speech justified "assessments on officeholders, mainly on the ground that the Democrats levied them in 1860, in the last days of Buchanan, when the party was in the lowest depths of degradation." *Nation*, XXXV, No. 899 (September 21, 1882), 231. The "Jelly-Fish" was a man who hesitated "to vote decisively for or against the Machine." *Ibid.*, XXXII, No. 833 (June 16, 1881), 415.

XIV

DECLINE OF THE MOVEMENT

Reformers remained alert after the passage of the Pendleton bill, which was signed by President Arthur January 16, 1883. Recalling somewhat bitterly that only his private secretary and Carl Schurz had supported his reform efforts, former President Hayes questioned whether enactment of the Pendleton law represented a genuine conversion of Congress. Hayes feared that the Senate revealed its true sentiments when it cut the salaries of the commissioners and predicted that "many who now *acquiesce* will do all they dare do to defeat the practical success of the measure—many more who supported it will be glad to see it fail—to see it become unpopular." Hayes urged "vigilance" and warned that reaction would "be supported most eagerly by a host of shrewd people." Reformers agreed and also conceded that the Pendleton Act was not a complete remedy—it would cripple the bosses of states with urban centers, but rural bosses would remain untouched by its provisions. Aside from offices in Washington, the act applied only to customhouses and post offices in the largest cities. The vast majority of federal civil servants and every municipal and state employee in the country was still unprotected by civil service regulations.[1]

---

[1] Rutherford B. Hayes to Silas W. Burt, Fremont, Ohio, January 12, 1883, Burt Collection, New York Historical Society. Hayes was a more ardent reformer out of office than in office. C. G. Howland to the editor of the *Nation*, Lawrence, Kansas, January 8, 1883, in "The Civil Service and the Local Bosses," *Nation* (New York), XXXVI, No. 916 (January 18, 1883), 57. For details of the civil service reform movement after 1883, see Frank Mann Stewart, *The National Civil Service Reform League* (Austin, Texas, 1929); A. Bower Sageser, *The First Two Decades of the Pendleton Act* (Lincoln, Nebraska, 1935); William Dudley Foulke, *Fighting the Spoilsmen* (New York, 1919). For an analysis of the impact of the Pendleton Act, see Ari Hoogenboom, "The Pendleton Act and the Civil Service," *American Historical Review* (Washington), LXIV, No. 2 (January, 1959), 301–318.

I

Democrats seemed eager to fulfill Hayes's prediction. They appeared hostile both to civil service reform and to Pendleton. In his own state, they were particularly unkind to him and attempted "to drive him out of public life." Democrats in the lower house of the Ohio legislature opposed a resolution congratulating Pendleton on the passage of his bill, while the Democratic press of Ohio roundly denounced and ridiculed both Pendleton and his measure.[2]

While Democrats read Pendleton "savage lectures," President Arthur aroused apprehension among reformers. His delay in appointing a civil service commission made them fear he intended to please spoilsmen. Once made, however, appointments were reassuring. The three commissioners were Dorman B. Eaton, who had been chairman of the Grant Civil Service Commission, John M. Gregory, first president of the University of Illinois, and Leroy D. Thoman, a young Democratic newspaperman who had lost the Ohio gubernatorial race to William McKinley.[3]

But the President had not stepped over into the reform camp. Both the continuation of spoils appointments in Cleveland and the delayed reappointment of Silas W. Burt as New York naval officer caused concern among reformers. Arthur and Burt had gone to the same college and had worked together in the New York Customhouse, where they became estranged when Burt refused to pay a political assessment. Reformers regarded Burt's reappointment in 1883 as "the crucial test of the President's sincerity," since effective reform in the customhouse had resulted from Burt's diligence. In February Arthur appointed Surveyor Charles K. Graham, a man "unfriendly to reform," naval officer, and nominated Burt chief examiner for the commission at a salary of $3,000, which was $5,000 less than his salary as naval officer. Resolving not to fall into what he thought were Arthur's plans to injure him and to hamper reform in the

---

[2] Hayes to Burt, Fremont, January 12, 1883, Burt Collection; *Nation*, XXXVI, No. 916 (January 18, 1883), 48; "The Ohio Democrats," *ibid.*, No. 939 (June 28, 1883), 544; George F. Edmunds to Chester A. Arthur, Washington, January 26, 1883, Arthur Papers, Library of Congress.

[3] Carl Schurz, "A Clear Alternative," *Nation*, XXXVI, No. 920 (February 15, 1883), 140; *ibid.*, No. 921 (February 22, 1883), 159. On Gregory, see Allene Gregory, *John Milton Gregory* (Chicago, 1923), *passim*, and on Thoman, who was Pendleton's choice as commissioner, see "Leroy D. Thoman," *The National Cyclopaedia of American Biography* (New York, 1892–1955), XII, 131.

New York Customhouse, Burt indignantly rejected both the President's appointment and Eaton's pressure on him to accept the position. The *Nation* considered Arthur's "discreditable" action to have been inspired by his political henchmen and questioned the sincerity of his civil service reform professions. "Your removal," Curtis wrote Burt, "is a crime against the cause and a stupid blunder. Of course it ends everything at the Custom House." [4]

To the surprise of many reformers, in early May Arthur adopted the commission's rules with only minor changes. Applying the principles of the Pendleton Act to the civil service had been largely Eaton's accomplishment. He wrote Curtis of "the manifold protracted—*repeated,* WEARYING discussions, not merely of vital & debateable [*sic*] points, but of points *we* have regarded as long since settled,—which has been a part of my experience with my fellow commissioners—one of them of the opposite party & neither of them with a training in OUR literature or technicalities." By August, Curtis, overlooking but not forgetting Arthur's shabby treatment of Burt, commended the President for his friendly administration of reform. The commission's first report contained abundant testimony favoring the act from heads of departments, post offices, and customhouses. Senator Joseph Hawley, Connecticut Republican and chairman of the committee that had reported the Pendleton bill, emphatically declared that it was a success and claimed in December, 1883, that he had not heard a congressman complain of it.[5]

[4] L. B. Tuckerman to the editor of the *Nation,* Cleveland, March 6, 1883, in "Civil-Service Reform in Ohio," *Nation,* XXXVI, No. 924 (March 15, 1883), 232; Silas Wright Burt, "Writings: Civil Service Reform 1886–1900" (Binder's title of a 158 page manuscript sketch of Arthur's political career), pp. 53–57, 141–143, Burt Writings, New York Public Library; Burt to Carl Schurz, February 2 and 7, 1883, Schurz Papers, Library of Congress; Eaton to Burt, Washington, March 13, 1883, and Curtis to Burt, West New Brighton, New York, March 4, 1883, Burt Collection; *Nation,* XXXVI, No. 923 (March 8, 1883), 199; "Meeting of the National League," *Civil Service Record* (Boston), II, No. 10 (March, 1883), 84.

[5] "The Civil Service Rules and Regulations," *ibid.,* II, No. 12 (May, 1883), 95–98; Eaton to Curtis, Washington, April 15, 1883, Schurz Papers. Curtis forwarded Eaton's letter to Schurz. Gregory resented Eaton's attitude, and, if his daughter's filiopietistic biography is to be taken seriously, Gregory all but ran the Civil Service Commission singlehandedly. Gregory, *op. cit.,* pp. 307–309. Charles Eliot Norton, ed., *Orations and Addresses of George William Curtis* (New York, 1894), II, 236–237; *Civil Service Record,* III, No. 10 (March, 1884), 71–76; Hawley to Johnson T. Platt, Washington, December 13, 1883, Civil Service Reform Association Papers, Collection of Regional History, Cornell University.

Having secured national legislation, civil service reformers worked for legislation on the state and municipal level. Local patronage, which these laws would control, was probably more essential to the boss system than federal patronage. Local offices were numerous, lucrative, and regularly assessed. The New York County clerk, for instance, retained as part of his annual salary $80,000 in fees. Local offices tided political machines over lean periods of federal patronage and provided local bosses with a source of independent strength. When the Pendleton bill became law, the legislative committee of the New York Civil Service Reform Association adapted it for use on the state level. This bill was introduced on January 16, 1883, in the New York legislature, and the reform association applied pressure in its favor. Association members journeyed to Albany to testify at committee hearings, amassed 6,000 signatures favoring the bill, and at crucial times employed a lobbyist to push reform.[6]

State legislators' attitude toward civil service reform was similar to that of national legislators. In New York the Democrats, who were in power, showed an "ill-concealed hostility" to reform, and Republicans favored reform largely because they were out of office. Although a debate on April 9, 1883, discouraged reformers, their forces led by youthful Theodore Roosevelt were eventually successful. Collapse of the opposition, the *Nation* reported, had not resulted from a sudden conversion but rather because "most of those politicians thought it prudent to make this concession to public opinion for the time being."[7]

The bill as enacted resembled the Pendleton Act. It created a board of three commissioners with many the same powers as the federal commission; this board was designed primarily to supervise

---

[6] Frederick Law Olmsted to Charles Eliot Norton, Brookline, Massachusetts, August 14, 1883, Norton Papers, Harvard University; *Nation*, XXXVIII, No. 977 (March 20, 1884), 243; "Minutes of the Executive Committee of the New York Civil Service Reform Association," December 6, 1882, January 10 and 16, February 7, March 7, April 4, May 2 and 3, 1883, National Civil Service League Papers, New York, hereafter cited as "Minutes." Everett P. Wheeler claimed that he and Edward M. Shepard drafted the New York bill. Everett P. Wheeler, *Sixty Years of American Life* (New York, 1917), p. 281.

[7] "The Civil Service Bill in New York," *Civil Service Record*, II, No. 11 (April, 1883), 85–86; "Debate in the New York Assembly," *ibid.*, pp. 91–92; *Nation*, XXXVI, No. 932 (May 10, 1883), 391. Henry Pringle, *Theodore Roosevelt* (New York, 1931), p. 75, claims Roosevelt was actually lukewarm to civil service reform in 1883, but Carleton Putnam, *Theodore Roosevelt* (New York, 1958), pp. 280–282, portrays Roosevelt as an ardent reformer..

a system of competitive examinations for appointments. The levying of political assessments on any state or local officer was forbidden. In addition, mayors of cities with populations exceeding 50,000 persons could apply civil service regulations to their cities, if they desired. This provision was left optional lest an immediate attempt to include these municipal offices arouse opposition. Reformers reasoned that public opinion would eventually force mayors to extend the merit system. The bill applied to officers employed in connection with canals, public works, prisons, asylums, and reformatories.[8]

The New York bill was at first conscientiously enforced. Cleveland unhesitatingly appointed an excellent commission and named Silas W. Burt as chief examiner—a position which Burt felt he could accept without loss of face. In addition, Mayors Seth Low of Brooklyn and Franklin Edson of New York adopted codes for their cities prepared by Burt under the state civil service act. Even though the chaotic condition of the New York State civil service delayed the application of rules until December 6, 1883, reform was off to an auspicious start.[9]

The New York legislature made further advances. In the spring of 1884, it passed legislation that required mayors to extend civil service rules to the state's twenty-five cities and included city police, health, fire, and law departments under the reform law. The same session of the legislature also pushed through the "Roosevelt" bills reorganizing the governments of New York City and County.[10]

Reform flourished in Massachusetts as well as in New York. The Massachusetts Civil Service Reform League wrote a reform bill and agitated for its passage. This bill, although based upon the Pendle-

---

[8] Everett P. Wheeler, "New York Civil Service Reform Bill," *Civil Service Record*, III, No. 1 (June, 1883), 1; "The New York Bill," *ibid.*, pp. 6–8, reprints the bill.

[9] *Ibid.*, III, No. 8 (January, 1884), 54–60; Silas Wright Burt, "A Brief History of the Civil Service Reform Movement in the United States," [1906, revised in 1908], p. S, Burt Writings, New York Public Library; Curtis to Burt, West New Brighton, June 3, 1883, Burt Collection. For a conflicting view of the author of New York and Brooklyn's codes, see Wheeler, *Sixty Years of American Life*, pp. 284–285.

[10] "What New York Is Doing," *Civil Service Record*, III, No. 12 (May, 1884), 89. A supplementary act is reprinted in "The New York Supplementary Act," *ibid.*, IV, No. 1 (June, 1884), 3. See also *Nation*, XXXVIII, No. 990 (June 19, 1884), 517. These advances pleased most reformers, but some did not wish to go too far too fast. Dorman B. Eaton to Burt, Washington, March 3, 1884, Burt Collection. On the "Roosevelt" bills, see Putnam, *op. cit.*, pp. 392–405.

ton and the New York acts, had distinctive features. It was to apply
to all twenty-two cities in the state and rules were to be drawn up
and administered by the state civil service commission instead of
city commissions as was done in New York State. In addition, the
bill would affect laborers. The senate passed the bill, but in the
house it met determined opposition from the Democrats and from
a former Republican collector of Boston. On June 3, 1884, a substitute measure was passed which strongly resembled the Pendleton
Act but which retained the essential features of the senate bill.[11]

Reformers further demonstrated their power in the campaign of
1884. When the Republican party nominated James G. Blaine many
of them deserted it and helped elect Grover Cleveland President.
Cleveland's administration of reform in New York State particularly
gratified reformers, while Blaine's attitude toward reform made
him abhorrent to them. Cleveland carried New York by a small
margin and thus won the election. Although a number of factors
contributed to the Republican defeat, the revolt of Republican reformers was of paramount importance.[12]

Despite their joy over Cleveland's election, reformers wondered
whether he could withstand the pressure that would be exerted
by Democratic spoilsmen after being out of office for twenty-
four lean years. Reformers were especially anxious to have the
Pendleton Act survive a change of parties. On December 29, 1884,
Cleveland reassured reformers by pledging himself not only to execute the act in good faith but also to be guided by its principles
with respect to the entire service. Reformers were ecstatic in their
response. Five months after Cleveland took office, Curtis proudly
stated that the hold of reform on the popular mind had enabled
the President to prevent a "clean sweep." The civil service reform
movement had reached its peak.[13]

[11] "Civil Service Reform in Massachusetts," Civil Service Record, III, No. 9
(February, 1884), 65–67; "Action of the Massachusetts Legislature," ibid., No. 12
(May, 1884), 88. Both George William Curtis and Eaton opposed including
laborers under the bill for fear of attempting too much. For amplification of
the Massachusetts bill, see Bliss Perry, Richard Henry Dana, 1851–1931 (Boston,
1933), pp. 147–148.
[12] Reformers' part in the election of 1884 has been adequately covered elsewhere. The best treatment, written from a reform point of view, is Allan
Nevins, Grover Cleveland (New York, 1933), pp. 156–188.
[13] George William Curtis, president, National Civil Service Reform League,
et al. to Cleveland, New York, December 20, 1884, and Cleveland to Curtis et al.,
Albany, December 29, 1884, in "The Policy of the Administration," Civil Service

II

The triumph of civil service reform was short-lived. Even while victories were being won, signs of decline appeared. Ohio Democrats defeated Pendleton in January, 1884, and bills were introduced in Congress to repeal the Pendleton Act. Many reformers had become complacent after securing reform legislation. Attendance at association and league meetings began to fall off precipitously. The annual league meeting in 1884 "was small" and Curtis feared that future meetings would be no larger "now that the reformed system has passed into politics." [14]

Despite this complacency, the National Civil Service Reform League pushed for further objectives. It strove to repeal the federal four-year laws, which facilitated removals by fixing the terms of about 3,500 of the most important and highest paid officers in the civil service. Postmasters earning more than $1,000 annually, high customs officials, and numerous officials in the Interior Department were affected by these laws. Failure to reappoint one of these officers quietly and effectively removed him from office; his position then could be given to a partisan. Thus removals were made with no stigma attached.

When Congress met in December, 1883, a bill repealing the four-year statutes was introduced in both the House and the Senate. Petitions were presented, and delegates from the league and local associations appeared in support of the bill. The House Committee on Reform in the Civil Service submitted a unanimous report favoring the bill. Yet on April 21, 1884, the House defeated it 146 to 99. Patronage-starved Democrats, now in power, constituted all but twenty-seven of the majority and conspicuously opposed the measure. Reformers periodically called for repeal of these statutes but with declining vigor; there was even lack of unanimity among them on the subject. [15]

Record, IV, No. 8 (January, 1885), 63; Curtis to Burt, West New Brighton, January 1, 1885, and George Lewis Prentiss to Burt, New York, January 3, 1885, Burt Collection; Norton, *op. cit.*, II, 284–285.

[14] Curtis to Burt, Ashfield, Massachusetts, August 13, 1884, Burt Collection. Pendleton was defeated by Henry B. Payne, who was all but impeached on evidence of bribery. *Nation*, XXXVII, No. 692 (December 6, 1883), 459–460; *ibid.*, XXXVIII, No. 968 (January 17, 1884), 43.

[15] Norton, *op. cit.*, II, 258–264; *Nation*, XXXVIII, No. 982 (April 24, 1884), 353. President Charles W. Eliot of Harvard thought the four-year statutes provided means for gracefully getting rid of undesirable officers, and therefore were useful.

The drive for reform on the state level also bogged down. Bills introduced in Rhode Island, New Jersey, Pennsylvania, Maryland, Virginia, Ohio, Indiana, Illinois, Wisconsin, Missouri, and California failed to pass,[16] and a determined counterattack upon civil service reform was made in New York and Massachusetts. From 1885 to 1894, enforcement of the New York rules was so loose that "a large percentage of the persons admitted to the service had never been on any eligible list." In December, 1896, these rules were revised to form what Carl Schurz called "the corruptest embodiment of the civil service reform idea so far attempted in any State." The attack on reform was bipartisan. Upon becoming governor of New York a few weeks later, Republican Frank S. Black announced he would "take the starch out of the civil service" and proceeded to do so. The "Black Act" amended the civil service law nearly out of existence. In 1887, the Massachusetts legislature provided that veterans could be appointed without examination. This amendent seriously crippled the act, and Massachusetts reformers had difficulty preventing further exemptions from examinations.

On the municipal level, reform advances were small and frequently illusory. Philadelphia applied the merit system to a limited portion of its municipal service in 1885, but it "was never honestly enforced and was detrimental for that reason." On the other hand, Milwaukee that same year established civil service rules for the police and fire departments which were "faithfully enforced." Civil service reform associations functioned in both these cities. Other municipalities outside of New York and Massachusetts showed little interest in reform.[17]

While reform suffered setbacks on state and local levels, the federal classified service increased rapidly. The merit system advanced not because of further action by Congress, which remained hostile to reform, but because of executive action. Ironically, executive action stemmed more from a desire to place fellow party members perma-

---

"Annual Meeting of the National League," *Civil Service Record*, V, No. 3 (August, 1885), 23. See Appendix B for the officers affected.

[16] *Civil Service Record*, II–X (June, 1883–June, 1891), *passim*. After passage of the Massachusetts civil service reform act in 1884, over twenty years elapsed before the next states—Wisconsin and Illinois—enacted reform bills. Stewart, *op. cit.*, p. 143.

[17] Burt, "Brief History . . . ," pp. W, BB–CC, FF–GG, Burt Writings. In 1892, one-sixth of all Massachusetts appointees were veterans exempt from examination. *Civil Service Record*, XI, No. 8 (February, 1892), 66.

nently in the civil service than from a wish to reform. The process involved replacing all political enemies with political friends in a branch of the unclassified, or unreformed, service and then extending the rules to cover it. This process was hastened by the alternation of party control in the 1880's and 1890's, which led Presidents every four years to make additions to the classified list. The irony was compounded. The advance of the merit system stimulated rapacious spoils methods in the unclassified service, and the civil service reform movement itself languished.

National politics proved a frustrating experience for reformers. Although they helped elect Presidents from 1884 through 1896, these Presidents always disappointed reformers until they inevitably extended the merit system just as they were leaving the White House. Although Cleveland at first pleased reformers, he alienated many of them during his first term. His administration of the Pendleton Act was scrupulous, but by 1888 he had swept Republicans from the unclassified service. Reformers thought this action violated his promise that the principles of the Pendleton Act would guide him respecting the entire service. They despondently referred to the "low tide" of reform. "Cleveland's course," wrote Curtis, "has left all of us Mugwumps [term applied to the Independents who deserted the Republican party to support Cleveland] in an apparently disagreeable position. . . . It has certainly discredited civil service reform and chilled those who were his most earnest supporters in 1884." [18]

Civil service reform was ignored for the most part during the campaign of 1888; Benjamin Harrison was elected President on the tariff issue, although his platform contained a civil service plank. Many reformers gave Cleveland lukewarm support—more for his stand on the tariff than for his civil service reform policies. But Indiana reformers and Henry C. Lea of Philadelphia refused to subordinate civil service reform to the tariff question. They vehemently opposed Cleveland for "betraying the cause on which he

[18] Curtis to Burt, Ashfield. October 2, 1887, and West New Brighton, December 30, 1887, and March 5, 1888, Burt Collection. Moorfield Storey maintained that reformers had only themselves to blame for Cleveland's course. They all agreed with Schurz that no Mugwump should accept office from Cleveland lest they be suspected of supporting him for spoils. Mark Anthony De Wolfe Howe, *Portrait of an Independent* (Boston, 1932), pp. 178–179. For a charitable reform view of Cleveland, see Perry, *op. cit.*, p. 151.

was elected." Lea's opposition enraged Cleveland. After his defeat, he called Lea a "base calumniator" who "ought to be horsewhipped, with the rest of the dirty mendacious gang who come to the surface" during a political campaign.

"I am not disturbed," Cleveland wrote, "by the accusation that I have violated party obligations and turned a deaf ear to partisan requirements. I calmly undergo the 'I told you so' of those who attribute failure to these things. But the treatment I have received from the advocates of Civil Service Reform makes my blood boil. Never in the history of the world has a public man been treated more unjustly and hostilely.

"I should have thrown aside all effort to do more than keep within the strict letter of the law long ago, if I had not believed in the spirit as well as the letter. I know what I have done and what I have suffered in this cause and with that I am satisfied as I retire from the struggle. I hope the next man will be better trusted by those who assume to be apostles of the Reform. The cause is worth much—very much; but the people who stand ready to attribute every mistake in the selection of officers to wanton violation of principle and assume to know more of the conditions, motives and intents than those charged with responsibility, are worth nothing." [19] Cleveland's civil service policy was not as innocent as he claimed, but Harrison was to prove even more disappointing to reformers.

As was feared, a "clean sweep" of the unclassified service followed Harrison's inauguration, and the reform plank in the Republican platform, which promised extension of the classified service, was ignored. Reformers were angered by Harrison's failure to reappoint reform favorites such as New York Naval Officer Silas W. Burt, whom Cleveland had reinstated, New York Postmaster Henry G. Pearson, and Boston Collector Leverett Saltonstall. Unlike Cleveland, Harrison removed many officers even before they completed their four-year terms. Within two years, First Assistant Postmaster J. S. "Headsman" Clarkson removed one-half of the

[19] Some of Cleveland's local appointments were particularly obnoxious to Indiana reformers, and Cleveland had sinned doubly in Lea's eyes; unlike most reformers, Lea was an ardent protectionist. Lucius B. Swift to Lea, Indianapolis, November 13, 1888, and Lea to Wendell Phillips Garrison, Cape May, New Jersey, July 17, 1888, Lea Papers, University of Pennsylvania; Charles R. Codman to Burt, Brookline, April 27, 1886, and Cleveland to Burt, no place, December 6, 1888, copy in Burt Collection.

postmasters in the United States. "Nearly two years of the present administration have elapsed," wrote a reformer in December, 1890, "and thus far the President has not extended the classified service to a single place, and, so far as appears from his message just delivered, he does not intend to do anything. A more flagrant case of the violation of a promise can scarcely be imagined." [20]

The Democrats again returned to office under Cleveland in 1893 and repeated the familiar process. Even though financial problems beset the administration, reformers continued to express their concern over the civil service. Once again they were disappointed; this time by one of their own. Josiah Quincy, a founder of the National Civil Service Reform League and a direct descendant and namesake of one of the earliest advocates of reform, was appointed Assistant Secretary of State. A few months after taking office, he had replaced over one-third of the Republican consular officials with Democrats. When the Massachusetts Reform Club invited Quincy to explain these changes, he "frankly admitted that he had removed former and appointed new United States consuls at a rate more rapid than ever before" and confessed that "as far as he was aware, a similar policy of rapid changes had been carried out in all noncompetitive positions of the other departments." In addition, Cleveland let certain congressmen control patronage in order to push through financial legislation, particularly the repeal of the Sherman Silver-Purchase Act.[21]

As time went on the civil service reform movement grew weaker. Since 1872 both parties had supported reform—at least in theory— but in 1896 Democrats under William Jennings Bryan boldly attacked the merit system. Republicans under William McKinley supported civil service reform but won the election on the sound money issue. Immediately President McKinley was pressed to revoke Cleveland's extensive additions to the classified list. McKinley resisted this pressure for two years, although during this time the law was poorly administered in the Treasury, Justice, Interior, and

[20] Stewart, op. cit., p. 53; Curtis to Burt, West New Brighton, November 9, 1888, April 22, 1889, and Ashfield, September 10, 1889, Burt Collection; Curtis to Norton, West New Brighton, April 22, 1889, Curtis Papers; William Dudley Foulke to Lea, Washington, December 2, 1890, Lea Papers.

[21] Quincy was not wholly to blame. He acted on orders from either Cleveland or Secretary of State Walter Q. Gresham. Nevins, op. cit., p. 517; Perry, op. cit., pp. 156–157; Howe, op. cit., p. 182. On patronage and the repeal of the Silver Purchase Act, see Nevins, op. cit., pp. 523–548.

Post Office Departments. The National Civil Service Reform League gathered evidence showing McKinley's quiet but constant efforts to abandon the civil service rules. His refusal to touch abuses of the partisan census scheme and his exempting, by executive order, deputy collectors of internal revenue from the civil service regulations are examples of his laxity. Finally, on May 29, 1899, McKinley withdrew several thousand offices from the rules. Although this reaction—"the first backward step in the history of the competitive merit system"—left reformers disheartened, defeat was only temporary. Assassination once again aided reform by placing Theodore Roosevelt in McKinley's chair. Besides improving the civil service system, Roosevelt extensively widened the classified service. When he came into office 46 per cent of the service was classified; when he left office 66 per cent was under the rules. Succeeding Presidents have also used this method to keep their partisans in office.[22]

Although the merit system made some gains on the state and local levels after 1895, the civil service reform movement continued to languish. Reformers bickered among themselves. Many reformers, particularly Curtis, Burt, and Godkin, disliked Eaton for his belief in gradualism and his willingness to compromise with politicians. In the autumn of 1885 Godkin insisted, "We must get him out of office, and get rid of him in his representative capacity," and Burt urged Cleveland to remove Eaton from the commission. "It will be a happy day for civil service reform," he wrote Cleveland's secretary, "when this impracticable, impractical and indiscreet man is out of the Commission. This has been thought by many others, and while freely acknowledging his zeal and good intentions we have also believed that he is dangerous as an administrator of the law." Burt's arguments convinced Cleveland, but Eaton resigned before he was removed.[23]

Reformers even disagreed over methods of reform. When New-

---

[22] Stewart, *op. cit.*, pp. 60–62, 65; Sageser, *op. cit.*, pp. 219–220; Perry, *op. cit.*, p. 161; Burt, "Brief History . . . ," pp. FF, HH, Burt Writings.

[23] *Ibid.*, pp. EE–GG; Godkin to Burt, New York, November 13, 1885, Burt Collection; Burt to Daniel Scott Lamont, New York, November 5, 1885, Cleveland Papers, Library of Congress; Cleveland to Burt, no place, November 8, 1885, copy in Burt Collection. Eaton's beating by thugs when he was a counsel for the Erie Railroad had left him with serious head injuries. His fellow commissioners attributed Eaton's "inability to cooperate effectively" to his ill-health. Gregory, *op. cit.*, pp. 307–309.

ton Martin Curtis introduced into the New York legislature a bill which George William Curtis claimed would "fill the service with ex-soldiers and . . . exclude everybody else," the New York association was "so divided" that it could "take no part for or against" it. George William Curtis found it hard to write annual reports for the league that his fellow leaders would endorse. It was difficult to move in unison.[24]

"All the societies report very low tide," Curtis lamented in 1887. Association membership fell off sharply. For example, the Brooklyn association declined from 351 members in 1882 to 161 in 1890. More than half of its members had dropped out in eight years. Only ninety who were members in 1882 remained in 1890. Although the tenacious ninety showed the same equal division between professional and business classes, there were nevertheless differences in the composition of the association. The new recruits were drawn largely from businessmen. The occupations of 117 of the 161 members in 1890 were ascertained. Of these, seventy-three were connected with business pursuits while only forty-four were professional men. Interest declined most markedly among lawyers, clergymen, and journalists. In 1882, membership included fifty-four lawyers, thirteen clergymen, and seven journalists; in 1890, there were only eighteen lawyers, four clergymen, and one journalist. Surprisingly, among the professional men, medical doctors retained interest longer than the others. There were seventeen doctors in 1890 in comparison to twenty-six in 1882. Among businessmen, merchants still predominated, but more manufacturers belonged to the Brooklyn association in 1890 than in 1882. The civil service reform movement was becoming both a businessmen's movement and a moribund movement at the same time.[25]

Not only did membership of associations decline, but entire associations collapsed as well. In December, 1883, there were fifty-nine civil service reform associations; nine years later in 1892, there were but thirty-five. These associations still centered in the Northeast, especially in New York and Massachusetts, but the area in-

---

[24] Curtis to Burt, West New Brighton, January 23, 1886, Burt Collection; Curtis to Norton, West New Brighton, November 29, 1886, and February 8, 1887, Curtis Papers.

[25] Curtis to Burt, Ashfield, July 27, 1887, Burt Collection. Names were found in *Address of the President and Report of the Secretary of the Civil-Service Reform Association of Brooklyn Read at Its Annual Meeting: February 20, 1890*, pp. 13–16; occupations were located in the *Brooklyn Directory*, 1890.

terested in civil service reform was shrinking. Not only were out-
posts in San Francisco and New Oreans lost, but also even those
in Louisville, Kentucky, and Norfolk, Virginia. By 1892, there
were no civil service reform associations north of Massachusetts,
south of Maryland, or west of Kansas. Dwindling membership
placed an extra burden on those who remained. In 1889, the treasurer of the National Civil Service Reform League pleaded that
the extensive work planned for the next year required at least
$12,000 and lamented that the "number to whom we can appeal
for financial aid is comparatively small." [26]

Failure left its mark on reformers, who were growing old and
weary. Their meager faith in democracy, declining since Reconstruction days, was all but gone by the end of the nineteenth century. The public evidenced little interest in their cherished reform.
Lifetimes devoted to purifying politics had barely improved conditions. In 1892, a few months before he died, Curtis expressed
admiration of Alexander Hamilton "and his scorn of the spurious
Democracy which is always found in all American parties." Godkin
was even more despondent. By 1896, he was tired both of editing
the New York *Evening Post* and of American politics and predicted "very evil times" for democracy. Two years later, Godkin
commented to Norton, "about democracy. . . . I have pretty much
given it up as a contribution to the world's moral progress. . . .
I too tremble at the thought of having a large navy and the war
making power, lodged in the hands of such puerile and thoughtless
people—100,000,000 strong. It is an awful prospect for the world,
and I am glad to be so near the end of my career." Norton wrote
to Godkin that "no one has shared more completely in the beliefs
of the best Americans of the middle of the century, and of their
gradual disillusion," and Silas Burt admired Godkin's "appreciation of the progressive political and civic degeneracy . . . in this
country." [27]

---

[26] *Civil Service Record*, III, No. 7 (December, 1883), 52; *ibid.*, XI, No. 12 (June,
1892), 106; Ira Bursley to Henry C. Lea, New York, December, 1889, Lea Papers,
University of Pennsylvania. The big plans never materialized. The league received $3,655 and spent only $1,654.63. The year 1890, however, proved to be a
better year financially than those immediately preceding and following it. Re-
ceipts and expenditures of the National Civil Service Reform League are printed
in Stewart, *op. cit.*, p. 277.

[27] Curtis to John J. Pinkerton, West New Brighton, May 14, 1892, Curtis Collection in the possession of Charles Pinkerton, Mount Kisco, New York; Edwin

The pessimistic mood of the 1890's did not long continue. Reformers who survived these years wrote more cheerfully in the next decade concerning the eventual defeat of the spoilsmen and the success of the civil service reform movement.[28] Their optimism was not a product of the revival of their organizations, which continued to decline; it resulted rather from advances made by the merit system on national and local levels under the impetus of the more powerful and broader Progressive movement. Progressives, while similar in some respects, were in many ways distinct from civil service reformers. They were more aware of the economic forces shaping the destiny of the United States than were civil service reformers. Furthermore, they optimistically believed that man was capable of governing himself. To them, the merit system would not curtail democracy but would extend it by breaking the unholy alliance between politics and business. Paradoxically, both Progressives and spoilsmen advanced the merit system while the civil service reform associations withered away.[29]

Lawrence Godkin to Norton, North East Harbor, Maine, July 7, 1896, and New York, November 29, 1898, Norton Papers; Norton to Godkin, Cambridge, January 6, 1900, and Burt to Godkin, New York, December 31, 1899, Godkin Papers, Harvard University.

[28] Burt, "Brief History . . . ," p. II, Burt Writings; Charles W. Eliot to Burt, Cambridge, April 30, 1910, Burt Collection. Nevertheless Burt and Eliot were conscious of the tremendous task still to be accomplished.

[29] The civil service reform movement did not completely wither away. The National Civil Service League with headquarters in New York is still very much alive, but the reform movement has had no vital hold on the American people since the 1880's.

BIBLIOGRAPHY

I. Source Materials

A. Manuscript Collections

Arthur, Chester A., Papers, Library of Congress.

———, Letterbooks, New York Historical Society.

Bright, John, Papers, British Museum.

Bryant, William Cullen–Parke Godwin Collection, New York Public Library.

Burt, Silas W., Collection, New York Historical Society.

———, Writings, New York Public Library.

Civil Service Reform Association Papers, Cornell's Collection of Regional History and University Archives, Cornell University.

Clarke, James Freeman, Family Papers, Harvard University.

Cleveland, Grover, Papers, Library of Congress.

Cox, Jacob Dolson, Papers, Oberlin College, Oberlin, Ohio.

Curtis, George William, Papers, Harvard University.

———, Collection, The Rutherford B. Hayes Library, Fremont, Ohio.

———, Collection, The Staten Island Institute of Arts and Sciences, Staten Island, New York.

———, Collection in the possession of Charles Pinkerton, Mount Kisco, New York.

Dawes, Henry L., Papers, Library of Congress.

Elliott, E. B., Papers, Library of the United States Civil Service Commission.

Fairchild, Charles Stebbins, Papers, New York Historical Society.

Fish, Hamilton, Papers, Library of Congress.

Garfield, James A., Papers, Library of Congress.

Godkin, Edwin L., Papers, Harvard University.

Grant, Ulysses S., Papers, The Rutherford B. Hayes Library, Fremont, Ohio.

Hayes, Rutherford B., Papers, The Rutherford B. Hayes Library, Fremont, Ohio.

Jenckes, Thomas A., Papers, Library of Congress.

Lea, Henry C., Papers, University of Pennsylvania.

Lieber, Francis, Papers, Henry E. Huntington Library, San Marino, California.

Logan, John A., Papers, Library of Congress.
Lowell, James Russell, Papers, Harvard University.
————, Papers, Rantoul Collection, Harvard University.
Marble, Manton, Papers, Library of Congress.
McKim, James Miller, Papers, Margaret Sarah McKim Maloney Memorial Collection, New York Public Library.
Miscellaneous Papers, New York Public Library.
National Civil Service League Papers, National Civil Service League, New York.
Norton, Charles Eliot, Papers, Harvard University.
Schurz, Carl, Papers, Library of Congress.
Sherman, John, Papers, Library of Congress.
Smith, William Henry, Papers, Indiana Historical Society, Indianapolis.
Sumner, Charles, Papers, Harvard University.
Trumbull, Lyman, Papers, Library of Congress.
United States Civil Service Commission Papers, Library of the United States Civil Service Commission.
United States Senate, Committee on Civil Service and Retrenchment Papers, National Archives.
Villard, Henry, Papers, Harvard University.
Wells, David A., Papers, New York Public Library.
White, Andrew Dickson, Papers, Cornell's Collection of Regional History and University Archives, Cornell University.

B. Civil Service Reform Association Publications

Civil Service Reform Association, Boston, *Annual Report,* 1881–83.
————, Brooklyn, *Annual Report,* 1881–90.
————, California, *Secretary's Annual Report and List of Members, April 6, 1885.* San Francisco: C. A. Murdock & Co., Printers, 1885.
————, New York, *Annual Report,* 1880–83.
————, New York, *Documents Relating to the Removal from Office of General N. M. Curtis and to His Indictment for Levying and Receiving Political Assessments.* New York: G. P. Putnam's Sons, 1882.
National Civil Service Reform League, *Proceedings,* 1881–93.

C. Federal Government Publications

Congressional Globe, The, 1853–73.
Congressional Record, The, 1873–83.
Eaton, Dorman B., "Civil Service Reform in the New York City Post Office and Custom-House," *House Executive Documents,* 46 Cong., 3 sess., XXVIII, No. 94 (March 1, 1881). 59 pp.
Richardson, James D., *A Compilation of the Messages and Papers of the Presidents 1789–1897.* Washington: Government Printing Office, 1896–99. 10 vols.
U. S. Congress, House of Representatives, Select Committee on Retrenchment, "Retrenchment-Reorganization of Executive Departments," *Reports,* 27 Cong., 2 sess., IV, No. 741 (May 23, 1842). 240 pp.

———, "The Revenue System of the United States," *Executive Documents,* 39 Cong., 1 sess., VII, No. 34 (January 29, 1866). 132 pp.

———, Joint Select Committee on Retrenchment, "Civil Service of the United States," *Reports,* 39 Cong., 2 sess., I, No. 8 (January 31, 1867). 114 pp.

———, Joint Select Committee on Retrenchment, "Civil Service of the United States," *Reports,* 40 Cong., 2 sess., II, No. 47 (May 25, 1868). 220 pp.

———, "Commissions to Examine Certain Custom-Houses of the United States," *Executive Documents,* 45 Cong., 1 sess., I, No. 8 (October 25, 1877). 137 pp.

U. S. Congress, Senate, *Journal of the Executive Proceedings of the Senate of the United States of America.* Washington: Government Printing Office, 1828–1948. 90 vols.

———, *A Bill to Regulate the Civil Service of the United States, and Promote the Efficiency Thereof,* 39 Cong., 1 sess., Senate No. 430.

———, Joint Select Committee on Retrenchment, "Report [to accompany Bill S. No. 587]," *Reports,* 40 Cong., 2 sess., No. 154 (July 2, 1868). 27 pp.

———, Joint Select Committee on Retrenchment, "Report," *Reports,* 41 Cong., 3 sess., No. 380 (March 3, 1871). 169 pp.

———, Committee on Investigation and Retrenchment, "Report," *Reports,* 42 Cong., 2 sess., IV (in 3 parts), No. 227 (June 4, 1872).

———, Select Committee to Examine the Several Branches of the Civil Service, "The Regulation and Improvement of the Civil Service," *Reports,* 46 Cong., 3 sess., I, No. 872 (February 16, 1881). 46 pp.

———, Committee on Civil Service and Retrenchment, "Report [to accompany Bill S. 133]," *Reports,* 47 Cong., 1 sess., III, No. 576 (May 15, 1882). 227 pp.

U. S. Department of Commerce, Bureau of the Census, *Historical Statistics of the United States, 1789–1945: A Supplement to the Statistical Abstract of the United States.* Washington: Government Printing Office, 1949. 363 pp.

U. S. Department of the Interior, *Register of Officers and Agents, Civil, Military, and Naval, in the Service of the United States, on the Thirtieth, September* . . . Washington: Government Printing Office, 1866–68.

D. Published Letters, Diaries, Speeches, and Articles

Adams, Henry Brooks, "Civil-Service Reform," *The North American Review* (Boston), CIX, No. 225 (October, 1869), 443–475.

———, "The Session," *The North American Review,* CVIII, No. 223 (April, 1869), 610–640.

Bancroft, Frederic, ed., *Speeches, Correspondence and Political Papers of Carl Schurz.* New York: G. P. Putnam's Sons, 1913. 6 vols.

Beale, Howard K., ed., *Diary of Gideon Welles: Secretary of the Navy. Under Lincoln and Johnson.* New York: W. W. Norton & Company, 1960. 3 vols.

Bing, Julius, "Civil Service of the United States," *The North American Review,* CV, No. 217 (October, 1867), 478–495.

Bing, Julius, "Our Civil Service," *Putnam's Magazine* (New York), New Series, II, No. 8 (August, 1868), 233–244.

Bradford, Gamaliel, "Congressional Reform," *The North American Review*, CXI, No. 229 (October, 1870), 330–351.

Cater, Harold Dean, ed., *Henry Adams and His Friends: A Collection of His Unpublished Letters*. Boston: Houghton Mifflin Company, 1947. 797 pp.

Cox, Jacob Dolson, "How Judge Hoar Ceased to Be Attorney-General," *The Atlantic Monthly, a Magazine of Literature, Science, Art, and Politics* (Boston), LXXVI, No. 454 (August, 1895), 162–173.

Dennett, Tyler, ed., *Lincoln and the Civil War, in the Diaries and Letters of John Hay*. New York: Dodd, Mead & Company, 1939. 348 pp.

Eaton, Dorman B., *Civil Service in Great Britain: A History of Abuses and Reforms and Their Bearing upon American Politics*. New York: Harper & Brothers, 1880. 469 pp.

———, *The Experiment of Civil Service Reform in the United States: Paper . . . Read Before the American Social Science Association at Detroit*, May, 1875. 37 pp.

Ford, Worthington Chauncey, ed., *Letters of Henry Adams (1858–1891)*. Boston: Houghton Mifflin Company, 1930. 552 pp.

Hay, John, *Letters and Extracts from the Diary of John Hay*. Washington: Privately Printed, 1908. 3 vols.

Krock, Arthur, ed., *The Editorials of Henry Watterson: Compiled with an Introduction and Notes*. Louisville, Kentucky: The Louisville Courier-Journal Company, 1923. 430 pp.

Morison, Elting E., John M. Blum, and John J. Buckley, eds., *The Letters of Theodore Roosevelt*. Cambridge: Harvard University Press, 1951–54. 8 vols.

Norton, Charles Eliot, ed., *Orations and Addresses of George William Curtis*. New York: Harper & Brothers Publishers, 1894. 3 vols.

Norton, Sara, and Mark Anthony DeWolfe Howe, *Letters of Charles Eliot Norton with Biographical Comment*. Boston: Houghton Mifflin Company, 1913. 2 vols.

Parton, James, "The Government of the City of New York," *The North American Review*, CIII, No. 213 (October, 1866), 413–465.

Schafer, Joseph, ed., *Intimate Letters of Carl Schurz, 1841–1869* (Publications of the State Historical Society of Wisconsin Collections, XXX). Madison: State Historical Society of Wisconsin, 1928. 476 pp.

Sumner, Charles, *The Works of Charles Sumner*. Boston: Lee and Shepard, 1870–83. 15 vols.

Thoron, Ward, ed., *The Letters of Mrs. Henry Adams, 1865–1883*. Boston: Little, Brown, and Company, 1936. 587 pp.

Villard, Henry, "Historical Sketch of Social Science," *Journal of Social Science: Containing the Transactions of the American Association* (New York), No. 1 (June, 1869), 5–10.

Williams, Charles Richard, ed., *Diary and Letters of Rutherford Birchard Hayes: Nineteenth President of the United States*. Columbus: The Ohio State Archaeological and Historical Society, 1924. 5 vols.

E. Memoirs, Reminiscences

Adams, Henry, *The Education of Henry Adams*. New York: The Modern Library, 1931. 517 pp.

Bancroft, Frederic, and William A. Dunning, eds., *The Reminiscences of Carl Schurz*. New York: McClure Company, 1907–08. 3 vols.

Foulke, William Dudley, *Fighting the Spoilsmen: Reminiscences of the Civil Service Reform Movement*. New York: G. P. Putnam's Sons, 1919. 348 pp.

Sherman, John, *Recollections of Forty Years in the House, Senate and Cabinet*. Chicago: The Werner Company, 1895. 2 vols.

Watterson, Henry, *"Marse Henry": An Autobiography*. New York: George H. Doran Company, 1919. 2 vols.

Wheeler, Everett P., *Sixty Years of American Life: Taylor to Roosevelt, 1850–1910*. New York: E. P. Dutton & Company, 1917. 489 pp.

White, Andrew Dickson, *Autobiography of Andrew Dickson White*. New York: The Century Co., 1905. 2 vols.

F. Serial Publications

Atlanta Constitution, 1881–82.

Boston Directory, 1882–83.

Brooklyn Directory, 1882–83, 1890.

Civil Service Record (Boston), 1881–92.

Evening Post (New York), 1866–81.

Harper's Weekly (New York), 1866–82.

Nation (New York), 1865–84.

New York City Directory, 1877–83.

New York Herald, 1866–68.

New York Times, 1866–82.

New York Tribune, 1866–81.

Philadelphia Inquirer, 1881–82.

Philadelphia Record, 1882–83.

Press (Philadelphia), 1866–67.

Rocky Mountain News (Denver), 1881.

San Francisco Chronicle, 1881–82.

World (New York), 1867–81.

G. Miscellaneous

Commager, Henry Steele, ed., *Documents of American History*, 5th edition. New York: Appleton-Century-Crofts, Inc., 1949. 2 vols.

The Republican Campaign Text Book for 1882. Washington: Republican Congressional Committee, 1882. 240 pp.

II. Secondary Accounts

A. General Works

Channing, Edward, *A History of the United States*. New York: The Macmillan Company, 1905–25. 6 vols.

Oberholtzer, Ellis Paxson, *A History of the United States Since the Civil War*. New York: The Macmillan Company, 1917–37. 5 vols.

Rhodes, James Ford, *History of the United States from the Compromise of 1850 to the Final Restoration of Home Rule at the South in 1877.* New York: The Macmillan Company, 1906. 7 vols.

B. *Short Biographical Accounts*

Brown, John Howard, ed., *Lamb's Biographical Dictionary of the United States.* Boston: Federal Book Company, 1900–1903. 7 vols.
Harvard University Quinquennial Catalogue of the Officers and Graduates 1636–1930. Cambridge: The University Press, 1930. 1463 pp.
Johnson, Allen, and Dumas Malone, eds., *Dictionary of American Biography.* New York: Charles Scribner's Sons, 1928–36. 20 vols.
Morris, Charles, ed., *Makers of New York, an Historical Work, Giving Portraits and Sketches of the Most Eminent Citizens of New York.* Philadelphia: L. R. Hamersly & Company, 1895. 348 pp.
The National Cyclopaedia of American Biography. New York: James T. White & Company, 1892–1955. 40 vols.
Obituary Record of the Graduates of Bowdoin College and the Medical School of Maine for the Year Ending 1 June 1896, Second Series, No. 7. Brunswick: Published by the College, 1890. pp. 279–342.
University of Pennsylvania Biographical Catalogue of the Matriculates of the College 1749–1893. Philadelphia: Society of the Alumni, 1894. 567 pp.
Who Was Who in America. Vol. I, 1897–1942. Chicago: A. N. Marquis Company, 1942.
Who's Who in New York City and State, 1st, 3rd editions. New York: L. R. Hamersly & Company, 1904, 1907. 2 vols.
Wilson, James Grant, and John Fiske, eds., *Appleton's Cyclopaedia of American Biography.* New York: D. Appleton and Company, 1888–89. 6 vols.

C. *Monographs*

Armstrong, William M., *E. L. Godkin and American Foreign Policy, 1865–1900.* New York: Bookman Associates, 1957. 268 pp.
Barclay, Thomas S., *The Liberal Republican Movement in Missouri: 1865–1871.* Columbia: State Historical Society of Missouri, 1926. 288 pp.
Barnard, Harry, *Rutherford B. Hayes and His America.* Indianapolis: The Bobbs-Merrill Company, Inc., 1954. 606 pp.
Barrows, Chester Leonard, *William M. Evarts: Lawyer, Diplomat, Statesman.* Chapel Hill: University of North Carolina Press, 1941. 587 pp.
Beale, Howard Kennedy, *The Critical Year: A Study of Andrew Johnson and Reconstruction.* New York: Harcourt, Brace and Company, 1930. 454 pp.
Belden, Thomas Graham, and Marva Robins Belden, *So Fell the Angels.* Boston: Little, Brown and Company, 1956. 401 pp.
Berens, Ruth McMurry, "Blueprint for Reform: Curtis, Eaton, and Schurz." University of Chicago: Unpublished Master's Dissertation, 1943. 284 pp.
Blake, Nelson Morehouse, *William Mahone of Virginia, Soldier and Political Insurgent.* Richmond: Garrett & Massie, Inc., 1935. 323 pp.
Bowen, Catherine Drinker, *The Lion and the Throne: The Life and Times of Sir Edward Coke (1552–1634).* Boston: Little, Brown and Company, 1957. 652 pp.

Carman, Harry James, and Reinhard Henry Luthin, *Lincoln and the Patronage.* New York: Columbia University Press, 1943. 375 pp.

Cary, Edward, *George William Curtis.* Boston: Houghton Mifflin and Company, 1894. 343 pp.

Chidsey, Donald Barr, *The Gentleman from New York: A Life of Roscoe Conkling.* New Haven: Yale University Press, 1935. 438 pp.

Clapp, Margaret, *Forgotten First Citizen: John Bigelow.* Boston: Little, Brown and Company, 1947. 390 pp.

Conkling, Alfred R., *The Life and Letters of Roscoe Conkling, Orator, Statesman, Advocate.* New York: Charles L. Webster & Company, 1889. 709 pp.

Cortissoz, Royal, *The Life of Whitelaw Reid.* New York: Charles Scribner's Sons, 1921. 2 vols.

Donald, David, *Lincoln Reconsidered.* New York: Alfred A. Knopf, 1956. 200 pp.

Donovan, Robert J., *The Assassins.* New York: Harper & Brothers, 1955. 300 pp.

Dorfman, Joseph, *The Economic Mind in American Civilization: Volume Three 1865–1918.* New York: Viking Press, 1949. 494 pp.

Eckenrode, H. J., *Rutherford B. Hayes, Statesman of Reunion.* New York: Dodd, Mead & Company, 1930. 363 pp.

Fish, Carl Russell, *The Civil Service and the Patronage.* Cambridge: Harvard University Press, 1920. 280 pp.

Fuess, Claude Moore, *Carl Schurz: Reformer (1829–1906).* New York: Dodd, Mead & Company, 1932. 421 pp.

Gosnell, Harold F., *Boss Platt and His New York Machine: A Study of the Political Leadership of Thomas C. Platt, Theodore Roosevelt, and Others.* Chicago: University of Chicago Press, 1924. 370 pp.

Gregory, Allene, *John Milton Gregory: A Biography.* Chicago: Covici-McGee Co., 1923. 372 pp.

Gutheim, Marjorie Frye, "John Lothrop Motley." Columbia University: Unpublished Doctoral Dissertation, 1955. 425 pp.

Hartman, William J., "Politics and Patronage: The New York Custom House, 1852–1902." Columbia University: Unpublished Doctoral Dissertation, 1952. 367 pp.

Hesseltine, William Best, *Ulysses S. Grant: Politician.* New York: Dodd, Mead & Company, 1935. 480 pp.

Hill, Louise Biles, *Joseph E. Brown and the Confederacy.* Chapel Hill: University of North Carolina Press, 1939. 360 pp.

Hofstadter, Richard, *The Age of Reform: From Bryan to F. D. R.* New York: Alfred A. Knopf, 1955. 328 pp.

Howe, George Frederick, *Chester A. Arthur: A Quarter-Century of Machine Politics.* New York: Dodd, Mead & Company, 1934. 307 pp.

Howe, Mark Anthony DeWolfe, *Portrait of an Independent: Moorfield Storey, 1845–1929.* Boston: Houghton Mifflin Company, 1932. 384 pp.

In Memoriam: Thomas Allen Jenckes, Born November 2, 1818. Died November 4, 1875. Providence, 1876. 75 pp.

Josephson, Matthew, *The Politicos, 1865–1896.* New York: Harcourt, Brace and Company, 1938. 760 pp.

Kingsley, J. Donald, *Representative Bureaucracy: An Interpretation of the British Civil Service.* Yellow Springs, Ohio: Antioch Press, 1944. 324 pp.

Lowitt, Richard, *A Merchant Prince of the Nineteenth Century: William E. Dodge.* New York: Columbia University Press, 1954. 384 pp.

McKitrick, Eric L., *Andrew Johnson and Reconstruction.* Chicago: University of Chicago Press, 1960. 534 pp.

Maxwell, William Quentin, *Lincoln's Fifth Wheel: The Political History of the United States Sanitary Commission.* New York: Longmans, Green & Company, 1956. 372 pp.

Merriam, George S., *The Life and Times of Samuel Bowles.* New York: The Century Company, 1885. 2 vols.

Milne, Gordon, *George William Curtis & the Genteel Tradition.* Bloomington: Indiana University Press, 1956. 294 pp.

Moses, Robert, *The Civil Service of Great Britain* (Columbia University Studies in History, Economics and Public Law, LVII, No. 1). New York: Columbia University, 1914. 324 pp.

Mott, Frank Luther, *A History of American Magazines, 1741–1885.* Cambridge: Harvard University Press, 1938. 3 vols.

Nevins, Allan, *Abram S. Hewitt, with Some Account of Peter Cooper.* New York: Harper & Brothers, 1935. 623 pp.

———, *Grover Cleveland: A Study in Courage.* New York: Dodd, Mead & Company, 1933. 832 pp.

———, *Hamilton Fish: The Inner History of the Grant Administration.* New York: Dodd, Mead & Company, 1937. 932 pp.

Ogden, Rollo, ed., *Life and Letters of Edwin Lawrence Godkin.* New York: Macmillan Company, 1907. 2 vols.

Perry, Bliss, *Richard Henry Dana, 1851–1931.* Boston: Houghton Mifflin Company, 1933. 265 pp.

Pierce, Edward L., *Memoir and Letters of Charles Sumner.* Boston: Roberts Brothers, 1877–93. 4 vols.

Pringle, Henry F., *Theodore Roosevelt: A Biography.* New York: Harcourt, Brace and Company, 1931. 627 pp.

Putnam, Carleton, *Theodore Roosevelt: The Formative Years, 1858–1886.* New York: Charles Scribner's Sons, 1958. 626 pp.

Ross, Earle Dudley, *The Liberal Republican Movement.* New York: Henry Holt and Company, 1919. 267 pp.

Ross, Ishbel, *Proud Kate: Portrait of an Ambitious Woman.* New York: Harper & Brothers, 1953. 309 pp.

Sageser, A. Bower, *The First Two Decades of the Pendleton Act: A Study of Civil Service Reform* (The University Studies of the University of Nebraska, XXXIV–XXXV). Lincoln: University of Nebraska, 1935. 274 pp.

Schattschneider, E. E., *Party Government.* New York: Farrar and Rinehart, Inc., 1942. 219 pp.

Schlesinger, Arthur M., Jr., *The Age of Jackson.* Boston: Little, Brown and Company, 1946. 545 pp.

Smith, Theodore Clark, *The Life and Letters of James Abram Garfield.* New Haven: Yale University Press, 1925. 2 vols.

Stewart, Frank Mann, *The National Civil Service Reform League: History, Activities, and Problems.* Austin: University of Texas, 1929. 304 pp.

Swanberg, W. A., *Sickles the Incredible.* New York: Charles Scribner's Sons, 1956. 433 pp.

Tansill, Charles Callan, *The Congressional Career of Thomas Francis Bayard, 1869–1885.* Washington: Georgetown University Press, 1946. 362 pp.

Thatcher, John Howard, "Public Discussion of Civil Service Reform, 1864–1883." Cornell University: Unpublished Doctoral Dissertation, 1943. 267 pp.

Van Deusen, Glyndon G., *Horace Greeley: Nineteenth Century Crusader.* Philadelphia: University of Pennsylvania Press, 1953. 445 pp.

Van Riper, Paul P., *History of the United States Civil Service.* Evanston, Illinois: Row, Peterson and Company, 1958. 588 pp.

Wall, Joseph Frazier, *Henry Watterson: Reconstructed Rebel.* New York: Oxford University Press, 1956. 362 pp.

White, Leonard D., *The Federalists: A Study in Administrative History.* New York: Macmillan Company, 1948. 538 pp.

————, *The Jacksonians: A Study in Administrative History, 1829–1861.* New York: Macmillan Company, 1954. 593 pp.

————, *The Jeffersonians: A Study in Administrative History, 1801–1829.* New York: Macmillan Company, 1951. 572 pp.

————, *The Republican Era, 1869–1901.* New York: Macmillan Company, 1958. 406 pp.

Williams, Charles Richard, *The Life of Rutherford Birchard Hayes: Nineteenth President of the United States.* Columbus: Ohio State Archaeological and Historical Society, 1928. 2 vols.

Williams, T. Harry, *Lincoln and the Radicals.* Madison: University of Wisconsin Press, 1941. 413 pp.

Woodward, C. Vann, *Reunion and Reaction: The Compromise of 1877 and the End of Reconstruction,* 2nd edition, revised. Garden City, New York: Doubleday & Company, 1956. 297 pp.

Younger, Edward, *John A. Kasson: Politics and Diplomacy from Lincoln to McKinley.* Iowa City: State Historical Society of Iowa, 1955. 450 pp.

D. Articles in Periodicals

Hartman, William J., "Pioneer in Civil Service Reform: Silas W. Burt and the New York Custom House," *The New York Historical Society Quarterly,* XXXIX, No. 4 (October, 1955), 369–379.

Hirsch, Mark D., "Samuel J. Tilden: The Story of a Lost Opportunity," *The American Historical Review* (Washington), LVI, No. 4 (July, 1951), 788–802.

Hoogenboom, Ari, "The Pendleton Act and the Civil Service," *The American Historical Review,* LXIV, No. 2 (January, 1959), 301–318.

Lardner, John, "That Was New York: Martyrdom of Bill the Butcher," *The New Yorker* (New York), XXX, Nos. 4, 5 (March 20 and 27, 1954, 41–56 and 38–59 respectively).

Mallam, William D., "The Grant-Butler Relationship," *The Mississippi*

Valley Historical Review (Cedar Rapids), XLI, No. 2 (September, 1954), 259–276.

Mowry, George E., "The California Progressive and His Rationale: A Study in Middle-Class Politics," *The Mississippi Valley Historical Review*, XXXVI, No. 2 (September, 1949), 239–250.

Murphy, Lionel V., "The First Federal Civil Service Commission: 1871–75 . . . ," *Public Personnel Review* (Chicago), III, Nos. 1, 3, 4 (January, July, October, 1942), 29–39, 218–231, 299–323.

APPENDIX A

Federal Civil Employment Statistics 1792–1901 [1]

Year	Total Population	Total Employed	Classified Positions	Persons Examined	Persons Passed	Persons Appointed
1790	3,929,214					
1792		780				
1800	5,308,483					
1801		3,000				
1810	7,239,881					
1816		6,327				
1820	9,638,453					
1821		8,211				
1830	12,866,020					
1831		19,800				
1840	17,069,453					
1841		23,700				
1850	23,191,876					
1851		33,300				
1860	31,443,321					
1861		49,200				
1870	38,558,371					
1871		53,900				
1880	50,155,783					
1881		107,000				
1884		131,208	13,780	3,542	2,044	489
1885			15,590	6,347	4,141	1,800
1886			17,273	7,602	5,034	1,881
1887			19,345	15,852	10,746	4,442
1888			22,577	11,281	6,868	2,616
1889			29,650	19,060	11,978	3,781
1890	62,947,714		30,626	22,994	13,947	5,182
1891		166,000	33,873	19,074	12,786	5,395
1892		171,000	37,523	19,460	12,160	3,961
1893		176,000	43,915	24,838	14,008	4,291
1894		180,000	45,821	37,379	22,131	4,704
1895		189,000	54,222	31,036	19,811	4,793
1896			87,044	31,179	20,714	5,086
1897		192,000	85,886	50,571	29,474	3,047
1898			89,306	45,712	30,600	7,870
1899		208,000	93,144	49,164	36,312	9,557
1900	75,994,575		94,893	46,602	34,965	9,889
1901		256,000	106,205	48,093	33,521	10,291

[1] For 1792 and 1801, see Leonard D. White, *The Federalists: A Study in Administrative History* (New York, 1948), p. 255. The remaining figures were drawn from U.S. Department of Commerce, Bureau of the Census, *Historical Statistics of the United States, 1789–1945* (Washington, 1949), pp. 25, 294. Civil service statistics are frequently contradictory and must be used with caution. See Paul P. Van Riper, *History of the United States Civil Service* (Evanston, Illinois, 1958), pp. 56–59.

APPENDIX B

Officers Affected by the Four-Year Laws in 1886 [1]

Postmasters:

New York City "special"	1
First Class	80
Second Class	404
Third Class	1,836
	2,321

Assistant Treasurers	9

Customs Service:

Collectors, Naval Officers, Surveyors, Appraisers, Assistant Appraisers, and Examiners of Drugs	198

Interior Department:

Pensions Agents	18
Surveyors-General	16
Indian Agents	64
Registers of United States Land Offices	104
Governors of Territories	8
Secretaries of Territories	8
Indian Inspectors	81
Receivers of Public Money	104
	403

Judicial:

Justices of Supreme Court of Territories	27
District Attorneys	69
Marshals	69
	165

Total	3,096

"To this list might be added four hundred and twenty-four deputies in the customs service whose appointments cannot extend beyond the terms of their superiors, and so are four years or less. The Director of the Mint and the Controller of the Currency are each appointed for a term of five years."

[1] The table and the quotation may be found in "Work for the Future," *Civil Service Record* (Boston), V, No. 10 (April, 1886), 83.

INDEX

Abolitionism, 63, 191, 201

Abolitionists: civil service reformers and, 21–22, 193; methods of used by civil service reformers, 186–187; mentioned, viii, 40n, 64, 197n

Adams, Brooks, 222

Adams, Charles Francis, Sr.: and presidential nomination of 1872, 111, 113–114; of 1876, 138; mentioned, 21

Adams, Charles Francis, Jr.: seeks office, 63; works for unity among reformers, 127–128; and Ohio gubernatorial election, 137; supports Tilden, 144; mentioned, 22n

Adams, Henry: on Sumner and R. H. Dana, Jr., 22, 23n; on majority, 26; on Grant's Cabinet, 52; on Grant's administration, 62–63; espouses civil service reform, 63; ideas on civil service reform, 65–68; works for revenue reform and free trade, 74; leaves Washington for Boston, 78; asks Schurz to write article, 83; attends conference sponsored by Free Trade League, 84; on Grant's annual message of 1870, 85; organizes civil service reformers, 136; and Ohio gubernatorial election, 137; supports Bristow, 138; on Schurz, 141; on Hayes, 141; supports Tilden,

144; on presidential nomination of 1880, 180n; on civil service reformers' exploitation of Garfield's assassination, 212; on Arthur and Garfield, 214; on Congress and Pendleton bill, 252; mentioned, 71, 141n, 148

Adams, John, 5

Adams, John Quincy (1767–1848), 5, 7

Adams, John Quincy (1833–1894), 63

Adams, Marian Hooper (Mrs. Henry): on Congress, 236; on civil service reform, 240; on Joseph E. Brown, 241

Agriculture, Department of, 224

Akerman, Amos T.: appointed Attorney General, 75; opinion of on appointing power, 92–95

Alabama claims, 91

Albany Customhouse, 51

Allen, William, 137

Allison, William B., 236n

American Free Trade League, 64, 83–85

American Revolution, 4, 5, 104–105

American Social Science Association: agitates for civil service reform, 55–56, 64–65, 74; addressed by Eaton, 134; mentioned, 21, 63

American Wood Paper Company, 14

ILLINI BOOKS

IB-1	Grierson's Raid: A Cavalry Adventure of the Civil War	D. Alexander Brown	$1.75
IB-2	The Mars Project	Wernher von Braun	$ .95
IB-3	The New Exploration: A Philosophy of Regional Planning	Benton MacKaye, with an Introduction by Lewis Mumford	$1.75
IB-4	Tragicomedy: Its Origin and Development in Italy, France, and England	Marvin T. Herrick	$1.95
IB-5	Themes in Greek and Latin Epitaphs	Richmond Lattimore	$1.95
IB-6	The Doctrine of Responsible Party Government: Its Origins and Present State	Austin Ranney	$1.25
IB-7	An Alternative to War or Surrender	Charles E. Osgood	$1.45
IB-8	Reference Books in the Mass Media	Eleanor Blum	$1.50
IB-9	Life in a Mexican Village: Tepoztlán Restudied	Oscar Lewis	$2.95
IB-10	*Three Presidents and Their Books: The Reading of Jefferson, Lincoln, and Franklin D. Roosevelt	Arthur E. Bestor, David C. Mearns, and Jonathan Daniels	$ .95
IB-11	Cultural Sciences: Their Origin and Development	Florian Znaniecki	$2.25
IB-12	The Legend of Noah: Renaissance Rationalism in Art, Science, and Letters	Don Cameron Allen	$1.45
IB-13	*The Mathematical Theory of Communication	Claude E. Shannon and Warren Weaver	$ .95
IB-14	Philosophy and Ordinary Language	Charles E. Caton, ed.	$1.95
IB-15	Four Theories of the Press	Fred S. Siebert, Theodore Peterson, and Wilbur Schramm	$1.25
IB-16	Constitutional Problems Under Lincoln	James G. Randall	$2.95
IB-17	Viva Mexico!	Charles Macomb Flandrau, edited and with an introduction by C. Harvey Gardiner	$1.95
IB-18	Comic Theory in the Sixteenth Century	Marvin T. Herrick	$1.75

* *Also available in clothbound editions.*

* Also available in clothbound editions.

University of Illinois Press Urbana, Chicago, and London